The Oxford Poetry 🖉 **P9-BJF-216**

GENERAL EDITOR: FRANK KERMODE

JOHN MILTON was born on 9 December 1608 in Cheapside, London. He published little until the appearance of *Poems of Mr John Milton, both English and Latin* in 1646, when he was thirty-seven. By this time he was deeply committed to a political vocation, and became an articulate and increasingly indispensable spokesman for the Independent cause. He wrote the crucial justifications for the trial and execution of Charles I, and, as Secretary for Foreign Tongues to the Council of State, was the voice of the English revolution to the world at large. After the failure of the Commonwealth he was briefly imprisoned; blind and in straitened circumstances he returned to poetry, and in 1667 published a ten-book version of *Paradise Lost*, his biblical epic written, as he put it, after 'long choosing, and beginning late'. In 1671, *Paradise Regained* and *Samson Agonistes* appeared, followed two years later by an expanded edition of his shorter poems. The canon was completed in 1674, the year of his death, with the appearance of the twelve-book *Paradise Lost*, which became a classic almost immediately. His influence on English poetry and criticism has been incalculable.

JONATHAN GOLDBERG is the Sir William Osler Professor of English Literature at the Johns Hopkins University. He is the author of *Endlesse Worke: Spenser and the Structures of Discourse, James I and the Politics of Literature, Voice Terminal Echo: Postmodernism and English Renaissance Texts,* and *Writing Matter: From the Hands of the English Renaissance.* His most recent book is *Sodometries: Renaissance Texts, Modern Sexualities,* and he is the editor of *Queering the Renaissance* and *Reclaiming Sodom.*

STEPHEN ORGEL is the Jackson Eli Reynolds Professor of Humanities at Stanford University, and has also taught at Johns Hopkins, Berkeley, and Harvard. His books include *The Jonsonian Masque, The Illusion of Power,* and, in collaboration with Sir Roy Strong, *Inigo Jones.* He has edited Ben Jonson's masques, the poems and translations of Christopher Marlowe, and, for the Oxford Shakespeare, *The Tempest.*

FRANK KERMODE, retired King Edward VII Professor of English Literature at Cambridge, is the author of many books, including *Romantic Image, The Sense of an Ending, The Classic, The Genesis of Secrecy, Forms of Attention,* and *History and Value*; he is co-editor with John Hollander of *The Oxford Anthology of English Literature.*

THE OXFORD POETRY LIBRARY

GENERAL EDITOR: FRANK KERMODE

Matthew Arnold	*Miriam Allott*
William Blake	*Michael Mason*
Byron	*Jerome McGann*
Samuel Taylor Coleridge	*Heather Jackson*
John Dryden	*Keith Walker*
Thomas Hardy	*Samuel Hynes*
George Herbert	*Louis Martz*
Gerard Manley Hopkins	*Catherine Phillips*
Ben Jonson	*Ian Donaldson*
John Keats	*Elizabeth Cook*
Andrew Marvell	*Frank Kermode and Keith Walker*
John Milton	*Jonathan Goldberg and Stephen Orgel*
Alexander Pope	*Pat Rogers*
Sir Philip Sidney	*Katherine Duncan-Jones*
Henry Vaughan	*Louis Martz*
William Wordsworth	*Stephen Gill and Duncan Wu*

The Oxford Poetry Library

John Milton

Edited by
JONATHAN GOLDBERG
and
STEPHEN ORGEL

Oxford   New York
OXFORD UNIVERSITY PRESS
1994

Oxford University Press, Walton Street, Oxford OX2 6DP

Oxford New York Toronto
Delhi Bombay Calcutta Madras Karachi
Kuala Lumpur Singapore Hong Kong Tokyo
Nairobi Dar es Salaam Cape Town
Melbourne Auckland Madrid
and associated companies in
Berlin Ibadan

Oxford is a trade mark of Oxford University Press

Introduction, selection, and editorial material
© Jonathan Goldberg and Stephen Orgel 1994

This selection first published in the Oxford Poetry Library 1994

British Library Cataloguing in Publication Data

Data available

Library of Congress Cataloging in Publication Data

Milton, John, 1608–1674.
[Poems. Selections]
John Milton / edited by Stephen Orgel and Jonathan Goldberg.
p. cm. — (The Oxford poetry library)
Selection of poems.
Includes bibliographical references and index.
I. Orgel, Stephen. II. Goldberg, Jonathan.
III. Title. IV. Series.
PR3552.O74 1994 821'.4—dc20 93–45625
ISBN 0–19–282304–3

1 3 5 7 9 10 8 6 4 2

Typeset by J&L Composition Ltd, Filey, North Yorkshire
Printed in Great Britain by
Biddles Ltd
Guildford and King's Lynn

Contents

Introduction

MILTON'S place in the canon of English literature rests upon *Paradise Lost*. Yet, it is worth pondering the likelihood that the poem first published in 1667 as a ten-book epic, and finally recast in twelve books shortly before Milton's death in 1674, is not the same as the poem Milton had announced he was writing early in the 1640s. *Paradise Lost* first appeared when Milton was some 60 years old, an advanced age in the period. Indeed, one could almost say that Milton had chanced his life in postponing the writing of the poem 'doctrinal and exemplary to a nation' that he had promised the readers of his *Reason of Church Government* in 1642 would soon be forthcoming. The delay in its writing can most fully be explained by the revolutionary conditions of the 1640s and 1650s: Milton had entered the pamphlet wars of the 1640s on the side of the Presbyterians; by the end of the decade, he had parted company with them, and was arguing for the death of the king; after Charles I was executed in 1649, Milton became Oliver Cromwell's Latin Secretary, a position he held in the Commonwealth until the 1660 Restoration of the Stuarts. The point, however, is not that the political upheavals in which he was continually involved interrupted the writing of the epic. It is, rather, that the Revolution and its defeat are implicit in the form that *Paradise Lost* finally took.

One cannot know, of course, what *Paradise Lost* would have been —what epic, if that was where Milton was heading in the early 1640s (his notes suggest that path or the writing of a drama on the subject of 'Adam Unparadised'), he might have written had there been no Revolution or if it had ultimately succeeded. One can notice, however, that his early poems, compositions of the late 1620s and 1630s, gathered and published under his name for the first time in 1645, reveal a writer who had spent the previous decade trying out many of the forms and conventions of earlier poetry, always in complicated ways. Poems like *On the Morning of Christ's Nativity*, written in 1629 when Milton was 21, which opened the 1645 volume (serving thereby as an announcement of poetic coming of age as much as a celebration of the birth of the holy child), bear resemblance to poems written by Donne or Herbert, that is, to Anglican celebrations of moments in the Christian calendar. They suggest that at the opening of the 1630s, at least, Milton's religion may not have been especially revolutionary, and his poetic ambitions may have been like those of other churchmen. He had, in fact, been 'destined' to a Church career, as he noted in a review of his life in *Reason of Church Government*, a destination to which his grammar school education at St Paul's and his 1632 MA at Cambridge would readily have led. Similarly disturbing to any sense that *Paradise Lost* represents the inevitable outcome of his earlier work as a poet is the poem that closed the 1645 volume, the *Masque Presented at Ludlow Castle* usually known by its eighteenth-century title, *Comus*, written in the most royalist of forms, the court masque, and accompanied by music by Henry Lawes, no less than Charles I's musician, 'Gentleman of the King's Chapel, and one of his Majesty's Private Music,' as the title-page in fact boasts. What such a poem—the longest Milton had written to that point—suggests is not only literary ambitions best realized in a courtly milieu, but reminds us that the conditions of courtly and aristocratic patronage for writing that prevailed up to the 1640s were disrupted by the Revolution and, after the Restoration, no longer available to Milton.

The 1645 volume, as we have suggested, displays Milton's engagement with earlier poets. Marlowe's famous lyric, 'Come live with me and be my love', is one of the precedents for 'L'Allegro' and 'Il Penseroso', for instance, while Milton's sonnets are a somewhat belated exercise in one of the genres that characterized the Elizabethan period—indeed, several of them were written in Italian, thereby glancing at the origin of the form. It is above all Spenser who places his mark on the poet. *Comus* is, among other things, a response to Book III of *The Faerie Queene*, while *Lycidas*, arguably Milton's most ambitious and accomplished poem of his early years, is indebted in many ways to Spenser's *Shepheardes Calender* and to the traditions of pastoral in which it participates. When in the opening lines of Book IX of *Paradise Lost*, Milton explicitly rejected some of the conventions of epic form, he most obviously recalls the precedent of Spenser's epic poem, with its knights engaged in chivalric quests. (The influence of Spenser, on the other hand, is most overtly registered in the allegorical figures of Sin and Death who first appear in Book II, and who derive from the figure of Error in Book I of *The Faerie Queene*.) Whether the repudiation of Spenserian epic in Book IX of *Paradise Lost* also points to a denial of the epic Milton had first planned to write cannot be answered definitively, although there are indications he had envisioned writing an Arthurian epic like Spenser's, while his *History of Britain* (1670), indebted as it is to such sources as Geoffrey of Monmouth, displays his knowledge of the (pseudo)-historical accounts that also helped shape Spenser's poem. It is none the less the case that the rejection of Spenser in the lines opening Book IX of *Paradise Lost* invokes a model necessary to be overcome in Milton's writing of an epic; more than that, however, it suggests ways in which a poem 'doctrinal and exemplary to a nation' could no longer take the form that *The Faerie Queene*, which shares those ambitions, did. *The Faerie Queene* is a not entirely straightforward encomium to Elizabeth I, and its blending of epic and romance testifies not only to the influence of Ariosto's *Orlando Furioso*, but to the melding of romance and allegory that character-ized Elizabethan court entertainments and pageants as well. The gentleman or nobleman that Spenser sought to 'fashion', as he put it in a prefatory letter to Sir Walter Ralegh that accompanied the publication of the first three books of *The Faerie Queene* in 1590, could not be Milton's intended reader, nor could his epic imagine the nation in the terms that Spenser had done. For, simply put, after 1660, Milton no longer could write as the poet of the state and its religion.

Decisive as the Revolution was to Milton's career, and to the deferral of *Paradise Lost*, a subject arrived at after 'long choosing, and beginning late' (*PL* IX. 25), it is worth noting that the early poems, as much as they engage the work of contemporary and preceding poets, also self-consciously mark a distance from their models. Even more to the point, when one looks at a poem like sonnet 7, which begins 'How soon hath time the subtle thief of youth, | Stol'n on his wing my three and twentieth year!', one encounters a text that records a sense of belatedness, a failure even at the age of 24 to produce an accomplishment worthy of his years. Perhaps this can easily be dismissed as a characteristic lament of an ambitious young man, but it tallies with a reading of Milton's life in the 1630s as a period marked by delay. He did not enter the Church after he received his MA; rather, he spent the following years at family estates, pursuing a programme of reading, capped by a trip to the continent in 1638–9, a prototype for the Grand Tour that soon became a requisite in the life of a gentleman. Even the return to England—and, for the first time, just past the age of 30, to a life not in his parents' house—was not quite undertaken, as he would later claim, at the prompting of the stirrings of revolution at home. Or so, in a merciless set of sentences, Samuel Johnson opines, in the account of Milton that he offered in his *Lives of the Poets* (1779):

Let not our veneration for Milton forbid us to look with some degree of merriment on great promises and small performance, on the man who hastens home because his countrymen are contending for their liberty, and, when he reaches the scene of action, vapors away his patriotism in a private boarding school.

As Dr Johnson notes, Milton's first employment was as a teacher in London, educating boys, including his nephews, John and Edward Phillips (his sister's children), in his lodgings. Johnson had little sympathy with Milton's politics—'His political notions were those of an acrimonious and surly republican,' he writes—and even less with Cromwell or with Milton's services during the period of the Commonwealth, which Johnson regarded as a betrayal of the very liberty that Milton defended: 'Nothing can be more just than that rebellion should end in slavery; that he, who had justified the murder of his king, for some acts which to him seemed unlawful, should now sell his services, and his flatteries, to a tyrant, of whom it was evident that he could do nothing lawful.' Hence, he found it impossible to sympathize with Milton in his old age, after the failure of the Revolution: 'the time was come in which regicides could no longer boast their wickedness,' he asserts. Johnson's swipes at Milton's initial delay were meant to belittle Milton's commitment to the cause, which he saw more as an index to Milton's egotism than anything else, and, as is clear from these citations, the cause itself was for Johnson unmitigated 'wickedness'. More fairly, and more to the point, Milton's delay in entering the pamphlet wars, as much as his growing alienation from the Presbyterians he at first supported, might suggest that the 'long choosing' of a topic for *Paradise Lost* is part of a career characterized by deferral and delay, a career increasingly dependent upon the realization of the Revolution.

When Milton ended *Lycidas* by referring to its speaker as an 'uncouth swain' (l. 185), his choice of adjective pointed both to his obscurity ('uncouth' means unknown) but also, even in this culminating poem of the 1630s, to his immaturity and incapacity. *Lycidas* records the death in 1637 of one of Milton's fellow students, Edward King, cut off in his youth; it also, more obliquely, must eulogize the death of his mother, Sara, in the same year, if only in its insistently displaced vision of the inability of Orpheus's mother to save him from death; more overtly, it mourns the state of the Church, and thereby the impossibility that Milton would take up the career which his fellow student had pursued. But this disidentification with King only masks a stronger sense of identification of himself as at an end before he had even begun. In sonnet 7, which faced a similar crisis some half a dozen years earlier, Milton had resigned himself to God; in *Lycidas*, the speaker is forever being pre-empted by the authoritative voices of gods and saints; as late as sonnet 16, the poem on his blindness—and how late that poem is it is difficult to determine, since it bears signs of rewriting over the course of the 1640s and 1650s—Milton famously resigns himself to the position of those who 'also serve who only stand and wait'. Waiting for the Revolution to be accomplished. Waiting, perhaps, for a miracle: that the blind man might see again, that the old man might remain young enough to write the poem deferred for decades. As early as sonnet 7, Milton had wondered whether his 'semblance might deceive the truth, | That I to manhood am arrived so near'. The 'uncouth swain' was thirty years old. To the close of the 1630s, indeed up to the time of writing *Paradise Lost*, Milton occupied this position of not yet arriving at 'manhood'. The writer of *Paradise Lost* had, indeed, hedged his bets: counting on a temporality perhaps not measured by the calendar, on vision that did not depend upon sight.

When *Paradise Lost* did appear, it was hardly from a position of strength that Milton wrote, except perhaps the strength of a survivor who had virtually outlived himself, as is more than suggested by some of the autobiographical passages in the epic, particularly those that open Books III, VII, and IX. Whatever the nation imagined as an audience for the poem in 1642 had been, or whose emergence Milton had anticipated and waited for, the nation of the 1660s to Milton could only have been a nightmare, the return of the regime whose end he had celebrated. The choice of subject for the poem was, indeed, doctrinal, classical epic put in the service of the Bible; yet, in the course of years, whatever Milton's relation to scripture might earlier have been, it had become anything but doctrinal, as Milton makes clear in *De Doctrina Christiana*, a long prose tract that he was composing at the same time as he was writing the epic, but which was not printed until it appeared with an accompanying English translation early in the nineteenth century. Even then it still would have been regarded as

radical for its heresies, among them mortalism, the belief that the
soul dies along with the body; materialism, a refusal to understand
spirit as different in kind from matter; anti-trinitarianism, including
a denial of the equality of the Father and Son. In the nation that he
conceived and for which he laboured, such positions were the
outgrowth of the Protestant belief in the ability of individual
conscience to hammer out its own salvation, a tenet of faith radically
extended by Milton. Yet, Milton's poem, no doubt written out of
the extraordinary strength of his belief in individual conscience,
does not espouse overtly its radical beliefs (though something of his
materialism can be seen in the insistence on angelic digestion and
sex, and the mortalism may be heard in the anxious dialogue
between God and the Son in Book III, hardly a conversation,
moreover, between equals); nor, with a God conceived of as
beleaguered monarch or, to Satan's eyes, a suspect tyrant, does the
poem easily project on to heaven the kind of political regime Milton
might have seen as divinely ordained (the debates in hell, however,
might well have been modelled on a parliament in which Milton
had less and less faith and, more generally, may reflect his disgust
at the factionalism of the 1650s against which he had attempted to
rally the revolutionary cause).

The precariousness, indeed, the virtual impossibility of Milton's
position, as he increasingly represented himself as virtually the sole
repository of a revolutionary spirit that had been abandoned and
betrayed, may best be represented in the hero of *Samson Agonistes*
(1671), the last poem Milton published. Like *Paradise Lost*, this
'final' poem reflects years of rewriting and revision dating back to
the 1640s; Samson's relation to Dalila, for instance, represents a
recasting of Milton's marriage to Mary Powell, the first of his three
wives—he married her in 1642; she almost immediately left him,
returning to her Royalist parents for several years, finally rejoining
Milton to bear him the three daughters whom he used notoriously
as his readers and amanuenses in his later years; Mary Powell
Milton died in 1652. Samson's deliverance of the nation, and
delivery of himself into the hands of his God, is the ultimate
sacrifice, the long deferred event against which Milton had wagered
his life.

If Samson's success is, at the same time, his defeat, this condition
may also characterize the writing and delivery of *Paradise Lost*; the
poem deferred by the Revolution and written in its defeat. Yet,
paradoxically, Milton's poem, because of the very conditions of its

continual rewriting and deferred delivery, is a revolutionary one or, even more to the point, a modern one. Written not merely after the Revolution and after its ineffaceable disruption of the past (the Restoration of the Stuarts soon led to another 'revolution'—the so-called 'Glorious Revolution' of 1688—and the installation of a monarch under the control of parliament; thus the lasting effect of the revolutionary years was its contribution to modern bourgeois liberalism), Milton's poem achieves its force through the radicality of its displacements. No longer legible within the designs of Spenserian epic, no longer answerable to a Revolution that had failed but which might also have led Milton to write a poem far more didactic and chastened than the one he did write, Milton's poem can only imagine a futurity it cannot possibly inhabit and which it only incipiently imagines (Adam and Eve, it has been often noted, seem like a proto-bourgeois couple or, at times, are almost novelistic in their presentation). If one name for Milton's strength is, arguably, individualism (a privilege that cannot be separated from his gender, race, or social position), it emerges in the characteristic form of modern individualism, expressed as the antagonism between individual and society. That this opposi-tional stance derives from Milton's years during the so-called Interregnum cannot be doubted. But what this means, too, is that the canonical force of *Paradise Lost* is not bound by the ways in which it anticipates the kinds of social settlement represented by the Glorious Revolution; the poem also houses disruptive energies, those revolutionary principles that the Glorious Revolution betrayed. That such disruptiveness marks Milton's writing could be noticed even in the earliest *alter ego* he chose—the Herculean child of *On the Morning of Christ's Nativity*—and it remains the case with Samson. This stance is arguably the one continuity that overrides the deferrals, delays, and refusals of the career we have sketched. What it suggests, as we have already implied, is a double legacy, at the least, of *Paradise Lost*.

On the one hand, one could look to even the earliest of Milton's readers and critics, Dryden for instance, to see how much the poem had to be defended against even as it was embraced. Thus, in 1674, the very year that *Paradise Lost* appeared in its final twelve-book incarnation, Dryden rewrote it as an opera, recast it into rhymed couplets, refashioned it to meet contemporary literary formal and generic demands. If this made Milton's epic seem instantly old-fashioned, it was also by ascribing to it a pastness that Dryden could locate its value, praising it, for instance in a poem accompanying the 1688 edition of the epic, as equal in stature to Homer or Virgil. The very effort to push Milton's epic into the remote past—to deny its contemporaneity—attributes to it, however, enormous force. For, by relocating *Paradise Lost* in antiquity, it is made a classic text. The conferral of canonical status on the poem is thus an attempt on Dryden's part to distance himself from it. What is involved is not simply aesthetic distance, however; the defence against the poem registers not merely its literary accomplishment but perhaps even more its disquieting energies.

Some of this can be seen in Dryden's critical estimation of *Paradise Lost* in the preface to his operatic rewriting of the epic, *The State of Innocence*, as 'one of the greatest, most noble, and most sublime poems which either this age or nation has produced'. The coupling of such terms as 'noble' and 'sublime' ascribes to the poem quasi-aristocratic value; the epic becomes exemplary of its kind, the highest of forms, and the coupling of generic and class markers 'elevates' the poem in ways that safeguard it against revolutionary or republican readings. This is perhaps even more the case in the series of essays on the poem that Addison contributed to *The Spectator* in 1712. Treating the poem as a supreme instance of 'the highest kind' of poetry, an epic that deserved to be called 'divine', Addison sought at the same time to make it normative, the realization of its genre and, beyond that, the embodiment of a comfortable and conforming Christianity. For Addison, the poem is 'universal' in its scope—and 'useful' too, for it teaches the great moral of obedience. Everywhere, Addison notes what makes the poem 'proper'; even the 'sublimity of his thoughts', which Addison believed was the source of the poem's greatness, is treated as part of its propriety, its ability, for instance to raise 'some glorious image or sentiment, proper to inflame the mind of the reader'. Addison's *Paradise Lost* exhibits a refining and subliming fire, capable of bringing readers up to a level of critical judgement and of belief that is no different from their social refinement. In his twelve essays on the 'beauties' of each book of *Paradise Lost*, Addison was at pains to show the meanings that 'ordinary' readers might miss, and to guide them to what is 'capable of pleasing the most delicate reader' and to raise his readers to that 'delicate' capacity. Thus, for instance, Addison's readers learn that Eve is 'soft and womanish', while Adam is 'more masculine and elevated'; what Addison terms the 'universal' is never far from a very restricted and hierarchized vision of a gendered social decorum.

As we have suggested, one legacy of the Revolution and thereby of the revolutionary poem might well have been the modern bourgeois state and its attendant liberal values. Addison makes *Paradise Lost* a poem that is legible in those terms, a site of 'sentiments' that are always 'conformable to their respective characters', conformable, that is, both to the character of a sublime poem and to the character of their exemplary characters. 'His subject', Addison sums up, 'is the noblest that could have entered into the thoughts of man.' What this means, among other things, is that Milton's imagination is 'conformable to . . . Scripture', 'finely imagined, and grounded upon what is delivered in sacred story'. Hence 'the more the reader examines the justness and delicacy of its sentiments, the more he will find himself pleased with it'. The poem, then, is educative, at once teaching what is best in poetry, best to believe, best if one is to reform oneself into that which makes one most noble and elevated, in a word, socially decorous and refined in taste and sensibility. For Milton, Addison assured his readers, 'took the greatest care to avoid anything that might be offensive to religion or good manners'.

Through complicated byways, views like Addison's have continued to prevail in Milton criticism and scholarship, if not quite in the same terms, none the less in the sense that Milton's poem represents enduring values, saving beliefs, comfort, and consolation. In that respect much Milton criticism supports a view of canonical literature which assumes that such texts instil time-transcending universal values, that what the Bible or the classics teach are entirely dehistoricized truths. In Addison and Dryden one can see the invention of that critical belief as part of the post-revolutionary settlement and as a reaction to, as much as a reading of, Milton's poem.

But, as we have suggested, there is, and virtually from the start, another legacy of the poem, one that finds the poem far less comfortable. It can be seen, for instance, in Richard Bentley's 1732 edition of *Paradise Lost*, which regards the poem as hardly perfect in execution or exemplary in its meanings. Bentley desired to save the poem's faults from Milton, and thus ascribed its supposed errors to an editor or to the printer. On the one hand, this saving gesture seeks to elevate Milton and Miltonic individualism above the vagaries of the material text. But on the other hand—since the 'errors' that Bentley found in the text were in fact Milton's—Bentley's reading of the poem confronts much in it that is unassimilable to the conforming response of Addison and his followers. So William Empson argued in *Some Versions of Pastoral* (1935), in an essay that reclaimed the errors of Bentley for a contemporary reading project, in Empson's case, one directed as much against prevailing orthodox readings of Milton (which became the standard academic critical tradition) as against a new orthodoxy, the rejection of the poet advanced by modernist critics. These followed the lead of T. S. Eliot, who, in his 1921 essay on 'The Metaphysical Poets', condemned Milton as the writer who had introduced a 'dissociation of sensibility' that Eliot saw as his task to repair. Modernist rejections of Milton that followed (including, famously, F. R. Leavis's attempt to rewrite the canon of English literature without Milton in it) depended precisely on a reading of Milton as a deadly upholder of calcified poetic form and language. That is, modernist readings depended on the Milton that the tradition of Addison espoused. Yet just below the surface of the assaults of Eliot or Leavis can be seen something else: a defence against Milton, a dislike of his wresting of language away from the ordinary, of his stretching of literary form to the breaking-point, and, hence, of the revolutionary politics that underlies the formal features of the poem. And ironically, as is more than suggested by Eliot's final recantation in a 1947 essay that somewhat grudgingly acknowledged Milton as a great poet, what modernist criticism wanted from Milton was precisely what it also claimed he did not offer: the consolations of order and art against the depradations of ordinary life. When Eliot found himself at home in the Established Church, he was willing to admit Milton into the literary pantheon after all. Both the rejection and the admission of Milton were couched, as we have been suggesting, in the terms laid out much earlier by Dryden and Addison. Or, as Empson astutely noted, both those academic critics who rallied around Milton as the embodiment of eternal values, and those modernist critics who followed in the wake of Eliot, were united in their neo-Christianity and social conservatism.

The terms for modern literary criticism were invented in the eighteenth century, and it was around Milton (and Shakespeare and Spenser) that its programme developed. Empson, arguably the greatest critic of Milton in the twentieth century, looked back not only to the extravagant example of Milton's early editors. Implicitly, his arguments about the poem have everything to do with Dr Johnson, the most brilliant eighteenth-century critic of Milton. In some respects, Johnson shared the normative views of his predecessors, and there are passages in his life of Milton that could be put beside Addison, as, for instance, his claim that *Paradise Lost* is a 'useful' text that shows 'the reasonableness of religion, and the necessity of obedience to the Divine Law'. We have had occasion already to note Johnson's resistance to Milton's politics, and we could easily recall some of his most famous—and most defensive —judgements about Milton's poems, notably his estimation of *Lycidas* as 'easy, vulgar and therefore disgusting', an evaluation seemingly motivated by pastoral as a genre but no doubt informed by the overt political reading of pastoral that the poem insists on in its subtitle. Johnson's resistance to Milton is valuable to notice because it suggests how hard won his admiration for *Paradise Lost* was. His reading of the poem testifies to its overwhelming force— the reader of the poem is described, for instance, as 'harassed and overburdened'—its imposition on him the weight not merely of its learning, but its vast abilities to displace the forms it inhabits. Also, and perhaps most important to Empson, Johnson measures the material force of Milton's language, its refusals of the protocols of sense, its joining of abstract and concrete, 'the confusion of spirit and matter' that Johnson saw as the consequence of one dilemma that Milton faced, 'the description of what cannot be described, the agency of spirits'. Although Johnson assumed that Milton shared his view of the separation of matter and spirit, what Johnson responds to is the materiality of a language that refuses to mark spirit as different in kind from matter; this is the representational equivalent of the poet's heretical materialism. It is from this point not an easy or inevitable leap to the arguments of Empson's *Milton's God* (1961), which suggested nothing less than the ways in which the poem's beliefs are anything but normative, that Milton puts God on trial and he comes off wanting, but it can almost be heard even in the course of Johnson's most normative account of the poem, for what he described as the most 'useful' aim of the poem, its instilling of reasonable belief and obedience to divine law, he also recognized as 'most arduous: "to vindicate the ways of God to man"'.

Empson's reading could be assimilated to the romantics' Milton, to Blake's proclamation in *The Marriage of Heaven and Hell* that Milton 'was of the Devil's party without knowing it', for instance. Such a belief is not unprecedented, however; Dryden had much earlier opined that *Paradise Lost* failed precisely in so far as it had made Satan its hero. Empson was close enough to eighteenth-century views to want what he saw as the truth about Milton's God to have been what Milton intended, to assault the values of Christianity; that is, Empson read the poem as an attack on Christianity written from within its beliefs. The poem is assumed to express Milton's conflicts, and, beyond that, the inherent conflicts within Christianity. 'As a rule,' Empson wrote in his essay on 'Milton and Bentley', 'if Milton's sympathies were divided, he understood the conflict he was dramatising, and if the result is hard to explain, it is easy to feel.' There is much in Milton's theology that supports Empson's views.

One can also trace a path from the romantics back to Dr Johnson. For Johnson's response to the poem suggests the ways in which it compels in him beliefs that run counter to his own, counter to the normalizing tendencies that marked earlier eighteenth-century critics like Dryden and Addison. Thus, for instance, Johnson echoes Addison in describing the poem as sublime; but for him, unlike Addison, this does not mean that the poem elevates one to a higher plane of civilized and polite consciousness. Rather, Johnson sees that the poem is profoundly inhuman, not merely because its task is to represent spirits, but also because until their fall even Adam and Eve are not human beings we can ever hope to approximate, not the basis for characters that one might find in a novel; hence, the poem gives 'little assistance to human conduct'. There is, Johnson claims, a 'want of human interest' throughout the poem, and the sublimity of the poem lies in the ways in which it stretches the reader to a breaking-point. Johnson can be wickedly nasty about this, as when he reports that '*Paradise Lost* is one of the books which the reader admires and lays down, and forgets to take up again', and concludes, 'none ever wished it longer than it is'. (This does not mean, however, that he would have approved of the excerpting of the poem that will be found in this edition.) This all too human response to the poem also serves to register its demands. And indeed the sublimity of the poem is captured in descriptions that seem proto-romantic, as the poem becomes a virtually ungraspable landscape of highs and lows, light and darkness, too vast to fill any mind except, as Johnson repeats over and again, the capacious imagination of a poet at home in 'the power of displaying the vast, illuminating the splendid, enforcing the awful, darkening the gloomy, and aggravating the dreadful'. Given these qualities, Johnson continues, Milton 'chose a subject on which too much could not be said, on which he might tire his fancy without the censure of extravagance'. Indeed, despite Johnson's attempts to find fault with the poem, he continued to register the fact that what he calls its weaknesses are at the same time signs of its inhuman strength.

Johnson recalls Addison's estimation that 'our language sunk under him', and recasts this as he describes the reader of the poem 'in captivity to a higher and nobler mind'; 'criticism', he concluded, 'sinks in admiration'. Johnson's response to the sublimity of the poem entailed this fall of the reader and critic before the heights of the poem's accomplishment, an inversion of the sublime effect of the poem's mingling of heights and depths. Whereas in Addison, the poem's elevation of the reader served a profoundly social function, Johnson's reader/critic is the site of a displacement by a poem that 'crowds the imagination', a dislocation that makes the scene of the reception of the poem a struggle between the Miltonic mind and the reader's. If this serves further to elevate and distance Milton it also paves the way for the privatization of the reading experience, conferring on any literate, cultivated reader the additional burden of a privacy that affords one the luxury of the agonized measuring of one's own individual imaginative capacities. It is in this sense that Johnson leads the way towards romantic criticism and provides another path to modern criticism—indeed to the so-called New Criticism—with its dehistoricizing valuation of the ability of literature to increase the reader's stock in imaginative responsiveness. Or, to shift terms slightly, Johnson's reader labours under the burden of achieving possession of an interiority that is the measure of what Pierre Bourdieu would call one's cultural capital.

If Johnson's criticism holds out this legacy, it also leads, as we have been suggesting, to Empson, and Empson, in turn, and especially through the intervention represented by *Milton's God*, could lead to a project of reading that would continually engage the resistance that Milton's *Paradise Lost* offers to privatizing, normalizing, and simply adulatory responses to the poem. The effect of such readings would not be necessarily to decanonize Milton, as modernist critics sought to do, but to be asking all the time what the effects of canonization are, in whose interests monuments like *Paradise Lost* are written, and what agendas they may serve or be made to subvert—or, perhaps even more to the point, to a recognition that canonicity does not necessarily name the value or the meaning of the text. One can be reminded of this, for instance, by what Malcolm X made of *Paradise Lost*, as he recounts in his autobiography:

In either volume 43 or 44 of The Harvard Classics, I read Milton's *Paradise Lost*. The devil, kicked out of Paradise, was trying to regain possession. He was using the forces of Europe, personified by the Popes, Charlemagne, Richard the Lionhearted, and other knights. I interpreted this to show that the Europeans were motivated and led by the devil, or the personification of the devil. So Milton and Mr Elijah Muhammad were actually saying the same thing.

Malcolm read the poem as an exposure of, rather than, an exaltation of the Western tradition, particularly in its inextricable relationship to those forces which, demonically, in the name of Christianity, have sought to enslave non-Christian, Muslim, and Black cultures. In recent years, feminist criticism has provided another powerful site of reading, so much so that Eve, these days, is the character to which most revisionary criticism is drawn (this impulse can be found in Empson, too, who describes Eve as 'set up' by the scheme of the poem and its religion; indeed even Johnson excoriates the poet's masculinism, his 'Turkish contempt of females, as subordinate and inferior beings', though it is of course noteworthy that Johnson would have such behaviour characterize Islamic rather than Western European cultures). Empson's desire to embed Milton's critique within his Christianity leads the way to a further historicizing of the poem, not least because theological issues do not merely count as religious but are sites for the most contested struggles in seventeenth-century England, at the centre of debates over social relations and institutions. The full effect of the poem as the product of a revolutionary consciousness—and its continuing possibilities for disruption—remain to be measured (Christopher Hill is perhaps the best guide on this question). Milton 'thought woman made only for obedience, and man only for rebellion', Johnson opines, pointing to a gendered division of labour in his work which everywhere shapes and deforms its imaginative project. Johnson's remark none the less inevitably suggests not merely a critical project of resistance to Miltonic designs but the very ways in which his rebelliousness must be read against efforts to contain his work, whether its aim is taken to be the justification of God or the exaltation of individual imagination. Rather, one might do well to read *Paradise Lost* following Empson, with an awareness that Milton gives 'every action a nightmare importance' and that what is thereby displayed is 'the Western temper at its height'. In this crisis-ridden text, Empson located the 'insane disproportion' between the biblical story of transgression—the eating of the forbidden fruit—and its fatal consequences. Building upon this description, one could generalize further to suggest (and to hold out this prospect to readers of Milton now) that the 'insane disproportion' of *Paradise Lost* guarantees that it can never be contained, that it will remain a site of reading that must be probed in terms of the vast overdeterminations that produced it and that have continued to produce it differently over the course of the past centuries.

Acknowledgements

LIKE every editor of Milton, our greatest debt is to previous editors. In particular, the *Variorum Milton*, the editions of Merritt Y. Hughes, John Carey, and Alastair Fowler, and the relevant volumes of the great Yale Milton *Prose* have been our constant companions. Our work has been greatly assisted by Fellowships at the Humanities Research Centre of the Australian National University in Canberra, and at the J. Paul Getty Center in Santa Monica; we gratefully acknowledge the superlative working conditions, the hospitality of our hosts, and the opportunity to discuss Milton over an extended period with two distinguished groups of Fellows. For enlightenment on particular points we are indebted to Philip Brett, Ian Donaldson, J. Martin Evans, Marcie Frank, Stanley Fish, Christopher Highley, Jonathan Brody Kramnick, Robert Mandelbaum, Bradley Rubidge, and Gary Spear. John Shawcross deserves a sentence to himself for his invaluable assistance on bibliographical matters. The general editor has been an unfailingly helpful guide, and many of his suggestions have been silently incorporated. Finally, the care, goodwill, and especially the patience of Judith Luna at the Oxford University Press seem to us beyond praise.

Chronology

1608   9 December: John Milton born in Cheapside, London, first son of John Milton, scrivener and musician, and his wife Sara.

c. 1615/17–24   Attends St Paul's School, London.

1625   Enters Christ's College, Cambridge.

1626   Probably rusticated (suspended) from Cambridge for part of Lent term.

1629   BA.

1632   MA; Milton's first published poem, 'On Shakespeare', appears in the dedicatory verses to the second Shakespeare folio.

1632–4   Lives at the family home in Hammersmith.

1634   *A Masque Presented at Ludlow Castle* ('*Comus*') performed.

1635–8   Lives at the family's country house at Horton, Bucks.

1637   Death of Sara Milton. Milton's classmate Edward King drowned.

1638–9   Travels in Italy.

1638   Publication of *Lycidas* in a volume of elegies for Edward King. Milton's closest friend, Charles Diodati, dies in August and is memorialized in *Epitaphium Damonis*.

1639   Milton returns to England and lives and teaches in London.

1640   Long Parliament convened 3 November.

1641   Publication of Milton's first political tracts: *Of Reformation, Of Prelatical Episcopacy, Animadversions upon the Remonstrant's Defence against Smectymnuus*.

1642   Civil War begins 22 August. Publication of *The Reason of Church Government, Apology for Smectymnuus*. Milton marries Mary Powell, who several months later returns to her family.

1643   Publication of *The Doctrine and Discipline of Divorce*.

1644   *Of Education, The Judgement of Martin Bucer Concerning Divorce, Areopagitica*, and a revised and enlarged edition of *Doctrine and Discipline* published.

1645	Publication of *Tetrachordon* and *Colasterion*. Mary Powell Milton returns to live with Milton.
1646	*Poems of Mr John Milton* (dated 1645) published. Milton's daughter Anne born.
1647	Death of John Milton, Sen.
1648	Milton's daughter Mary born.
1649	King Charles executed. Publication of *The Tenure of Kings and Magistrates* and *Eikonoklastes*. Milton appointed Secretary for Foreign Tongues by the Council of State.
1651	Publication of *Defensio pro Populo Anglicano*. Milton's son John born.
1652	Milton becomes totally blind. His wife Mary dies after giving birth to their daughter Deborah. His son John dies.
1654	*Defensio Secunda* published. Cromwell becomes Protector.
1655	*Pro Se Defensio* published.
1656	Marries Katherine Woodcock.
1657	Birth of a daughter, who dies six months later.
1658	Death of Katherine Woodcock Milton. Death of Cromwell.
1659	Publication of *A Treatise of Civil Power* and *Considerations touching the Likeliest Means to Remove Hirelings out of the Church*.
1660	Publication of *The Ready and Easy Way to Establish a Free Commonwealth*. Charles II enters London. Milton arrested and imprisoned; released seven months later.
1663	Marries Elizabeth Minshull.
1667	*Paradise Lost* published in a ten-book version.
1670	*The History of Britain* published.
1671	*Paradise Regained* and *Samson Agonistes* published.
1673	Revised and enlarged edition of *Poems* (1645) published. *Of True Religion* published.
1674	*Paradise Lost* published in a twelve-book version. Milton dies 8 November.

Note on the Text

MODERNIZATION of Milton's spelling has been carried out according to the principles established by Stanley Wells in *Modernizing Shakespeare's Spelling* (Oxford, 1979). This has meant a loss of quaintness—e.g. sovran, quire, and faery have become sovereign, choir, and fairy—but it is hoped that most readers will agree with us that Milton in his own time was not quaint. In the spelling of proper names, an uneasy compromise has been attempted. Where the modern spelling leaves pronunciation and rhythm unaffected, we have modernized; but Milton's biblical names are those of the Vulgate, not the Authorized Version, and his geography cannot be brought up to date. Hence we retain Dalila, Fesole, Rhene, Danaw, but we use Moloch (not Moloc), Moscow (not Mosco), Astrakhan (not Astracan). In general, the sound of English has changed so much since Milton's time that it has seemed pointless, if not positively misleading, to retain old spellings merely because they seem to preserve a particular Miltonic pronunciation. Punctuation is a more complex matter, and one to which Milton paid careful attention. His practice is not entirely consistent, but to modernize it is to lose not only a good deal of rhetorical force, but often his most individual syntax. Here again, the language has changed, and grammatical structures that were possible, and even commonplace, in the seventeenth century are now solecisms. For example, a question mark does not invariably indicate the end of a sentence for Milton; to capitalize the lower-case word following the question mark, as most modern editors routinely do, constitutes a grammatical change. In general, we have undertaken to alter the original punctuation only when it seemed patently incorrect or when not to modernize it would be confusing or misleading. We have not attempted to produce a Milton in modern syntax.

In our arrangement of the poems, we have undertaken to follow the order established by Milton himself, in so far as it was feasible to do so, rather than the arrangement according to dates of composition, often putative, usual in modern editions. We have undertaken, that is, to present Milton as he presented himself, feeling that this is an essential element in understanding his career. We have, therefore, kept the 1645 *Poems* together as a unit, and have in most instances preferred its readings to those of the 1673 text, which editorial opinion has generally considered less authoritative. In the case of the *Ode on the Morning of Christ's Nativity*, however, the 1673 text includes revisions that are clearly authorial, and therefore that is the text we have followed (the variants are given in the notes). For the text of *A Masque* (*Comus*), we have been persuaded by the editorial argument most forcefully maintained by John Shawcross that the 1673

revision of lines 166–9 is unlikely to be Milton's, and we have therefore
retained the 1645 reading. Poems added in the 1673 edition, and the few
uncollected poems, have been placed after the 1645 poems.

POEMS 1645

On the Morning of Christ's Nativity

I

This is the month, and this the happy morn
Wherein the son of heaven's eternal king,
Of wedded maid, and virgin mother born,
Our great redemption from above did bring;
For so the holy sages once did sing,
　　That he our deadly forfeit should release,
And with his father work us a perpetual peace.

II

That glorious form, that light unsufferable,
And that far-beaming blaze of majesty,
Wherewith he wont at heaven's high council-table,　　10
To sit the midst of trinal unity,
He laid aside; and here with us to be,
　　Forsook the courts of everlasting day,
And chose with us a darksome house of mortal clay.

III

Say heavenly muse, shall not thy sacred vein
Afford a present to the infant God?
Hast thou no verse, no hymn, or solemn strain,
To welcome him to this his new abode,
Now while the heaven by the sun's team untrod,
　　Hath took no print of the approaching light,　　20
And all the spangled host keep watch in squadrons bright?

IV

See how from far upon the eastern road
The star-led wizards haste with odours sweet,
O run, prevent them with thy humble ode,
And lay it lowly at his blessèd feet;
Have thou the honour first thy Lord to greet,

And join thy voice unto the angel choir,
From out his secret altar touched with hallowed fire.

THE HYMN

I

It was the winter wild,
While the heaven-born-child   30
   All meanly wrapped in the rude manger lies;
Nature in awe to him
Had doffed her gaudy trim,
   With her great master so to sympathize:
It was no season then for her
To wanton with the sun her lusty paramour.

II

Only with speeches fair
She woos the gentle air
   To hide her guilty front with innocent snow,
And on her naked shame,   40
Pollute with sinful blame,
   The saintly veil of maiden white to throw,
Confounded, that her maker's eyes
Should look so near upon her foul deformities.

III

But he her fears to cease,
Sent down the meek-eyed Peace,
   She crowned with olive green, came softly sliding
Down through the turning sphere
His ready harbinger,
   With turtle wing the amorous clouds dividing,   50
And waving wide her myrtle wand,
She strikes a universal peace through sea and land.

IV

No war, or battle's sound
Was heard the world around
   The idle spear and shield were high up hung,
The hookèd chariot stood
Unstained with hostile blood,

The trumpet spake not to the armèd throng,
And kings sat still with awful eye,
As if they surely knew their sovereign Lord was by.   60

V

But peaceful was the night
Wherein the prince of light
   His reign of peace upon the earth began:
The winds with wonder whist,
Smoothly the waters kissed,
   Whispering new joys to the mild ocean,
Who now hath quite forgot to rave,
While birds of calm sit brooding on the charmèd wave.

VI

The stars with deep amaze
Stand fixed in steadfast gaze,   70
   Bending one way their precious influence,
And will not take their flight,
For all the morning light,
   Or Lucifer that often warned them thence;
But in their glimmering orbs did glow,
Until their Lord himself bespake, and bid them go.

VII

And though the shady gloom
Had given day her room,
   The sun himself withheld his wonted speed,
And hid his head for shame,   80
As his inferior flame,
   The new enlightened world no more should need;
He saw a greater sun appear
Than his bright throne, or burning axle-tree could bear.

VIII

The shepherds on the lawn,
Or ere the point of dawn,
   Sat simply chatting in a rustic row;
Full little thought they then,
That the mighty Pan
   Was kindly come to live with them below;   90

Perhaps their loves, or else their sheep,
Was all that did their silly thoughts so busy keep.

IX

When such music sweet
Their hearts and ears did greet,
   As never was by mortal finger strook,
Divinely-warbled voice
Answering the stringèd noise,
   As all their souls in blissful rapture took:
The air such pleasure loth to lose,
With thousand echoes still prolongs each heavenly close.   100

X

Nature that heard such sound
Beneath the hollow round
   Of Cynthia's seat, the airy region thrilling,
Now was almost won
To think her part was done,
   And that her reign had here its last fulfilling;
She knew such harmony alone
Could hold all heaven and earth in happier union.

XI

At last surrounds their sight
A globe of circular light,   110
   That with long beams the shamefaced night arrayed,
The helmèd cherubim
And sworded seraphim,
   Are seen in glittering ranks with wings displayed,
Harping in loud and solemn choir,
With unexpressive notes to heaven's newborn heir.

XII

Such music (as 'tis said)
Before was never made,
   But when of old the sons of morning sung,
While the creator great   120
His constellations set,
   And the well-balanced world on hinges hung,

And cast the dark foundations deep,
And bid the welt'ring waves their oozy channel keep.

XIII

Ring out, ye crystal spheres,
Once bless our human ears
   (If ye have power to touch our senses so),
And let your silver chime
Move in melodious time;
   And let the base of heaven's deep organ blow,   130
And with your ninefold harmony
Make up full consort to the angelic symphony.

XIV

For if such holy song
Enwrap our fancy long,
   Time will run back, and fetch the age of gold,
And speckled vanity
Will sicken soon and die,
   And lep'rous sin will melt from earthly mould,
And hell itself will pass away,
And leave her dolorous mansions to the peering day.   140

XV

Yea Truth, and Justice then
Will down return to men,
   Orbed in a rainbow; and like glories wearing
Mercy will sit between,
Throned in celestial sheen,
   With radiant feet the tissued clouds down steering,
And heaven as at some festival,
Will open wide the gates of her high palace hall.

XVI

But wisest fate says no,
This must not yet be so,   150
   The babe lies yet in smiling infancy,
That on the bitter cross
Must redeem our loss;
   So both himself and us to glorify:

Yet first to those ychained in sleep,
The wakeful trump of doom must thunder through the deep.

XVII

With such a horrid clang
As on Mount Sinai rang
  While the red fire, and smould'ring clouds out brake:
The agèd earth aghast   160
With terror of that blast,
  Shall from the surface to the centre shake;
When at the world's last session,
The dreadful judge in middle air shall spread his throne.

XVIII

And then at last our bliss
Full and perfect is,
  But now begins; for from this happy day
The old dragon underground
In straiter limits bound,
  Not half so far casts his usurpèd sway,   170
And wroth to see his kingdom fail,
Swinges the scaly horror of his folded tail.

XIX

The oracles are dumb,
No voice or hideous hum
  Runs through the archèd roof in words deceiving.
Apollo from his shrine
Can no more divine,
  With hollow shriek the steep of Delphos leaving.
No nightly trance, or breathèd spell,
Inspires the pale-eyed priest from the prophetic cell.   180

XX

The lonely mountains o'er,
And the resounding shore,
  A voice of weeping heard, and loud lament;
From haunted spring, and dale
Edged with poplar pale,
  The parting genius is with sighing sent,

With flower-inwoven tresses torn
The nymphs in twilight shade of tangled thickets mourn.

XXI

In consecrated earth,
And on the holy hearth,   190
    The lars, and lemures moan with midnight plaint,
In urns, and altars round,
A drear and dying sound
    Affrights the flamens at their service quaint;
And the chill marble seems to sweat,
While each peculiar power forgoes his wonted seat.

XXII

Peor, and Baalim,
Forsake their temples dim,
    With that twice battered god of Palestine,
And moonèd Ashtaroth,   200
Heaven's queen and mother both,
    Now sits not girt with tapers' holy shrine,
The Libyc Hammon shrinks his horn,
In vain the Tyrian maids their wounded Thammuz mourn.

XXIII

And sullen Moloch fled,
Hath left in shadows dread,
    His burning idol all of blackest hue;
In vain with cymbals' ring,
They call the grisly king,
    In dismal dance about the furnace blue;   210
The brutish gods of Nile as fast,
Isis and Orus, and the dog Anubis haste.

XXIV

Nor is Osiris seen
In Memphian grove, or green,
    Trampling the unshowered grass with lowings loud:
Nor can he be at rest
Within his sacred chest,
    Nought but profoundest hell can be his shroud,

In vain with timbrelled anthems dark
The sable-stolèd sorcerers bear his worshipped ark.   220

XXV

He feels from Judah's land
The dreaded infant's hand,
    The rays of Bethlehem blind his dusky eyn;
Nor all the gods beside,
Longer dare abide,
    Not Typhon huge ending in snaky twine:
Our babe to show his Godhead true,
Can in his swaddling bands control the damnèd crew.

XXVI

So when the sun in bed,
Curtained with cloudy red,   230
    Pillows his chin upon an orient wave,
The flocking shadows pale,
Troop to the infernal jail,
    Each fettered ghost slips to his several grave,
And the yellow-skirted fays,
Fly after the night-steeds, leaving their moon-loved maze.

XXVII

But see the virgin blest,
Hath laid her babe to rest.
    Time is our tedious song should here have ending:
Heaven's youngest teemèd star,   240
Hath fixed her polished car,
    Her sleeping Lord with handmaid lamp attending:
And all about the courtly stable,
Bright-harnessed angels sit in order serviceable.

On Time

    Fly envious Time, till thou run out thy race,
    Call on the lazy leaden-stepping hours,
    Whose speed is but the heavy plummet's pace;
    And glut thyself with what thy womb devours,

Which is no more than what is false and vain,
And merely mortal dross;
So little is our loss,
So little is thy gain.
For whenas each thing bad thou hast entombed,
And last of all, thy greedy self consumed,   10
Then long eternity shall greet our bliss
With an individual kiss;
And joy shall overtake us as a flood,
When everything that is sincerely good
And perfectly divine,
With truth, and peace, and love shall ever shine
About the supreme throne
Of him, t' whose happy-making sight alone,
When once our heavenly-guided soul shall climb,
Then all this earthy grossness quit,   20
Attired with stars, we shall for ever sit,
    Triumphing over Death, and Chance, and thee O Time.

At a Solemn Music

Blest pair of sirens, pledges of heaven's joy,
Sphere-born harmonious sisters, Voice, and Verse,
Wed your divine sounds, and mixed power employ
Dead things with inbreathed sense able to pierce,
And to our high-raised fantasy present,
That undisturbèd song of pure concent,
Ay sung before the sapphire-coloured throne
To him that sits thereon
With saintly shout, and solemn jubilee,
Where the bright seraphim in burning row   10
Their loud uplifted angel trumpets blow,
And the cherubic host in thousand choirs
Touch their immortal harps of golden wires,
With those just spirits that wear victorious palms,
Hymns devout and holy psalms
Singing everlastingly;
That we on earth with undiscording voice
May rightly answer that melodious noise;

As once we did, till disproportioned sin
Jarred against nature's chime, and with harsh din   20
Broke the fair music that all creatures made
To their great Lord, whose love their motion swayed
In perfect diapason, whilst they stood
In first obedience, and their state of good.
Oh may we soon again renew that song,
And keep in tune with heaven, till God ere long
To his celestial consort us unite,
To live with him, and sing in endless morn of light.

On Shakespeare. *1630*

What needs my Shakespeare for his honoured bones,
The labour of an age in pilèd stones,
Or that his hallowed relics should be hid
Under a star-ypointing pyramid?
Dear son of memory, great heir of fame,
What need'st thou such weak witness of thy name?
Thou in our wonder and astonishment
Hast built thyself a live-long monument.
For whilst to th' shame of slow-endeavouring art,
Thy easy numbers flow, and that each heart   10
Hath from the leaves of thy unvalued book,
Those Delphic lines with deep impression took,
Then thou our fancy of itself bereaving,
Dost make us marble with too much conceiving;
And so sepulchred in such pomp dost lie,
That kings for such a tomb would wish to die.

L'Allegro

Hence loathèd Melancholy
  Of Cerberus, and blackest Midnight born,
In Stygian cave forlorn
  'Mongst horrid shapes, and shrieks, and sights unholy,
Find out some uncouth cell,

Where brooding Darkness spreads his jealous wings,
And the night-raven sings;
  There under ebon shades, and low-browed rocks,
As ragged as thy locks,
  In dark Cimmerian desert ever dwell.   10
But come thou goddess fair and free,
In heaven yclept Euphrosyne,
And by men, heart-easing Mirth,
Whom lovely Venus at a birth
With two sister Graces more
To ivy-crownèd Bacchus bore;
Or whether (as some sager sing)
The frolic wind that breathes the spring,
Zephyr with Aurora playing,
As he met her once a-Maying,   20
There on beds of violets blue,
And fresh-blown roses washed in dew,
Filled her with thee a daughter fair,
So buxom, blithe, and debonair.
Haste thee nymph, and bring with thee
Jest and youthful jollity,
Quips and cranks, and wanton wiles,
Nods, and becks, and wreathèd smiles,
Such as hang on Hebe's cheek,
And love to live in dimple sleek;   30
Sport that wrinkled Care derides,
And Laughter holding both his sides.
Come, and trip it as ye go
On the light fantastic toe,
And in thy right hand lead with thee,
The mountain nymph, sweet Liberty;
And if I give thee honour due,
Mirth, admit me of thy crew
To live with her, and live with thee,
In unreprovèd pleasures free;   40
To hear the lark begin his flight,
And singing startle the dull night,
From his watch-tower in the skies,
Till the dappled dawn doth rise;
Then to come in spite of sorrow,
And at my window bid good morrow,

Through the sweet-briar, or the vine,
Or the twisted eglantine.
While the cock with lively din,
Scatters the rear of darkness thin,   50
And to the stack, or the barn door,
Stoutly struts his dames before,
Oft list'ning how the hounds and horn
Cheerly rouse the slumb'ring morn,
From the side of some hoar hill,
Through the high wood echoing shrill.
Sometime walking not unseen
By hedgerow elms, on hillocks green,
Right against the eastern gate,
Where the great sun begins his state,   60
Robed in flames, and amber light,
The clouds in thousand liveries dight,
While the ploughman near at hand,
Whistles o'er the furrowed land,
And the milkmaid singeth blithe,
And the mower whets his scythe,
And every shepherd tells his tale
Under the hawthorn in the dale.
Straight mine eye hath caught new pleasures
Whilst the landscape round it measures,   70
Russet lawns, and fallows grey,
Where the nibbling flocks do stray,
Mountains on whose barren breast
The labouring clouds do often rest:
Meadows trim with daisies pied,
Shallow brooks, and rivers wide,
Towers, and battlements it sees
Bosomed high in tufted trees,
Where perhaps some beauty lies,
The cynosure of neighbouring eyes.   80
Hard by, a cottage chimney smokes,
From betwixt two agèd oaks,
Where Corydon and Thyrsis met,
Are at their savoury dinner set
Of herbs, and other country messes,
Which the neat-handed Phyllis dresses;
And then in haste her bower she leaves,

With Thestylis to bind the sheaves;
Or if the earlier season lead
To the tanned haycock in the mead,   90
Sometimes with secure delight
The upland hamlets will invite,
When the merry bells ring round,
And the jocund rebecks sound
To many a youth, and many a maid,
Dancing in the chequered shade;
And young and old come forth to play
On a sunshine holiday,
Till the livelong daylight fail,
Then to the spicy nut-brown ale,   100
With stories told of many a feat,
How fairy Mab the junkets eat,
She was pinched, and pulled she said,
And he by friar's lantern led
Tells how the drudging goblin sweat,
To earn his cream-bowl duly set,
When in one night, ere glimpse of morn,
His shadowy flail hath threshed the corn,
That ten day-labourers could not end;
Then lies him down the lubber fiend.   110
And stretched out all the chimney's length,
Basks at the fire his hairy strength;
And crop-full out of doors he flings,
Ere the first cock his matin rings.
Thus done the tales, to bed they creep,
By whispering winds soon lulled asleep.
Towered cities please us then,
And the busy hum of men,
Where throngs of knights and barons bold,
In weeds of peace high triumphs hold,   120
With store of ladies, whose bright eyes
Rain influence, and judge the prize
Of wit, or arms, while both contend
To win her grace, whom all commend.
There let Hymen oft appear
In saffron robe, with taper clear,
And pomp, and feast, and revelry,
With masque, and antique pageantry,

Such sights as youthful poets dream
On summer eves by haunted stream.   130
Then to the well-trod stage anon,
If Jonson's learnèd sock be on,
Or sweetest Shakespeare fancy's child,
Warble his native wood-notes wild,
And ever against eating cares,
Lap me in soft Lydian airs,
Married to immortal verse
Such as the meeting soul may pierce
In notes, with many a winding bout
Of linkèd sweetness long drawn out,   140
With wanton heed, and giddy cunning,
The melting voice through mazes running;
Untwisting all the chains that tie
The hidden soul of harmony.
That Orpheus' self may heave his head
From golden slumber on a bed
Of heaped Elysian flowers, and hear
Such strains as would have won the ear
Of Pluto, to have quite set free
His half-regainèd Eurydice.   150
These delights, if thou canst give,
Mirth with thee, I mean to live.

Il Penseroso

Hence vain deluding joys,
   The brood of folly without father bred,
How little you bestead,
   Or fill the fixèd mind with all your toys;
Dwell in some idle brain,
   And fancies fond with gaudy shapes possess,
As thick and numberless
   As the gay motes that people the sunbeams,
Or likest hovering dreams
   The fickle pensioners of Morpheus' train.   10
But hail thou goddess, sage and holy,
Hail divinest Melancholy,

Whose saintly visage is too bright
To hit the sense of human sight;
And therefore to our weaker view,
O'erlaid with black staid wisdom's hue.
Black, but such as in esteem,
Prince Memnon's sister might beseem,
Or that starred Ethiop queen that strove
To set her beauty's praise above   20
The sea-nymphs', and their powers offended.
Yet thou art higher far descended,
Thee bright-haired Vesta long of yore,
To solitary Saturn bore;
His daughter she (in Saturn's reign,
Such mixture was not held a stain)
Oft in glimmering bowers, and glades
He met her, and in secret shades
Of woody Ida's inmost grove,
While yet there was no fear of Jove.   30
Come pensive nun, devout and pure,
Sober, steadfast, and demure,
All in a robe of darkest grain,
Flowing with majestic train,
And sable stole of cypress lawn,
Over thy decent shoulders drawn.
Come, but keep thy wonted state,
With even step, and musing gait,
And looks commercing with the skies,
Thy rapt soul sitting in thine eyes: 40
There held in holy passion still,
Forget thyself to marble, till
With a sad leaden downward cast,
Thou fix them on the earth as fast.
And join with thee calm Peace, and Quiet,
Spare Fast, that oft with gods doth diet,
And hears the muses in a ring,
Ay round about Jove's altar sing.
And add to these retired Leisure,
That in trim gardens takes his pleasure;   50
But first, and chiefest, with thee bring,
Him that yon soars on golden wing,
Guiding the fiery-wheelèd throne,

The cherub Contemplation,
And the mute Silence hist along,
'Less Philomel will deign a song,
In her sweetest, saddest plight,
Smoothing the rugged brow of night,
While Cynthia checks her dragon yoke,
Gently o'er th' accustomed oak;   60
Sweet bird that shunn'st the noise of folly,
Most musical, most melancholy!
Thee chauntress oft the woods among,
I woo to hear thy even-song;
And missing thee, I walk unseen
On the dry smooth-shaven green,
To behold the wandering moon,
Riding near her highest noon,
Like one that had been led astray
Through the heaven's wide pathless way;   70
And oft, as if her head she bowed,
Stooping through a fleecy cloud.
Oft on a plat of rising ground,
I hear the far-off curfew sound,
Over some wide-watered shore,
Swinging slow with sullen roar;
Or if the air will not permit,
Some still removèd place will fit,
Where glowing embers through the room
Teach light to counterfeit a gloom,   80
Far from all resort of mirth,
Save the cricket on the hearth,
Or the bellman's drowsy charm,
To bless the doors from nightly harm:
Or let my lamp at midnight hour,
Be seen in some high lonely tower,
Where I may oft outwatch the Bear,
With thrice great Hermes, or unsphere
The spirit of Plato to unfold
What worlds, or what vast regions hold   90
The immortal mind that hath forsook
Her mansion in this fleshly nook:
And of those daemons that are found
In fire, air, flood, or underground,

Whose power hath a true consent
With planet, or with element.
Sometimes let gorgeous Tragedy
In sceptred pall come sweeping by,
Presenting Thebes, or Pelops' line,
Or the tale of Troy divine. 100
Or what (though rare) of later age,
Ennobled hath the buskined stage.
But, O sad virgin, that thy power
Might raise Musaeus from his bower,
Or bid the soul of Orpheus sing
Such notes as warbled to the string,
Drew iron tears down Pluto's cheek,
And made hell grant what love did seek.
Or call up him that left half-told
The story of Cambuscan bold, 110
Of Camball, and of Algarsife,
And who had Canace to wife,
That owned the virtuous ring and glass,
And of the wondrous horse of brass,
On which the Tartar king did ride;
And if aught else, great bards beside,
In sage and solemn tunes have sung,
Of tourneys and of trophies hung;
Of forests, and enchantments drear,
Where more is meant than meets the ear. 120
Thus Night oft see me in thy pale career,
Till civil-suited Morn appear,
Not tricked and frounced as she was wont,
With the Attic boy to hunt,
But kerchiefed in a comely cloud,
While rocking winds are piping loud,
Or ushered with a shower still,
When the gust hath blown his fill,
Ending on the rustling leaves,
With minute drops from off the eaves. 130
And when the sun begins to fling
His flaring beams, me goddess bring
To archèd walks of twilight groves,
And shadows brown that Sylvan loves
Of pine, or monumental oak,

Where the rude axe with heavèd stroke,
Was never heard the nymphs to daunt,
Or fright them from their hallowed haunt.
There in close covert by some brook,
Where no profaner eye may look,   140
Hide me from day's garish eye,
While the bee with honied thigh,
That at her flowery work doth sing,
And the waters murmuring
With such consort as they keep,
Entice the dewy-feathered Sleep;
And let some strange mysterious dream,
Wave at his wings in airy stream,
Of lively portraiture displayed,
Softly on my eyelids laid.   150
And as I wake, sweet music breathe
Above, about, or underneath,
Sent by some spirit to mortals good,
Or th' unseen genius of the wood.
But let my due feet never fail,
To walk the studious cloister's pale,
And love the high embowèd roof,
With antic pillars' massy proof,
And storied windows richly dight,
Casting a dim religious light.   160
There let the pealing organ blow,
To the full-voiced choir below,
In service high, and anthems clear,
As may with sweetness, through mine ear,
Dissolve me into ecstasies,
And bring all heaven before mine eyes.
And may at last my weary age
Find out the peaceful hermitage,
The hairy gown and mossy cell,
Where I may sit and rightly spell,   170
Of every star that heaven doth shew,
And every herb that sips the dew;
Till old experience do attain
To something like prophetic strain.
These pleasures Melancholy give,
And I with thee will choose to live.

Sonnet *1*

O nightingale, that on yon bloomy spray
   Warblest at eve, when all the woods are still,
   Thou with fresh hope the lover's heart dost fill,
   While the jolly hours lead on propitious May,
Thy liquid notes that close the eye of day,
   First heard before the shallow cuckoo's bill
   Portend success in love; O if Jove's will
   Have linked that amorous power to thy soft lay,
Now timely sing, ere the rude bird of hate
   Foretell my hopeless doom in some grove nigh: 10
   As thou from year to year hast sung too late
For my relief; yet hadst no reason why,
   Whether the muse, or Love call thee his mate,
   Both them I serve, and of their train am I.

Sonnet *7*

How soon hath time the subtle thief of youth,
   Stol'n on his wing my three and twentieth year!
   My hasting days fly on with full career,
   But my late spring no bud or blossom shew'th.
Perhaps my semblance might deceive the truth,
   That I to manhood am arrived so near,
   And inward ripeness doth much less appear,
   That some more timely-happy spirits endueth.
Yet be it less or more, or soon or slow,
   It shall be still in strictest measure even,   10
   To that same lot, however mean or high,
Toward which time leads me, and the will of heaven;
   All is, if I have grace to use it so,
   As ever in my great task-master's eye.

Sonnet 8

Captain or colonel, or knight in arms,
  Whose chance on these defenceless doors may seize,
  If ever deed of honour did thee please,
  Guard them, and him within protect from harms,
He can requite thee, for he knows the charms
  That call fame on such gentle acts as these,
  And he can spread thy name o'er lands and seas,
  Whatever clime the sun's bright circle warms.
Lift not thy spear against the muses' bower,
  The great Emathian conqueror bid spare   10
  The house of Pindarus, when temple and tower
Went to the ground: and the repeated air
  Of sad Electra's poet had the power
  To save the Athenian walls from ruin bare.

Sonnet 9

Lady, that in the prime of earliest youth,
  Wisely hast shunned the broad way and the green,
  And with those few are eminently seen,
  That labour up the hill of heavenly truth,
The better part with Mary and with Ruth,
  Chosen thou hast, and they that overween,
  And at thy growing virtues fret their spleen,
  No anger find in thee, but pity and ruth.
Thy care is fixed, and zealously attends
  To fill thy odorous lamp with deeds of light,   10
  And hope that reaps not shame. Therefore be sure
Thou, when the bridegroom with his feastful friends
  Passes to bliss at the mid-hour of night,
  Hast gained thy entrance, virgin wise and pure.

Sonnet 10

Daughter to that good earl, once president
    Of England's council, and her treasury,
    Who lived in both, unstained with gold or fee,
    And left them both, more in himself content,
Till the sad breaking of that parliament
    Broke him, as that dishonest victory
    At Chaeronea, fatal to liberty
    Killed with report that old man eloquent,
Though later born, than to have known the days
    Wherein your father flourished, yet by you,   10
    Madam, methinks I see him living yet;
So well your words his noble virtues praise,
    That all both judge you to relate them true,
    And to possess them, honoured Margaret.

Lycidas

In this monody the author bewails a learned friend, unfortunately drowned in his passage from Chester on the Irish Seas, 1637. And by occasion foretells the ruin of our corrupted clergy then in their height.

Yet once more, O ye laurels, and once more
Ye myrtles brown, with ivy never sere,
I come to pluck your berries harsh and crude,
And with forced fingers rude,
Shatter your leaves before the mellowing year.
Bitter constraint, and sad occasion dear,
Compels me to disturb your season due:
For Lycidas is dead, dead ere his prime,
Young Lycidas, and hath not left his peer:
Who would not sing for Lycidas? he knew   10
Himself to sing, and build the lofty rhyme.
He must not float upon his watery bier
Unwept, and welter to the parching wind,
Without the meed of some melodious tear.
    Begin then, sisters of the sacred well,
That from beneath the seat of Jove doth spring,

Begin, and somewhat loudly sweep the string.
Hence with denial vain, and coy excuse,
So may some gentle muse
With lucky words favour my destined urn,   20
And as he passes turn,
And bid fair peace be to my sable shroud.
For we were nursed upon the self-same hill,
Fed the same flock; by fountain, shade, and rill.
    Together both, ere the high lawns appeared
Under the opening eyelids of the morn,
We drove afield, and both together heard
What time the grey-fly winds her sultry horn,
Battening our flocks with the fresh dews of night,
Oft till the star that rose, at evening, bright   30
Toward heaven's descent had sloped his westering wheel.
Meanwhile the rural ditties were not mute,
Tempered to the oaten flute,
Rough satyrs danced, and fauns with cloven heel,
From the glad sound would not be absent long,
And old Damoetas loved to hear our song.
    But O the heavy change, now thou art gone,
Now thou art gone, and never must return!
Thee shepherd, thee the woods, and desert caves,
With wild thyme and the gadding vine o'ergrown,   40
And all their echoes mourn.
The willows, and the hazel copses green,
Shall now no more be seen,
Fanning their joyous leaves to thy soft lays.
As killing as the canker to the rose,
Or taint-worm to the weanling herds that graze,
Or frost to flowers, that their gay wardrobe wear,
When first the whitethorn blows;
Such, Lycidas, thy loss to shepherd's ear.
    Where were ye nymphs when the remorseless deep   50
Closed o'er the head of your loved Lycidas?
For neither were ye playing on the steep,
Where your old bards, the famous Druids lie,
Nor on the shaggy top of Mona high,
Nor yet where Deva spreads her wizard stream:
Ay me, I fondly dream!
Had ye been there ... for what could that have done?

What could the muse herself that Orpheus bore,
The muse herself, for her enchanting son
Whom universal nature did lament,   60
When by the rout that made the hideous roar,
His gory visage down the stream was sent,
Down the swift Hebrus to the Lesbian shore.
  Alas! What boots it with uncessant care
To tend the homely slighted shepherd's trade,
And strictly meditate the thankless muse,
Were it not better done as others use,
To sport with Amaryllis in the shade,
Or with the tangles of Neaera's hair?
Fame is the spur that the clear spirit doth raise   70
(That last infirmity of noble mind)
To scorn delights, and live laborious days;
But the fair guerdon when we hope to find,
And think to burst out into sudden blaze,
Comes the blind Fury with th' abhorrèd shears,
And slits the thin-spun life. But not the praise,
Phoebus replied, and touched my trembling ears;
Fame is no plant that grows on mortal soil,
Nor in the glistering foil
Set off to the world, nor in broad rumour lies,   80
But lives and spreads aloft by those pure eyes,
And perfect witness of all-judging Jove;
As he pronounces lastly on each deed,
Of so much fame in heaven expect thy meed.
  O fountain Arethuse, and thou honoured flood,
Smooth-sliding Mincius, crowned with vocal reeds,
That strain I heard was of a higher mood:
But now my oat proceeds,
And listens to the herald of the sea
That came in Neptune's plea,   90
He asked the waves, and asked the felon winds,
What hard mishap hath doomed this gentle swain?
And questioned every gust of rugged wings
That blows from off each beakèd promontory;
They knew not of his story,
And sage Hippotades their answer brings,
That not a blast was from his dungeon strayed,
The air was calm, and on the level brine,

Sleek Panope with all her sisters played.
It was that fatal and perfidious bark   100
Built in th' eclipse, and rigged with curses dark,
That sunk so low that sacred head of thine.
   Next Camus, reverend sire, went footing slow,
His mantle hairy, and his bonnet sedge,
Inwrought with figures dim, and on the edge
Like to that sanguine flower inscribed with woe.
Ah! who hath reft (quoth he) my dearest pledge?
Last came, and last did go,
The pilot of the Galilean lake,
Two massy keys he bore of metals twain   110
(The golden opes, the iron shuts amain),
He shook his mitred locks, and stern bespake,
How well could I have spared for thee, young swain,
Enow of such as for their bellies' sake,
Creep and intrude, and climb into the fold?
Of other care they little reckoning make,
Than how to scramble at the shearers' feast,
And shove away the worthy bidden guest.
Blind mouths! that scarce themselves know how to hold
A sheep-hook, or have learned aught else the least   120
That to the faithful herdman's art belongs!
What recks it them? What need they? They are sped;
And when they list, their lean and flashy songs
Grate on their scrannel pipes of wretched straw,
The hungry sheep look up, and are not fed,
But swoll'n with wind, and the rank mist they draw,
Rot inwardly, and foul contagion spread:
Besides what the grim wolf with privy paw
Daily devours apace, and nothing said,
But that two-handed engine at the door,   130
Stands ready to smite once, and smite no more.
   Return Alpheus, the dread voice is past,
That shrunk thy streams; return Sicilian muse,
And call the vales, and bid them hither cast
Their bells, and flowrets of a thousand hues.
Ye valleys low where the mild whispers use,
Of shades and wanton winds, and gushing brooks,
On whose fresh lap the swart star sparely looks,
Throw hither all your quaint enamelled eyes,

That on the green turf suck the honied showers,   140
And purple all the ground with vernal flowers.
Bring the rathe primrose that forsaken dies,
The tufted crow-toe, and pale jessamine,
The white pink, and the pansy freaked with jet,
The glowing violet,
The musk-rose, and the well-attired woodbine,
With cowslips wan that hang the pensive head,
And every flower that sad embroidery wears:
Bid amaranthus all his beauty shed,
And daffodillies fill their cups with tears,   150
To strew the laureate hearse where Lycid lies.
For so to interpose a little ease,
Let our frail thoughts dally with false surmise.
Ay me! Whilst thee the shores, and sounding seas
Wash far away, where'er thy bones are hurled,
Whether beyond the stormy Hebrides
Where thou perhaps under the whelming tide
Visit'st the bottom of the monstrous world;
Or whether thou to our moist vows denied,
Sleep'st by the fable of Bellerus old,   160
Where the great vision of the guarded mount
Looks toward Namancos and Bayona's hold;
Look homeward angel now, and melt with ruth.
And, O ye dolphins, waft the hapless youth.
   Weep no more, woeful shepherds weep no more,
For Lycidas your sorrow is not dead,
Sunk though he be beneath the watery floor,
So sinks the day-star in the ocean bed,
And yet anon repairs his drooping head,
And tricks his beams, and with new spangled ore,   170
Flames in the forehead of the morning sky:
So Lycidas sunk low, but mounted high,
Through the dear might of him that walked the waves,
Where other groves, and other streams along,
With nectar pure his oozy locks he laves,
And hears the unexpressive nuptial song,
In the blest kingdoms meek of joy and love.
There entertain him all the saints above,
In solemn troops, and sweet societies
That sing, and singing in their glory move,   180

And wipe the tears for ever from his eyes.
Now Lycidas the shepherds weep no more;
Henceforth thou art the genius of the shore,
In thy large recompense, and shalt be good
To all that wander in that perilous flood.

    Thus sang the uncouth swain to th' oaks and rills,
While the still morn went out with sandals grey,
He touched the tender stops of various quills,
With eager thought warbling his Doric lay:
And now the sun had stretched out all the hills,   190
And now was dropped into the western bay;
At last he rose, and twitched his mantle blue:
Tomorrow to fresh woods, and pastures new.

A Masque of the same Author
Presented at Ludlow Castle, 1634
Before the Earl of Bridgewater
Then President of Wales
['Comus']

THE PERSONS

The Attendant Spirit, afterwards in the habit of Thyrsis.
Comus, with his crew.
The Lady.
First Brother.
Second Brother.
Sabrina the Nymph.

The chief persons which presented, were
The Lord Brackley,
Master Thomas Egerton his brother,
The Lady Alice Egerton.

    The first scene discovers a wild wood.
      The Attendant Spirit descends or enters.

Before the starry threshold of Jove's court
My mansion is, where those immortal shapes
Of bright aerial spirits live ensphered

In regions mild of calm and serene air,
Above the smoke and stir of this dim spot,
Which men call earth, and, with low-thoughted care
Confined, and pestered in this pinfold here,
Strive to keep up a frail, and feverish being
Unmindful of the crown that virtue gives
After this mortal change, to her true servants   10
Amongst the enthroned gods on sainted seats.
Yet some there be that by due steps aspire
To lay their just hands on that golden key
That opes the palace of eternity:
To such my errand is, and but for such,
I would not soil these pure ambrosial weeds,
With the rank vapours of this sin-worn mould.
   But to my task. Neptune besides the sway
Of every salt flood, and each ebbing stream,
Took in by lot 'twixt high and nether Jove,   20
Imperial rule of all the sea-girt isles
That like to rich and various gems inlay
The unadornèd bosom of the deep,
Which he to grace his tributary gods
By course commits to several government,
And gives them leave to wear their sapphire crowns,
And wield their little tridents, but this isle
The greatest, and the best of all the main
He quarters to his blue-haired deities,
And all this tract that fronts the falling sun   30
A noble peer of mickle trust, and power
Has in his charge, with tempered awe to guide
An old, and haughty nation proud in arms:
Where his fair offspring nursed in princely lore,
Are coming to attend their father's state,
And new-entrusted sceptre, but their way
Lies through the perplexed paths of this drear wood,
The nodding horror of whose shady brows
Threats the forlorn and wandering passenger.
And here their tender age might suffer peril,   40
But that by quick command from sovereign Jove
I was dispatched for their defence, and guard;
And listen why, for I will tell you now
What never yet was heard in tale or song

From old, or modern bard in hall, or bower.
  Bacchus that first from out the purple grape,
Crushed the sweet poison of misusèd wine
After the Tuscan mariners transformed
Coasting the Tyrrhene shore, as the winds listed,
On Circe's island fell (who knows not Circe   50
The daughter of the Sun? Whose charmèd cup
Whoever tasted, lost his upright shape,
And downward fell into a grovelling swine);
This nymph that gazed upon his clustering locks,
With ivy berries wreathed, and his blithe youth,
Had by him, ere he parted thence, a son
Much like his father, but his mother more,
Whom therefore she brought up and Comus named,
Who ripe, and frolic of his full-grown age,
Roving the Celtic, and Iberian fields,   60
At last betakes him to this ominous wood,
And in thick shelter of black shades embowered,
Excels his mother at her mighty art,
Offering to every weary traveller,
His orient liquor in a crystal glass,
To quench the drought of Phoebus, which as they taste
(For most do taste through fond intemperate thirst)
Soon as the potion works, their human countenance,
The express resemblance of the gods, is changed
Into some brutish form of wolf, or bear,   70
Or ounce, or tiger, hog, or bearded goat,
All other parts remaining as they were,
And they, so perfect is their misery,
Not once perceive their foul disfigurement,
But boast themselves more comely than before
And all their friends, and native home forget
To roll with pleasure in a sensual sty.
Therefore when any favoured of high Jove,
Chances to pass through this advent'rous glade,
Swift as the sparkle of a glancing star,   80
I shoot from heaven to give him safe convoy,
As now I do: but first I must put off
These my sky-robes spun out of Iris' woof,
And take the weeds and likeness of a swain,
That to the service of this house belongs,

Who with his soft pipe, and smooth-dittied song,
Well knows to still the wild winds when they roar,
And hush the waving woods, nor of less faith,
And in this office of his mountain watch,
Likeliest, and nearest to the present aid   90
Of this occasion. But I hear the tread
Of hateful steps, I must be viewless now.

*Comus enters with a charming-rod in one hand, his glass in the other, with
him a rout of monsters, headed like sundry sorts of wild beasts, but otherwise
like men and women, their apparel glistering, they come in making a riotous
and unruly noise, with torches in their hands.*

Comus. The star that bids the shepherd fold,
Now the top of heaven doth hold,
And the gilded car of day,
His glowing axle doth allay
In the steep Atlantic stream,
And the slope sun his upward beam
Shoots against the dusky pole,
Pacing toward the other goal   100
Of his chamber in the east.
Meanwhile, welcome joy, and feast,
Midnight shout, and revelry,
Tipsy dance, and jollity.
Braid your locks with rosy twine
Dropping odours, dropping wine.
Rigour now is gone to bed,
And Advice with scrupulous head,
Strict Age, and sour Severity,
With their grave saws in slumber lie.   110
We that are of purer fire
Imitate the starry choir,
Who in their nightly watchful spheres,
Lead in swift round the months and years.
The sounds, and seas with all their finny drove
Now to the moon in wavering morris move,
And on the tawny sands and shelves,
Trip the pert fairies and the dapper elves;
By dimpled brook, and fountain-brim,
The wood-nymphs decked with daisies trim,   120
Their merry wakes and pastimes keep:

What hath night to do with sleep?
Night hath better sweets to prove,
Venus now wakes, and wakens Love.
Come let us our rites begin,
'Tis only daylight that makes sin
Which these dun shades will ne'er report.
Hail goddess of nocturnal sport
Dark-veiled Cotytto, to whom the secret flame
Of midnight torches burns; mysterious dame   130
That ne'er art called, but when the dragon womb
Of Stygian darkness spits her thickest gloom,
And makes one blot of all the air,
Stay thy cloudy ebon chair,
Wherein thou rid'st with Hecat', and befriend
Us thy vowed priests, till utmost end
Of all thy dues be done, and none left out,
Ere the blabbing eastern scout,
The nice morn on th' Indian steep
From her cabined loophole peep,   140
And to the tell-tale sun descry
Our concealed solemnity.
Come, knit hands, and beat the ground,
In a light fantastic round.

The Measure

Break off, break off, I feel the different pace
Of some chaste footing near about this ground.
Run to your shrouds, within these brakes and trees;
Our number may affright: some virgin sure
(For so I can distinguish by mine art)
Benighted in these woods. Now to my charms,   150
And to my wily trains; I shall ere long
Be well stocked with as fair a herd as grazed
About my mother Circe. Thus I hurl
My dazzling spells into the spongy air,
Of power to cheat the eye with blear illusion,
And give it false presentments, lest the place
And my quaint habits breed astonishment,
And put the damsel to suspicious flight,
Which must not be, for that's against my course;
I under fair pretence of friendly ends,   160

And well-placed words of glozing courtesy
Baited with reasons not unplausible
Wind me into the easy-hearted man,
And hug him into snares. When once her eye
Hath met the virtue of this magic dust,
I shall appear some harmless villager
Whom thrift keeps up about his country gear;
But here she comes, I fairly step aside
And hearken, if I may, her business here.

The Lady enters

Lady. This way the noise was, if mine ear be true,   170
My best guide now, methought it was the sound
Of riot, and ill-managed merriment,
Such as the jocund flute, or gamesome pipe
Stirs up among the loose unlettered hinds,
When for their teeming flocks, and granges full,
In wanton dance they praise the bounteous Pan,
And thank the gods amiss. I should be loath
To meet the rudeness, and swilled insolence
Of such late wassailers; yet O where else
Shall I inform my unacquainted feet   180
In the blind mazes of this tangled wood?
My brothers when they saw me wearied out
With this long way, resolving here to lodge
Under the spreading favour of these pines,
Stepped as they said to the next thicket-side
To bring me berries, or such cooling fruit
As the kind hospitable woods provide.
They left me then, when the grey-hooded Even
Like a sad votarist in palmer's weed
Rose from the hindmost wheels of Phoebus' wain.   190
But where they are, and why they came not back,
Is now the labour of my thoughts; 'tis likeliest
They had engaged their wand'ring steps too far,
And envious darkness, ere they could return,
Had stole them from me, else O thievish Night
Why shouldst thou, but for some felonious end,
In thy dark lantern thus close up the stars,
That Nature hung in heaven, and filled their lamps
With everlasting oil, to give due light

To the misled and lonely traveller?   200
This is the place, as well as I may guess,
Whence even now the tumult of loud mirth
Was rife, and perfect in my listening ear,
Yet nought but single darkness do I find.
What might this be? A thousand fantasies
Begin to throng into my memory
Of calling shapes, and beckoning shadows dire,
And airy tongues, that syllable men's names
On sands, and shores, and desert wildernesses.
These thoughts may startle well, but not astound   210
The virtuous mind, that ever walks attended
By a strong siding champion Conscience—
O welcome pure-eyed Faith, white-handed Hope,
Thou hovering angel girt with golden wings,
And thou unblemished form of Chastity,
I see ye visibly, and now believe
That he, the Supreme Good, t' whom all things ill
Are but as slavish officers of vengeance,
Would send a glistering guardian if need were
To keep my life and honour unassailed.   220
Was I deceived, or did a sable cloud
Turn forth her silver lining on the night?
I did not err, there does a sable cloud
Turn forth her silver lining on the night,
And casts a gleam over this tufted grove.
I cannot hallo to my brothers, but
Such noise as I can make to be heard farthest
I'll venture, for my new-enlivened spirits
Prompt me; and they perhaps are not far off.

SONG

Sweet Echo, sweetest nymph that liv'st unseen   230
    Within thy airy shell
  By slow Meander's margent green,
And in the violet-embroidered vale
   Where the love-lorn nightingale
Nightly to thee her sad song mourneth well,
Canst thou not tell me of a gentle pair
   That likest thy Narcissus are?
     O if thou have

    Hid them in some flowery cave,
       Tell me but where   240
    Sweet queen of parley, daughter of the sphere.
    So mayst thou be translated to the skies,
And give resounding grace to all heaven's harmonies.

Comus. Can any mortal mixture of earth's mould
Breathe such divine enchanting ravishment?
Sure something holy lodges in that breast,
And with these raptures moves the vocal air
To testify his hidden residence;
How sweetly did they float upon the wings
Of silence, through the empty-vaulted night   250
At every fall smoothing the raven down
Of darkness till it smiled: I have oft heard
My mother Circe with the Sirens three,
Amidst the flowery-kirtled Naiades
Culling their potent herbs, and baleful drugs,
Who as they sung, would take the prisoned soul,
And lap it in Elysium; Scylla wept,
And chid her barking waves into attention,
And fell Charybdis murmured soft applause:
Yet they in pleasing slumber lulled the sense,   260
And in sweet madness robbed it of itself,
But such a sacred, and home-felt delight,
Such sober certainty of waking bliss
I never heard till now. I'll speak to her
And she shall be my queen. Hail foreign wonder
Whom certain these rough shades did never breed
Unless the goddess that in rural shrine
Dwell'st here with Pan, or Sylvan, by blest song
Forbidding every bleak unkindly fog
To touch the prosperous growth of this tall wood.   270
Lady. Nay gentle shepherd ill is lost that praise
That is addressed to unattending ears,
Not any boast of skill, but extreme shift
How to regain my severed company
Compelled me to awake the courteous Echo
To give me answer from her mossy couch.
Comus. What chance good lady hath bereft you thus?
Lady. Dim darkness, and this leafy labyrinth.

Comus. Could that divide you from near-ushering guides?
Lady. They left me weary on a grassy turf.   280
Comus. By falsehood, or discourtesy, or why?
Lady. To seek i' the valley some cool friendly spring.
Comus. And left your fair side all unguarded lady?
Lady. They were but twain, and purposed quick return.
Comus. Perhaps forestalling night prevented them.
Lady. How easy my misfortune is to hit!
Comus. Imports their loss, beside the present need?
Lady. No less than if I should my brothers lose.
Comus. Were they of manly prime, or youthful bloom?
Lady. As smooth as Hebe's their unrazored lips.   290
Comus. Two such I saw, what time the laboured ox
In his loose traces from the furrow came,
And the swinked hedger at his supper sat;
I saw them under a green mantling vine
That crawls along the side of yon small hill,
Plucking ripe clusters from the tender shoots,
Their port was more than human as they stood;
I took it for a fairy vision
Of some gay creatures of the element
That in the colours of the rainbow live   300
And play i' the plighted clouds. I was awestruck,
And as I passed, I worshipped; if those you seek
It were a journey like the path to heaven,
To help you find them.
Lady.   Gentle villager
What readiest way would bring me to that place?
Comus. Due west it rises from this shrubby point.
Lady. To find out that, good shepherd, I suppose,
In such a scant allowance of starlight,
Would overtask the best land-pilot's art,
Without the sure guess of well-practised feet.   310
Comus. I know each lane, and every alley green,
Dingle, or bushy dell of this wild wood,
And every bosky bourn from side to side
My daily walks and ancient neighbourhood,
And if your stray attendance be yet lodged,
Or shroud within these limits, I shall know
Ere morrow wake, or the low-roosted lark
From her thatched pallet rouse; if otherwise,

I can conduct you lady to a low
But loyal cottage, where you may be safe   320
Till further quest.
Lady.   Shepherd I take thy word,
And trust thy honest-offered courtesy,
Which oft is sooner found in lowly sheds
With smoky rafters, than in tap'stry halls
And courts of princes, where it first was named,
And yet is most pretended: in a place
Less warranted than this, or less secure
I cannot be, that I should fear to change it;
Eye me blest Providence, and square my trial
To my proportioned strength. Shepherd lead on. —   330

The two Brothers

Eld. Bro. Unmuffle ye faint stars, and thou fair moon
That wont'st to love the traveller's benison,
Stoop thy pale visage through an amber cloud,
And disinherit Chaos, that reigns here
In double night of darkness, and of shades;
Or if your influence be quite dammed up
With black usurping mists, some gentle taper
Though a rush-candle from the wicker hole
Of some clay habitation visit us
With thy long levelled rule of streaming light,   340
And thou shalt be our star of Arcady,
Or Tyrian Cynosure.
Sec. Bro.   Or if our eyes
Be barred that happiness, might we but hear
The folded flocks penned in their wattled cotes,
Or sound of pastoral reed with oaten stops,
Or whistle from the lodge, or village cock
Count the night-watches to his feathery dames,
'Twould be some solace yet some little cheering
In this close dungeon of innumerous boughs.
But O that hapless virgin our lost sister   350
Where may she wander now, whither betake her
From the chill dew, amongst rude burrs and thistles?
Perhaps some cold bank is her bolster now
Or 'gainst the rugged bark of some broad elm
Leans her unpillowed head fraught with sad fears;

What if in wild amazement, and affright,
Or while we speak within the direful grasp
Of savage hunger, or of savage heat?
Eld. Bro. Peace brother, be not over-exquisite
To cast the fashion of uncertain evils;   360
For grant they be so, while they rest unknown,
What need a man forestall his date of grief,
And run to meet what he would most avoid?
Or if they be but false alarms of fear,
How bitter is such self-delusion!
I do not think my sister so to seek,
Or so unprincipled in virtue's book,
And the sweet peace that goodness bosoms ever,
As that the single want of light and noise
(Not being in danger, as I trust she is not)   370
Could stir the constant mood of her calm thoughts,
And put them into misbecoming plight.
Virtue could see to do what Virtue would
By her own radiant light, though sun and moon
Were in the flat sea sunk. And Wisdom's self
Oft seeks to sweet retired solitude,
Where with her best nurse Contemplation
She plumes her feathers, and lets grow her wings
That in the various bustle of resort
Were all to-ruffled, and sometimes impaired.   380
He that has light within his own clear breast
May sit i' the centre, and enjoy bright day,
But he that hides a dark soul, and foul thoughts
Benighted walks under the midday sun;
Himself is his own dungeon.
Sec. Bro.   'Tis most true
That musing Meditation most affects
The pensive secrecy of desert cell,
Far from the cheerful haunt of men, and herds,
And sits as safe as in a senate-house,
For who would rob a hermit of his weeds,   390
His few books, or his beads, or maple dish,
Or do his grey hairs any violence?
But Beauty like the fair Hesperian tree
Laden with blooming gold, had need the guard
Of dragon-watch with unenchanted eye,

To save her blossoms, and defend her fruit
From the rash hand of bold Incontinence.
You may as well spread out the unsunned heaps
Of miser's treasure by an outlaw's den,
And tell me it is safe, as bid me hope   400
Danger will wink on opportunity,
And let a single helpless maiden pass
Uninjured in this wild surrounding waste.
Of night, or loneliness it recks me not,
I fear the dread events that dog them both,
Lest some ill-greeting touch attempt the person
Of our unowned sister.
Eld. Bro.   I do not, brother,
Infer, as if I thought my sister's state
Secure without all doubt, or controversy:
Yet where an equal poise of hope and fear   410
Does arbitrate the event, my nature is
That I incline to hope, rather than fear,
And gladly banish squint suspicion.
My sister is not so defenceless left
As you imagine, she has a hidden strength
Which you remember not.
Sec. Bro.   What hidden strength,
Unless the strength of heaven, if you mean that?
Eld. Bro. I mean that too, but yet a hidden strength
Which if heaven gave it, may be termed her own:
'Tis chastity, my brother, chastity: 420
She that has that, is clad in complete steel,
And like a quivered nymph with arrows keen
May trace huge forests, and unharboured heaths,
Infamous hills, and sandy perilous wilds,
Where through the sacred rays of chastity,
No savage fierce, bandit, or mountaineer
Will dare to soil her virgin purity,
Yea there, where very desolation dwells
By grots, and caverns shagged with horrid shades,
She may pass on with unblenched majesty,   430
Be it not done in pride, or in presumption.
Some say no evil thing that walks by night
In fog, or fire, by lake, or moorish fen,
Blue meagre hag, or stubborn unlaid ghost,

That breaks his magic chains at curfew time,
No goblin, or swart fairy of the mine,
Hath hurtful power o'er true virginity.
Do ye believe me yet, or shall I call
Antiquity from the old schools of Greece
To testify the arms of chastity?   440
Hence had the huntress Dian her dread bow
Fair silver-shafted queen for ever chaste,
Wherewith she tamed the brinded lioness
And spotted mountain pard, but set at nought
The frivolous bolt of Cupid; gods and men
Feared her stern frown, and she was queen o' the woods.
What was that snaky-headed Gorgon shield
That wise Minerva wore, unconquered virgin,
Wherewith she freezed her foes to congealed stone?
But rigid looks of chaste austerity,   450
And noble grace that dashed brute violence
With sudden adoration, and blank awe.
So dear to heaven is saintly chastity,
That when a soul is found sincerely so,
A thousand liveried angels lackey her,
Driving far off each thing of sin and guilt,
And in clear dream, and solemn vision
Tell her of things that no gross ear can hear,
Till oft converse with heavenly habitants
Begin to cast a beam on the outward shape,   460
The unpolluted temple of the mind,
And turns it by degrees to the soul's essence,
Till all be made immortal: but when lust
By unchaste looks, loose gestures, and foul talk,
But most by lewd and lavish act of sin,
Lets in defilement to the inward parts,
The soul grows clotted by contagion,
Embodies, and imbrutes, till she quite lose
The divine property of her first being.
Such are those thick and gloomy shadows damp   470
Oft seen in charnel-vaults, and sepulchres
Lingering, and sitting by a new-made grave,
As loath to leave the body that it loved,
And linked itself by carnal sensuality
To a degenerate and degraded state.

Sec. Bro. How charming is divine philosophy!
Not harsh, and crabbèd as dull fools suppose,
But musical as is Apollo's lute,
And a perpetual feast of nectared sweets,
Where no crude surfeit reigns. 480
Eld. Bro. List, list, I hear
Some far-off hallo break the silent air.
Sec. Bro. Methought so too; what should it be?
Eld. Bro. For certain
Either some one like us night-foundered here,
Or else some neighbour woodman, or at worst,
Some roving robber calling to his fellows.
Sec. Bro. Heaven keep my sister, again, again, and near,
Best draw, and stand upon our guard.
Eld. Bro. I'll hallo,
If he be friendly he comes well, if not,
Defence is a good cause, and heaven be for us.

The Attendant Spirit habited like a shepherd.

That hallo I should know, what are you? speak; 490
Come not too near, you fall on iron stakes else.
Spir. What voice is that, my young lord? speak again.
Sec. Bro. O brother, 'tis my father's shepherd sure.
Eld. Bro. Thyrsis? Whose artful strains have oft delayed
The huddling brook to hear his madrigal,
And sweetened every musk-rose of the dale,
How cam'st thou here good swain? hath any ram
Slipped from the fold, or young kid lost his dam,
Or straggling wether the pent flock forsook?
How couldst thou find this dark sequestered nook? 500
Spir. O my loved master's heir, and his next joy,
I came not here on such a trivial toy
As a strayed ewe, or to pursue the stealth
Of pilfering wolf; not all the fleecy wealth
That doth enrich these downs is worth a thought
To this my errand, and the care it brought.
But O my virgin Lady, where is she?
How chance she is not in your company?
Eld. Bro. To tell thee sadly shepherd, without blame,
Or our neglect, we lost her as we came. 510
Spir. Ay me unhappy then my fears are true.

Eld. Bro. What fears good Thyrsis? Prithee briefly show.
Spir. I'll tell ye, 'tis not vain or fabulous
(Though so esteemed by shallow ignorance),
What the sage poets taught by the heavenly Muse,
Storied of old in high immortal verse
Of dire chimeras and enchanted isles,
And rifted rocks whose entrance leads to hell,
For such there be, but unbelief is blind.
    Within the navel of this hideous wood,   520
Immured in cypress shades a sorcerer dwells
Of Bacchus, and of Circe born, great Comus,
Deep skilled in all his mother's witcheries,
And here to every thirsty wanderer,
By sly enticement gives his baneful cup,
With many murmurs mixed, whose pleasing poison
The visage quite transforms of him that drinks,
And the inglorious likeness of a beast
Fixes instead, unmoulding reason's mintage
Charactered in the face; this have I learnt   530
Tending my flocks hard by i' the hilly crofts,
That brow this bottom glade, whence night by night
He and his monstrous rout are heard to howl
Like stabled wolves, or tigers at their prey,
Doing abhorrèd rites to Hecate
In their obscurèd haunts of inmost bowers,
Yet have they many baits, and guileful spells
To inveigle and invite the unwary sense
Of them that pass unweeting by the way.
This evening late by then the chewing flocks   540
Had ta'en their supper on the savoury herb
Of knot-grass dew-besprent, and were in fold,
I sat me down to watch upon a bank
With ivy canopied, and interwove
With flaunting honeysuckle, and began
Wrapt in a pleasing fit of melancholy
To meditate my rural minstrelsy,
Till fancy had her fill, but ere a close
The wonted roar was up amidst the woods,
And filled the air with barbarous dissonance   550
At which I ceased, and listened them a while,
Till an unusual stop of sudden silence

Gave respite to the drowsy frighted steeds
That draw the litter of close-curtained sleep;
At last a soft and solemn-breathing sound
Rose like a steam of rich distilled perfumes,
And stole upon the air, that even Silence
Was took ere she was ware, and wished she might
Deny her nature, and be never more
Still to be so displaced. I was all ear,   560
And took in strains that might create a soul
Under the ribs of death, but O ere long
Too well I did perceive it was the voice
Of my most honoured lady, your dear sister.
Amazed I stood, harrowed with grief and fear,
And O poor hapless nightingale thought I,
How sweet thou sing'st, how near the deadly snare!
Then down the lawns I ran with headlong haste
Through paths, and turnings often trod by day,
Till guided by mine ear I found the place   570
Where that damned wizard hid in sly disguise
(For so by certain signs I knew) had met
Already, ere my best speed could prevent,
The aidless innocent Lady his wished prey,
Who gently asked if he had seen such two,
Supposing him some neighbour villager;
Longer I durst not stay, but soon I guessed
Ye were the two she meant, with that I sprung
Into swift flight, till I had found you here,
But further know I not.   580
Sec. Bro.   O night and shades,
How are ye joined with hell in triple knot
Against the unarmed weakness of one virgin
Alone, and helpless! Is this the confidence
You gave me brother?
Eld. Bro.   Yes, and keep it still,
Lean on it safely, not a period
Shall be unsaid for me: against the threats
Of malice or of sorcery, or that power
Which erring men call chance, this I hold firm,
Virtue may be assailed, but never hurt,
Surprised by unjust force, but not enthralled,   590
Yea even that which mischief meant most harm

Shall in the happy trial prove most glory.
But evil on itself shall back recoil,
And mix no more with goodness, when at last
Gathered like scum, and settled to itself
It shall be in eternal restless change
Self-fed, and self-consumed; if this fail,
The pillared firmament is rottenness,
And earth's base built on stubble. But come, let's on;
Against the opposing will and arm of heaven   600
May never this just sword be lifted up,
But for that damned magician, let him be girt
With all the grisly legions that troop
Under the sooty flag of Acheron,
Harpies and hydras, or all the monstrous forms
'Twixt Africa and Ind, I'll find him out,
And force him to restore his purchase back,
Or drag him by the curls, to a foul death,
Cursed as his life.
Spir.   Alas good venturous youth,
I love thy courage yet, and bold emprise,   610
But here thy sword can do thee little stead,
Far other arms, and other weapons must
Be those that quell the might of hellish charms,
He with his bare wand can unthread thy joints,
And crumble all thy sinews.
Eld. Bro.   Why prithee shepherd
How durst thou then thyself approach so near
As to make this relation?
Spir.   Care and utmost shifts
How to secure the Lady from surprisal,
Brought to my mind a certain shepherd lad
Of small regard to see to, yet well skilled   620
In every virtuous plant and healing herb
That spreads her verdant leaf to the morning ray,
He loved me well, and oft would beg me sing,
Which when I did, he on the tender grass
Would sit, and hearken even to ecstasy,
And in requital ope his leathern scrip,
And show me simples of a thousand names
Telling their strange and vigorous faculties;
Amongst the rest a small unsightly root,

But of divine effect, he culled me out;   630
The leaf was darkish, and had prickles on it,
But in another country, as he said,
Bore a bright golden flower, but not in this soil:
Unknown, and like esteemed, and the dull swain
Treads on it daily with his clouted shoon,
And yet more med'cinal is it than that moly
That Hermes once to wise Ulysses gave;
He called it haemony, and gave it me,
And bade me keep it as of sovereign use
'Gainst all enchantments, mildew blast, or damp   640
Or ghastly Furies' apparition;
I pursed it up, but little reckoning made,
Till now that this extremity compelled,
But now I find it true; for by this means
I knew the foul enchanter though disguised,
Entered the very lime-twigs of his spells,
And yet came off: if you have this about you
(As I will give you when we go) you may
Boldly assault the necromancer's hall;
Where if he be, with dauntless hardihood,   650
And brandished blade rush on him, break his glass,
And shed the luscious liquor on the ground,
But seize his wand, though he and his cursed crew
Fierce sign of battle make, and menace high,
Or like the sons of Vulcan vomit smoke,
Yet will they soon retire, if he but shrink.
Eld. Bro. Thyrsis lead on apace, I'll follow thee,
And some good angel bear a shield before us.

The scene changes to a stately palace, set out with all manner of deliciousness: soft music, tables spread with all dainties. Comus appears with his rabble, and the Lady set in an enchanted chair, to whom he offers his glass, which she puts by, and goes about to rise.

Comus. Nay lady sit; if I but wave this wand,
Your nerves are all chained up in alabaster,   660
And you a statue, or as Daphne was
Root-bound, that fled Apollo.
Lady.   Fool do not boast,
Thou canst not touch the freedom of my mind
With all thy charms, although this corporal rind

Thou hast immanacled, while heaven sees good.
Comus. Why are you vexed Lady? why do you frown?
Here dwell no frowns, nor anger, from these gates
Sorrow flies far: see, here be all the pleasures
That fancy can beget on youthful thoughts,
When the fresh blood grows lively, and returns   670
Brisk as the April buds in primrose season.
And first behold this cordial julep here
That flames, and dances in his crystal bounds
With spirits of balm, and fragrant syrups mixed.
Not that nepenthes which the wife of Thone,
In Egypt gave to Jove-born Helena,
Is of such power to stir up joy as this,
To life so friendly, or so cool to thirst.
Why should you be so cruel to yourself,
And to those dainty limbs which Nature lent   680
For gentle usage, and soft delicacy?
But you invert the covenants of her trust,
And harshly deal like an ill borrower
With that which you received on other terms,
Scorning the unexempt condition
By which all mortal frailty must subsist,
Refreshment after toil, ease after pain,
That have been tired all day without repast,
And timely rest have wanted, but fair virgin
This will restore all soon.
Lady.   'Twill not false traitor,   690
'Twill not restore the truth and honesty
That thou hast banished from thy tongue with lies,
Was this the cottage, and the safe abode
Thou told'st me of? What grim aspects are these,
These ugly-headed monsters? Mercy guard me!
Hence with thy brewed enchantments, foul deceiver,
Hast thou betrayed my credulous innocence
With vizored falsehood, and base forgery,
And wouldst thou seek again to trap me here
With lickerish baits fit to ensnare a brute?   700
Were it a draught for Juno when she banquets,
I would not taste thy treasonous offer; none
But such as are good men can give good things,
And that which is not good, is not delicious

To a well-governed and wise appetite.
Comus. O foolishness of men! That lend their ears
To those budge doctors of the Stoic fur,
And fetch their precepts from the Cynic tub,
Praising the lean and sallow Abstinence.
Wherefore did Nature pour her bounties forth,   710
With such a full and unwithdrawing hand,
Covering the earth with odours, fruits, and flocks,
Thronging the seas with spawn innumerable,
But all to please, and sate the curious taste?
And set to work millions of spinning worms,
That in their green shops weave the smooth-haired silk
To deck her sons, and that no corner might
Be vacant of her plenty, in her own loins
She hutched the all-worshipped ore, and precious gems
To store her children with; if all the world   720
Should in a pet of temperance feed on pulse,
Drink the clear stream, and nothing wear but frieze,
The all-giver would be unthanked, would be unpraised,
Not half his riches known, and yet despised,
And we should serve him as a grudging master,
As a penurious niggard of his wealth,
And live like Nature's bastards, not her sons,
Who would be quite surcharged with her own weight,
And strangled with her waste fertility;
The earth cumbered, and the winged air darked with plumes,   730
The herds would over-multitude their lords,
The sea o'erfraught would swell, and the unsought diamonds
Would so emblaze the forehead of the deep,
And so bestud with stars, that they below
Would grow inured to light, and come at last
To gaze upon the sun with shameless brows.
List Lady be not coy, and be not cozened
With that same vaunted name virginity,
Beauty is Nature's coin, must not be hoarded,
But must be current, and the good thereof   740
Consists in mutual and partaken bliss,
Unsavoury in the enjoyment of itself,
If you let slip time, like a neglected rose
It withers on the stalk with languished head.
Beauty is Nature's brag, and must be shown

In courts, at feasts, and high solemnities
Where most may wonder at the workmanship;
It is for homely features to keep home,
They had their name thence; coarse complexions
And cheeks of sorry grain will serve to ply   750
The sampler, and to tease the housewife's wool.
What need a vermeil-tinctured lip for that,
Love-darting eyes, or tresses like the morn?
There was another meaning in these gifts,
Think what, and be advised, you are but young yet.
Lady. I had not thought to have unlocked my lips
In this unhallowed air, but that this juggler
Would think to charm my judgement, as mine eyes
Obtruding false rules pranked in reason's garb.
I hate when vice can bolt her arguments,   760
And virtue has no tongue to check her pride:
Imposter do not charge most innocent Nature,
As if she would her children should be riotous
With her abundance, she good cateress
Means her provision only to the good
That live according to her sober laws,
And holy dictate of spare temperance:
If every just man that now pines with want
Had but a moderate and beseeming share
Of that which lewdly-pampered luxury   770
Now heaps upon some few with vast excess,
Nature's full blessings would be well-dispensed
In unsuperfluous even proportion,
And she no whit encumbered with her store,
And then the giver would be better thanked,
His praise due paid, for swinish gluttony
Ne'er looks to heaven amidst his gorgeous feast,
But with besotted base ingratitude
Crams, and blasphemes his feeder. Shall I go on?
Or have I said enough? To him that dares   780
Arm his profane tongue with contemptuous words
Against the sun-clad power of chastity;
Fain would I something say, yet to what end?
Thou hast nor ear, nor soul to apprehend
The sublime notion, and high mystery
That must be uttered to unfold the sage

And serious doctrine of virginity,
And thou art worthy that thou shouldst not know
More happiness than this thy present lot.
Enjoy your dear wit, and gay rhetoric   790
That hath so well been taught her dazzling fence,
Thou art not fit to hear thyself convinced;
Yet should I try, the uncontrollèd worth
Of this pure cause would kindle my rapt spirits
To such a flame of sacred vehemence,
That dumb things would be moved to sympathize,
And the brute Earth would lend her nerves, and shake,
Till all thy magic structures reared so high,
Were shattered into heaps o'er thy false head.
Comus. She fables not, I feel that I do fear   800
Her words set off by some superior power;
And though not mortal, yet a cold shuddering dew
Dips me all o'er, as when the wrath of Jove
Speaks thunder, and the chains of Erebus
To some of Saturn's crew. I must dissemble,
And try her yet more strongly. Come, no more,
This is mere moral babble, and direct
Against the canon laws of our foundation;
I must not suffer this, yet 'tis but the lees
And settlings of a melancholy blood;   810
But this will cure all straight, one sip of this
Will bathe the drooping spirits in delight
Beyond the bliss of dreams. Be wise, and taste.—

*The Brothers rush in with swords drawn, wrest his glass out of his hand, and
break it against the ground; his rout make sign of resistance but are all driven in.
The Attendant Spirit comes in.*

Spir. What, have you let the false enchanter scape?
O ye mistook, ye should have snatched his wand
And bound him fast; without his rod reversed,
And backward mutters of dissevering power,
We cannot free the Lady that sits here
In stony fetters fixed, and motionless;
Yet stay, be not disturbed, now I bethink me,   820
Some other means I have which may be used,
Which once of Meliboeus old I learnt,
The soothest shepherd that e'er piped on plains.

There is a gentle nymph not far from hence,
That with moist curb sways the smooth Severn stream,
Sabrina is her name, a virgin pure,
Whilom she was the daughter of Locrine,
That had the sceptre from his father Brute.
The guiltless damsel flying the mad pursuit
Of her enragèd stepdame Guendolen,   830
Commended her fair innocence to the flood
That stayed her flight with his cross-flowing course,
The water nymphs that in the bottom played,
Held up their pearlèd wrists and took her in,
Bearing her straight to agèd Nereus' hall,
Who piteous of her woes, reared her lank head,
And gave her to his daughters to imbathe
In nectared lavers strewed with asphodel,
And through the porch and inlet of each sense
Dropped in ambrosial oils till she revived,   840
And underwent a quick immortal change
Made goddess of the river; still she retains
Her maiden gentleness, and oft at eve
Visits the herds along the twilight meadows,
Helping all urchin blasts, and ill-luck signs
That the shrewd meddling elf delights to make,
Which she with precious vialed liquors heals.
For which the shepherds at their festivals
Carol her goodness loud in rustic lays,
And throw sweet garland wreaths into her stream   850
Of pansies, pinks, and gaudy daffodils.
And, as the old swain said, she can unlock
The clasping charm, and thaw the numbing spell,
If she be right invoked in warbled song,
For maidenhood she loves, and will be swift
To aid a virgin such as was herself
In hard-besetting need, this will I try,
And add the power of some adjuring verse.

SONG

Sabrina fair
   Listen where thou art sitting   860
Under the glassy, cool, translucent wave,
   In twisted braids of lilies knitting

The loose train of thy amber-dropping hair,
 Listen for dear honour's sake,
 Goddess of the silver lake,
  Listen and save.

Listen and appear to us
In name of great Oceanus,
By the earth-shaking Neptune's mace,
And Tethys' grave majestic pace,   870
By hoary Nereus' wrinkled look,
And the Carpathian wizard's hook,
By scaly Triton's winding shell,
And old soothsaying Glaucus' spell,
By Leucothea's lovely hands,
And her son that rules the strands,
By Thetis' tinsel-slippered feet,
And the songs of sirens sweet,
By dead Parthenope's dear tomb,
And fair Ligea's golden comb,   880
Wherewith she sits on diamond rocks
Sleeking her soft alluring locks,
By all the nymphs that nightly dance
Upon thy streams with wily glance,
Rise, rise, and heave thy rosy head
From thy coral-paven bed,
And bridle in thy headlong wave,
Till thou our summons answered have.
                        Listen and save.

Sabrina rises, attended by water nymphs, and sings.

By the rushy-fringèd bank,   890
Where grows the willow and the osier dank,
 My sliding chariot stays,
Thick set with agate, and the azurn sheen
Of turquoise blue, and emerald green
  That in the channel strays,
Whilst from off the waters fleet
Thus I set my printless feet
O'er the cowslip's velvet head,
 That bends not as I tread,
Gentle swain at thy request   900

I am here.
Spir. Goddess dear
We implore thy powerful hand
To undo the charmèd band
Of true virgin here distressed,
Through the force, and through the wile
Of unblessed enchanter vile.
Sabr. Shepherd 'tis my office best
To help ensnared chastity;
Brightest Lady look on me,   910
Thus I sprinkle on thy breast
Drops that from my fountain pure
I have kept of precious cure,
Thrice upon thy finger's tip,
Thrice upon thy rubied lip,
Next this marble venomed seat
Smeared with gums of glutinous heat
I touch with chaste palms moist and cold,
Now the spell hath lost his hold,
And I must haste ere morning hour   920
To wait in Amphitrite's bower.

Sabrina descends, and the Lady rises out of her seat.

Spir. Virgin, daughter of Locrine,
Sprung of old Anchises' line,
May thy brimmèd waves for this
Their full tribute never miss
From a thousand petty rills,
That tumble down the snowy hills;
Summer drought, or singèd air
Never scorch thy tresses fair,
Nor wet October's torrent flood   930
Thy molten crystal fill with mud,
May thy billows roll ashore
The beryl, and the golden ore,
May thy lofty head be crowned
With many a tower and terrace round,
And here and there thy banks upon
With groves of myrrh, and cinnamon.
Come Lady while heaven lends us grace,
Let us fly this cursèd place,

Lest the sorcerer us entice   940
With some other new device.

Not a waste or needless sound
Till we come to holier ground,
I shall be your faithful guide
Through this gloomy covert wide,
And not many furlongs thence
Is your father's residence,
Where this night are met in state
Many a friend to gratulate
His wished presence, and beside   950
All the swains that there abide,
With jigs, and rural dance resort,
We shall catch them at their sport,
And our sudden coming there
Will double all their mirth and cheer;
Come let us haste, the stars grow high,
But night sits monarch yet in the mid sky.

*The scene changes, presenting Ludlow town and the President's castle; then come
in country dancers, after them the Attendant Spirit, with the two Brothers and
the Lady.*

SONG

Spir. Back, shepherds, back, enough your play,
Till next sunshine holiday,
Here be without duck or nod   960
Other trippings to be trod
Of lighter toes, and such court guise
As Mercury did first devise
With the mincing Dryades
On the lawns, and on the leas.

This second song presents them to their father and mother.

Noble lord, and lady bright,
I have brought ye new delight,
Here behold so goodly grown
Three fair branches of your own,
Heaven hath timely tried their youth,   970
Their faith, their patience, and their truth,
And sent them here through hard assays

With a crown of deathless praise,
To triumph in victorious dance
O'er sensual folly, and intemperance.

The dances ended, the Spirit epiloguizes.

Spir. To the ocean now I fly,
And those happy climes that lie
Where day never shuts his eye,
Up in the broad fields of the sky:
There I suck the liquid air   980
All amidst the gardens fair
Of Hesperus, and his daughters three
That sing about the golden tree:
Along the crispèd shades and bowers
Revels the spruce and jocund Spring,
The Graces, and the rosy-bosomed Hours,
Thither all their bounties bring,
That there eternal summer dwells,
And west winds, with musky wing
About the cedarn alleys fling   990
Nard, and cassia's balmy smells.
Iris there with humid bow,
Waters the odorous banks that blow
Flowers of more mingled hue
Than her purfled scarf can show,
And drenches with Elysian dew
(List mortals if your ears be true)
Beds of hyacinth, and roses,
Where young Adonis oft reposes,
Waxing well of his deep wound   1000
In slumber soft, and on the ground
Sadly sits the Assyrian queen;
But far above in spangled sheen
Celestial Cupid her famed son advanced,
Holds his dear Psyche sweet entranced
After her wandering labours long,
Till free consent the gods among
Make her his eternal bride,
And from her fair unspotted side
Two blissful twins are to be born,   1010
Youth and Joy; so Jove hath sworn.

But now my task is smoothly done,
I can fly, or I can run
Quickly to the green earth's end,
Where the bowed welkin slow doth bend,
And from thence can soar as soon
To the corners of the moon.
   Mortals that would follow me,
Love Virtue, she alone is free,
She can teach ye how to climb   1020
Higher than the sphery chime;
Or if Virtue feeble were,
Heaven itself would stoop to her.

Sonnet 11

A book was writ of late called *Tetrachordon*;
   And woven close, both matter, form and style;
   The subject new: it walked the town awhile,
   Numbering good intellects; now seldom pored on.
Cries the stall-reader, Bless us! what a word on
   A title-page is this! And some in file
   Stand spelling false, while one might walk to Mile-
   End Green. Why is it harder sirs than Gordon,
Colkitto, or Macdonnel, or Galasp?
   Those rugged names to our like mouths grow sleek   10
   That would have made Quintilian stare and gasp.
Thy age, like ours, O soul of Sir John Cheke,
   Hated not learning worse than toad or asp;
   When thou taught'st Cambridge, and King Edward Greek.

Sonnet 12
On the Same

I did but prompt the age to quit their clogs
   By the known rules of ancient liberty,
   When straight a barbarous noise environs me
   Of owls and cuckoos, asses, apes and dogs.
As when those hinds that were transformed to frogs
   Railed at Latona's twin-born progeny
   Which after held the sun and moon in fee.
   But this is got by casting pearl to hogs;
That bawl for freedom in their senseless mood,
   And still revolt when truth would set them free.   10
   Licence they mean when they cry liberty;
For who loves that, must first be wise and good;
   But from that mark how far they rove we see
   For all this waste of wealth, and loss of blood.

Sonnet 13
To Mr H. Lawes, on his Airs

Harry whose tuneful and well-measured song
  First taught our English music how to span
  Words with just note and accent, not to scan
  With Midas' ears, committing short and long;
Thy worth and skill exempts thee from the throng,
  With praise enough for envy to look wan;
  To after age thou shalt be writ the man,
  That with smooth air couldst humour best our tongue.
Thou honour'st verse, and verse must lend her wing
  To honour thee, the priest of Phoebus' choir   10
  That tun'st their happiest lines in hymn, or story.
Dante shall give fame leave to set thee higher
  Than his Casella, whom he wooed to sing
  Met in the milder shades of Purgatory.

Sonnet 14

When faith and love which parted from thee never,
  Had ripened thy just soul to dwell with God,
  Meekly thou didst resign this earthy load
  Of death, called life; which us from life doth sever.
Thy works and alms and all thy good endeavour
  Stayed not behind, nor in the grave were trod;
  But as faith pointed with her golden rod,
  Followed thee up to joy and bliss forever.
Love led them on, and faith who knew them best
  Thy handmaids, clad them o'er with purple beams   10
  And azure wings, that up they flew so dressed,
And speak the truth of thee on glorious themes
  Before the judge, who thenceforth bid thee rest
  And drink thy fill of pure immortal streams.

Sonnet 15
On the Late Massacre in Piedmont

Avenge O Lord thy slaughtered saints, whose bones
  Lie scattered on the Alpine mountains cold,
  Even them who kept thy truth so pure of old
  When all our fathers worshipped stocks and stones,
Forget not: in thy book record their groans
  Who were thy sheep and in their ancient fold
  Slain by the bloody Piedmontese that rolled
  Mother with infant down the rocks. Their moans
The vales redoubled to the hills, and they
  To heaven. Their martyred blood and ashes sow   10
  O'er all the Italian fields where still doth sway
The triple tyrant: that from these may grow
  A hundredfold, who having learnt thy way
  Early may fly the Babylonian woe.

Sonnet 16

When I consider how my light is spent,
  Ere half my days, in this dark world and wide,
  And that one talent which is death to hide,
  Lodged with me useless, though my soul more bent
To serve therewith my maker, and present
  My true account, lest he returning chide,
  Doth God exact day-labour, light denied,
  I fondly ask; but patience to prevent
That murmur, soon replies, God doth not need
  Either man's work or his own gifts, who best   10
  Bear his mild yoke, they serve him best, his state
Is kingly. Thousands at his bidding speed
  And post o'er land and ocean without rest:
  They also serve who only stand and wait.

Sonnet 17

Lawrence of virtuous father virtuous son,
  Now that the fields are dank, and ways are mire,
  Where shall we sometimes meet, and by the fire
  Help waste a sullen day; what may be won
From the hard season gaining: time will run
  On smoother, till Favonius reinspire
  The frozen earth; and clothe in fresh attire
  The lily and rose, that neither sowed nor spun.
What neat repast shall feast us, light and choice,
  Of Attic taste, with wine, whence we may rise   10
  To hear the lute well touched, or artful voice
Warble immortal notes and Tuscan air?
  He who of those delights can judge, and spare
  To interpose them oft, is not unwise.

Sonnet 18

Cyriack, whose grandsire on the royal bench
  Of British Themis, with no mean applause
  Pronounced and in his volumes taught our laws,
  Which others at their bar so often wrench;
Today deep thoughts resolve with me to drench
  In mirth, that after no repenting draws;
  Let Euclid rest and Archimedes pause,
  And what the Swede intend, and what the French.
To measure life, learn thou betimes, and know
  Toward solid good what leads the nearest way;   10
  For other things mild heaven a time ordains,
And disapproves that care, though wise in show,
  That with superfluous burden loads the day,
  And when God sends a cheerful hour, refrains.

Sonnet 19

Methought I saw my late espousèd saint
  Brought to me like Alcestis from the grave,
  Whom Jove's great son to her glad husband gave,
  Rescued from death by force though pale and faint.
Mine as whom washed from spot of childbed taint,
  Purification in the old law did save,
  And such, as yet once more I trust to have
  Full sight of her in heaven without restraint,
Came vested all in white, pure as her mind:
  Her face was veiled, yet to my fancied sight,   10
  Love, sweetness, goodness in her person shined
So clear, as in no face with more delight.
  But O as to embrace me she inclined
  I waked, she fled, and day brought back my night.

On the New Forcers of Conscience
under the Long Parliament

Because you have thrown off your prelate lord,
  And with stiff vows renounced his liturgy
  To seize the widowed whore plurality
  From them whose sin ye envied, not abhorred,
Dare ye for this adjure the civil sword
  To force our consciences that Christ set free,
  And ride us with a classic hierarchy
  Taught ye by mere A. S. and Rutherford?
Men whose life, learning, faith and pure intent
  Would have been held in high esteem with Paul   10
  Must now be named and printed heretics
By shallow Edwards and Scotch What-d'ye-call:
  But we do hope to find out all your tricks,
  Your plots and packing worse than those of Trent,
    That so the Parliament
May with their wholesome and preventive shears

Clip your phylacteries, though balk your ears,
    And succour our just fears
When they shall read this clearly in your charge,
New *Presbyter* is but old *Priest* writ large.   20

UNCOLLECTED ENGLISH POEMS

On the Lord General Fairfax at the Siege of Colchester

Fairfax, whose name in arms through Europe rings
   Filling each mouth with envy, or with praise,
   And all her jealous monarchs with amaze,
   And rumours loud, that daunt remotest kings,
Thy firm unshaken virtue ever brings
   Victory home, though new rebellions raise
   Their hydra heads, and the false north displays
   Her broken league, to imp their serpent wings,
O yet a nobler task awaits thy hand;
   For what can war, but endless war still breed,   10
   Till truth, and right from violence be freed,
And public faith cleared from the shameful brand
   Of public fraud. In vain doth valour bleed
   While avarice, and rapine share the land.

To the Lord General Cromwell

Cromwell, our chief of men, who through a cloud
   Not of war only, but detractions rude,
   Guided by faith and matchless fortitude
   To peace and truth thy glorious way hast ploughed,
And on the neck of crownèd fortune proud
   Hast reared God's trophies and his work pursued,
   While Darwen stream with blood of Scots imbrued,
   And Dunbar field resounds thy praises loud,
And Worcester's laureate wreath; yet much remains
   To conquer still; peace hath her victories   10
   No less renowned than war, new foes arise
Threatening to bind our souls with secular chains:
   Help us to save free conscience from the paw
   Of hireling wolves whose gospel is their maw.

To Sir Henry Vane the Younger

Vane, young in years, but in sage counsel old,
  Than whom a better senator ne'er held
  The helm of Rome, when gowns not arms repelled
  The fierce Epirot and the African bold:
Whether to settle peace or to unfold
  The drift of hollow states, hard to be spelled,
  Then to advise how war may best, upheld,
  Move by her two main nerves, iron and gold
In all her equipage: besides to know
  Both spiritual power and civil, what each means,   10
  What severs each, thou hast learned, which few have done.
The bounds of either sword to thee we owe;
  Therefore on thy firm hand Religion leans
  In peace, and reckons thee her eldest son.

To Mr Cyriack Skinner Upon his Blindness

Cyriack, this three years' day these eyes, though clear
  To outward view, of blemish or of spot,
  Bereft of light their seeing have forgot,
  Nor to their idle orbs doth sight appear
Of sun or moon or star throughout the year,
  Or man or woman. Yet I argue not
  Against heaven's hand or will, nor bate a jot
  Of heart or hope; but still bear up and steer
Right onward. What supports me dost thou ask?
  The conscience, friend, to have lost them overplied   10
  In liberty's defence, my noble task,
Of which all Europe talks from side to side.
  This thought might lead me through the world's vain mask
  Content though blind, had I no better guide.

PARADISE LOST

Book I

Of man's first disobedience, and the fruit
Of that forbidden tree, whose mortal taste
Brought death into the world, and all our woe,
With loss of Eden, till one greater man
Restore us, and regain the blissful seat,
Sing heavenly muse, that on the secret top
Of Oreb, or of Sinai, didst inspire
That shepherd, who first taught the chosen seed,
In the beginning how the heavens and earth
Rose out of chaos: or if Sion hill   10
Delight thee more, and Siloa's brook that flowed
Fast by the oracle of God; I thence
Invoke thy aid to my adventurous song,
That with no middle flight intends to soar
Above the Aonian mount, while it pursues
Things unattempted yet in prose or rhyme.
And chiefly thou O Spirit, that dost prefer
Before all temples the upright heart and pure,
Instruct me, for thou know'st; thou from the first
Wast present, and with mighty wings outspread   20
Dove-like sat'st brooding on the vast abyss
And mad'st it pregnant: what in me is dark
Illumine, what is low raise and support;
That to the height of this great argument
I may assert eternal providence,
And justify the ways of God to men.
      Say first, for heaven hides nothing from thy view
Nor the deep tract of hell, say first what cause
Moved our grand parents in that happy state,
Favoured of heaven so highly, to fall off   30
From their creator, and transgress his will
For one restraint, lords of the world besides?
Who first seduced them to that foul revolt?

The infernal serpent; he it was, whose guile
Stirred up with envy and revenge, deceived
The mother of mankind, what time his pride
Had cast him out from heaven, with all his host
Of rebel angels, by whose aid aspiring
To set himself in glory above his peers,
He trusted to have equalled the most high,   40
If he opposed; and with ambitious aim
Against the throne and monarchy of God
Raised impious war in heaven and battle proud
With vain attempt. Him the almighty power
Hurled headlong flaming from the ethereal sky
With hideous ruin and combustion down
To bottomless perdition, there to dwell
In adamantine chains and penal fire,
Who durst defy the omnipotent to arms.
Nine times the space that measures day and night   50
To mortal men, he with his horrid crew
Lay vanquished, rolling in the fiery gulf
Confounded though immortal: but his doom
Reserved him to more wrath; for now the thought
Both of lost happiness and lasting pain
Torments him; round he throws his baleful eyes
That witnessed huge affliction and dismay
Mixed with obdurate pride and steadfast hate:
At once as far as angels' ken he views
The dismal situation waste and wild,   60
A dungeon horrible, on all sides round
As one great furnace flamed, yet from those flames
No light, but rather darkness visible
Served only to discover sights of woe,
Regions of sorrow, doleful shades, where peace
And rest can never dwell, hope never comes
That comes to all; but torture without end
Still urges, and a fiery deluge, fed
With ever-burning sulphur unconsumed:
Such place eternal justice had prepared   70
For those rebellious, here their prison ordained
In utter darkness, and their portion set
As far removed from God and light of heaven
As from the centre thrice to the utmost pole.

O how unlike the place from whence they fell!
There the companions of his fall, o'erwhelmed
With floods and whirlwinds of tempestuous fire,
He soon discerns, and weltering by his side
One next himself in power, and next in crime,
Long after known in Palestine, and named   80
Beelzebub. To whom the arch-enemy,
And thence in heaven called Satan, with bold words
Breaking the horrid silence thus began.
    If thou beest he; but O how fallen! how changed
From him, who in the happy realms of light
Clothed with transcendent brightness didst outshine
Myriads though bright: if he whom mutual league,
United thoughts and counsels, equal hope
And hazard in the glorious enterprise,
Joined with me once, now misery hath joined   90
In equal ruin: into what pit thou seest
From what height fallen, so much the stronger proved
He with his thunder: and till then who knew
The force of those dire arms? yet not for those,
Nor what the potent victor in his rage
Can else inflict, do I repent or change,
Though changed in outward lustre; that fixed mind
And high disdain, from sense of injured merit,
That with the mightiest raised me to contend,
And to the fierce contention brought along   100
Innumerable force of spirits armed
That durst dislike his reign, and me preferring,
His utmost power with adverse power opposed
In dubious battle on the plains of heaven,
And shook his throne. What though the field be lost?
All is not lost; the unconquerable will,
And study of revenge, immortal hate,
And courage never to submit or yield:
And what is else not to be overcome?
That glory never shall his wrath or might   110
Extort from me. To bow and sue for grace
With suppliant knee, and deify his power,
Who from the terror of this arm so late
Doubted his empire, that were low indeed,
That were an ignominy and shame beneath

This downfall; since by fate the strength of gods
And this empyreal substance cannot fail,
Since through experience of this great event
In arms not worse, in foresight much advanced,
We may with more successful hope resolve   120
To wage by force or guile eternal war
Irreconcilable, to our grand foe,
Who now triumphs, and in the excess of joy
Sole reigning holds the tyranny of heaven.
    So spake the apostate angel, though in pain,
Vaunting aloud, but racked with deep despair:
And him thus answered soon his bold compeer.
    O prince, O chief of many thronèd powers,
That led the embattled seraphim to war
Under thy conduct, and in dreadful deeds   130
Fearless, endangered heaven's perpetual king;
And put to proof his high supremacy,
Whether upheld by strength, or chance, or fate,
Too well I see and rue the dire event,
That with sad overthrow and foul defeat
Hath lost us heaven, and all this mighty host
In horrible destruction laid thus low,
As far as gods and heavenly essences
Can perish: for the mind and spirit remains
Invincible, and vigour soon returns,   140
Though all our glory extinct, and happy state
Here swallowed up in endless misery.
But what if he our conqueror (whom I now
Of force believe almighty, since no less
Than such could have o'erpowered such force as ours)
Have left us this our spirit and strength entire
Strongly to suffer and support our pains,
That we may so suffice his vengeful ire,
Or do him mightier service as his thralls
By right of war, whate'er his business be   150
Here in the heart of hell to work in fire,
Or do his errands in the gloomy deep;
What can it then avail though yet we feel
Strength undiminished, or eternal being
To undergo eternal punishment?
Whereto with speedy words the arch-fiend replied.

Fallen cherub, to be weak is miserable
Doing or suffering: but of this be sure,
To do aught good never will be our task,
But ever to do ill our sole delight,   160
As being the contrary to his high will
Whom we resist. If then his providence
Out of our evil seek to bring forth good,
Our labour must be to pervert that end,
And out of good still to find means of evil;
Which oft-times may succeed, so as perhaps
Shall grieve him, if I fail not, and disturb
His inmost counsels from their destined aim.
But see the angry victor hath recalled
His ministers of vengeance and pursuit   170
Back to the gates of heaven: the sulphurous hail
Shot after us in storm, o'erblown hath laid
The fiery surge, that from the precipice
Of heaven received us falling, and the thunder,
Winged with red lightning and impetuous rage,
Perhaps hath spent his shafts, and ceases now
To bellow through the vast and boundless deep.
Let us not slip the occasion, whether scorn,
Or satiate fury yield it from our foe.
Seest thou yon dreary plain, forlorn and wild,   180
The seat of desolation, void of light,
Save what the glimmering of these livid flames
Casts pale and dreadful? Thither let us tend
From off the tossing of these fiery waves,
There rest, if any rest can harbour there,
And reassembling our afflicted powers,
Consult how we may henceforth most offend
Our enemy, our own loss how repair,
How overcome this dire calamity,
What reinforcement we may gain from hope,   190
If not what resolution from despair.
    Thus Satan talking to his nearest mate
With head uplift above the wave, and eyes
That sparkling blazed, his other parts besides
Prone on the flood, extended long and large
Lay floating many a rood, in bulk as huge
As whom the fables name of monstrous size,

Titanian, or Earth-born, that warred on Jove,
Briareos or Typhon, whom the den
By ancient Tarsus held, or that sea-beast   200
Leviathan, which God of all his works
Created hugest that swim the ocean stream:
Him haply slumbering on the Norway foam
The pilot of some small night-foundered skiff,
Deeming some island, oft, as seamen tell,
With fixèd anchor in his scaly rind
Moors by his side under the lee, while night
Invests the sea, and wishèd morn delays:
So stretched out huge in length the arch-fiend lay
Chained on the burning lake, nor ever thence   210
Had risen or heaved his head, but that the will
And high permission of all-ruling heaven
Left him at large to his own dark designs,
That with reiterated crimes he might
Heap on himself damnation, while he sought
Evil to others, and enraged might see
How all his malice served but to bring forth
Infinite goodness, grace and mercy shown
On man by him seduced, but on himself
Treble confusion, wrath and vengeance poured.   220
Forthwith upright he rears from off the pool
His mighty stature; on each hand the flames
Driven backward slope their pointing spires, and rolled
In billows, leave i' the midst a horrid vale.
Then with expanded wings he steers his flight
Aloft, incumbent on the dusky air
That felt unusual weight, till on dry land
He lights, if it were land that ever burned
With solid, as the lake with liquid fire;
And such appeared in hue, as when the force   230
Of subterranean wind transports a hill
Torn from Pelorus, or the shattered side
Of thundering Aetna, whose combustible
And fuelled entrails thence conceiving fire,
Sublimed with mineral fury, aid the winds,
And leave a singèd bottom all involved
With stench and smoke: such resting found the sole
Of unblessed feet. Him followed his next mate,

Both glorying to have scaped the Stygian flood
As gods, and by their own recovered strength,   240
Not by the sufferance of supernal power.
   Is this the region, this the soil, the clime,
Said then the lost archangel, this the seat
That we must change for heaven, this mournful gloom
For that celestial light? Be it so, since he
Who now is sovereign can dispose and bid
What shall be right: furthest from him is best
Whom reason hath equalled, force hath made supreme
Above his equals. Farewell, happy fields
Where joy forever dwells: hail horrors, hail   250
Infernal world, and thou profoundest hell
Receive thy new possessor: one who brings
A mind not to be changed by place or time.
The mind is its own place, and in itself
Can make a heaven of hell, a hell of heaven.
What matter where, if I be still the same,
And what I should be, all but less than he
Whom thunder hath made greater? Here at least
We shall be free; the almighty hath not built
Here for his envy, will not drive us hence: 260
Here we may reign secure, and in my choice
To reign is worth ambition though in hell:
Better to reign in hell, than serve in heaven.
But wherefore let we then our faithful friends,
The associates and copartners of our loss
Lie thus astonished on the oblivious pool,
And call them not to share with us their part
In this unhappy mansion, or once more
With rallied arms to try what may be yet
Regained in heaven, or what more lost in hell?   270
   So Satan spake, and him Beelzebub
Thus answered. Leader of those armies bright,
Which but the omnipotent none could have foiled,
If once they hear that voice, their liveliest pledge
Of hope in fears and dangers, heard so oft
In worst extremes, and on the perilous edge
Of battle when it raged, in all assaults
Their surest signal, they will soon resume
New courage and revive, though now they lie

Grovelling and prostrate on yon lake of fire,   280
As we erewhile, astounded and amazed,
No wonder, fallen such a pernicious height.
    He scarce had ceased when the superior fiend
Was moving toward the shore; his ponderous shield
Ethereal temper, massy, large, and round,
Behind him cast; the broad circumference
Hung on his shoulders like the moon, whose orb
Through optic glass the Tuscan artist views
At evening from the top of Fesole,
Or in Valdarno, to descry new lands,   290
Rivers or mountains in her spotty globe.
His spear, to equal which the tallest pine
Hewn on Norwegian hills, to be the mast
Of some great admiral, were but a wand,
He walked with to support uneasy steps
Over the burning marl, not like those steps
On heaven's azure, and the torrid clime
Smote on him sore besides, vaulted with fire;
Natheless he so endured, till on the beach
Of that inflamèd sea, he stood and called   300
His legions, angel forms, who lay entranced
Thick as autumnal leaves that strew the brooks
In Vallombrosa, where the Etrurian shades
High overarched imbower; or scattered sedge
Afloat, when with fierce winds Orion armed
Hath vexed the Red Sea coast, whose waves o'erthrew
Busiris and his Memphian chivalry,
While with perfidious hatred they pursued
The sojourners of Goshen, who beheld
From the safe shore their floating carcasses   310
And broken chariot wheels, so thick bestrewn
Abject and lost lay these, covering the flood,
Under amazement of their hideous change.
He called so loud, that all the hollow deep
Of hell resounded. Princes, potentates,
Warriors, the flower of heaven, once yours, now lost,
If such astonishment as this can seize
Eternal spirits; or have ye chosen this place
After the toil of battle to repose
Your wearied virtue, for the ease you find   320

To slumber here, as in the vales of heaven?
Or in this abject posture have ye sworn
To adore the conqueror? who now beholds
Cherub and seraph rolling in the flood
With scattered arms and ensigns, till anon
His swift pursuers from heaven gates discern
The advantage, and descending tread us down
Thus drooping, or with linkèd thunderbolts
Transfix us to the bottom of this gulf.
Awake, arise, or be forever fallen.   330
   They heard, and were abashed, and up they sprung
Upon the wing, as when men wont to watch
On duty, sleeping found by whom they dread,
Rouse and bestir themselves ere well awake.
Nor did they not perceive the evil plight
In which they were, or the fierce pains not feel;
Yet to their general's voice they soon obeyed
Innumerable. As when the potent rod
Of Amram's son in Egypt's evil day
Waved round the coast, up called a pitchy cloud   340
Of locusts, warping on the eastern wind,
That o'er the realm of impious Pharaoh hung
Like night, and darkened all the land of Nile:
So numberless were those bad angels seen
Hovering on wing under the cope of hell
'Twixt upper, nether, and surrounding fires;
Till, as a signal given, the uplifted spear
Of their great sultan waving to direct
Their course, in even balance down they light
On the firm brimstone, and fill all the plain;   350
A multitude, like which the populous north
Poured never from her frozen loins, to pass
Rhene or the Danaw, when her barbarous sons
Came like a deluge on the south, and spread
Beneath Gibralter to the Lybian sands.
Forthwith from every squadron and each band
The heads and leaders thither haste where stood
Their great commander; godlike shapes and forms
Excelling human, princely dignities,
And powers that erst in heaven sat on thrones;   360
Though of their names in heavenly records now

Be no memorial, blotted out and razed
By their rebellion, from the books of life.
Nor had they yet among the sons of Eve
Got them new names, till wandering o'er the earth,
Through God's high sufferance for the trial of man,
By falsities and lies the greatest part
Of mankind they corrupted to forsake
God their creator, and the invisible
Glory of him that made them, to transform   370
Oft to the image of a brute, adorned
With gay religions full of pomp and gold,
And devils to adore for deities:
Then were they known to men by various names,
And various idols through the heathen world.
Say, muse, their names then known, who first, who last,
Roused from the slumber, on that fiery couch,
At their great emperor's call, as next in worth
Came singly where he stood on the bare strand,
While the promiscuous crowd stood yet aloof?   380
The chief were those who from the pit of hell
Roaming to seek their prey on earth, durst fix
Their seats long after next the seat of God,
Their altars by his altar, gods adored
Among the nations round, and durst abide
Jehovah thundering out of Sion, throned
Between the cherubim; yea, often placed
Within his sanctuary itself their shrines,
Abominations; and with cursèd things
His holy rites, and solemn feasts profaned,   390
And with their darkness durst affront his light.
First Moloch, horrid king besmeared with blood
Of human sacrifice, and parents' tears,
Though for the noise of drums and timbrels loud
Their children's cries unheard, that passed through fire
To his grim idol. Him the Ammonite
Worshipped in Rabba and her watery plain,
In Argob and in Basan, to the stream
Of utmost Arnon. Nor content with such
Audacious neighbourhood, the wisest heart   400
Of Solomon he led by fraud to build
His temple right against the temple of God

On that opprobrious hill, and made his grove
The pleasant valley of Hinnom, Tophet thence
And black Gehenna called, the type of hell.
Next Chemos, the obscene dread of Moab's sons,
From Aroar to Nebo, and the wild
Of southmost Abarim; in Hesebon
And Horonaim, Seon's realm, beyond
The flowery dale of Sibma clad with vines,   410
And Eleale to the Asphaltic Pool.
Peor his other name, when he enticed
Israel in Sittim, on their march from Nile,
To do him wanton rites; which cost them woe.
Yet thence his lustful orgies he enlarged
Even to that hill of scandal, by the grove
Of Moloch homicide, lust hard by hate;
Till good Josiah drove them thence to hell.
With these came they, who from the bordering flood
Of old Euphrates to the brook that parts   420
Egypt from Syrian ground, had general names
Of Baalim and Ashtaroth, those male,
These feminine. For spirits when they please
Can either sex assume, or both; so soft
And uncompounded is their essence pure,
Not tied or manacled with joint or limb,
Nor founded on the brittle strength of bones,
Like cumbrous flesh; but in what shape they choose
Dilated or condensed, bright or obscure,
Can execute their airy purposes,   430
And works of love or enmity fulfil.
For those the race of Israel oft forsook
Their living strength, and unfrequented left
His righteous altar, bowing lowly down
To bestial gods; for which their heads as low
Bowed down in battle, sunk before the spear
Of despicable foes. With these in troop
Came Astoreth, whom the Phoenicians called
Astarte, queen of heaven, with crescent horns;
To whose bright image nightly by the moon   440
Sidonian virgins paid their vows and songs,
In Sion also not unsung, where stood
Her temple on the offensive mountain, built

By that uxorious king, whose heart though large,
Beguiled by fair idolatresses, fell
To idols foul. Thammuz came next behind,
Whose annual wound in Lebanon allured
The Syrian damsels to lament his fate
In amorous ditties all a summer's day,
While smooth Adonis from his native rock   450
Ran purple to the sea, supposed with blood
Of Thammuz yearly wounded: the love-tale
Infected Sion's daughters with like heat,
Whose wanton passions in the sacred porch
Ezekiel saw, when by the vision led
His eye surveyed the dark idolatries
Of alienated Judah. Next came one
Who mourned in earnest, when the captive ark
Maimed his brute image, heads and hands lopped off
In his own temple, on the groundsel edge,   460
Where he fell flat, and shamed his worshippers:
Dagon his name, sea monster, upward man
And downward fish: yet had his temple high
Reared in Azotus, dreaded through the coast
Of Palestine, in Gath and Ascalon
And Accaron and Gaza's frontier bounds.
Him followed Rimmon, whose delightful seat
Was fair Damascus, on the fertile banks
Of Abbana and Pharphar, lucid streams.
He also against the house of God was bold: 470
A leper once he lost and gained a king,
Ahaz his sottish conqueror, whom he drew
God's altar to disparage and displace
For one of Syrian mode, whereon to burn
His odious offerings, and adore the gods
Whom he had vanquished. After these appeared
A crew who under names of old renown,
Osiris, Isis, Orus and their train
With monstrous shapes and sorceries abused
Fanatic Egypt and her priests, to seek   480
Their wanderings gods disguised in brutish forms
Rather than human. Nor did Israel scape
The infection when their borrowed gold composed
The calf in Oreb: and the rebel king

Doubled that sin in Bethel and in Dan,
Likening his maker to the grazèd ox,
Jehovah, who in one night when he passed
From Egypt marching, equalled with one stroke
Both her first born and all her bleating gods.
Belial came last, than whom a spirit more lewd   490
Fell not from heaven, or more gross to love
Vice for itself: to him no temple stood
Or altar smoked; yet who more oft than he
In temples and at altars, when the priest
Turns atheist, as did Eli's sons, who filled
With lust and violence the house of God.
In courts and palaces he also reigns
And in luxurious cities, where the noise
Of riot ascends above their loftiest towers,
And injury and outrage: and when night   500
Darkens the streets, then wander forth the sons
Of Belial, flown with insolence and wine.
Witness the streets of Sodom, and that night
In Gibeah, when the hospitable door
Exposed a matron to avoid worse rape.
These were the prime in order and in might;
The rest were long to tell, though far renowned,
The Ionian gods, of Javan's issue held
Gods, yet confessed later than Heaven and Earth
Their boasted parents; Titan Heaven's first born   510
With his enormous brood, and birthright seized
By younger Saturn, he from mightier Jove
His own and Rhea's son like measure found;
So Jove usurping reigned: these first in Crete
And Ida known, thence on the snowy top
Of cold Olympus ruled the middle air
Their highest heaven; or on the Delphian cliff,
Or in Dodona, and through all the bounds
Of Doric land; or who with Saturn old
Fled over Adria to the Hesperian fields,   520
And o'er the Celtic roamed the utmost isles.
All these and more came flocking; but with looks
Downcast and damp, yet such wherein appeared
Obscure some glimpse of joy, to have found their chief
Not in despair, to have found themselves not lost

In loss itself; which on his countenance cast
Like doubtful hue: but he his wonted pride
Soon recollecting, with high words, that bore
Semblance of worth, not substance, gently raised
Their fainting courage, and dispelled their fears. 530
Then straight commands that at the warlike sound
Of trumpets loud and clarions be upreared
His mighty standard; that proud honour claimed
Azazel as his right, a cherub tall:
Who forthwith from the glittering staff unfurled
The imperial ensign, which full high advanced
Shone like a meteor streaming to the wind
With gems and golden lustre rich emblazed,
Seraphic arms and trophies: all the while
Sonorous metal blowing martial sounds: 540
At which the universal host upsent
A shout that tore hell's concave, and beyond
Frighted the reign of Chaos and old Night.
All in a moment through the gloom were seen
Ten thousand banners rise into the air
With orient colours waving: with them rose
A forest huge of spears: and thronging helms
Appeared, and serried shields in thick array
Of depth immeasurable: anon they move
In perfect phalanx to the Dorian mode 550
Of flutes and soft recorders; such as raised
To height of noblest temper heroes old
Arming to battle, and instead of rage
Deliberate valour breathed, firm and unmoved
With dread of death to flight or foul retreat,
Nor wanting power to mitigate and swage
With solemn touches, troubled thoughts, and chase
Anguish and doubt and fear and sorrow and pain
From mortal or immortal minds. Thus they
Breathing united force with fixèd thought 560
Moved on in silence to soft pipes that charmed
Their painful steps o'er the burnt soil; and now
Advanced in view, they stand, a horrid front
Of dreadful length and dazzling arms, in guise
Of warriors old with ordered spear and shield,
Awaiting what command their mighty chief

Had to impose: he through the armèd files
Darts his experienced eye, and soon traverse
The whole battalion views, their order due,
Their visages and stature as of gods,   570
Their number last he sums. And now his heart
Distends with pride, and hardening in his strength
Glories: for never since created man,
Met such embodied force, as named with these
Could merit more than that small infantry
Warred on by cranes: though all the Giant brood
Of Phlegra with the heroic race were joined
That fought at Thebes and Ilium, on each side
Mixed with auxiliar gods; and what resounds
In fable or romance of Uther's son   580
Begirt with British and Armoric knights;
And all who since, baptized or infidel
Jousted in Aspramont or Montalban,
Damasco, or Morocco, or Trebizond,
Or whom Bizerta sent from Afric shore
When Charlemagne with all his peerage fell
By Fontarabia. Thus far these beyond
Compare of mortal prowess, yet observed
Their dread commander: he above the rest
In shape and gesture proudly eminent   590
Stood like a tower; his form had yet not lost
All her original brightness, nor appeared
Less than archangel ruined, and the excess
Of glory obscured: as when the sun new risen
Looks through the horizontal misty air
Shorn of his beams, or from behind the moon
In dim eclipse disastrous twilight sheds
On half the nations, and with fear of change
Perplexes monarchs. Darkened so, yet shone
Above them all the archangel: but his face   600
Deep scars of thunder had intrenched, and care
Sat on his faded cheek, but under brows
Of dauntless courage, and considerate pride
Waiting revenge: cruel his eye, but cast
Signs of remorse and passion to behold
The fellows of his crime, the followers rather
(Far other once beheld in bliss) condemned

Forever now to have their lot in pain,
Millions of spirits for his fault amerced
Of heaven, and from eternal splendours flung   610
For his revolt, yet faithful how they stood,
Their glory withered. As when heaven's fire
Hath scathed the forest oaks, or mountain pines,
With singèd top their stately growth though bare
Stands on the blasted heath. He now prepared
To speak; whereat their doubled ranks they bend
From wing to wing, and half enclose him round
With all his peers: attention held them mute.
Thrice he essayed, and thrice in spite of scorn,
Tears such as angels weep burst forth: at last   620
Words interwove with sighs found out their way.
   O myriads of immortal spirits, O powers
Matchless, but with the almighty, and that strife
Was not inglorious, though the event was dire,
As this place testifies, and this dire change
Hateful to utter: but what power of mind
Foreseeing or presaging, from the depth
Of knowledge past or present, could have feared,
How such united force of gods, how such
As stood like these, could ever know repulse?   630
For who can yet believe, though after loss,
That all these puissant legions, whose exile
Hath emptied heaven, shall fail to reascend
Self-raised, and repossess their native seat?
For me be witness all the host of heaven,
If counsels different, or danger shunned
By me, have lost our hopes. But he who reigns
Monarch in heaven, till then as one secure
Sat on his throne, upheld by old repute,
Consent or custom, and his regal state   640
Put forth at full, but still his strength concealed,
Which tempted our attempt, and wrought our fall.
Henceforth his might we know, and know our own
So as not either to provoke, or dread
New war, provoked; our better part remains
To work in close design, by fraud or guile
What force effected not: that he no less
At length from us may find, who overcomes

By force, hath overcome but half his foe.
Space may produce new worlds; whereof so rife   650
There went a fame in heaven that he ere long
Intended to create, and therein plant
A generation, whom his choice regard
Should favour equal to the sons of heaven:
Thither, if but to pry, shall be perhaps
Our first eruption, thither or elsewhere:
For this infernal pit shall never hold
Celestial spirits in bondage, nor the abyss
Long under darkness cover. But these thoughts
Full counsel must mature: peace is despaired,   660
For who can think submission? War then, war
Open or understood must be resolved.
    He spake: and to confirm his words, outflew
Millions of flaming swords, drawn from the thighs
Of mighty cherubim; the sudden blaze
Far round illumined hell: highly they raged
Against the highest, and fierce with graspèd arms
Clashed on their sounding shields the din of war,
Hurling defiance toward the vault of heaven.
    There stood a hill not far whose grisly top   670
Belched fire and rolling smoke; the rest entire
Shone with a glossy scurf, undoubted sign
That in his womb was hid metallic ore,
The work of sulphur. Thither winged with speed
A numerous brigade hastened. As when bands
Of pioneers with spade and pickaxe armed
Forerun the royal camp, to trench a field,
Or cast a rampart. Mammon led them on,
Mammon, the least erected spirit that fell
From heaven, for even in heaven his looks and thoughts   680
Were always downward bent, admiring more
The riches of heaven's pavement, trodden gold,
Than aught divine or holy else enjoyed
In vision beatific: by him first
Men also, and by his suggestion taught,
Ransacked the centre, and with impious hands
Rifled the bowels of their mother earth
For treasures better hid. Soon had his crew
Opened into the hill a spacious wound

And digged out ribs of gold. Let none admire   690
That riches grow in hell; that soil may best
Deserve the precious bane. And here let those
Who boast in mortal things, and wondering tell
Of Babel, and the works of Memphian kings
Learn how their greatest monuments of fame,
And strength and art are easily outdone
By spirits reprobate, and in an hour
What in an age they with incessant toil
And hands innumerable scarce perform.
Nigh on the plain in many cells prepared,   700
That underneath had veins of liquid fire
Sluiced from the lake, a second multitude
With wondrous art founded the massy ore,
Severing each kind, and scummed the bullion dross:
A third as soon had formed within the ground
A various mould, and from the boiling cells
By strange conveyance filled each hollow nook,
As in an organ from one blast of wind
To many a row of pipes the sound-board breathes.
Anon out of the earth a fabric huge   710
Rose like an exhalation, with the sound
Of dulcet symphonies and voices sweet,
Built like a temple, where pilasters round
Were set, and Doric pillars overlaid
With golden architrave; nor did there want
Cornice or frieze, with bossy sculptures graven,
The roof was fretted gold. Not Babylon,
Nor great Alcairo such magnificence
Equalled in all their glories, to enshrine
Belus or Serapis their gods, or seat   720
Their kings, when Egypt with Assyria strove
In wealth and luxury. The ascending pile
Soon fixed her stately height, and straight the doors
Opening their brazen folds discover wide
Within her ample spaces, o'er the smooth
And level pavement: from the archèd roof
Pendent by subtle magic many a row
Of starry lamps and blazing cressets fed
With naphtha and asphaltus yielded light
As from a sky. The hasty multitude   730

Admiring entered, and the work some praise
And some the architect: his hand was known
In heaven by many a towered structure high,
Where sceptred angels held their residence,
And sat as princes, whom the supreme king
Exalted to such power, and gave to rule,
Each in his hierarchy, the orders bright.
Nor was his name unheard or unadored
In ancient Greece; and in Ausonian land
Men called him Mulciber; and how he fell   740
From heaven, they fabled, thrown by angry Jove
Sheer o'er the crystal battlements; from morn
To noon he fell, from noon to dewy eve,
A summer's day; and with the setting sun
Dropped from the zenith like a falling star,
On Lemnos the Aegaean isle: thus they relate,
Erring; for he with this rebellious rout
Fell long before; nor aught availed him now
To have built in heaven high towers; nor did he scape
By all his engines, but was headlong sent   750
With his industrious crew to build in hell.
Meanwhile the wingèd heralds by command
Of sovereign power, with awful ceremony
And trumpets' sound throughout the host proclaim
A solemn council forthwith to be held
At Pandaemonium, the high capital
Of Satan and his peers: their summons called
From every band and squarèd regiment
By place or choice the worthiest; they anon
With hundreds and with thousands trooping came   760
Attended: all access was thronged, the gates
And porches wide, but chief the spacious hall
(Though like a covered field, where champions bold
Wont ride in armed, and at the soldan's chair
Defied the best of paynim chivalry
To mortal combat or career with lance)
Thick swarmed, both on the ground and in the air,
Brushed with the hiss of rustling wings. As bees
In springtime, when the sun with Taurus rides,
Pour forth their populous youth about the hive   770
In clusters; they among fresh dews and flowers

Fly to and fro, or on the smoothèd plank,
The suburb of their straw-built citadel,
New rubbed with balm, expatiate and confer
Their state affairs. So thick the airy crowd
Swarmed and were straitened; till the signal given,
Behold a wonder! they but now who seemed
In bigness to surpass Earth's giant sons
Now less than smallest dwarfs, in narrow room
Throng numberless, like that pygmean race   780
Beyond the Indian mount, or fairy elves,
Whose midnight revels, by a forest side
Or fountain some belated peasant sees,
Or dreams he sees, while overhead the moon
Sits arbitress, and nearer to the earth
Wheels her pale course, they on their mirth and dance
Intent, with jocund music charm his ear;
At once with joy and fear his heart rebounds.
Thus incorporeal spirits to smallest forms
Reduced their shapes immense, and were at large,   790
Though without number still amidst the hall
Of that infernal court. But far within
And in their own dimensions like themselves
The great seraphic lords and cherubim
In close recess and secret conclave sat
A thousand demigods on golden seats,
Frequent and full. After short silence then
And summons read, the great consult began.

From Book II

. . . .

The Stygian council thus dissolved; and forth
In order came the grand infernal peers,
Midst came their mighty paramount, and seemed
Alone the antagonist of heaven, nor less
Than hell's dread emperor with pomp supreme,   510
And Godlike imitated state; him round
A globe of fiery seraphim enclosed
With bright emblazonry, and horrent arms.

Then of their session ended they bid cry
With trumpets' regal sound the great result:
Toward the four winds four speedy cherubim
Put to their mouths the sounding alchemy
By herald's voice explained: the hollow abyss
Heard far and wide, and all the host of hell
With deafening shout returned them loud acclaim.   520
Thence more at ease their minds and somewhat raised
By false presumptuous hope, the rangèd powers
Disband, and wandering, each his several way
Pursues, as inclination or sad choice
Leads him perplexed, where he may likeliest find
Truce to his restless thoughts, and entertain
The irksome hours, till this great chief return.
Part on the plain, or in the air sublime
Upon the wing, or in swift race contend,
As at the Olympian games or Pythian fields;   530
Part curb their fiery steeds, or shun the goal
With rapid wheels, or fronted brigades form.
As when to warn proud cities war appears
Waged in the troubled sky, and armies rush
To battle in the clouds, before each van
Prick forth the airy knights, and couch their spears
Till thickest legions close; with feats of arms
From either end of heaven the welkin burns.
Others with vast Typhoean rage more fell
Rend up both rocks and hills, and ride the air   540
In whirlwind; hell scarce holds the wild uproar.
As when Alcides from Oechalia crowned
With conquest, felt the envenomed robe, and tore
Through pain up by the roots Thessalian pines,
And Lichas from the top of Oeta threw
Into the Euboic sea. Others more mild,
Retreated in a silent valley, sing
With notes angelical to many a harp
Their own heroic deeds and hapless fall
By doom of battle; and complain that fate   550
Free virtue should enthral to force or chance.
Their song was partial, but the harmony
(What could it less when spirits immortal sing?)
Suspended hell, and took with ravishment

The thronging audience. In discourse more sweet
(For eloquence the soul, song charms the sense,)
Others apart sat on a hill retired,
In thoughts more elevate, and reasoned high
Of providence, foreknowledge, will and fate,
Fixed fate, free will, foreknowledge absolute,   560
And found no end, in wandering mazes lost.
Of good and evil much they argued then,
Of happiness and final misery,
Passion and apathy, and glory and shame,
Vain wisdom all, and false philosophy:
Yet with a pleasing sorcery could charm
Pain for a while or anguish, and excite
Fallacious hope, or arm the obdurèd breast
With stubborn patience as with triple steel.
Another part in squadrons and gross bands,   570
On bold adventure to discover wide
That dismal world, if any clime perhaps
Might yield them easier habitation, bend
Four ways their flying march, along the banks
Of four infernal rivers that disgorge
Into the burning lake their baleful streams;
Abhorrèd Styx the flood of deadly hate,
Sad Acheron of sorrow, black and deep;
Cocytus, named of lamentation loud
Heard on the rueful stream; fierce Phlegethon   580
Whose waves of torrent fire inflame with rage.
Far off from these a slow and silent stream,
Lethe the river of oblivion rolls
Her watery labyrinth, whereof who drinks,
Forthwith his former state and being forgets,
Forgets both joy and grief, pleasure and pain.
Beyond this flood a frozen continent
Lies dark and wild, beat with perpetual storms
Of whirlwind and dire hail, which on firm land
Thaws not, but gathers heap, and ruin seems   590
Of ancient pile; all else deep snow and ice,
A gulf profound as that Serbonian bog
Betwixt Damietta and Mount Casius old,
Where armies whole have sunk: the parching air
Burns frore, and cold performs the effect of fire.

Thither by harpy-footed Furies haled,
At certain revolutions all the damned
Are brought: and feel by turns the bitter change
Of fierce extremes, extremes by change more fierce,
From beds of raging fire to starve in ice   600
Their soft ethereal warmth, and there to pine
Immovable, infixed, and frozen round,
Periods of time, thence hurried back to fire.
They ferry over this Lethean sound
Both to and fro, their sorrow to augment,
And wish and struggle, as they pass, to reach
The tempting stream, with one small drop to lose
In sweet forgetfulness all pain and woe,
All in one moment, and so near the brink;
But fate withstands, and to oppose the attempt   610
Medusa with gorgonian terror guards
The ford, and of itself the water flies
All taste of living wight, as once it fled
The lip of Tantalus. Thus roving on
In confused march forlorn, the adventurous bands
With shuddering horror pale, and eyes aghast
Viewed first their lamentable lot, and found
No rest: through many a dark and dreary vale
They passed, and many a region dolorous,
O'er many a frozen, many a fiery alp,   620
Rocks, caves, lakes, fens, bogs, dens, and shades of death,
A universe of death, which God by curse
Created evil, for evil only good,
Where all life dies, death lives, and nature breeds,
Perverse, all monstrous, all prodigious things,
Abominable, inutterable, and worse
Than fables yet have feigned, or fear conceived,
Gorgons and hydras, and chimeras dire.
    Meanwhile the adversary of God and man,
Satan with thoughts inflamed of highest design,   630
Puts on swift wings, and towards the gates of hell
Explores his solitary flight; sometimes
He scours the right hand coast, sometimes the left,
Now shaves with level wing the deep, then soars
Up to the fiery concave towering high.
As when far off at sea a fleet descried

Hangs in the clouds, by equinoctial winds
Close sailing from Bengala, or the isles
Of Ternate and Tidore, whence merchants bring
Their spicy drugs: they on the trading flood   640
Through the wide Ethiopian to the Cape
Ply stemming nightly toward the pole. So seemed
Far off the flying fiend: at last appear
Hell bounds high reaching to the horrid roof,
And thrice threefold the gates; three folds were brass,
Three iron, three of adamantine rock,
Impenetrable, impaled with circling fire,
Yet unconsumed. Before the gates there sat
On either side a formidable shape;
The one seemed woman to the waist, and fair,   650
But ended foul in many a scaly fold
Voluminous and vast, a serpent armed
With mortal sting: about her middle round
A cry of hell hounds never ceasing barked
With wide Cerberian mouths full loud, and rung
A hideous peal: yet, when they list, would creep,
If aught disturbed their noise, into her womb,
And kennel there, yet there still barked and howled,
Within unseen. Far less abhorred than these
Vexed Scylla bathing in the sea that parts   660
Calabria from the hoarse Trinacrian shore:
Nor uglier follow the Night-hag, when called
In secret, riding through the air she comes
Lured with the smell of infant blood, to dance
With Lapland witches, while the labouring moon
Eclipses at their charms. The other shape,
If shape it might be called that shape had none
Distinguishable in member, joint, or limb,
Or substance might be called that shadow seemed,
For each seemed either; black it stood as night,   670
Fierce as ten Furies, terrible as hell,
And shook a dreadful dart; what seemed his head
The likeness of a kingly crown had on.
Satan was now at hand, and from his seat
The monster moving onward came as fast
With horrid strides, hell trembled as he strode.
The undaunted fiend what this might be admired,

Admired, not feared; God and his son except,
Created thing nought valued he nor shunned;
And with disdainful look thus first began.   680

　　Whence and what art thou, execrable shape,
That darest, though grim and terrible, advance
Thy miscreated front athwart my way
To yonder gates? through them I mean to pass,
That be assured, without leave asked of thee:
Retire, or taste thy folly, and learn by proof,
Hell-born, not to contend with spirits of heaven.

　　To whom the goblin full of wrath replied,
Art thou that traitor angel, art thou he,
Who first broke peace in heaven and faith, till then   690
Unbroken, and in proud rebellious arms
Drew after him the third part of heaven's sons
Conjured against the highest, for which both thou
And they outcast from God, are here condemned
To waste eternal days in woe and pain?
And reckon'st thou thyself with spirits of heaven,
Hell-doomed, and breath'st defiance here and scorn
Where I reign king, and to enrage thee more,
Thy king and lord? Back to thy punishment,
False fugitive, and to thy speed add wings,   700
Lest with a whip of scorpions I pursue
Thy lingering, or with one stroke of this dart
Strange horror seize thee, and pangs unfelt before.

　　So spake the grisly terror, and in shape,
So speaking and so threatening, grew tenfold
More dreadful and deform: on the other side
Incensed with indignation Satan stood
Unterrified, and like a comet burned,
That fires the length of Ophiuchus huge
In the Arctic sky, and from his horrid hair   710
Shakes pestilence and war. Each at the head
Levelled his deadly aim; their fatal hands
No second stroke intend, and such a frown
Each cast at the other, as when two black clouds
With heaven's artillery fraught, come rattling on
Over the Caspian, then stand front to front
Hovering a space, till winds the signal blow
To join their dark encounter in midair:

So frowned the mighty combatants, that hell
Grew darker at their frown, so matched they stood;   720
For never but once more was either like
To meet so great a foe: and now great deeds
Had been achieved, whereof all hell had rung,
Had not the snaky sorceress that sat
Fast by hell gate, and kept the fatal key,
Risen, and with hideous outcry rushed between.
    O father, what intends thy hand, she cried,
Against thy only son? What fury O son,
Possesses thee to bend that mortal dart
Against thy father's head? and know'st for whom;   730
For him who sits above and laughs the while
At thee ordained his drudge, to execute
Whate'er his wrath, which he calls justice, bids,
His wrath which one day will destroy ye both.
    She spake, and at her words the hellish pest
Forbore, then these to her Satan returned:
    So strange thy outcry, and thy words so strange
Thou interposest, that my sudden hand
Prevented spares to tell thee yet by deeds
What it intends; till first I know of thee,   740
What thing thou art, thus double-formed, and why
In this infernal vale first met thou call'st
Me father, and that phantasm call'st my son?
I know thee not, nor ever saw till now
Sight more detestable than him and thee.
    To whom thus the portress of hell gate replied;
Hast thou forgot me then, and do I seem
Now in thine eye so foul, once deemed so fair
In heaven, when at the assembly, and in sight
Of all the seraphim with thee combined   750
In bold conspiracy against heaven's king,
All on a sudden miserable pain
Surprised thee, dim thine eyes, and dizzy swum
In darkness, while thy head flames thick and fast
Threw forth, till on the left side opening wide,
Likest to thee in shape and countenance bright,
Then shining heavenly fair, a goddess armed
Out of thy head I sprung: amazement seized
All the host of heaven; back they recoiled afraid

At first, and called me Sin, and for a sign   760
Portentous held me; but familiar grown,
I pleased, and with attractive graces won
The most averse, thee chiefly, who full oft
Thyself in me thy perfect image viewing
Becam'st enamoured, and such joy thou took'st
With me in secret, that my womb conceived
A growing burden. Meanwhile war arose,
And fields were fought in heaven; wherein remained
(For what could else) to our almighty foe
Clear victory, to our part loss and rout   770
Through all the empyrean: down they fell
Driven headlong from the pitch of heaven, down
Into this deep, and in the general fall
I also; at which time this powerful key
Into my hand was given, with charge to keep
These gates for ever shut, which none can pass
Without my opening. Pensive here I sat
Alone, but long I sat not, till my womb
Pregnant by thee, and now excessive grown
Prodigious motion felt and rueful throes.   780
At last this odious offspring whom thou seest
Thine own begotten, breaking violent way
Tore through my entrails, that with fear and pain
Distorted, all my nether shape thus grew
Transformed: but he my inbred enemy
Forth issued, brandishing his fatal dart
Made to destroy: I fled, and cried out Death;
Hell trembled at the hideous name, and sighed
From all her caves, and back resounded Death.
I fled, but he pursued (though more, it seems,   790
Inflamed with lust than rage) and swifter far,
Me overtook his mother all dismayed,
And in embraces forcible and foul
Engendering with me, of that rape begot
These yelling monsters that with ceaseless cry
Surround me, as thou sawest, hourly conceived
And hourly born, with sorrow infinite
To me, for when they list into the womb
That bred them they return, and howl and gnaw
My bowels, their repast; then bursting forth   800

Afresh with conscious terrors vex me round,
That rest or intermission none I find.
Before mine eyes in opposition sits
Grim Death my son and foe, who sets them on,
And me his parent would full soon devour
For want of other prey, but that he knows
His end with mine involved; and knows that I
Should prove a bitter morsel, and his bane,
Whenever that shall be; so fate pronounced.
But thou, O father, I forewarn thee, shun   810
His deadly arrow; neither vainly hope
To be invulnerable in those bright arms,
Though tempered heavenly, for that mortal dint,
Save he who reigns above, none can resist.
    She finished, and the subtle fiend his lore
Soon learned, now milder, and thus answered smooth.
Dear daughter, since thou claim'st me for thy sire,
And my fair son here show'st me, the dear pledge
Of dalliance had with thee in heaven, and joys
Then sweet, now sad to mention, through dire change   820
Befallen us unforeseen, unthought of, know
I come no enemy, but to set free
From out this dark and dismal house of pain,
Both him and thee, and all the heavenly host
Of spirits that in our just pretences armed
Fell with us from on high: from them I go
This uncouth errand sole, and one for all
Myself expose, with lonely steps to tread
The unfounded deep, and through the void immense
To search with wandering quest a place foretold   830
Should be, and, by concurring signs, ere now
Created vast and round, a place of bliss
In the purlieus of heaven, and therein placed
A race of upstart creatures, to supply
Perhaps our vacant room, though more removed,
Lest heaven surcharged with potent multitude
Might hap to move new broils: be this or aught
Than this more secret now designed, I haste
To know, and this once known, shall soon return,
And bring ye to the place where thou and Death   840
Shall dwell at ease, and up and down unseen

Wing silently the buxom air, embalmed
With odours; there ye shall be fed and filled
Immeasurably, all things shall be your prey.
He ceased, for both seemed highly pleased, and Death
Grinned horrible a ghastly smile, to hear
His famine should be filled, and blessed his maw
Destined to that good hour: no less rejoiced
His mother bad, and thus bespake her sire.
    The key of this infernal pit by due,   850
And by command of heaven's all-powerful king
I keep, by him forbidden to unlock
These adamantine gates; against all force
Death ready stands to interpose his dart,
Fearless to be o'ermatched by living might.
But what owe I to his commands above
Who hates me, and hath hither thrust me down
Into this gloom of Tartarus profound,
To sit in hateful office here confined,
Inhabitant of heaven, and heavenly-born,   860
Here in perpetual agony and pain,
With terrors and with clamours compassed round
Of mine own brood, that on my bowels feed:
Thou art my father, thou my author, thou
My being gav'st me; whom should I obey
But thee, whom follow? thou wilt bring me soon
To that new world of light and bliss, among
The gods who live at ease, where I shall reign
At thy right hand voluptuous, as beseems
Thy daughter and thy darling, without end.   870
    Thus saying, from her side the fatal key,
Sad instrument of all our woe, she took;
And towards the gate rolling her bestial train,
Forthwith the huge portcullis high updrew,
Which but her self, not all the Stygian powers
Could once have moved; then in the keyhole turns
The intricate wards, and every bolt and bar
Of massy iron or solid rock with ease
Unfastens: on a sudden open fly
With impetuous recoil and jarring sound   880
The infernal doors, and on their hinges grate
Harsh thunder, that the lowest bottom shook

Of Erebus. She opened, but to shut
Excelled her power; the gates wide open stood,
That with extended wings a bannered host
Under spread ensigns marching might pass through
With horse and chariots ranked in loose array;
So wide they stood, and like a furnace mouth
Cast forth redounding smoke and ruddy flame.
Before their eyes in sudden view appear   890
The secrets of the hoary deep, a dark
Illimitable ocean without bound,
Without dimension, where length, breadth, and height,
And time and place are lost; where eldest Night
And Chaos, ancestors of Nature, hold
Eternal anarchy, amidst the noise
Of endless wars, and by confusion stand.
For Hot, Cold, Moist, and Dry, four champions fierce
Strive here for mastery, and to battle bring
Their embryon atoms; they around the flag   900
Of each his faction, in their several clans,
Light-armed or heavy, sharp, smooth, swift or slow,
Swarm populous, unnumbered as the sands
Of Barca or Cyrene's torrid soil,
Levied to side with warring winds, and poise
Their lighter wings. To whom these most adhere,
He rules a moment; Chaos umpire sits,
And by decision more embroils the fray
By which he reigns: next him high arbiter
Chance governs all. Into this wild abyss,   910
The womb of nature and perhaps her grave,
Of neither sea, nor shore, nor air, nor fire,
But all these in their pregnant causes mixed
Confus'dly, and which thus must ever fight,
Unless the almighty maker them ordain
His dark materials to create more worlds,
Into this wild abyss the wary fiend
Stood on the brink of hell and looked awhile,
Pondering his voyage; for no narrow frith
He had to cross. Nor was his ear less pealed   920
With noises loud and ruinous (to compare
Great things with small) than when Bellona storms,
With all her battering engines bent to raze

Some capital city; or less than if this frame
Of heaven were falling, and these elements
In mutiny had from her axle torn
The steadfast earth. At last his sail-broad vans
He spreads for flight, and in the surging smoke
Uplifted spurns the ground, thence many a league
As in a cloudy chair ascending rides   930
Audacious, but that seat soon failing, meets
A vast vacuity: all unawares
Fluttering his pennons vain plumb down he drops
Ten thousand fathom deep, and to this hour
Down had been falling, had not by ill chance
The strong rebuff of some tumultuous cloud
Instinct with fire and nitre hurried him
As many miles aloft: that fury stayed,
Quenched in a boggy Syrtis, neither sea,
Nor good dry land: nigh foundered on he fares,   940
Treading the crude consistence, half on foot,
Half flying; behoves him now both oar and sail.
As when a griffin through the wilderness
With wingèd course o'er hill or moory dale,
Pursues the Arimaspian, who by stealth
Had from his wakeful custody purloined
The guarded gold: so eagerly the fiend
O'er bog or steep, through straight, rough, dense, or rare,
With head, hands, wings or feet pursues his way,
And swims or sinks, or wades, or creeps, or flies: 950
At length a universal hubbub wild
Of stunning sounds and voices all confused
Borne through the hollow dark assaults his ear
With loudest vehemence: thither he plies,
Undaunted to meet there whatever power
Or spirit of the nethermost abyss
Might in that noise reside, of whom to ask
Which way the nearest coast of darkness lies
Bordering on light; when straight behold the throne
Of Chaos, and his dark pavilion spread   960
Wide on the wasteful deep; with him enthroned
Sat sable-vested Night, eldest of things,
The consort of his reign; and by them stood
Orcus and Ades, and the dreaded name

Of Demogorgon; Rumour next and Chance,
And Tumult and Confusion all embroiled,
And Discord with a thousand various mouths.
    To whom Satan turning boldly, thus. Ye powers
And spirits of this nethermost abyss,
Chaos and ancient Night, I come no spy,   970
With purpose to explore or to disturb
The secrets of your realm, but by constraint
Wandering this darksome desert, as my way
Lies through your spacious empire up to light,
Alone, and without guide, half lost, I seek
What readiest path leads where your gloomy bounds
Confine with heaven; or if some other place
From your dominion won, the ethereal king
Possesses lately, thither to arrive
I travel this profound, direct my course;   980
Directed no mean recompense it brings
To your behoof, if I that region lost,
All usurpation thence expelled, reduce
To her original darkness and your sway
(Which is my present journey) and once more
Erect the standard there of ancient Night;
Yours be the advantage all, mine the revenge.
    Thus Satan; and him thus the anarch old
With faltering speech and visage incomposed
Answered. I know thee, stranger, who thou art,   990
That mighty leading angel, who of late
Made head against heaven's king, though overthrown.
I saw and heard, for such a numerous host
Fled not in silence through the frighted deep
With ruin upon ruin, rout on rout,
Confusion worse confounded; and heaven gates
Poured out by millions her victorious bands
Pursuing. I upon my frontiers here
Keep residence; if all I can will serve,
That little which is left so to defend,   1000
Encroached on still through our intestine broils
Weakening the sceptre of old Night: first hell
Your dungeon stretching far and wide beneath;
Now lately heaven and earth, another world
Hung o'er my realm, linked in a golden chain

To that side heaven from whence your legions fell:
If that way be your walk, you have not far;
So much the nearer danger; go and speed;
Havoc and spoil and ruin are my gain.

    He ceased; and Satan stayed not to reply,   1010
But glad that now his sea should find a shore,
With fresh alacrity and force renewed
Springs upward like a pyramid of fire
Into the wild expanse, and through the shock
Of fighting elements, on all sides round
Environed wins his way; harder beset
And more endangered, than when Argo passed
Through Bosphorus, betwixt the jostling rocks:
Or when Ulysses on the larboard shunned
Charybdis, and by the other whirlpool steered.   1020
So he with difficulty and labour hard
Moved on, with difficulty and labour he;
But he once past, soon after when man fell,
Strange alteration! Sin and Death amain
Following his track, such was the will of heaven,
Paved after him a broad and beaten way
Over the dark abyss, whose boiling gulf
Tamely endured a bridge of wondrous length
From hell continued reaching the utmost orb
Of this frail world; by which the spirits perverse   1030
With easy intercourse pass to and fro
To tempt or punish mortals, except whom
God and good angels guard by special grace.
But now at last the sacred influence
Of light appears, and from the walls of heaven
Shoots far into the bosom of dim night
A glimmering dawn; here nature first begins
Her farthest verge, and Chaos to retire
As from her outmost works a broken foe
With tumult less and with less hostile din,   1040
That Satan with less toil, and now with ease
Wafts on the calmer wave by dubious light
And like a weather-beaten vessel holds
Gladly the port, though shrouds and tackle torn;
Or in the emptier waste, resembling air,
Weighs his spread wings, at leisure to behold

Far off the empyreal heaven, extended wide
In circuit, undetermined square or round,
With opal towers and battlements adorned
Of living sapphire, once his native seat;   1050
And fast by hanging in a golden chain
This pendent world, in bigness as a star
Of smallest magnitude close by the moon.
Thither full fraught with mischievous revenge,
Accursed, and in a cursèd hour he hies.

From Book III

Hail holy light, offspring of heaven first-born,
Or of the eternal co-eternal beam
May I express thee unblamed? since God is light,
And never but in unapproachèd light
Dwelt from eternity, dwelt then in thee,
Bright effluence of bright essence increate.
Or hear'st thou rather pure ethereal stream,
Whose fountain who shall tell? before the sun,
Before the heavens thou wert, and at the voice
Of God, as with a mantle didst invest   10
The rising world of waters dark and deep,
Won from the void and formless infinite.
Thee I revisit now with bolder wing,
Escaped the Stygian pool, though long detained
In that obscure sojourn, while in my flight
Through utter and through middle darkness borne
With other notes than to the Orphean lyre
I sung of Chaos and eternal Night,
Taught by the heavenly Muse to venture down
The dark descent, and up to reascend,   20
Though hard and rare: thee I revisit safe,
And feel thy sovereign vital lamp; but thou
Revisit'st not these eyes, that roll in vain
To find thy piercing ray, and find no dawn;
So thick a drop serene hath quenched their orbs,
Or dim suffusion veiled. Yet not the more
Cease I to wander where the muses haunt

Clear spring, or shady grove, or sunny hill,
Smit with the love of sacred song; but chief
Thee Sion and the flowery brooks beneath   30
That wash thy hallowed feet, and warbling flow,
Nightly I visit: nor sometimes forget
Those other two equalled with me in fate,
So were I equalled with them in renown,
Blind Thamyris, and blind Maeonides,
And Tiresias and Phineus prophets old.
Then feed on thoughts, that voluntary move
Harmonious numbers; as the wakeful bird
Sings darkling, and in shadiest covert hid
Tunes her nocturnal note. Thus with the year   40
Seasons return, but not to me returns
Day, or the sweet approach of even or morn,
Or sight of vernal bloom, or summer's rose,
Or flocks, or herds, or human face divine;
But cloud instead, and ever-during dark
Surrounds me, from the cheerful ways of men
Cut off, and for the book of knowledge fair
Presented with a universal blank
Of nature's works to me expunged and razed,
And wisdom at one entrance quite shut out.   50
So much the rather thou celestial light
Shine inward, and the mind through all her powers
Irradiate, there plant eyes, all mist from thence
Purge and disperse, that I may see and tell
Of things invisible to mortal sight.
    Now had the almighty Father from above,
From the pure empyrean where he sits
High throned above all height, bent down his eye,
His own works and their works at once to view:
About him all the sanctities of heaven   60
Stood thick as stars, and from his sight received
Beatitude past utterance; on his right
The radiant image of his glory sat,
His only son; on earth he first beheld
Our two first parents, yet the only two
Of mankind, in the happy garden placed,
Reaping immortal fruits of joy and love,
Uninterrupted joy, unrivalled love

In blissful solitude; he then surveyed
Hell and the gulf between, and Satan there   70
Coasting the wall of heaven on this side night
In the dun air sublime, and ready now
To stoop with wearied wings, and willing feet
On the bare outside of this world, that seemed
Firm land embosomed without firmament,
Uncertain which, in ocean or in air.
Him God beholding from his prospect high,
Wherein past, present, future he beholds,
Thus to his only son foreseeing spake.
   Only begotten Son, seest thou what rage   80
Transports our adversary, whom no bounds
Prescribed, no bars of hell, nor all the chains
Heaped on him there, nor yet the main abyss
Wide interrupt can hold; so bent he seems
On desperate revenge, that shall redound
Upon his own rebellious head. And now
Through all restraint broke loose he wings his way
Not far off heaven, in the precincts of light,
Directly towards the new created world,
And man there placed, with purpose to assay   90
If him by force he can destroy, or worse,
By some false guile pervert; and shall pervert
For man will hearken to his glozing lies,
And easily transgress the sole command,
Sole pledge of his obedience: so will fall,
He and his faithless progeny: whose fault?
Whose but his own? ingrate, he had of me
All he could have; I made him just and right,
Sufficient to have stood, though free to fall.
Such I created all the ethereal powers   100
And spirits, both them who stood and them who failed;
Freely they stood who stood, and fell who fell.
Not free, what proof could they have given sincere
Of true allegiance, constant faith or love,
Where only what they needs must do, appeared,
Not what they would? what praise could they receive?
What pleasure I from such obedience paid,
When will and reason (reason also is choice)
Useless and vain, of freedom both despoiled,

Made passive both, had served necessity,   110
Not me. They therefore as to right belonged,
So were created, nor can justly accuse
Their maker, or their making, or their fate,
As if predestination overruled
Their will, disposed by absolute decree
Or high foreknowledge; they themselves decreed
Their own revolt, not I: if I foreknew,
Foreknowledge had no influence on their fault,
Which had no less proved certain unforeknown.
So without least impulse or shadow of fate,   120
Or aught by me immutably foreseen,
They trespass, authors to themselves in all
Both what they judge and what they choose; for so
I formed them free, and free they must remain,
Till they enthrall themselves: I else must change
Their nature, and revoke the high decree
Unchangeable, eternal, which ordained
Their freedom, they themselves ordained their fall.
The first sort by their own suggestion fell,
Self-tempted, self-depraved: man falls deceived   130
By the other first: man therefore shall find grace,
The other none: in mercy and justice both,
Through heaven and earth, so shall my glory excel,
But mercy first and last shall brightest shine.
    Thus while God spake, ambrosial fragrance filled
All heaven, and in the blessèd spirits elect
Sense of new joy ineffable diffused:
Beyond compare the Son of God was seen
Most glorious, in him all his father shone
Substantially expressed, and in his face   140
Divine compassion visibly appeared,
Love without end, and without measure grace,
Which uttering thus he to his father spake.
    O father, gracious was that word which closed
Thy sovereign sentence, that man should find grace;
For which both heaven and earth shall high extol
Thy praises, with the innumerable sound
Of hymns and sacred songs, wherewith thy throne
Encompassed shall resound thee ever blessed.
For should man finally be lost, should man   150

Thy creature late so loved, thy youngest son
Fall circumvented thus by fraud, though joined
With his own folly? that be from thee far,
That far be from thee, Father, who art judge
Of all things made, and judgest only right.
Or shall the adversary thus obtain
His end, and frustrate thine, shall he fulfil
His malice, and thy goodness bring to naught,
Or proud return though to his heavier doom,
Yet with revenge accomplished and to hell   160
Draw after him the whole race of mankind,
By him corrupted? or wilt thou thyself
Abolish thy creation, and unmake,
For him, what for thy glory thou hast made?
So should thy goodness and thy greatness both
Be questioned and blasphemed without defence.
    To whom the great creator thus replied.
O Son, in whom my soul hath chief delight,
Son of my bosom, Son who art alone
My word, my wisdom, and effectual might,   170
All hast thou spoken as my thoughts are, all
As my eternal purpose hath decreed:
Man shall not quite be lost, but saved who will,
Yet not of will in him, but grace in me
Freely vouchsafed; once more I will renew
His lapsèd powers, though forfeit and enthralled
By sin to foul exorbitant desires;
Upheld by me, yet once more he shall stand
On even ground against his mortal foe
By me upheld, that he may know how frail   180
His fallen condition is, and to me owe
All his deliverance, and to none but me.
Some I have chosen of peculiar grace
Elect above the rest; so is my will:
The rest shall hear me call, and oft be warned
Their sinful state, and to appease betimes
The incensèd deity, while offered grace
Invites; for I will clear their senses dark,
What may suffice, and soften stony hearts
To pray, repent, and bring obedience due.   190
To prayer, repentance, and obedience due,

Though but endeavoured with sincere intent,
Mine ear shall not be slow, mine eye not shut.
And I will place within them as a guide
My umpire conscience, whom if they will hear,
Light after light well used they shall attain,
And to the end persisting, safe arrive.
This my long sufferance and my day of grace
They who neglect and scorn, shall never taste;
But hard be hardened, blind be blinded more,   200
That they may stumble on, and deeper fall;
And none but such from mercy I exclude.
But yet all is not done; man disobeying,
Disloyal breaks his fealty, and sins
Against the high supremacy of heaven,
Affecting godhead, and so losing all,
To expiate his treason hath naught left,
But to destruction sacred and devote,
He with his whole posterity must die,
Die he or justice must; unless for him   210
Some other able, and as willing, pay
The rigid satisfaction, death for death.
Say heavenly powers, where shall we find such love,
Which of ye will be mortal to redeem
Man's mortal crime, and just the unjust to save,
Dwells in all heaven charity so dear?
    He asked, but all the heavenly choir stood mute,
And silence was in heaven: on man's behalf
Patron or intercessor none appeared,
Much less that durst upon his own head draw   220
The deadly forfeiture, and ransom set.
And now without redemption all mankind
Must have been lost, adjudged to death and hell
By doom severe, had not the Son of God,
In whom the fulness dwells of love divine,
His dearest mediation thus renewed.
    Father, thy word is past, man shall find grace;
And shall grace not find means, that finds her way,
The speediest of thy winged messengers,
To visit all thy creatures, and to all   230
Comes unprevented, unimplored, unsought,
Happy for man, so coming; he her aid

Can never seek, once dead in sins and lost;
Atonement for himself or offering meet,
Indebted and undone, hath none to bring:
Behold me then, me for him, life for life
I offer, on me let thine anger fall;
Account me man; I for his sake will leave
Thy bosom, and this glory next to thee
Freely put off, and for him lastly die .   240
Well pleased, on me let Death wreak all his rage;
Under his gloomy power I shall not long
Lie vanquished; thou hast given me to possess
Life in myself forever, by thee I live,
Though now to Death I yield, and am his due
All that of me can die, yet that debt paid,
Thou wilt not leave me in the loathsome grave
His prey, nor suffer my unspotted soul
Forever with corruption there to dwell;
But I shall rise victorious, and subdue   250
My vanquisher, spoiled of his vaunted spoil;
Death his death's wound shall then receive, and stoop
Inglorious, of his mortal sting disarmed.
I through the ample air in triumph high
Shall lead hell captive maugre hell, and show
The powers of darkness bound. Thou at the sight
Pleased, out of heaven shalt look down and smile,
While by thee raised I ruin all my foes,
Death last, and with his carcass glut the grave:
Then with the multitude of my redeemed   260
Shall enter heaven long absent, and return,
Father, to see thy face, wherein no cloud
Of anger shall remain, but peace assured,
And reconcilement; wrath shall be no more
Thenceforth, but in thy presence joy entire.
    His words here ended, but his meek aspect
Silent yet spake, and breathed immortal love
To mortal men, above which only shone
Filial obedience: as a sacrifice
Glad to be offered, he attends the will   270
Of his great father. Admiration seized
All heaven, what this might mean, and whither tend
Wondering; but soon the almighty thus replied:

O thou in heaven and earth the only peace
Found out for mankind under wrath, O thou
My sole complacence! well thou know'st how dear
To me are all my works, nor man the least
Though last created, that for him I spare
Thee from my bosom and right hand, to save,
By losing thee awhile, the whole race lost.   280
Thou therefore whom thou only canst redeem,
Their nature also to thy nature join;
And be thyself man among men on earth,
Made flesh, when time shall be, of virgin seed,
By wondrous birth: be thou in Adam's room
The head of all mankind, though Adam's son.
As in him perish all men, so in thee
As from a second root shall be restored,
As many as are restored, without thee none.
His crime makes guilty all his sons, thy merit   290
Imputed shall absolve them who renounce
Their own both righteous and unrighteous deeds,
And live in thee transplanted, and from thee
Receive new life. So man, as is most just,
Shall satisfy for man, be judged and die,
And dying rise, and rising with him raise
His brethren, ransomed with his own dear life.
So heavenly love shall outdo hellish hate
Giving to death, and dying to redeem,
So dearly to redeem what hellish hate   300
So easily destroyed, and still destroys
In those who, when they may, accept not grace.
Nor shalt thou by descending to assume
Man's nature, lessen or degrade thine own.
Because thou hast, though throned in highest bliss
Equal to God, and equally enjoying
Godlike fruition, quitted all to save
A world from utter loss, and hast been found
By merit more than birthright Son of God,
Found worthiest to be so by being good,   310
Far more than great or high; because in thee
Love hath abounded more than glory abounds,
Therefore thy humiliation shall exalt
With thee thy manhood also to this throne;

Here shalt thou sit incarnate, here shalt reign
Both God and man, Son both of God and man,
Anointed universal king; all power
I give thee, reign for ever, and assume
Thy merits; under thee as head supreme
Thrones, princedoms, powers, dominions I reduce: 320
All knees to thee shall bow, of them that bide
In heaven, or earth, or under earth in hell,
When thou attended gloriously from heaven
Shalt in the sky appear, and from thee send
The summoning archangels to proclaim
Thy dread tribunal: forthwith from all winds
The living, and forthwith the cited dead
Of all past ages to the general doom
Shall hasten, such a peal shall rouse their sleep.
Then all thy saints assembled, thou shalt judge   330
Bad men and angels, they arraigned shall sink
Beneath thy sentence; hell her numbers full,
Thenceforth shall be forever shut. Meanwhile
The world shall burn, and from her ashes spring
New heaven and earth, wherein the just shall dwell,
And after all their tribulations long
See golden days, fruitful of golden deeds,
With joy and love triumphing, and fair truth.
Then thou thy regal sceptre shalt lay by,
For regal sceptre then no more shall need,   340
God shall be all in all. But all ye gods,
Adore him, who to compass all this dies,
Adore the Son, and honour him as me.

   .   .   .   .

Meanwhile upon the firm opacous globe
Of this round world, whose first convex divides
The luminous inferior orbs, enclosed   420
From Chaos and the inroad of darkness old,
Satan alighted walks: a globe far off
It seemed, now seems a boundless continent
Dark, waste, and wild, under the frown of night
Starless exposed, and ever-threatening storms
Of Chaos blustering round, inclement sky;
Save on that side which from the wall of heaven
Though distant far some small reflection gains

Of glimmering air less vexed with tempest loud:
Here walked the fiend at large in spacious field.   430
As when a vulture on Imaus bred,
Whose snowy ridge the roving Tartar bounds,
Dislodging from a region scarce of prey
To gorge the flesh of lambs or yeanling kids
On hills where flocks are fed, flies toward the springs
Of Ganges or Hydaspes, Indian streams;
But in his way lights on the barren plains
Of Sericana, where Chineses drive
With sails and wind their cany wagons light:
So on this windy sea of land, the fiend   440
Walked up and down alone bent on his prey,
Alone, for other creatures in this place
Living or lifeless to be found was none,
None yet, but store hereafter from the earth
Up hither like aerial vapours flew
Of all things transitory and vain, when sin
With vanity had filled the works of men:
Both all things vain, and all who in vain things
Built their fond hopes of glory or lasting fame,
Or happiness in this or the other life;   450
All who have their reward on earth, the fruits
Of painful superstition and blind zeal,
Nought seeking but the praise of men, here find
Fit retribution, empty as their deeds;
All the unaccomplished works of nature's hand,
Abortive, monstrous, or unkindly mixed,
Dissolved on earth, fleet hither, and in vain,
Till final dissolution, wander here,
Not in the neighbouring moon, as some have dreamed;
Those argent fields more likely habitants,   460
Translated saints, or middle spirits hold
Betwixt the angelical and human kind:
Hither of ill-joined sons and daughters born
First from the ancient world those Giants came
With many a vain exploit, though then renowned:
The builders next of Babel on the plain
Of Sennaar, and still with vain design
New Babels, had they wherewithal, would build:
Others came single; he who to be deemed

A god, leaped fondly into Aetna flames,   470
Empedocles, and he who to enjoy
Plato's Elysium, leaped into the sea,
Cleombrotus, and many more too long,
Embryos and idiots, eremites and friars
White, black and grey, with all their trumpery.
Here pilgrims roam, that strayed so far to seek
In Golgotha him dead, who lives in heaven;
And they who to be sure of Paradise
Dying put on the weeds of Dominic,
Or in Franciscan think to pass disguised;   480
They pass the planets seven, and pass the fixed,
And that crystalline sphere whose balance weighs
The trepidation talked, and that first moved;
And now Saint Peter at heaven's wicket seems
To wait them with his keys, and now at foot
Of heaven's ascent they lift their feet, when lo
A violent cross wind from either coast
Blows them transverse ten thousand leagues awry
Into the devious air; then might ye see
Cowls, hoods and habits with their wearers tossed   490
And fluttered into rags, then relics, beads,
Indulgences, dispenses, pardons, bulls,
The sport of winds: all these upwhirled aloft
Fly o'er the backside of the world far off
Into a limbo large and broad, since called
The Paradise of Fools, to few unknown
Long after, now unpeopled, and untrod;
All this dark globe the fiend found as he passed,
And long he wandered, till at last a gleam
Of dawning light turned thitherward in haste   500
His travelled steps; far distant he descries
Ascending by degrees magnificent
Up to the wall of heaven a structure high,
At top whereof, but far more rich appeared
The work as of a kingly palace gate
With frontispiece of diamond and gold
Embellished, thick with sparkling orient gems
The portal shone, inimitable on earth
By model, or by shading pencil drawn.
The stairs were such as whereon Jacob saw   510

Angels ascending and descending, bands
Of guardians bright, when he from Esau fled
To Padan-Aram in the field of Luz,
Dreaming by night under the open sky,
And waking cried, *This is the gate of heaven.*
Each stair mysteriously was meant, nor stood
There always, but drawn up to heaven sometimes
Viewless, and underneath a bright sea flowed
Of jasper, or of liquid pearl, whereon
Who after came from earth, sailing arrived,   520
Wafted by angels, or flew o'er the lake
Rapt in a chariot drawn by fiery steeds.
The stairs were then let down, whether to dare
The fiend by easy ascent, or aggravate
His sad exclusion from the doors of bliss.
Direct against which opened from beneath,
Just o'er the blissful seat of Paradise,
A passage down to the earth, a passage wide,
Wider by far than that of after-times
Over Mount Sion, and, though that were large,   530
Over the Promised Land to God so dear,
By which, to visit oft those happy tribes,
On high behests his angels to and fro
Passed frequent, and his eye with choice regard
From Paneas the fount of Jordan's flood
To Beersaba, where the Holy Land
Borders on Egypt and the Arabian shore;
So wide the opening seemed, where bounds were set
To darkness, such as bound the ocean wave.
Satan from hence now on the lower stair   540
That scaled by steps of gold to heaven gate
Looks down with wonder at the sudden view
Of all this world at once. As when a scout
Through dark and desert ways with peril gone
All night; at last by break of cheerful dawn
Obtains the brow of some high-climbing hill,
Which to his eye discovers unaware
The goodly prospect of some foreign land
First-seen, or some renowned metropolis
With glistering spires and pinnacles adorned,   550
Which now the rising sun gilds with his beams.

Such wonder seized, though after heaven seen,
The spirit malign, but much more envy seized
At sight of all this world beheld so fair.
Round he surveys, and well might, where he stood
So high above the circling canopy
Of night's extended shade; from eastern point
Of Libra to the fleecy star that bears
Andromeda far off Atlantic seas
Beyond the horizon; then from pole to pole   560
He views in breadth, and without longer pause
Down right into the world's first region throws
His flight precipitant, and winds with ease
Through the pure marble air his oblique way
Amongst innumerable stars, that shone
Stars distant, but nigh hand seemed other worlds,
Or other worlds they seemed, or happy isles,
Like those Hesperian gardens famed of old,
Fortunate fields, and groves and flowery vales,
Thrice happy isles, but who dwelt happy there   570
He stayed not to inquire: above them all
The golden sun in splendour likest heaven
Allured his eye: thither his course he bends
Through the calm firmament; but up or down
By centre, or eccentric, hard to tell,
Or longitude, where the great luminary
Aloof the vulgar constellations thick,
That from his lordly eye keep distance due,
Dispenses light from far; they as they move
Their starry dance in numbers that compute   580
Days, months, and years, towards his all-cheering lamp
Turn swift their various motions, or are turned
By his magnetic beam, that gently warms
The universe, and to each inward part
With gentle penetration, though unseen,
Shoots invisible virtue even to the deep:
So wondrously was set his station bright.
There lands the fiend, a spot like which perhaps
Astronomer in the sun's lucent orb
Through his glazed optic tube yet never saw.   590
The place he found beyond expression bright,
Compared with aught on earth, metal or stone;

Not all parts like, but all alike informed
With radiant light, as glowing iron with fire;
If metal, part seemed gold, part silver clear;
If stone, carbuncle most or chrysolite,
Ruby or topaz, to the twelve that shone
In Aaron's breastplate, and a stone besides
Imagined rather oft than elsewhere seen,
That stone, or like to that which here below   600
Philosophers in vain so long have sought,
In vain, though by their powerful art they bind
Volatile Hermes, and call up unbound
In various shapes old Proteus from the sea,
Drained through a limbeck to his native form.
What wonder then if fields and regions here
Breathe forth elixir pure, and rivers run
Potable gold, when with one virtuous touch
The arch-chemic sun so far from us remote
Produces with terrestrial humour mixed   610
Here in the dark so many precious things
Of colour glorious and effect so rare?
Here matter new to gaze the devil met
Undazzled, far and wide his eye commands,
For sight no obstacle found here, nor shade,
But all sunshine, as when his beams at noon
Culminate from the equator, as they now
Shot upward still direct, whence no way round
Shadow from body opaque can fall, and the air,
Nowhere so clear, sharpened his visual ray   620
To objects distant far, whereby he soon
Saw within ken a glorious angel stand,
The same whom John saw also in the sun:
His back was turned, but not his brightness hid;
Of beaming sunny rays, a golden tiar
Circled his head, nor less his locks behind
Illustrious on his shoulders fledge with wings
Lay waving round; on some great charge employed
He seemed, or fixed in cogitation deep.
Glad was the spirit impure; as now in hope   630
To find who might direct his wandering flight
To Paradise the happy seat of man,
His journey's end and our beginning woe.

But first he casts to change his proper shape,
Which else might work him danger or delay:
And now a stripling cherub he appears,
Not of the prime, yet such as in his face
Youth smiled celestial, and to every limb
Suitable grace diffused, so well he feigned;
Under a coronet his flowing hair   640
In curls on either cheek played, wings he wore
Of many a coloured plume sprinkled with gold,
His habit fit for speed succinct, and held
Before his decent steps a silver wand.
He drew not nigh unheard, the angel bright,
Ere he drew nigh, his radiant visage turned,
Admonished by his ear, and straight was known
The archangel Uriel, one of the seven
Who in God's presence, nearest to his throne
Stand ready at command, and are his eyes   650
That run through all the heavens, or down to the earth
Bear his swift errands over moist and dry,
O'er sea and land: him Satan thus accosts.
   Uriel, for thou of those seven spirits that stand
In sight of God's high throne, gloriously bright,
The first art wont his great authentic will
Interpreter through highest heaven to bring,
Where all his sons thy embassy attend;
And here art likeliest by supreme decree
Like honour to obtain, and as his eye   660
To visit oft this new creation round;
Unspeakable desire to see, and know
All these his wondrous works, but chiefly man,
His chief delight and favour, him for whom
All these his works so wondrous he ordained,
Hath brought me from the choirs of cherubim
Alone thus wandering. Brightest seraph tell
In which of all these shining orbs hath man
His fixèd seat, or fixèd seat hath none,
But all these shining orbs his choice to dwell;   670
That I may find him, and with secret gaze,
Or open admiration him behold
On whom the great creator hath bestowed
Worlds, and on whom hath all these graces poured;

That both in him and all things, as is meet,
The universal maker we may praise;
Who justly hath driven out his rebel foes
To deepest hell, and to repair that loss
Created this new happy race of men
To serve him better: wise are all his ways.   680
    So spake the false dissembler unperceived;
For neither man nor angel can discern
Hypocrisy, the only evil that walks
Invisible, except to God alone,
By his permissive will, through heaven and earth:
And oft though wisdom wake, suspicion sleeps
At wisdom's gate, and to simplicity
Resigns her charge, while goodness thinks no ill
Where no ill seems: which now for once beguiled
Uriel, though regent of the sun, and held   690
The sharpest sighted spirit of all in heaven;
Who to the fraudulent imposter foul
In his uprightness answer thus returned.
Fair angel, thy desire which tends to know
The works of God, thereby to glorify
The great work-master, leads to no excess
That reaches blame, but rather merits praise
The more it seems excess, that led thee hither
From thy empyreal mansion thus alone,
To witness with thine eyes what some perhaps   700
Contented with report hear only in heaven:
For wonderful indeed are all his works,
Pleasant to know, and worthiest to be all
Had in remembrance always with delight;
But what created mind can comprehend
Their number, or the wisdom infinite
That brought them forth, but hid their causes deep.
I saw when at his word the formless mass,
This world's material mould, came to a heap:
Confusion heard his voice, and wild uproar   710
Stood ruled, stood vast infinitude confined;
Till at his second bidding darkness fled,
Light shone, and order from disorder sprung:
Swift to their several quarters hasted then
The cumbrous elements, earth, flood, air, fire,

And this ethereal quintessence of heaven
Flew upward, spirited with various forms,
That rolled orbicular, and turned to stars
Numberless, as thou seest, and how they move;
Each had his place appointed, each his course,   720
The rest in circuit walls this universe.
Look downward on that globe whose hither side
With light from hence, though but reflected, shines;
That place is earth the seat of man, that light
His day, which else as the other hemisphere
Night would invade, but there the neighbouring moon
(So call that opposite fair star) her aid
Timely interposes, and her monthly round
Still ending, still renewing, through mid heaven;
With borrowed light her countenance triform   730
Hence fills and empties to enlighten the earth,
And in her pale dominion checks the night.
That spot to which I point is Paradise,
Adam's abode, those lofty shades his bower.
Thy way thou canst not miss, me mine requires.
     Thus said, he turned, and Satan bowing low,
As to superior spirits is wont in heaven,
Where honour due and reverence none neglects,
Took leave, and toward the coast of earth beneath,
Down from the ecliptic, sped with hoped success,   740
Throws his steep flight in many an airy wheel,
Nor stayed, till on Niphates' top he lights.

Book IV

O for that warning voice, which he who saw
The Apocalypse heard cry in heaven aloud,
Then when the dragon, put to second rout,
Came furious down to be revenged on men,
Woe to the inhabitants on earth! that now,
While time was, our first-parents had been warned
The coming of their secret foe, and scaped,
Haply so scaped his mortal snare; for now
Satan, now first inflamed with rage, came down,

The tempter ere the accuser of mankind,   10
To wreak on innocent frail man his loss
Of that first battle, and his flight to hell:
Yet not rejoicing in his speed, though bold,
Far off and fearless, nor with cause to boast,
Begins his dire attempt, which nigh the birth
Now rolling, boils in his tumultuous breast,
And like a devilish engine back recoils
Upon himself; horror and doubt distract
His troubled thoughts, and from the bottom stir
The hell within him, for within him hell   20
He brings, and round about him, nor from hell
One step no more than from himself can fly
By change of place: now conscience wakes despair
That slumbered, wakes the bitter memory
Of what he was, what is, and what must be
Worse; of worse deeds worse sufferings must ensue.
Sometimes towards Eden which now in his view
Lay pleasant, his grieved look he fixes sad,
Sometimes towards heaven and the full-blazing sun,
Which now sat high in his meridian tower: 30
Then much revolving, thus in sighs began.
    O thou that with surpassing glory crowned,
Look'st from thy sole dominion like the god
Of this new world; at whose sight all the stars
Hide their diminished heads; to thee I call,
But with no friendly voice, and add thy name
O sun, to tell thee how I hate thy beams
That bring to my remembrance from what state
I fell, how glorious once above thy sphere;
Till pride and worse ambition threw me down   40
Warring in heaven against heaven's matchless king:
Ah wherefore! he deserved no such return
From me, whom he created what I was
In that bright eminence, and with his good
Upbraided none; nor was his service hard.
What could be less than to afford him praise,
The easiest recompense, and pay him thanks,
How due! Yet all his good proved ill in me,
And wrought but malice; lifted up so high
I 'sdained subjection, and thought one step higher   50

Would set me highest, and in a moment quit
The debt immense of endless gratitude,
So burdensome still paying, still to owe;
Forgetful what from him I still received,
And understood not that a grateful mind
By owing owes not, but still pays, at once
Indebted and discharged; what burden then?
O had his powerful destiny ordained
Me some inferior angel, I had stood
Then happy; no unbounded hope had raised   60
Ambition. Yet why not? Some other power
As great might have aspired, and me though mean
Drawn to his part; but other powers as great
Fell not, but stand unshaken, from within
Or from without, to all temptations armed.
Hadst thou the same free will and power to stand?
Thou hadst: whom hast thou then or what to accuse,
But heaven's free love dealt equally to all?
Be then his love accursed, since love or hate,
To me alike, it deals eternal woe.   70
Nay cursed be thou; since against his thy will
Chose freely what it now so justly rues.
Me miserable! which way shall I fly
Infinite wrath, and infinite despair?
Which way I fly is hell; myself am hell;
And in the lowest deep a lower deep
Still threatening to devour me opens wide,
To which the hell I suffer seems a heaven.
O then at last relent: is there no place
Left for repentance, none for pardon left?   80
None left but by submission; and that word
Disdain forbids me, and my dread of shame
Among the spirits beneath, whom I seduced
With other promises and other vaunts
Than to submit, boasting I could subdue
The omnipotent. Ay me, they little know
How dearly I abide that boast so vain,
Under what torments inwardly I groan:
While they adore me on the throne of hell,
With diadem and sceptre high advanced   90
The lower still I fall, only supreme

In misery; such joy ambition finds.
But say I could repent and could obtain
By act of grace my former state; how soon
Would height recall high thoughts, how soon unsay
What feigned submission swore: ease would recant
Vows made in pain, as violent and void.
For never can true reconcilement grow
Where wounds of deadly hate have pierced so deep:
Which would but lead me to a worse relapse,   100
And heavier fall: so should I purchase dear
Short intermission bought with double smart.
This knows my punisher; therefore as far
From granting he, as I from begging peace:
All hope excluded thus, behold instead
Of us outcast, exiled, his new delight,
Mankind created, and for him this world.
So farewell hope, and with hope farewell fear,
Farewell remorse: all good to me is lost;
Evil be thou my good; by thee at least   110
Divided empire with heaven's king I hold
By thee, and more than half perhaps will reign;
As man ere long, and this new world shall know.
     Thus while he spake, each passion dimmed his face
Thrice changed with pale, ire, envy and despair,
Which marred his borrowed visage, and betrayed
Him counterfeit, if any eye beheld.
For heavenly minds from such distempers foul
Are ever clear. Whereof he soon aware,
Each perturbation smoothed with outward calm,   120
Artificer of fraud; and was the first
That practised falsehood under saintly show,
Deep malice to conceal, couched with revenge:
Yet not enough had practised to deceive
Uriel once warned; whose eye pursued him down
The way he went, and on the Assyrian mount
Saw him disfigured, more than could befall
Spirit of happy sort: his gestures fierce
He marked, and mad demeanour, then alone,
As he supposed, all unobserved, unseen.   130
So on he fares, and to the border comes,
Of Eden, where delicious Paradise,

Now nearer, crowns with her enclosure green,
As with a rural mound the champaign head
Of a steep wilderness, whose hairy sides
With thicket overgrown, grotesque and wild,
Access denied; and overhead up grew
Insuperable height of loftiest shade,
Cedar, and pine, and fir, and branching palm,
A sylvan scene, and as the ranks ascend   140
Shade above shade, a woody theatre
Of stateliest view. Yet higher than their tops
The verdurous wall of Paradise up sprung:
Which to our general sire gave prospect large
Into his nether empire neighbouring round.
And higher than that wall a circling row
Of goodliest trees loaden with fairest fruit,
Blossoms and fruits at once of golden hue
Appeared, with gay enamelled colours mixed:
On which the sun more glad impressed his beams   150
Than in fair evening cloud, or humid bow,
When God hath showered the earth; so lovely seemed
That landscape: and of pure now purer air
Meets his approach, and to the heart inspires
Vernal delight and joy, able to drive
All sadness but despair: now gentle gales
Fanning their odoriferous wings dispense
Native perfumes, and whisper whence they stole
Those balmy spoils. As when to them who sail
Beyond the Cape of Hope, and now are past   160
Mozambique, off at sea north-east winds blow
Sabean odours from the spicy shore
Of Araby the blest, with such delay
Well pleased they slack their course, and many a league
Cheered with the grateful smell old Ocean smiles.
So entertained those odorous sweets the fiend
Who came their bane, though with them better pleased
Than Asmodeus with the fishy fume,
That drove him, though enamoured, from the spouse
Of Tobit's son, and with a vengeance sent   170
From Media post to Egypt, there fast bound.
    Now to the ascent of that steep savage hill
Satan had journeyed on, pensive and slow;

But further way found none, so thick entwined,
As one continued brake, the undergrowth
Of shrubs and tangling bushes had perplexed
All path of man or beast that passed that way:
One gate there only was, and that looked east
On the other side: which when the arch-felon saw
Due entrance he disdained, and in contempt,   180
At one slight bound high overleaped all bound
Of hill or highest wall, and sheer within
Lights on his feet. As when a prowling wolf,
Whom hunger drives to seek new haunt for prey,
Watching where shepherds pen their flocks at eve
In hurdled cotes amid the field secure,
Leaps o'er the fence with ease into the fold:
Or as a thief bent to unhoard the cash
Of some rich burgher, whose substantial doors,
Cross-barred and bolted fast, fear no assault,   190
In at the window climbs, or o'er the tiles;
So clomb this first grand thief into God's fold:
So since into his church lewd hirelings climb.
Thence up he flew, and on the tree of life,
The middle tree and highest there that grew,
Sat like a cormorant; yet not true life
Thereby regained, but sat devising death
To them who lived; nor on the virtue thought
Of that life-giving plant, but only used
For prospect, what well used had been the pledge   200
Of immortality. So little knows
Any, but God alone, to value right
The good before him, but perverts best things
To worst abuse, or to their meanest use.
Beneath him with new wonder now he views
To all delight of human sense exposed
In narrow room nature's whole wealth, yea more,
A heaven on earth, for blissful Paradise
Of God the garden was, by him in the east
Of Eden planted; Eden stretched her line   210
From Auran eastward to the royal towers
Of great Seleucia, built by Grecian kings,
Or where the sons of Eden long before
Dwelt in Telassar: in this pleasant soil

His far more pleasant garden God ordained;
Out of the fertile ground he caused to grow
All trees of noblest kind for sight, smell, taste;
And all amid them stood the tree of life,
High eminent, blooming ambrosial fruit
Of vegetable gold; and next to life   220
Our death the tree of knowledge grew fast by,
Knowledge of good bought dear by knowing ill.
Southward through Eden went a river large,
Nor changed his course, but through the shaggy hill
Passed underneath engulfed, for God had thrown
That mountain as his garden mould high raised
Upon the rapid current, which through veins
Of porous earth with kindly thirst up drawn,
Rose a fresh fountain, and with many a rill
Watered the garden; thence united fell   230
Down the steep glade, and met the nether flood,
Which from his darksome passage now appears,
And now divided into four main streams,
Runs diverse, wandering many a famous realm
And country whereof here needs no account,
But rather to tell how, if art could tell,
How from that sapphire fount the crispèd brooks,
Rolling on orient pearl and sands of gold,
With mazy error under pendent shades
Ran nectar, visiting each plant, and fed   240
Flowers worthy of Paradise which not nice art
In beds and curious knots, but nature boon
Poured forth profuse on hill and dale and plain,
Both where the morning sun first warmly smote
The open field, and where the unpierced shade
Embrowned the noontide bowers: thus was this place,
A happy rural seat of various view;
Groves whose rich trees wept odorous gums and balm,
Others whose fruit burnished with golden rind
Hung amiable, Hesperian fables true,   250
If true, here only, and of delicious taste:
Betwixt them lawns, or level downs, and flocks
Grazing the tender herb, were interposed,
Or palmy hillock, or the flowery lap
Of some irriguous valley spread her store,

Flowers of all hue, and without thorn the rose:
Another side, umbrageous grots and caves
Of cool recess, o'er which the mantling vine
Lays forth her purple grape, and gently creeps
Luxuriant; meanwhile murmuring waters fall   260
Down the slope hills, dispersed, or in a lake,
That to the fringèd bank with myrtle crowned,
Her crystal mirror holds, unite their streams.
The birds their choir apply; airs, vernal airs,
Breathing the smell of field and grove, attune
The trembling leaves, while universal Pan
Knit with the Graces and the Hours in dance
Led on the eternal spring. Not that fair field
Of Enna, where Proserpin' gathering flowers
Herself a fairer flower by gloomy Dis   270
Was gathered, which cost Ceres all that pain
To seek her through the world; nor that sweet grove
Of Daphne by Orontes, and the inspired
Castalian spring, might with this Paradise
Of Eden strive; nor that Nyseian isle
Girt with the river Triton, where old Cham,
Whom Gentiles Ammon call and Lybian Jove,
His Amalthea and her florid son
Young Bacchus from his stepdame Rhea's eye;
Nor where Abassin kings their issue guard,   280
Mount Amara, though this by some supposed
True Paradise under the Ethiop line
By Nilus' head, enclosed with shining rock,
A whole day's journey high, but wide remote
From this Assyrian garden, where the fiend
Saw undelighted all delight, all kind
Of living creatures new to sight and strange:
Two of far nobler shape erect and tall,
Godlike erect, with native honour clad
In naked majesty seemed lords of all,   290
And worthy seemed, for in their looks divine
The image of their glorious maker shone,
Truth, wisdom, sanctitude severe and pure,
Severe but in true filial freedom placed;
Whence true authority in men; though both
Not equal, as their sex not equal seemed;

For contemplation he and valour formed,
For softness she and sweet attractive grace,
He for God only, she for God in him:
His fair large front and eye sublime declared   300
Absolute rule; and hyacinthine locks
Round from his parted forelock manly hung
Clustering, but not beneath his shoulders broad:
She as a veil down to the slender waist
Her unadornèd golden tresses wore
Dishevelled, but in wanton ringlets waved
As the vine curls her tendrils, which implied
Subjection, but required with gentle sway,
And by her yielded, by him best received,
Yielded with coy submission, modest pride,   310
And sweet reluctant amorous delay.
Nor those mysterious parts were then concealed,
Then was not guilty shame, dishonest shame
Of nature's works, honour dishonourable,
Sin-bred, how have ye troubled all mankind
With shows instead, mere shows of seeming pure,
And banished from man's life his happiest life,
Simplicity and spotless innocence.
So passed they naked on, nor shunned the sight
Of God or angel, for they thought no ill: 320
So hand in hand they passed, the loveliest pair
That ever since in love's embraces met,
Adam the goodliest man of men since born
His sons, the fairest of her daughters Eve.
Under a tuft of shade that on a green
Stood whispering soft, by a fresh fountain side
They sat them down, and after no more toil
Of their sweet gardening labour than sufficed
To recommend cool zephyr, and made ease
More easy, wholesome thirst and appetite   330
More grateful, to their supper fruits they fell,
Nectarine fruits which the compliant boughs
Yielded them, sidelong as they sat recline
On the soft downy bank damasked with flowers:
The savoury pulp they chew, and in the rind
Still as they thirsted scoop the brimming stream;
Nor gentle purpose, nor endearing smiles

Wanted, nor youthful dalliance as beseems
Fair couple, linked in happy nuptial league,
Alone as they. About them frisking played   340
All beasts of the earth, since wild, and of all chase
In wood or wilderness, forest or den;
Sporting the lion ramped, and in his paw
Dandled the kid; bears, tigers, ounces, pards,
Gambolled before them, the unwieldy elephant
To make them mirth used all his might, and wreathed
His lithe proboscis; close the serpent sly
Insinuating, wove with Gordian twine
His braided train, and of his fatal guile
Gave proof unheeded; others on the grass   350
Couched, and now filled with pasture gazing sat,
Or bedward ruminating: for the sun
Declined was hasting now with prone career
To the Ocean Isles, and in the ascending scale
Of heaven the stars that usher evening rose:
When Satan still in gaze, as first he stood,
Scarce thus at length failed speech recovered sad.
      O hell! what do mine eyes with grief behold,
Into our room of bliss thus high advanced
Creatures of other mould, earth-born perhaps,   360
Not spirits, yet to heavenly spirits bright
Little inferior; whom my thoughts pursue
With wonder, and could love, so lively shines
In them divine resemblance, and such grace
The hand that formed them on their shape hath poured.
Ah gentle pair, ye little think how nigh
Your change approaches, when all these delights
Will vanish and deliver ye to woe,
More woe, the more your taste is now of joy;
Happy, but for so happy ill secured   370
Long to continue, and this high seat your heaven
Ill fenced for heaven to keep out such a foe
As now is entered; yet no purposed foe
To you whom I could pity thus forlorn
Though I unpitied: league with you I seek,
And mutual amity so strait, so close,
That I with you must dwell, or you with me
Henceforth; my dwelling haply may not please

Like this fair Paradise, your sense, yet such
Accept your maker's work; he gave it me,   380
Which I as freely give; hell shall unfold,
To entertain you two, her widest gates,
And send forth all her kings; there will be room,
Not like these narrow limits, to receive,
Your numerous offspring; if no better place,
Thank him who puts me loath to this revenge
On you who wrong me not for him who wronged.
And should I at your harmless innocence
Melt, as I do, yet public reason just,
Honour and empire with revenge enlarged,   390
By conquering this new world, compels me now
To do what else though damned I should abhor.
    So spake the fiend, and with necessity,
The tyrant's plea, excused his devilish deeds.
Then from his lofty stand on that high tree
Down he alights among the sportful herd
Of those four-footed kinds, himself now one,
Now other, as their shape served best his end
Nearer to view his prey, and unespied
To mark what of their state he more might learn   400
By word or action marked: about them round
A lion now he stalks with fiery glare,
Then as a tiger, who by chance hath spied
In some purlieu two gentle fawns at play,
Straight couches close, then rising changes oft
His couchant watch, as one who chose his ground
Whence rushing he might surest seize them both
Gripped in each paw: when Adam first of men
To first of women Eve thus moving speech,
Turned him all ear to hear new utterance flow.   410
    Sole partner and sole part of all these joys,
Dearer thyself than all; needs must the power
That made us, and for us this ample world
Be infinitely good, and of his good
As liberal and free as infinite,
That raised us from the dust and placed us here
In all this happiness, who at his hand
Have nothing merited, nor can perform
Aught whereof he hath need, he who requires

From us no other service than to keep   420
This one, this easy charge, of all the trees
In Paradise that bear delicious fruit
So various, not to taste that only tree
Of knowledge, planted by the tree of life,
So near grows death to life, what e'er death is,
Some dreadful thing no doubt; for well thou know'st
God hath pronounced it death to taste that tree,
The only sign of our obedience left
Among so many signs of power and rule
Conferred upon us, and dominion given   430
Over all other creatures that possess
Earth, air, and sea. Then let us not think hard
One easy prohibition, who enjoy
Free leave so large to all things else, and choice
Unlimited of manifold delights:
But let us ever praise him, and extol
His bounty, following our delightful task
To prune these growing plants, and tend these flowers,
Which were it toilsome, yet with thee were sweet.
      To whom thus Eve replied. O thou for whom   440
And from whom I was formed flesh of thy flesh,
And without whom am to no end, my guide
And head, what thou hast said is just and right.
For we to him indeed all praises owe,
And daily thanks, I chiefly who enjoy
So far the happier lot, enjoying thee
Pre-eminent by so much odds, while thou
Like consort to thyself canst nowhere find.
That day I oft remember, when from sleep
I first awaked, and found myself reposed   450
Under a shade of flowers, much wondering where
And what I was, whence thither brought, and how.
Not distant far from thence a murmuring sound
Of waters issued from a cave and spread
Into a liquid plain, then stood unmoved
Pure as the expanse of heaven; I thither went
With unexperienced thought, and laid me down
On the green bank, to look into the clear
Smooth lake, that to me seemed another sky.
As I bent down to look, just opposite,   460

A shape within the watery gleam appeared
Bending to look on me, I started back,
It started back, but pleased I soon returned,
Pleased it returned as soon with answering looks
Of sympathy and love; there I had fixed
Mine eyes till now, and pined with vain desire,
Had not a voice thus warned me, What thou seest,
What there thou seest fair creature is thyself,
With thee it came and goes: but follow me,
And I will bring thee where no shadow stays   470
Thy coming, and thy soft embraces, he
Whose image thou art, him thou shall enjoy
Inseparably thine, to him shalt bear
Multitudes like thyself, and thence be called
Mother of human race: what could I do,
But follow straight, invisibly thus led?
Till I espied thee, fair indeed and tall,
Under a platan, yet methought less fair,
Less winning soft, less amiably mild,
Than that smooth watery image; back I turned,   480
Thou following cried'st aloud, Return fair Eve,
Whom fly'st thou? Whom thou fly'st, of him thou art,
His flesh, his bone; to give thee being I lent
Out of my side to thee, nearest my heart
Substantial life, to have thee by my side
Henceforth an individual solace dear;
Part of my soul I seek thee, and thee claim
My other half: with that thy gentle hand
Seized mine, I yielded, and from that time see
How beauty is excelled by manly grace   490
And wisdom, which alone is truly fair.
  So spake our general mother, and with eyes
Of conjugal attraction unreproved,
And meek surrender, half embracing leaned
On our first father, half her swelling breast
Naked met his under the flowing gold
Of her loose tresses hid: he in delight
Both of her beauty and submissive charms
Smiled with superior love, as Jupiter
On Juno smiles, when he impregns the clouds   500
That shed May flowers; and pressed her matron lip

With kisses pure: aside the devil turned
For envy, yet with jealous leer malign
Eyed them askance, and to himself thus plained.
    Sight hateful, sight tormenting! thus these two
Emparadised in one another's arms
The happier Eden, shall enjoy their fill
Of bliss on bliss, while I to hell am thrust,
Where neither joy nor love, but fierce desire,
Among our other torments not the least,   510
Still unfulfilled with pain of longing pines;
Yet let me not forget what I have gained
From their own mouths; all is not theirs it seems:
One fatal tree there stands of knowledge called,
Forbidden them to taste: knowledge forbidden?
Suspicious, reasonless. Why should their Lord
Envy them that? can it be sin to know,
Can it be death? and do they only stand
By ignorance, is that their happy state,
The proof of their obedience and their faith?   520
O fair foundation laid whereon to build
Their ruin! Hence I will excite their minds
With more desire to know, and to reject
Envious commands, invented with design
To keep them low whom knowledge might exalt
Equal with gods; aspiring to be such,
They taste and die: what likelier can ensue?
But first with narrow search I must walk round
This garden, and no corner leave unspied;
A chance but chance may lead where I may meet   530
Some wandering spirit of heaven, by fountain side,
Or in thick shade retired, from him to draw
What further would be learned. Live while ye may,
Yet happy pair; enjoy, till I return,
Short pleasures, for long woes are to succeed.
    So saying, his proud step he scornful turned,
But with sly circumspection, and began
Through wood, through waste, o'er hill, o'er dale his roam.
Meanwhile in utmost longitude, where heaven
With earth and ocean meets, the setting sun   540
Slowly descended, and with right aspect
Against the eastern gate of Paradise

Levelled his evening rays: it was a rock
Of alabaster, piled up to the clouds,
Conspicuous far, winding with one ascent
Accessible from earth, one entrance high;
The rest was craggy cliff, that overhung
Still as it rose, impossible to climb.
Betwixt these rocky pillars Gabriel sat
Chief of the angelic guards, awaiting night;   550
About him exercised heroic games
The unarmed youth of heaven, but nigh at hand
Celestial armoury, shields, helms, and spears,
Hung high with diamond flaming, and with gold.
Thither came Uriel, gliding through the even
On a sunbeam, swift as a shooting star
In autumn thwarts the night, when vapours fired
Impress the air, and shows the mariner
From what point of his compass to beware
Impetuous winds: he thus began in haste.   560
    Gabriel, to thee thy course by lot hath given
Charge and strict watch that to this happy place
No evil thing approach or enter in;
This day at height of noon came to my sphere
A spirit, zealous, as he seemed, to know
More of the almighty's works, and chiefly man
God's latest image: I described his way
Bent all on speed, and marked his airy gait;
But in the mount that lies from Eden north,
Where he first lighted, soon discerned his looks   570
Alien from heaven, with passions foul obscured:
Mine eye pursued him still, but under shade
Lost sight of him; one of the banished crew
I fear, hath ventured from the deep, to raise
New troubles; him thy care must be to find.
    To whom the wingèd warrior thus returned:
Uriel, no wonder if thy perfect sight,
Amid the sun's bright circle where thou sit'st,
See far and wide: in at this gate none pass
The vigilance here placed, but such as come   580
Well known from heaven; and since meridian hour
No creature thence: if spirit of other sort,
So minded, have o'erleaped these earthy bounds

On purpose, hard thou know'st it to exclude
Spiritual substance with corporeal bar.
But if within the circuit of these walks,
In whatsoever shape he lurk, of whom
Thou tell'st, by morrow dawning I shall know.
   So promised he, and Uriel to his charge
Returned on that bright beam, whose point now raised   590
Bore him slope downward to the sun now fallen
Beneath the Azores; whether the bright orb,
Incredible how swift, had thither rolled
Diurnal, or this less voluble earth
By shorter flight to the east, had left him there
Arraying with reflected purple and gold
The clouds that on his western throne attend:
Now came still evening on, and twilight grey
Had in her sober livery all things clad;
Silence accompanied, for beast and bird,   600
They to their grassy couch, these to their nests
Were slunk, all but the wakeful nightingale;
She all night long her amorous descant sung;
Silence was pleased: now glowed the firmament
With living sapphires: Hesperus that led
The starry host, rode brightest, till the moon
Rising in clouded majesty, at length
Apparent queen unveiled her peerless light,
And o'er the dark her silver mantle threw.
   When Adam thus to Eve: Fair consort, the hour   610
Of night, and all things now retired to rest
Mind us of like repose, since God hath set
Labour and rest, as day and night to men
Successive, and the timely dew of sleep
Now falling with soft slumbrous weight inclines
Our eyelids; other creatures all day long
Rove idle unemployed, and less need rest;
Man hath his daily work of body or mind
Appointed, which declares his dignity,
And the regard of heaven on all his ways;   620
While other animals unactive range,
And of their doings God takes no account.
Tomorrow ere fresh morning streak the east
With first approach of light, we must be risen,

And at our pleasant labour, to reform
Yon flowery arbours, yonder alleys green,
Our walk at noon, with branches overgrown,
That mock our scant manuring, and require
More hands than ours to lop their wanton growth:
Those blossoms also, and those dropping gums,   630
That lie bestrewn unsightly and unsmooth,
Ask riddance, if we mean to tread with ease;
Meanwhile, as nature wills, night bids us rest.
    To whom thus Eve with perfect beauty adorned.
My author and disposer, what thou bid'st
Unargued I obey; so God ordains,
God is thy law, thou mine: to know no more
Is woman's happiest knowledge and her praise.
With thee conversing I forget all time,
All seasons and their change, all please alike.   640
Sweet is the breath of morn, her rising sweet,
With charm of earliest birds; pleasant the sun
When first on this delightful land he spreads
His orient beams, on herb, tree, fruit, and flower,
Glistering with dew; fragrant the fertile earth
After soft showers; and sweet the coming on
Of grateful evening mild, then silent night
With this her solemn bird and this fair moon,
And these the gems of heaven, her starry train:
But neither breath of morn when she ascends   650
With charm of earliest birds, nor rising sun
On this delightful land, nor herb, fruit, flower,
Glistering with dew, nor fragrance after showers,
Nor grateful evening mild, nor silent night
With this her solemn bird, nor walk by moon,
Or glittering starlight without thee is sweet.
But wherefore all night long shine these, for whom
This glorious sight, when sleep hath shut all eyes?
    To whom our general ancestor replied.
Daughter of God and man, accomplished Eve,   660
Those have their course to finish, round the earth,
By morrow evening, and from land to land
In order, though to nations yet unborn,
Ministering light prepared, they set and rise;
Lest total darkness should by night regain

Her old possession, and extinguish life
In nature and all things, which these soft fires
Not only enlighten, but with kindly heat
Of various influence foment and warm,
Temper or nourish, or in part shed down   670
Their stellar virtue on all kinds that grow
On earth, made hereby apter to receive
Perfection from the sun's more potent ray.
These then, though unbeheld in deep of night,
Shine not in vain, nor think, though men were none,
That heaven would want spectators, God want praise;
Millions of spiritual creatures walk the earth
Unseen, both when we wake, and when we sleep:
All these with ceaseless praise his works behold
Both day and night: how often from the steep   680
Of echoing hill or thicket have we heard
Celestial voices to the midnight air,
Sole, or responsive each to other's note
Singing their great creator: oft in bands
While they keep watch, or nightly rounding walk
With heavenly touch of instrumental sounds
In full harmonic number joined, their songs
Divide the night, and lift our thoughts to heaven.
    Thus talking hand in hand alone they passed
On to their blissful bower; it was a place   690
Chosen by the sovereign planter, when he framed
All things to man's delightful use; the roof
Of thickest covert was inwoven shade
Laurel and myrtle, and what higher grew
Of firm and fragrant leaf; on either side
Acanthus, and each odorous bushy shrub
Fenced up the verdant wall; each beauteous flower,
Iris all hues, roses, and jessamine
Reared high their flourished heads between, and wrought
Mosaic; underfoot the violet,   700
Crocus, and hyacinth with rich inlay
Broidered the ground, more coloured than with stone
Of costliest emblem: other creature here
Beast, bird, insect, or worm durst enter none;
Such was their awe of man. In shadier bower
More sacred and sequestered, though but feigned,

Pan or Silvanus never slept, nor nymph,
Nor Faunus haunted. Here in close recess
With flowers, garlands, and sweet-smelling herbs
Espousèd Eve decked first her nuptial bed,   710
And heavenly choirs the hymenean sung,
What day the genial angel to our sire
Brought her in naked beauty more adorned,
More lovely than Pandora, whom the gods
Endowed with all their gifts, and O too like
In sad event, when to the unwiser son
Of Japhet brought by Hermes, she ensnared
Mankind with her fair looks, to be avenged
On him who had stole Jove's authentic fire.

   Thus at their shady lodge arrived, both stood,   720
Both turned, and under open sky adored
The God that made both sky, air, earth and heaven
Which they beheld, the moon's resplendent globe
And starry pole: Thou also mad'st the night,
Maker omnipotent, and thou the day,
Which we in our appointed work employed
Have finished happy in our mutual help
And mutual love, the crown of all our bliss
Ordained by thee, and this delicious place
For us too large, where thy abundance wants   730
Partakers, and uncropped falls to the ground.
But thou hast promised from us two a race
To fill the earth, who shall with us extol
Thy goodness infinite, both when we wake,
And when we seek, as now, thy gift of sleep.
   This said unanimous, and other rites
Observing none, but adoration pure
Which God likes best, into their inmost bower
Handed they went; and eased the putting off
These troublesome disguises which we wear,   740
Straight side by side were laid, nor turned I ween
Adam from his fair spouse, nor Eve the rites
Mysterious of connubial love refused:
Whatever hypocrites austerely talk
Of purity and place and innocence,
Defaming as impure what God declares
Pure, and commands to some, leaves free to all.

Our maker bids increase, who bids abstain
But our destroyer, foe to God and man?
Hail wedded love, mysterious law, true source   750
Of human offspring, sole propriety
In Paradise of all things common else.
By thee adulterous lust was driven from men
Among the bestial herds to range, by thee
Founded in reason, loyal, just, and pure,
Relations dear, and all the charities
Of father, son, and brother first were known.
Far be it, that I should write thee sin or blame,
Or think thee unbefitting holiest place,
Perpetual fountain of domestic sweets,   760
Whose bed is undefiled and chaste pronounced,
Present, or past, as saints and patriarchs used.
Here Love his golden shafts employs, here lights
His constant lamp, and waves his purple wings,
Reigns here and revels; not in the bought smile
Of harlots, loveless, joyless, unendeared,
Casual fruition, nor in court amours
Mixed dance, or wanton masque, or midnight ball,
Or serenade, which the starved lover sings
To his proud fair, best quitted with disdain.   770
These lulled by nightingales embracing slept,
And on their naked limbs the flowery roof
Showered roses, which the morn repaired. Sleep on
Blest pair; and O yet happiest if ye seek
No happier state, and know to know no more.
  Now had night measured with her shadowy cone
Halfway uphill this vast sublunar vault,
And from their ivory port the cherubim
Forth issuing at the accustomed hour stood armed
To their night watches in warlike parade,   780
When Gabriel to his next in power thus spake.
  Uzziel, half these draw off, and coast the south
With strictest watch; these other wheel the north,
Our circuit meets full west. As flame they part
Half wheeling to the shield, half to the spear.
From these, two strong and subtle spirits he called
That near him stood, and gave them thus in charge.
  Ithuriel and Zephon, with winged speed

Search through this garden, leave unsearched no nook,
But chiefly where those two fair creatures lodge,   790
Now laid perhaps asleep secure of harm.
This evening from the sun's decline arrived
Who tells of some infernal spirit seen
Hitherward bent (who could have thought?) escaped
The bars of hell, on errand bad no doubt:
Such where ye find, seize fast, and hither bring.
    So saying, on he led his radiant files,
Dazzling the moon; these to the bower direct
In search of whom they sought: him there they found
Squat like a toad, close at the ear of Eve;   800
Assaying by his devilish art to reach
The organs of her fancy, and with them forge
Illusions as he list, phantasms and dreams,
Or if, inspiring venom, he might taint
The animal spirits that from pure blood arise
Like gentle breaths from rivers pure, thence raise
At least distempered, discontented thoughts,
Vain hopes, vain aims, inordinate desires
Blown up with high conceits engendering pride.
Him thus intent Ithuriel with his spear   810
Touched lightly; for no falsehood can endure
Touch of celestial temper, but returns
Of force to its own likeness: up he starts
Discovered and surprised. As when a spark
Lights on a heap of nitrous powder, laid
Fit for the tun some magazine to store
Against a rumoured war, the smutty grain
With sudden blaze diffused, inflames the air:
So started up in his own shape the fiend.
Back stepped those two fair angels half amazed   820
So sudden to behold the grisly king;
Yet thus, unmoved with fear, accost him soon.
    Which of those rebel spirits adjudged to hell
Com'st thou, escaped thy prison, and transformed,
Why sat'st thou like an enemy in wait
Here watching at the head of these that sleep?
    Know ye not then said Satan, filled with scorn,
Know ye not me? Ye knew me once no mate
For you, there sitting where ye durst not soar;

Not to know me argues yourselves unknown,   830
The lowest of your throng; or if ye know,
Why ask ye, and superfluous begin
Your message, like to end as much in vain?
To whom thus Zephon, answering scorn with scorn.
Think not, revolted spirit, thy shape the same,
Or undiminished brightness, to be known
As when thou stood'st in heaven upright and pure;
That glory then, when thou no more wast good,
Departed from thee, and thou resemblest now
Thy sin and place of doom obscure and foul.   840
But come, for thou, be sure, shalt give account
To him who sent us, whose charge is to keep
This place inviolable, and these from harm.
     So spake the cherub, and his grave rebuke
Severe in youthful beauty, added grace
Invincible: abashed the devil stood,
And felt how awful goodness is, and saw
Virtue in her shape how lovely, saw, and pined
His loss; but chiefly to find here observed
His lustre visibly impaired; yet seemed   850
Undaunted. If I must contend, said he,
Best with the best, the sender not the sent,
Or all at once; more glory will be won,
Or less be lost. Thy fear, said Zephon bold,
Will save us trial what the least can do
Single against thee wicked, and thence weak.
     The fiend replied not, overcome with rage;
But like a proud steed reined, went haughty on,
Champing his iron curb: to strive or fly
He held it vain; awe from above had quelled   860
His heart, not else dismayed. Now drew they nigh
The western point, where those half-rounding guards
Just met, and closing stood in squadron joined
Awaiting next command. To whom their chief
Gabriel from the front thus called aloud.
     O friends, I hear the tread of nimble feet
Hasting this way, and now by glimpse discern
Ithuriel and Zephon through the shade,
And with them comes a third of regal port,
But faded splendour wan; who by his gait   870

And fierce demeanour seems the prince of hell,
Not likely to part hence without contest;
Stand firm, for in his look defiance lours.

He scarce had ended, when those two approached
And brief related whom they brought, where found,
How busied, in what form and posture couched.

To whom with stern regard thus Gabriel spake.
Why hast thou, Satan, broke the bounds prescribed
To thy transgressions, and disturbed the charge
Of others, who approve not to transgress   880
By thy example, but have power and right
To question thy bold entrance on this place;
Employed it seems to violate sleep, and those
Whose dwelling God hath planted here in bliss?

To whom thus Satan, with contemptuous brow.
Gabriel, thou hadst in heaven the esteem of wise,
And such I held thee; but this question asked
Puts me in doubt. Lives there who loves his pain?
Who would not, finding way, break loose from hell,
Though thither doomed? Thou wouldst thyself, no doubt,   890
And boldly venture to whatever place
Farthest from pain, where thou might'st hope to change
Torment with ease, and soonest recompense
Dole with delight, which in this place I sought;
To thee no reason, who know'st only good,
But evil hast not tried: and wilt object
His will who bound us? Let him surer bar
His iron gates, if he intends our stay
In that dark durance: thus much what was asked.
The rest is true, they found me where they say;   900
But that implies not violence or harm.

Thus he in scorn. The warlike angel moved,
Disdainfully half smiling thus replied.
O loss of one in heaven to judge of wise,
Since Satan fell, whom folly overthrew,
And now returns him from his prison scaped,
Gravely in doubt whether to hold them wise
Or not, who ask what boldness brought him hither
Unlicensed from his bounds in hell prescribed;
So wise he judges it to fly from pain   910
However, and to scape his punishment.

So judge thou still, presumptuous, till the wrath,
Which thou incurr'st by flying, meet thy flight
Sevenfold, and scourge that wisdom back to hell,
Which taught thee yet no better, that no pain
Can equal anger infinite provoked.
But wherefore thou alone? Wherefore with thee
Came not all hell broke loose? Is pain to them
Less pain, less to be fled, or thou than they
Less hardy to endure? Courageous chief,   920
The first in flight from pain, hadst thou alleged
To thy deserted host this cause of flight,
Thou surely hadst not come sole fugitive.
    To which the fiend thus answered frowning stern.
Not that I less endure, or shrink from pain,
Insulting angel, well thou know'st I stood
Thy fiercest, when in battle to thy aid
The blasting vollied thunder made all speed
And seconded thy else not dreaded spear.
But still thy words at random, as before,   930
Argue thy inexperience what behoves
From hard assays and ill successes past
A faithful leader, not to hazard all
Through ways of danger by himself untried,
I therefore, I alone first undertook
To wing the desolate abyss, and spy
This new created world, whereof in hell
Fame is not silent, here in hope to find
Better abode, and my afflicted powers
To settle here on earth, or in midair;   940
Though for possession put to try once more
What thou and thy gay legions dare against;
Whose easier business were to serve their Lord
High up in heaven, with songs to hymn his throne,
And practised distances to cringe, not fight.
    To whom the warrior angel soon replied.
To say and straight unsay, pretending first
Wise to fly pain, professing next the spy,
Argues no leader but a liar traced,
Satan, and couldst thou faithful add? O name,   950
O sacred name of faithfulness profaned!
Faithful to whom? to thy rebellious crew?

Army of fiends, fit body to fit head;
Was this your discipline and faith engaged,
Your military obedience, to dissolve
Allegiance to the acknowledged power supreme?
And thou sly hypocrite, who now wouldst seem
Patron of liberty, who more than thou
Once fawned, and cringed, and servilely adored
Heaven's awful monarch? wherefore but in hope   960
To dispossess him, and thy self to reign?
But mark what I aread thee now, avaunt;
Fly thither whence thou fled'st: if from this hour
Within these hallowed limits thou appear,
Back to the infernal pit I drag thee chained,
And seal thee so, as henceforth not to scorn
The facile gates of hell too slightly barred.
    So threatened he, but Satan to no threats
Gave heed, but waxing more in rage replied.
    Then when I am thy captive talk of chains,   970
Proud limitary cherub, but ere then
Far heavier load thyself expect to feel
From my prevailing arm, though heaven's king
Ride on thy wings, and thou with thy compeers,
Used to the yoke, draw'st his triumphant wheels
In progress through the road of heaven star-paved.
    While thus he spake, the angelic squadron bright
Turned fiery red, sharpening in moonèd horns
Their phalanx, and began to hem him round
With ported spears, as thick as when a field   980
Of Ceres ripe for harvest waving bends
Her bearded grove of ears, which way the wind
Sways them; the careful ploughman doubting stands
Lest on the threshing floor his hopeful sheaves
Prove chaff. On the other side Satan alarmed
Collecting all his might dilated stood,
Like Tenerife or Atlas unremoved:
His stature reached the sky, and on his crest
Sat horror plumed; nor wanted in his grasp
What seemed both spear and shield: now dreadful deeds   990
Might have ensued, nor only Paradise
In this commotion, but the starry cope
Of heaven perhaps, or all the elements

At least had gone to wrack, disturbed and torn
With violence of this conflict, had not soon
The eternal to prevent such horrid fray
Hung forth in heaven his golden scales, yet seen
Betwixt Astrea and the Scorpion sign,
Wherein all things created first he weighed,
The pendulous round earth with balanced air   1000
In counterpoise, now ponders all events,
Battles and realms: in these he put two weights
The sequel each of parting and of fight;
The latter quick up flew, and kicked the beam;
Which Gabriel spying, thus bespake the fiend.

   Satan, I know thy strength, and thou know'st mine,
Neither our own but given; what folly then
To boast what arms can do, since thine no more
Than heaven permits, nor mine, though doubled now
To trample thee as mire: for proof look up,   1010
And read thy lot in yon celestial sign
Where thou art weighed, and shown how light, how weak,
If thou resist. The fiend looked up and knew
His mounted scale aloft: nor more; but fled
Murmuring, and with him fled the shades of night.

From Book V

Now Morn her rosy steps in the eastern clime
Advancing, sowed the earth with orient pearl,
When Adam waked, so customed, for his sleep
Was airy light from pure digestion bred,
And temperate vapours bland, which the only sound
Of leaves and fuming rills, Aurora's fan,
Lightly dispersed, and the shrill matin song
Of birds on every bough; so much the more
His wonder was to find unwakened Eve
With tresses discomposed, and glowing cheek,   10
As through unquiet rest: he on his side
Leaning half-raised, with looks of cordial love
Hung over her enamoured, and beheld
Beauty, which whether waking or asleep,

Shot forth peculiar graces; then with voice
Mild, as when Zephyrus on Flora breathes,
Her hand soft touching, whispered thus. Awake
My fairest, my espoused, my latest found,
Heaven's last best gift, my ever new delight,
Awake, the morning shines, and the fresh field   20
Calls us, we lose the prime, to mark how spring
Our tended plants, how blows the citron grove,
What drops the myrrh, and what the balmy reed,
How nature paints her colours, how the bee
Sits on the bloom extracting liquid sweet.
    Such whispering waked her, but with startled eye
On Adam, whom embracing, thus she spake.
    O sole in whom my thoughts find all repose,
My glory, my perfection, glad I see
Thy face, and morn returned, for I this night,   30
Such night till this I never passed, have dreamed,
If dreamed, not as I oft am wont, of thee,
Works of day past, or morrow's next design,
But of offence and trouble, which my mind
Knew never till this irksome night; methought
Close at mine ear one called me forth to walk
With gentle voice, I thought it thine; it said,
Why sleep'st thou Eve? now is the pleasant time,
The cool, the silent, save where silence yields
To the night-warbling bird, that now awake   40
Tunes sweetest his love-laboured song; now reigns
Full-orbed the moon, and with more pleasing light
Shadowy sets off the face of things; in vain,
If none regard; heaven wakes with all his eyes,
Whom to behold but thee, nature's desire,
In whose sight all things joy, with ravishment
Attracted by thy beauty still to gaze.
I rose as at thy call, but found thee not;
To find thee I directed then my walk;
And on, methought, alone I passed through ways   50
That brought me on a sudden to the tree
Of interdicted knowledge: fair it seemed,
Much fairer to my fancy than by day:
And as I wondering looked, beside it stood
One shaped and winged like one of those from heaven

By us oft seen; his dewy locks distilled
Ambrosia; on that tree he also gazed;
And O fair plant, said he, with fruit surcharged,
Deigns none to ease thy load and taste thy sweet,
Nor God, nor man; is knowledge so despised?   60
Or envy, or what reserve forbids to taste?
Forbid who will, none shall from me withhold
Longer thy offered good, why else set here?
This said he paused not, but with venturous arm
He plucked, he tasted; me damp horror chilled
At such bold words vouched with a deed so bold:
But he thus overjoyed, O fruit divine,
Sweet of thy self, but much more sweet thus cropped,
Forbidden here, it seems, as only fit
For gods, yet able to make gods of men: 70
And why not gods of men, since good, the more
Communicated, more abundant grows,
The author not impaired, but honoured more?
Here, happy creature, fair angelic Eve,
Partake thou also; happy though thou art,
Happier thou mayst be, worthier canst not be:
Taste this, and be henceforth among the gods
Thyself a goddess, not to earth confined,
But sometimes in the air, as we, sometimes
Ascend to heaven, by merit thine, and see   80
What life the gods live there, and such live thou.
So saying, he drew nigh, and to me held,
Even to my mouth of that same fruit held part
Which he had plucked; the pleasant savoury smell
So quickened appetite, that I, methought,
Could not but taste. Forthwith up to the clouds
With him I flew, and underneath beheld
The earth outstretched immense, a prospect wide
And various: wondering at my flight and change
To this high exaltation; suddenly   90
My guide was gone, and I, methought, sunk down,
And fell asleep; but O how glad I waked
To find this but a dream!
      .   .   .   .

[ADAM CONVERSES WITH RAPHAEL]

   Thus when with meats and drinks they had sufficed,
Not burdened nature, sudden mind arose

In Adam, not to let the occasion pass
Given him by this great conference to know
Of things above his world, and of their being
Who dwell in heaven, whose excellence he saw
Transcend his own so far, whose radiant forms
Divine effulgence, whose high power so far
Exceeded human, and his wary speech
Thus to the empyreal minister he framed.   460
    Inhabitant with God, now know I well
Thy favour, in this honour done to man,
Under whose lowly roof thou hast vouchsafed
To enter, and these earthly fruits to taste,
Food not of angels, yet accepted so,
As that more willingly thou couldst not seem
At heaven's high feasts to have fed: yet what compare?
    To whom the winged hierarch replied.
O Adam, one almighty is, from whom
All things proceed, and up to him return,   470
If not depraved from good, created all
Such to perfection, one first matter all,
Indued with various forms, various degrees
Of substance, and in things that live, of life;
But more refined, more spiritous, and pure,
As nearer to him placed or nearer tending
Each in their several active spheres assigned,
Till body up to spirit work, in bounds
Proportioned to each kind. So from the root
Springs lighter the green stalk, from thence the leaves   480
More airy, last the bright consummate flower
Spirits odorous breathes: flowers and their fruit
Man's nourishment, by gradual scale sublimed
To vital spirits aspire, to animal,
To intellectual, give both life and sense,
Fancy and understanding, whence the soul
Reason receives, and reason is her being,
Discursive, or intuitive; discourse
Is oftest yours, the latter most is ours,
Differing but in degree, of kind the same.   490
Wonder not then, what God for you saw good
If I refuse not, but convert, as you,
To proper substance; time may come when men

With angels may participate, and find
No inconvenient diet, nor too light fare:
And from these corporal nutriments perhaps
Your bodies may at last turn all to spirit,
Improved by tract of time, and winged ascend
Ethereal, as we, or may at choice
Here or in heavenly paradises dwell;   500
If ye be found obedient, and retain
Unalterably firm his love entire
Whose progeny you are. Meanwhile enjoy
Your fill what happiness this happy state
Can comprehend, incapable of more.

. . . .

From Book VII

Descend from heaven Urania, by that name
If rightly thou art called, whose voice divine
Following, above the Olympian hill I soar,
Above the flight of Pegasean wing.
The meaning, not the name I call: for thou
Nor of the muses nine, nor on the top
Of old Olympus dwell'st, but heavenly born,
Before the hills appeared, or fountain flowed,
Thou with eternal wisdom didst converse,
Wisdom thy sister, and with her didst play   10
In presence of the almighty Father, pleased
With thy celestial song. Up led by thee
Into the heaven of heavens I have presumed,
An earthly guest, and drawn empyreal air,
Thy tempering; with like safety guided down
Return me to my native element:
Lest from this flying steed unreined, (as once
Bellerophon, though from a lower clime)
Dismounted, on the Aleian field I fall
Erroneous there to wander and forlorn.   20
Half yet remains unsung, but narrower bound
Within the visible diurnal sphere;
Standing on earth, not rapt above the pole,

More safe I sing with mortal voice, unchanged
To hoarse or mute, though fallen on evil days,
On evil days though fallen, and evil tongues;
In darkness, and with dangers compassed round,
And solitude; yet not alone, while thou
Visit'st my slumbers nightly, or when morn
Purples the east: still govern thou my song,   30
Urania, and fit audience find, though few.
But drive far off the barbarous dissonance
Of Bacchus and his revellers, the race
Of that wild rout that tore the Thracian bard
In Rhodope, where woods and rocks had ears
To rapture, till the savage clamour drowned
Both harp and voice; nor could the muse defend
Her son. So fail not thou, who thee implores:
For thou art heavenly, she an empty dream.

· · · · · · · ·

From Book VIII

[ADAM TO RAPHAEL]

For man to tell how human life began   250
Is hard; for who himself beginning knew?
Desire with thee still longer to converse
Induced me. As new waked from soundest sleep
Soft on the flowery herb I found me laid
In balmy sweat, which with his beams the sun
Soon dried, and on the reeking moisture fed.
Straight toward heaven my wondering eyes I turned,
And gazed awhile the ample sky, till raised
By quick instinctive motion up I sprung,
As thitherward endeavouring, and upright   260
Stood on my feet; about me round I saw
Hill, dale, and shady woods, and sunny plains,
And liquid lapse of murmuring streams; by these,
Creatures that lived, and moved, and walked, or flew,
Birds on the branches warbling; all things smiled,
With fragrance and with joy my heart o'erflowed.
My self I then perused, and limb by limb
Surveyed, and sometimes went, and sometimes ran

With supple joints, and lively vigour led:
But who I was, or where, or from what cause,   270
Knew not; to speak I tried, and forthwith spake,
My tongue obeyed and readily could name
Whate'er I saw. Thou sun, said I, fair light,
And thou enlightened earth, so fresh and gay,
Ye hills and dales, ye rivers, woods, and plains,
And ye that live and move, fair creatures, tell,
Tell, if ye saw, how came I thus, how here?
Not of myself; by some great maker then,
In goodness and in power pre-eminent;
Tell me, how may I know him, how adore,   280
From whom I have that thus I move and live,
And feel that I am happier than I know.
While thus I called, and strayed I knew not whither,
From where I first drew air, and first beheld
This happy light, when answer none returned,
On a green shady bank profuse of flowers
Pensive I sat me down; there gentle sleep
First found me, and with soft oppression seized
My drowsèd sense, untroubled, though I thought
I then was passing to my former state   290
Insensible, and forthwith to dissolve:
When suddenly stood at my head a dream,
Whose inward apparition gently moved
My fancy to believe I yet had being,
And lived: one came, methought, of shape divine,
And said, Thy mansion wants thee, Adam, rise,
First man, of men innumerable ordained
First father, called by thee I come thy guide
To the garden of bliss, thy seat prepared.
So saying, by the hand he took me raised,   300
And over fields and waters, as in air
Smooth sliding without step, last led me up
A woody mountain; whose high top was plain,
A circuit wide, enclosed, with goodliest trees
Planted, with walks, and bowers, that what I saw
Of earth before scarce pleasant seemed. Each tree
Loaden with fairest fruit that hung to the eye
Tempting, stirred in me sudden appetite
To pluck and eat; whereat I waked, and found

Before mine eyes all real, as the dream   310
Had lively shadowed: here had new begun
My wandering, had not he who was my guide
Up hither, from among the trees appeared
Presence divine. Rejoicing, but with awe
In adoration at his feet I fell
Submiss: he reared me, and Whom thou sought'st I am,
Said mildly, Author of all this thou seest
Above, or round about thee or beneath.
This Paradise I give thee, count it thine
To till and keep, and of the fruit to eat: 320
Of every tree that in the garden grows
Eat freely with glad heart; fear here no dearth:
But of the tree whose operation brings
Knowledge of good and ill, which I have set
The pledge of thy obedience and thy faith,
Amid the garden by the tree of life,
Remember what I warn thee, shun to taste,
And shun the bitter consequence: for know,
The day thou eat'st thereof, my sole command
Transgressed, inevitably thou shalt die;   330
From that day mortal, and this happy state
Shalt lose, expelled from hence into a world
Of woe and sorrow. Sternly he pronounced
The rigid interdiction, which resounds
Yet dreadful in mine ear, though in my choice
Not to incur; but soon his clear aspect
Returned and gracious purpose thus renewed.
Not only these fair bounds, but all the earth
To thee and to thy race I give; as lords
Possess it, and all things that therein live,   340
Or live in sea, or air, beast, fish, and fowl.

          .   .   .   .

To love thou blam'st me not, for love thou say'st
Leads up to heaven, is both the way and guide;
Bear with me then, if lawful what I ask;
Love not the heavenly spirits, and how their love
Express they, by looks only, or do they mix
Irradiance, virtual or immediate touch?
    To whom the angel with a smile that glowed
Celestial rosy red, love's proper hue,

Answered. Let it suffice thee that thou know'st   620
Us happy, and without love no happiness.
Whatever pure thou in the body enjoy'st
(And pure thou wert created) we enjoy
In eminence, and obstacle find none
Of membrane, joint, or limb, exclusive bars:
Easier than air with air, if spirits embrace,
Total they mix, union of pure with pure
Desiring; nor restrained conveyance need
As flesh to mix with flesh, or soul with soul.

. . . .

Book IX

No more of talk where God or angel guest
With man, as with his friend, familiar used
To sit indulgent, and with him partake
Rural repast, permitting him the while
Venial discourse unblamed: I now must change
Those notes to tragic; foul distrust, and breach
Disloyal on the part of man, revolt,
And disobedience: on the part of heaven
Now alienated, distance and distaste,
Anger and just rebuke, and judgment given,   10
That brought into this world a world of woe,
Sin and her shadow Death, and Misery
Death's harbinger: sad task, yet argument
Not less but more heroic than the wrath
Of stern Achilles on his foe pursued
Thrice fugitive about Troy wall; or rage
Of Turnus for Lavinia disespoused,
Or Neptune's ire or Juno's, that so long
Perplexed the Greek and Cytherea's son;
If answerable style I can obtain   20
Of my celestial patroness, who deigns
Her nightly visitation unimplored,
And dictates to me slumbering, or inspires
Easy my unpremeditated verse:
Since first this subject for heroic song
Pleased me long choosing, and beginning late;
Not sedulous by nature to indite

Wars, hitherto the only argument
Heroic deemed, chief mastery to dissect
With long and tedious havoc fabled knights   30
In battles feigned; the better fortitude
Of patience and heroic martyrdom
Unsung; or to describe races and games,
Or tilting furniture, emblazoned shields,
Impresas quaint, caparisons and steeds;
Bases and tinsel trappings, gorgeous knights
At joust and tournament; then marshalled feast
Served up in hall with sewers, and seneschals;
The skill of artifice or office mean,
Not that which justly gives heroic name   40
To person or to poem. Me of these
Nor skilled nor studious, higher argument
Remains, sufficient of itself to raise
That name, unless an age too late, or cold
Climate, or years damp my intended wing
Depressed, and much they may, if all be mine,
Not hers who brings it nightly to my ear.
      The sun was sunk, and after him the star
Of Hesperus, whose office is to bring
Twilight upon the earth, short arbiter   50
Twixt day and night, and now from end to end
Night's hemisphere had veiled the horizon round:
When Satan who late fled before the threats
Of Gabriel out of Eden, now improved
In meditated fraud and malice, bent
On man's destruction, maugre what might hap
Of heavier on himself, fearless returned.
By night he fled, and at midnight returned
From compassing the earth, cautious of day,
Since Uriel regent of the sun descried   60
His entrance, and forewarned the cherubim
That kept their watch; thence full of anguish driven,
The space of seven continued nights he rode
With darkness, thrice the equinoctial line
He circled, four times crossed the car of Night
From pole to pole, traversing each colure;
On the eighth returned, and on the coast averse
From entrance or cherubic watch, by stealth

Found unsuspected way. There was a place,
Now not, though sin, not time, first wrought the change,   70
Where Tigris at the foot of Paradise
Into a gulf shot underground, till part
Rose up a fountain by the tree of life;
In with the river sunk, and with it rose
Satan involved in rising mist, then sought
Where to lie hid; sea he had searched and land
From Eden over Pontus, and the pool
Maeotis, up beyond the river Ob;
Downward as far antarctic; and in length
West from Orontes to the ocean barred   80
At Darien, thence to the land where flows
Ganges and Indus: thus the orb he roamed
With narrow search; and with inspection deep
Considered every creature, which of all
Most opportune might serve his wiles, and found
The serpent subtlest beast of all the field.
Him after long debate, irresolute
Of thoughts revolved, his final sentence chose
Fit vessel, fittest imp of fraud, in whom
To enter, and his dark suggestions hide   90
From sharpest sight: for in the wily snake,
Whatever sleights none would suspicious mark,
As from his wit and native subtlety
Proceeding, which in other beasts observed
Doubt might beget of diabolic power
Active within beyond the sense of brute.
Thus he resolved, but first from inward grief
His bursting passion into plaints thus poured:
   O earth, how like to heaven, if not preferred
More justly, seat worthier of gods, as built   100
With second thoughts, reforming what was old!
For what god after better worse would build?
Terrestrial heaven, danced round by other heavens
That shine, yet bear their bright officious lamps,
Light above light, for thee alone, as seems,
In thee concentring all their precious beams
Of sacred influence: as God in heaven
Is centre, yet extends to all, so thou
Centring receiv'st from all those orbs; in thee,

Not in themselves, all their known virtue appears   110
Productive in herb, plant, and nobler birth
Of creatures animate with gradual life
Of growth, sense, reason, all summed up in man.
With what delight could I have walked thee round,
If I could joy in aught, sweet interchange
Of hill, and valley, rivers, woods and plains,
Now land, now sea, and shores with forest crowned,
Rocks, dens, and caves; but I in none of these
Find place or refuge; and the more I see
Pleasures about me, so much more I feel   120
Torment within me, as from the hateful siege
Of contraries; all good to me becomes
Bane, and in heaven much worse would be my state,
But neither here seek I, no nor in heaven
To dwell, unless by mastering heaven's supreme;
Nor hope to be myself less miserable
By what I seek, but others to make such
As I, though thereby worse to me redound:
For only in destroying I find ease
To my relentless thoughts; and him destroyed,   130
Or won to what may work his utter loss,
For whom all this was made, all this will soon
Follow, as to him linked in weal or woe,
In woe then; that destruction wide may range:
To me shall be the glory sole among
The infernal powers, in one day to have marred
What he almighty styled, six nights and days
Continued making, and who knows how long
Before had been contriving, though perhaps
Not longer than since I in one night freed   140
From servitude inglorious well-nigh half
The angelic name, and thinner left the throng
Of his adorers: he to be avenged
And to repair his numbers thus impaired,
Whether such virtue spent of old now failed
More angels to create, if they at least
Are his created, or to spite us more,
Determined to advance into our room
A creature formed of earth, and him endow,
Exalted from so base original,   150

With heavenly spoils, our spoils: what he decreed
He effected; man he made, and for him built
Magnificent this world, and earth his seat,
Him lord pronounced, and, O indignity!
Subjected to his service angel wings,
And flaming ministers to watch and tend
Their earthy charge: of these the vigilance
I dread, and to elude, thus wrapped in mist
Of midnight vapour glide obscure, and pry
In every bush and brake, where hap may find   160
The serpent sleeping, in whose mazy folds
To hide me, and the dark intent I bring.
O foul descent! that I who erst contended
With gods to sit the highest, am now constrained
Into a beast, and mixed with bestial slime,
This essence to incarnate and imbrute,
That to the height of deity aspired;
But what will not ambition and revenge
Descend to? Who aspires must down as low
As high he soared, obnoxious first or last   170
To basest things. Revenge, at first though sweet,
Bitter ere long back on itself recoils;
Let it; I reck not, so it light well aimed,
Since higher I fall short, on him who next
Provokes my envy, this new favourite
Of heaven, this man of clay, son of despite,
Whom us the more to spite his maker raised
From dust: spite then with spite is best repaid.
      So saying, through each thicket dank or dry,
Like a black mist low creeping, he held on   180
His midnight search, where soonest he might find
The serpent: him fast sleeping soon he found
In labyrinth of many a round self-rolled,
His head the midst, well stored with subtle wiles:
Not yet in horrid shade or dismal den,
Nor nocent yet, but on the grassy herb
Fearless unfeared he slept: in at his mouth
The devil entered, and his brutal sense,
In heart or head, possessing soon inspired
With act intelligential; but his sleep   190
Disturbed not, waiting close the approach of morn.

Now whenas sacred light began to dawn
In Eden on the humid flowers, that breathed
Their morning incense, when all things that breathe,
From the earth's great altar send up silent praise
To the creator, and his nostrils fill
With grateful smell, forth came the human pair
And joined their vocal worship to the choir
Of creatures wanting voice, that done, partake
The season, prime for sweetest scents and airs: 200
Then commune how that day they best may ply
Their growing work: for much their work outgrew
The hands' dispatch of two, gardening so wide.
And Eve first to her husband thus began.
     Adam, well may we labour still to dress
This garden, still to tend plant, herb and flower,
Our pleasant task enjoined, but till more hands
Aid us, the work under our labour grows,
Luxurious by restraint; what we by day
Lop overgrown, or prune, or prop, or bind,   210
One night or two with wanton growth derides
Tending to wild. Thou therefore now advise
Or hear what to my mind first thoughts present,
Let us divide our labours, thou where choice
Leads thee, or where most needs, whether to wind
The woodbine round this arbour, or direct
The clasping ivy where to climb, while I
In yonder spring of roses intermixed
With myrtle, find what to redress till noon:
For while so near each other thus all day   220
Our task we choose, what wonder if so near
Looks intervene and smiles, or object new
Casual discourse draw on, which intermits
Our day's work brought to little, though begun
Early, and the hour of supper comes unearned.
     To whom mild answer Adam thus returned.
Sole Eve, associate sole, to me beyond
Compare above all living creatures dear,
Well hast thou motioned, well thy thoughts employed
How we might best fulfil the work which here   230
God hath assigned us, nor of me shalt pass
Unpraised: for nothing lovelier can be found

In woman, than to study household good,
And good works in her husband to promote.
Yet not so strictly hath our Lord imposed
Labour, as to debar us when we need
Refreshment, whether food, or talk between,
Food of the mind, or this sweet intercourse
Of looks and smiles, for smiles from reason flow,
To brute denied, and are of love the food,   240
Love not the lowest end of human life.
For not to irksome toil, but to delight
He made us, and delight to reason joined.
These paths and bowers doubt not but our joint hands
Will keep from wilderness with ease, as wide
As we need walk, till younger hands ere long
Assist us: but if much converse perhaps
Thee satiate, to short absence I could yield.
For solitude sometimes is best society,
And short retirement urges sweet return.   250
But other doubt possesses me, lest harm
Befall thee severed from me; for thou know'st
What hath been warned us, what malicious foe
Envying our happiness, and of his own
Despairing, seeks to work us woe and shame
By sly assault; and somewhere nigh at hand
Watches, no doubt, with greedy hope to find
His wish and best advantage, us asunder,
Hopeless to circumvent us joined, where each
To other speedy aid might lend at need;   260
Whether his first design be to withdraw
Our fealty from God, or to disturb
Conjugal love, than which perhaps no bliss
Enjoyed by us excites his envy more;
Or this, or worse, leave not the faithful side
That gave thee being, still shades thee and protects.
The wife, where danger or dishonour lurks,
Safest and seemliest by her husband stays,
Who guards her, or with her the worst endures.
    To whom the virgin majesty of Eve,   270
As one who loves, and some unkindness meets,
With sweet austere composure thus replied.
    Offspring of heaven and earth, and all earth's lord,

That such an enemy we have, who seeks
Our ruin, both by thee informed I learn,
And from the parting angel overheard
As in a shady nook I stood behind,
Just then returned at shut of evening flowers.
But that thou shouldst my firmness therefore doubt
To God or thee, because we have a foe   280
May tempt it, I expected not to hear.
His violence thou fear'st not, being such,
As we, not capable of death or pain,
Can either not receive, or can repel.
His fraud is then thy fear, which plain infers
Thy equal fear that my firm faith and love
Can by his fraud be shaken or seduced;
Thoughts, which how found they harbour in thy breast
Adam, misthought of her to thee so dear?
   To whom with healing words Adam replied.   290
Daughter of God and man, immortal Eve,
For such thou art, from sin and blame entire:
Not diffident of thee do I dissuade
Thy absence from my sight, but to avoid
The attempt itself, intended by our foe.
For he who tempts, though in vain, at least asperses
The tempted with dishonour foul, supposed
Not incorruptible of faith, not proof
Against temptation: thou thyself with scorn
And anger wouldst resent the offered wrong,   300
Though ineffectual found: misdeem not then,
If such affront I labour to avert
From thee alone, which on us both at once
The enemy, though bold, will hardly dare,
Or daring, first on me the assault shall light.
Nor thou his malice and false guile contemn;
Subtle he needs must be, who could seduce
Angels, nor think superfluous others' aid.
I from the influence of thy looks receive
Access in every virtue, in thy sight   310
More wise, more watchful, stronger, if need were
Of outward strength; while shame, thou looking on,
Shame to be overcome or over-reached
Would utmost vigour raise, and raised unite.

Why shouldst not thou like sense within thee feel
When I am present, and thy trial choose
With me, best witness of thy virtue tried.
    So spake domestic Adam in his care
And matrimonial love; but Eve, who thought
Less attributed to her faith sincere,   320
Thus her reply with accent sweet renewed.
    If this be our condition, thus to dwell
In narrow circuit straitened by a foe,
Subtle or violent, we not endued
Single with like defence, wherever met,
How are we happy, still in fear of harm?
But harm precedes not sin: only our foe
Tempting affronts us with his foul esteem
Of our integrity: his foul esteem
Sticks no dishonour on our front, but turns   330
Foul on himself; then wherefore shunned or feared
By us? who rather double honour gain
From his surmise proved false, find peace within,
Favour from heaven, our witness from the event.
And what is faith, love, virtue unassayed
Alone, without exterior help sustained?
Let us not then suspect our happy state
Left so imperfect by the maker wise,
As not secure to single or combined.
Frail is our happiness, if this be so,   340
And Eden were no Eden thus exposed.
    To whom thus Adam fervently replied.
O woman, best are all things as the will
Of God ordained them, his creating hand
Nothing imperfect or deficient left
Of all that he created, much less man,
Or aught that might his happy state secure,
Secure from outward force; within himself
The danger lies, yet lies within his power:
Against his will he can receive no harm.   350
But God left free the will, for what obeys
Reason, is free, and reason he made right,
But bid her well beware, and still erect,
Lest by some fair-appearing good surprised
She dictate false, and misinform the will

To do what God expressly hath forbid.
Not then mistrust, but tender love enjoins,
That I should mind thee oft, and mind thou me.
Firm we subsist, yet possible to swerve,
Since reason not impossibly may meet   360
Some specious object by the foe suborned,
And fall into deception unaware,
Not keeping strictest watch, as she was warned.
Seek not temptation then, which to avoid
Were better, and most likely if from me
Thou sever not: trial will come unsought.
Wouldst thou approve thy constancy, approve
First thy obedience; the other who can know,
Not seeing thee attempted, who attest?
But if thou think, trial unsought may find   370
Us both securer than thus warned thou seem'st,
Go; for thy stay, not free, absents thee more;
Go in thy native innocence, rely
On what thou hast of virtue, summon all,
For God towards thee hath done his part, do thine.
    So spake the patriarch of mankind, but Eve
Persisted, yet submiss, though last, replied.
    With thy permission then, and thus forewarned
Chiefly by what thy own last reasoning words
Touched only, that our trial, when least sought,   380
May find us both perhaps far less prepared,
The willinger I go, nor much expect
A foe so proud will first the weaker seek;
So bent, the more shall shame him his repulse.
    Thus saying, from her husband's hand her hand
Soft she withdrew, and like a wood-nymph light
Oread or dryad, or of Delia's train,
Betook her to the groves, but Delia's self
In gait surpassed and goddess-like deport,
Though not as she with bow and quiver armed,   390
But with such gardening tools as art yet rude,
Guiltless of fire had formed, or angels brought.
To Pales, or Pomona thus adorned,
Likeliest she seemed, Pomona when she fled
Vertumnus, or to Ceres in her prime,
Yet virgin of Proserpina from Jove.

Her long with ardent look his eye pursued
Delighted, but desiring more her stay.
Oft he to her his charge of quick return
Repeated, she to him as oft engaged   400
To be returned by noon amid the bower,
And all things in best order to invite
Noontide repast, or afternoon's repose.
O much deceived, much failing, hapless Eve,
Of thy presumed return! event perverse!
Thou never from that hour in Paradise
Found'st either sweet repast, or sound repose;
Such ambush hid among sweet flowers and shades
Waited with hellish rancour imminent
To intercept thy way, or send thee back   410
Despoiled of innocence, of faith, of bliss.
For now, and since first break of dawn the fiend,
Mere serpent in appearance, forth was come,
And on his quest, where likeliest he might find
The only two of mankind, but in them
The whole included race, his purposed prey.
In bower and field he sought, where any tuft
Of grove or garden-plot more pleasant lay,
Their tendance or plantation for delight,
By fountain or by shady rivulet   420
He sought them both, but wished his hap might find
Eve separate, he wished, but not with hope
Of what so seldom chanced, when to his wish,
Beyond his hope, Eve separate he spies,
Veiled in a cloud of fragrance, where she stood,
Half spied, so thick the roses bushing round
About her glowed, oft stooping to support
Each flower of slender stalk, whose head though gay
Carnation, purple, azure, or specked with gold,
Hung drooping unsustained, them she upstays   430
Gently with myrtle band, mindless the while,
Herself, though fairest unsupported flower,
From her best prop so far, and storm so nigh.
Nearer he drew, and many a walk traversed
Of stateliest covert, cedar, pine, or palm,
Then voluble and bold, now hid, now seen
Among thick-woven arborets and flowers

Embordered on each bank, the hand of Eve:
Spot more delicious than those gardens feigned
Or of revived Adonis, or renowned   440
Alcinous, host of old Laertes' son,
Or that, not mystic, where the sapient king
Held dalliance with his fair Egyptian spouse.
Much he the place admired, the person more.
As one who long in populous city pent,
Where houses thick and sewers annoy the air,
Forth issuing on a summer's morn to breathe
Among the pleasant villages and farms
Adjoined, from each thing met conceives delight,
The smell of grain, or tedded grass, or kine,   450
Or dairy, each rural sight, each rural sound;
If chance with nymph-like step fair virgin pass,
What pleasing seemed, for her now pleases more,
She most, and in her look sums all delight.
Such pleasure took the serpent to behold
This flowery plat, the sweet recess of Eve
Thus early, thus alone; her heavenly form
Angelic, but more soft, and feminine,
Her graceful innocence, her every air
Of gesture or least action overawed   460
His malice, and with rapine sweet bereaved
His fierceness of the fierce intent it brought:
That space the evil one abstracted stood
From his own evil, and for the time remained
Stupidly good, of enmity disarmed,
Of guile, of hate, of envy, of revenge;
But the hot hell that always in him burns,
Though in mid-heaven, soon ended his delight,
And tortures him now more, the more he sees
Of pleasure not for him ordained: then soon   470
Fierce hate he recollects, and all his thoughts
Of mischief, gratulating, thus excites.
   Thoughts, whither have ye led me, with what sweet
Compulsion thus transported to forget
What hither brought us, hate, not love, nor hope
Of Paradise for hell, hope here to taste
Of pleasure, but all pleasure to destroy,
Save what is in destroying, other joy

To me is lost. Then let me not let pass
Occasion which now smiles, behold alone   480
The woman, opportune to all attempts,
Her husband, for I view far round, not nigh,
Whose higher intellectual more I shun,
And strength, of courage haughty, and of limb
Heroic built, though of terrestrial mould,
Foe not informidable, exempt from wound,
I not; so much hath hell debased, and pain
Enfeebled me, to what I was in heaven.
She fair, divinely fair, fit love for gods,
Not terrible, though terror be in love   490
And beauty, not approached by stronger hate,
Hate stronger, under show of love well feigned,
The way which to her ruin now I tend.
    So spake the enemy of mankind, enclosed
In serpent, inmate bad, and toward Eve
Addressed his way, not with indented wave,
Prone on the ground, as since, but on his rear,
Circular base of rising folds, that towered
Fold above fold a surging maze, his head
Crested aloft, and carbuncle his eyes;   500
With burnished neck of verdant gold, erect
Amidst his circling spires, that on the grass
Floated redundant: pleasing was his shape,
And lovely, never since of serpent kind
Lovelier, not those that in Illyria changed
Hermione and Cadmus, or the god
In Epidaurus; nor to which transformed
Ammonian Jove, or Capitoline was seen,
He with Olympias, this with her who bore
Scipio the height of Rome. With tract oblique   510
At first, as one who sought access, but feared
To interrupt, sidelong he works his way.
As when a ship by skilful steersman wrought
Nigh river's mouth or foreland, where the wind
Veers oft, as oft so steers, and shifts her sail;
So varied he, and of his tortuous train
Curled many a wanton wreath in sight of Eve,
To lure her eye; she busied heard the sound
Of rustling leaves, but minded not, as used

To such disport before her through the field,　　520
From every beast, more duteous at her call,
Than at Circean call the herd disguised.
He bolder now, uncalled before her stood;
But as in gaze admiring: oft he bowed
His turret crest, and sleek enamelled neck,
Fawning, and licked the ground whereon she trod.
His gentle dumb expression turned at length
The eye of Eve to mark his play; he glad
Of her attention gained, with serpent tongue
Organic, or impulse of vocal air,　　530
His fraudulent temptation thus began.
　　Wonder not, sovereign mistress, if perhaps
Thou canst, who art sole wonder, much less arm
Thy looks, the heaven of mildness, with disdain,
Displeased that I approach thee thus, and gaze
Insatiate, I thus single, nor have feared
Thy awful brow, more awful thus retired.
Fairest resemblance of thy maker fair,
Thee all things living gaze on, all things thine
By gift, and thy celestial beauty adore　　540
With ravishment beheld, there best beheld
Where universally admired; but here
In this enclosure wild, these beasts among,
Beholders rude, and shallow to discern
Half what in thee is fair, one man except,
Who sees thee? (and what is one?) who shouldst be seen
A goddess among gods, adored and served
By angels numberless, thy daily train.
　　So glozed the tempter, and his proem tuned;
Into the heart of Eve his words made way,　　550
Though at the voice much marvelling; at length
Not unamazed she thus in answer spake.
What may this mean? Language of man pronounced
By tongue of brute, and human sense expressed?
The first at least of these I thought denied
To beasts, whom God on their creation-day
Created mute to all articulate sound;
The latter I demur, for in their looks
Much reason, and in their actions oft appears.
Thee, serpent, subtlest beast of all the field　　560

I knew, but not with human voice endued;
Redouble then this miracle, and say,
How cam'st thou speakable of mute, and how
To me so friendly grown above the rest
Of brutal kind, that daily are in sight?
Say, for such wonder claims attention due.
    To whom the guileful tempter thus replied.
Empress of this fair world, resplendent Eve,
Easy to me it is to tell thee all
What thou command'st, and right thou shouldst be obeyed: 570
I was at first as other beasts that graze
The trodden herb, of abject thoughts and low,
As was my food, nor aught but food discerned
Or sex, and apprehended nothing high:
Till on a day roving the field, I chanced
A goodly tree far distant to behold
Loaden with fruit of fairest colours mixed,
Ruddy and gold: I nearer drew to gaze;
When from the boughs a savoury odour blown,
Grateful to appetite, more pleased my sense   580
Than smell of sweetest fennel, or the teats
Of ewe or goat dropping with milk at even,
Unsucked of lamb or kid, that tend their play.
To satisfy the sharp desire I had
Of tasting those fair apples, I resolved
Not to defer; hunger and thirst at once,
Powerful persuaders, quickened at the scent
Of that alluring fruit, urged me so keen.
About the mossy trunk I wound me soon,
For high from ground the branches would require   590
Thy utmost reach or Adam's: round the tree
All other beasts that saw, with like desire
Longing and envying stood, but could not reach.
Amid the tree now got, where plenty hung
Tempting so nigh, to pluck and eat my fill
I spared not, for such pleasure till that hour
At feed or fountain never had I found.
Sated at length, ere long I might perceive
Strange alteration in me, to degree
Of reason in my inward powers, and speech   600
Wanted not long, though to this shape retained.

Thenceforth to speculations high or deep
I turned my thoughts, and with capacious mind
Considered all things visible in heaven,
Or earth, or middle, all things fair and good;
But all that fair and good in thy divine
Semblance, and in thy beauty's heavenly ray
United I beheld; no fair to thine
Equivalent or second, which compelled
Me thus, though importune perhaps, to come   610
And gaze, and worship thee of right declared
Sovereign of creatures, universal dame.
    So talked the spirited sly snake; and Eve
Yet more amazed unwary thus replied.
    Serpent, thy overpraising leaves in doubt
The virtue of that fruit, in thee first proved:
But say, where grows the tree, from hence how far?
For many are the trees of God that grow
In Paradise, and various, yet unknown
To us, in such abundance lies our choice,   620
As leaves a greater store of fruit untouched,
Still hanging incorruptible, till men
Grow up to their provision, and more hands
Help to disburden nature of her birth.
    To whom the wily adder, blithe and glad.
Empress, the way is ready, and not long,
Beyond a row of myrtles, on a flat,
Fast by a fountain, one small thicket past
Of blowing myrrh and balm; if thou accept
My conduct, I can bring thee thither soon.   630
    Lead then, said Eve. He leading swiftly rolled
In tangles, and made intricate seem straight,
To mischief swift. Hope elevates, and joy
Brightens his crest, as when a wandering fire,
Compact of unctuous vapour, which the night
Condenses, and the cold environs round,
Kindled through agitation to a flame,
Which oft, they say, some evil spirit attends
Hovering and blazing with delusive light,
Misleads the amazed night-wanderer from his way   640
To bogs and mires, and oft through pond or pool,
There swallowed up and lost, from succour far.

So glistered the dire snake, and into fraud
Led Eve our credulous mother, to the tree
Of prohibition, root of all our woe;
Which when she saw, thus to her guide she spake.

   Serpent, we might have spared our coming hither,
Fruitless to me, though fruit be here to excess,
The credit of whose virtue rest with thee,
Wondrous indeed, if cause of such effects.   650
But of this tree we may not taste nor touch;
God so commanded, and left that command
Sole daughter of his voice; the rest, we live
Law to our selves, our reason is our law.

   To whom the tempter guilefully replied.
Indeed? hath God then said that of the fruit
Of all these garden trees ye shall not eat,
Yet lords declared of all in earth or air?

   To whom thus Eve yet sinless. Of the fruit
Of each tree in the garden we may eat,   660
But of the fruit of this fair tree amidst
The garden, God hath said, Ye shall not eat
Thereof, nor shall ye touch it, lest ye die.

   She scarce had said, though brief, when now more bold
The tempter, but with show of zeal and love
To man, and indignation at his wrong,
New part puts on, and as to passion moved,
Fluctuates disturbed, yet comely and in act
Raised, as of some great matter to begin.
As when of old some orator renowned   670
In Athens or free Rome, where eloquence
Flourished, since mute, to some great cause addressed,
Stood in himself collected, while each part,
Motion, each act won audience ere the tongue,
Sometimes in height began, as no delay
Of preface brooking through his zeal of right.
So standing, moving, or to height upgrown
The tempter all impassioned thus began.

   O sacred, wise, and wisdom-giving plant,
Mother of science, now I feel thy power   680
Within me clear, not only to discern
Things in their causes, but to trace the ways
Of highest agents, deemed however wise.

Queen of this universe, do not believe
Those rigid threats of death; ye shall not die:
How should ye? by the fruit? it gives you life
To knowledge: by the threatener? look on me,
Me who have touched and tasted, yet both live,
And life more perfect have attained than fate
Meant me, by venturing higher than my lot.   690
Shall that be shut to man, which to the beast
Is open? or will God incense his ire
For such a petty trespass, and not praise
Rather your dauntless virtue, whom the pain
Of death denounced, whatever thing death be,
Deterred not from achieving what might lead
To happier life, knowledge of good and evil;
Of good, how just? of evil, if what is evil
Be real, why not known, since easier shunned?
God therefore cannot hurt ye, and be just;   700
Not just, not God; not feared then, nor obeyed:
Your fear itself of death removes the fear.
Why then was this forbid? Why but to awe,
Why but to keep ye low and ignorant,
His worshipper; he knows that in the day
Ye eat thereof, your eyes that seem so clear,
Yet are but dim, shall perfectly be then
Opened and cleared, and ye shall be as gods,
Knowing both good and evil as they know.
That ye should be as gods, since I as man,   710
Internal man, is but proportion meet,
I of brute human, ye of human gods.
So ye shall die perhaps, by putting off
Human, to put on gods, death to be wished,
Though threatened, which no worse than this can bring.
And what are gods that man may not become
As they, participating godlike food?
The gods are first, and that advantage use
On our belief, that all from them proceeds;
I question it, for this fair earth I see,   720
Warmed by the sun, producing every kind,
Them nothing: if they all things, who enclosed
Knowledge of good and evil in this tree,
That whoso eats thereof, forthwith attains

Wisdom without their leave? and wherein lies
The offence, that man should thus attain to know?
What can your knowledge hurt him, or this tree
Impart against his will if all be his?
Or is it envy, and can envy dwell
In heavenly breasts? these, these and many more   730
Causes import your need of this fair fruit.
Goddess humane, reach then, and freely taste.

   He ended, and his words replete with guile
Into her heart too easy entrance won:
Fixed on the fruit she gazed, which to behold
Might tempt alone, and in her ears the sound
Yet rung of his persuasive words, impregned
With reason, to her seeming, and with truth;
Meanwhile the hour of noon drew on, and waked
An eager appetite, raised by the smell   740
So savoury of that fruit, which with desire,
Inclinable now grown to touch or taste,
Solicited her longing eye; yet first
Pausing a while, thus to her self she mused.

   Great are thy virtues, doubtless, best of fruits,
Though kept from man, and worthy to be admired,
Whose taste, too long forborne, at first assay
Gave elocution to the mute, and taught
The tongue not made for speech to speak thy praise:
Thy praise he also who forbids thy use,   750
Conceals not from us, naming thee the tree
Of knowledge, knowledge both of good and evil;
Forbids us then to taste, but his forbidding
Commends thee more, while it infers the good
By thee communicated, and our want:
For good unknown, sure is not had, or had
And yet unknown, is as not had at all.
In plain then, what forbids he but to know,
Forbids us good, forbids us to be wise?
Such prohibitions bind not. But if death   760
Bind us with after-bands, what profits then
Our inward freedom? In the day we eat
Of this fair fruit, our doom is, we shall die.
How dies the serpent? he hath eaten and lives,
And knows, and speaks, and reasons, and discerns,

Irrational till then. For us alone
Was death invented? or to us denied
This intellectual food, for beasts reserved?
For beasts it seems: yet that one beast which first
Hath tasted, envies not, but brings with joy   770
The good befallen him, author unsuspect,
Friendly to man, far from deceit or guile.
What fear I then, rather what know to fear
Under this ignorance of good and evil,
Of God or death, of law or penalty?
Here grows the cure of all, this fruit divine,
Fair to the eye, inviting to the taste,
Of virtue to make wise: what hinders then
To reach, and feed at once both body and mind?
    So saying, her rash hand in evil hour   780
Forth reaching to the fruit, she plucked, she ate:
Earth felt the wound, and nature from her seat
Sighing through all her works gave signs of woe,
That all was lost. Back to the thicket slunk
The guilty serpent, and well might, for Eve
Intent now wholly on her taste, naught else
Regarded, such delight till then, as seemed,
In fruit she never tasted, whether true
Or fancied so, through expectation high
Of knowledge, nor was godhead from her thought.   790
Greedily she engorged without restraint,
And knew not eating death: satiate at length,
And heightened as with wine, jocund and boon,
Thus to herself she pleasingly began.
    O sovereign, virtuous, precious of all trees
In Paradise, of operation blessed
To sapience, hitherto obscured, infamed,
And thy fair fruit let hang, as to no end
Created; but henceforth my early care,
Not without song, each morning, and due praise   800
Shall tend thee, and the fertile burden ease
Of thy full branches offered free to all;
Till dieted by thee I grow mature
In knowledge, as the gods who all things know;
Though others envy what they cannot give;
For had the gift been theirs, it had not here

Thus grown. Experience, next to thee I owe,
Best guide; not following thee, I had remained
In ignorance, thou open'st wisdom's way,
And giv'st access, though secret she retire.   810
And I perhaps am secret; heaven is high,
High and remote to see from thence distinct
Each thing on earth; and other care perhaps
May have diverted from continual watch
Our great forbidder, safe with all his spies
About him. But to Adam in what sort
Shall I appear? shall I to him make known
As yet my change, and give him to partake
Full happiness with me, or rather not,
But keep the odds of knowledge in my power   820
Without copartner? so to add what wants
In female sex, the more to draw his love,
And render me more equal, and perhaps,
A thing not undesirable, sometime
Superior; for inferior who is free?
This may be well: but what if God have seen,
And death ensue? then I shall be no more,
And Adam wedded to another Eve,
Shall live with her enjoying, I extinct;
A death to think. Confirmed then I resolve,   830
Adam shall share with me in bliss or woe:
So dear I love him, that with him all deaths
I could endure, without him live no life.

   So saying, from the tree her step she turned,
But first low reverence done, as to the power
That dwelt within, whose presence had infused
Into the plant sciential sap, derived
From nectar, drink of gods. Adam the while
Waiting desirous her return, had wove
Of choicest flowers a garland to adorn   840
Her tresses, and her rural labours crown,
As reapers oft are wont their harvest queen.
Great joy he promised to his thoughts, and new
Solace in her return, so long delayed;
Yet oft his heart, divine of something ill,
Misgave him; he the faltering measure felt;
And forth to meet her went, the way she took

That morn when first they parted; by the tree
Of knowledge he must pass, there he her met,
Scarce from the tree returning; in her hand   850
A bough of fairest fruit that downy smiled,
New gathered, and ambrosial smell diffused.
To him she hasted, in her face excuse
Came prologue, and apology to prompt,
Which with bland words at will she thus addressed.
    Hast thou not wondered, Adam, at my stay?
Thee I have missed, and thought it long, deprived
Thy presence, agony of love till now
Not felt, nor shall be twice, for never more
Mean I to try, what rash untried I sought,   860
The pain of absence from thy sight. But strange
Hath been the cause, and wonderful to hear:
This tree is not as we are told, a tree
Of danger tasted, nor to evil unknown
Opening the way, but of divine effect
To open eyes, and make them gods who taste;
And hath been tasted such: the serpent wise,
Or not restrained as we, or not obeying,
Hath eaten of the fruit, and is become,
Not dead, as we are threatened, but thenceforth   870
Endued with human voice and human sense,
Reasoning to admiration, and with me
Persuasively hath so prevailed, that I
Have also tasted, and have also found
The effects to correspond, opener mine eyes,
Dim erst, dilated spirits, ampler heart,
And growing up to godhead; which for thee
Chiefly I sought, without thee can despise.
For bliss, as thou hast part, to me is bliss,
Tedious, unshared with thee, and odious soon.   880
Thou therefore also taste, that equal lot
May join us, equal joy, as equal love;
Lest thou not tasting, different degree
Disjoin us, and I then too late renounce
Deity for thee, when fate will not permit.
    Thus Eve with countenance blithe her story told;
But in her cheek distemper flushing glowed.
On the other side, Adam, soon as he heard

The fatal trespass done by Eve, amazed,
Astonied stood and blank, while horror chill   890
Ran through his veins, and all his joints relaxed;
From his slack hand the garland wreathed for Eve
Down dropped, and all the faded roses shed:
Speechless he stood and pale, till thus at length
First to himself he inward silence broke.

    O fairest of creation, last and best
Of all God's works, creature in whom excelled
Whatever can to sight or thought be formed,
Holy, divine, good, amiable or sweet!
How art thou lost, how on a sudden lost,   900
Defaced, deflowered, and now to death devote?
Rather how hast thou yielded to transgress
The strict forbiddance, how to violate
The sacred fruit forbidden! some cursed fraud
Of enemy hath beguiled thee, yet unknown,
And me with thee hath ruined, for with thee
Certain my resolution is to die;
How can I live without thee, how forgo
Thy sweet converse and love so dearly joined,
To live again in these wild woods forlorn?   910
Should God create another Eve, and I
Another rib afford, yet loss of thee
Would never from my heart; no no, I feel
The link of nature draw me: flesh of flesh,
Bone of my bone thou art, and from thy state
Mine never shall be parted, bliss or woe.

    So having said, as one from sad dismay
Recomforted, and after thoughts disturbed
Submitting to what seemed remediless,
Thus in calm mood his words to Eve he turned.   920

    Bold deed thou hast presumed, adventurous Eve,
And peril great provoked, who thus hath dared
Had it been only coveting to eye
That sacred fruit, sacred to abstinence,
Much more to taste it under ban to touch.
But past who can recall, or done undo?
Not God omnipotent, nor fate, yet so
Perhaps thou shalt not die, perhaps the fact
Is not so heinous now, foretasted fruit,

Profaned first by the serpent, by him first   930
Made common and unhallowed ere our taste;
Nor yet on him found deadly, he yet lives,
Lives, as thou saidst, and gains to live as man
Higher degree of life, inducement strong
To us, as likely tasting to attain
Proportional ascent, which cannot be
But to be gods, or angels demigods.
Nor can I think that God, creator wise,
Though threatening, will in earnest so destroy
Us his prime creatures, dignified so high,   940
Set over all his works, which in our fall,
For us created, needs with us must fail,
Dependent made; so God shall uncreate,
Be frustrate, do, undo, and labour lose,
Not well conceived of God, who though his power
Creation could repeat, yet would be loath
Us to abolish, lest the adversary
Triumph and say, Fickle their state whom God
Most favours, who can please him long; me first
He ruined, now mankind; whom will he next?   950
Matter of scorn, not to be given the foe,
However I with thee have fixed my lot,
Certain to undergo like doom, if death
Consort with thee, death is to me as life;
So forcible within my heart I feel
The bond of nature draw me to my own,
My own in thee, for what thou art is mine;
Our state cannot be severed, we are one,
One flesh; to lose thee were to lose my self.

   So Adam, and thus Eve to him replied.   960
O glorious trial of exceeding love,
Illustrious evidence, example high!
Engaging me to emulate, but short
Of thy perfection, how shall I attain,
Adam, from whose dear side I boast me sprung,
And gladly of our union hear thee speak,
One heart, one soul in both; whereof good proof
This day affords, declaring thee resolved,
Rather than death or aught than death more dread
Shall separate us, linked in love so dear,   970

To undergo with me one guilt, one crime,
If any be, of tasting this fair fruit,
Whose virtue, for of good still good proceeds,
Direct, or by occasion hath presented
This happy trial of thy love, which else
So eminently never had been known.
Were it I thought death menaced would ensue
This my attempt, I would sustain alone
The worst, and not persuade thee rather die
Deserted, than oblige thee with a fact   980
Pernicious to thy peace, chiefly assured
Remarkably so late of thy so true,
So faithful love unequalled; but I feel
Far otherwise the event, not death, but life
Augmented, opened eyes, new hopes, new joys,
Taste so divine, that what of sweet before
Hath touched my sense, flat seems to this, and harsh.
On my experience, Adam, freely taste,
And fear of death deliver to the winds.
      So saying, she embraced him, and for joy   990
Tenderly wept, much won that he his love
Had so ennobled, as of choice to incur
Divine displeasure for her sake, or death.
In recompense (for such compliance bad
Such recompense best merits) from the bough
She gave him of that fair enticing fruit
With liberal hand: he scrupled not to eat
Against his better knowledge, not deceived,
But fondly overcome with female charm.
Earth trembled from her entrails, as again   1000
In pangs, and nature gave a second groan,
Sky loured and muttering thunder, some sad drops
Wept at completing of the mortal sin
Original; while Adam took no thought,
Eating his fill, nor Eve to iterate
Her former trespass feared, the more to soothe
Him with her loved society, that now
As with new wine intoxicated both
They swim in mirth, and fancy that they feel
Divinity within them breeding wings   1010
Wherewith to scorn the earth: but that false fruit

Far other operation first displayed,
Carnal desire inflaming, he on Eve
Began to cast lascivious eyes, she him
As wantonly repaid; in lust they burn:
Till Adam thus gan Eve to dalliance move.
  Eve, now I see thou art exact of taste,
And elegant, of sapience no small part,
Since to each meaning savour we apply,
And palate call judicious; I the praise   1020
Yield thee, so well this day thou hast purveyed.
Much pleasure we have lost, while we abstained
From this delightful fruit, nor known till now
True relish, tasting; if such pleasure be
In things to us forbidden, it might be wished,
For this one tree had been forbidden ten.
But come, so well refreshed, now let us play,
As meet is, after such delicious fare;
For never did thy beauty since the day
I saw thee first and wedded thee, adorned   1030
With all perfections, so inflame my sense
With ardour to enjoy thee, fairer now
Than ever, bounty of this virtuous tree.
  So said he, and forbore not glance or toy
Of amorous intent, well understood
Of Eve, whose eye darted contagious fire.
Her hand he seized, and to a shady bank,
Thick overhead with verdant roof embowered
He led her nothing loath; flowers were the couch,
Pansies, and violets, and asphodel,   1040
And hyacinth, earth's freshest softest lap.
There they their fill of love and love's disport
Took largely, of their mutual guilt the seal,
The solace of their sin, till dewy sleep
Oppressed them, wearied with their amorous play.
Soon as the force of that fallacious fruit,
That with exhilarating vapour bland
About their spirits had played, and inmost powers
Made err, was now exhaled, and grosser sleep
Bred of unkindly fumes, with conscious dreams   1050
Encumbered, now had left them, up they rose
As from unrest, and each the other viewing,

Soon found their eyes how opened, and their minds
How darkened; innocence, that as a veil
Had shadowed them from knowing ill, was gone,
Just confidence, and native righteousness
And honour from about them, naked left
To guilty shame he covered, but his robe
Uncovered more, so rose the Danite strong
Herculean Samson from the harlot-lap   1060
Of Philistean Dalilah, and waked
Shorn of his strength, they destitute and bare
Of all their virtue: silent, and in face
Confounded long they sat, as stricken mute,
Till Adam, though not less than Eve abashed,
At length gave utterance to these words constrained.
   O Eve, in evil hour thou didst give ear
To that false worm, of whomsoever taught
To counterfeit man's voice, true in our fall,
False in our promised rising; since our eyes   1070
Opened we find indeed, and find we know
Both good and evil, good lost, and evil got,
Bad fruit of knowledge, if this be to know,
Which leaves us naked thus, of honour void,
Of innocence, of faith, of purity,
Our wonted ornaments now soiled and stained,
And in our faces evident the signs
Of foul concupiscence; whence evil store;
Even shame, the last of evils; of the first
Be sure then. How shall I behold the face   1080
Henceforth of God or angel, erst with joy
And rapture so oft beheld? those heavenly shapes
Will dazzle now this earthly, with their blaze
Insufferably bright. O might I here
In solitude live savage, in some glade
Obscured, where highest woods impenetrable
To star or sunlight, spread their umbrage broad
And brown as evening: cover me ye pines,
Ye cedars, with innumerable boughs
Hide me, where I may never see them more.   1090
But let us now, as in bad plight, devise
What best may for the present serve to hide
The parts of each from other, that seem most

To shame obnoxious, and unseemliest seen,
Some tree whose broad smooth leaves together sewed,
And girded on our loins, may cover round
Those middle parts, that this newcomer, shame,
There sit not, and reproach us as unclean.
    So counselled he, and both together went
Into the thickest wood, there soon they chose   1100
The fig-tree, not that kind for fruit renowned,
But such as at this day to Indians known
In Malabar or Deccan spreads her arms
Branching so broad and long, that in the ground
The bended twigs take root, and daughters grow
About the mother tree, a pillared shade
High overarched, and echoing walks between;
There oft the Indian herdsman shunning heat
Shelters in cool, and tends his pasturing herds
At loopholes cut through thickest shade: those leaves   1110
They gathered, broad as Amazonian targe,
And with what skill they had, together sewed,
To gird their waist, vain covering if to hide
Their guilt and dreaded shame; O how unlike
To that first naked glory. Such of late
Columbus found the American so girt
With feathered cincture, naked else and wild
Among the trees on isles and woody shores.
Thus fenced, and as they thought, their shame in part
Covered, but not at rest or ease of mind,   1120
They sat them down to weep, nor only tears
Rained at their eyes, but high winds worse within
Began to rise, high passions, anger, hate,
Mistrust, suspicion, discord, and shook sore
Their inward state of mind, calm region once
And full of peace, now tossed and turbulent:
For understanding ruled not, and the will
Heard not her lore, both in subjection now
To sensual appetite, who from beneath
Usurping over sovereign reason claimed   1130
Superior sway: from thus distempered breast,
Adam, estranged in look and altered style,
Speech intermitted thus to Eve renewed.
    Would thou hadst hearkened to my words, and stayed

With me, as I besought thee, when that strange
Desire of wandering this unhappy morn,
I know not whence possessed thee; we had then
Remained still happy, not as now, despoiled
Of all our good, shamed, naked, miserable.
Let none henceforth seek needless cause to approve   1140
The faith they owe; when earnestly they seek
Such proof, conclude, they then begin to fail.
    To whom soon moved with touch of blame thus Eve.
What words have passed thy lips, Adam severe,
Imput'st thou that to my default, or will
Of wandering, as thou call'st it, which who knows
But might as ill have happened thou being by,
Or to thy self perhaps: hadst thou been there,
Or here the attempt, thou couldst not have discerned
Fraud in the serpent, speaking as he spake;   1150
No ground of enmity between us known,
Why he should mean me ill, or seek to harm.
Was I to have never parted from thy side?
As good have grown there still a lifeless rib.
Being as I am, why didst not thou the head
Command me absolutely not to go,
Going into such danger as thou saidst?
Too facile then thou didst not much gainsay,
Nay didst permit, approve, and fair dismiss.
Hadst thou been firm and fixed in thy dissent,   1160
Neither had I transgressed, nor thou with me.
    To whom then first incensed Adam replied,
Is this the love, is this the recompense
Of mine to thee, ingrateful Eve, expressed
Immutable when thou wert lost, not I,
Who might have lived and joyed immortal bliss,
Yet willingly chose rather death with thee:
And am I now upbraided, as the cause
Of thy transgressing? not enough severe,
It seems, in thy restraint: what could I more?   1170
I warned thee, I admonished thee, foretold
The danger, and the lurking enemy
That lay in wait; beyond this had been force,
And force upon free will hath here no place.
But confidence then bore thee on, secure

Either to meet no danger, or to find
Matter of glorious trial; and perhaps
I also erred in overmuch admiring
What seemed in thee so perfect, that I thought
No evil durst attempt thee, but I rue   1180
That error now, which is become my crime,
And thou the accuser. Thus it shall befall
Him who to worth in women overtrusting
Lets her will rule; restraint she will not brook,
And left to herself, if evil thence ensue,
She first his weak indulgence will accuse.
　　Thus they in mutual accusation spent
The fruitless hours, but neither self-condemning,
And of their vain contest appeared no end.

From Book X

[CHRIST DESCENDS TO EDEN]

Down he descended straight; the speed of gods   90
Time counts not, though with swiftest minutes winged.
Now was the sun in western cadence low
From noon, and gentle airs due at their hour
To fan the earth now waked, and usher in
The evening cool when he from wrath more cool
Came the mild judge and intercessor both
To sentence man: the voice of God they heard
Now walking in the garden, by soft winds
Brought to their ears, while day declined, they heard,
And from his presence hid themselves among   100
The thickest trees, both man and wife, till God
Approaching, thus to Adam called aloud.
　　Where art thou Adam, wont with joy to meet
My coming seen far off? I miss thee here,
Not pleased, thus entertained with solitude,
Where obvious duty erewhile appeared unsought:
Or come I less conspicuous, or what change
Absents thee, or what chance detains? Come forth.
He came, and with him Eve, more loath, though first

To offend, discountenanced both, and discomposed;
Love was not in their looks, either to God
Or to each other, but apparent guilt,
And shame, and perturbation, and despair,
Anger, and obstinacy, and hate, and guile.
Whence Adam faltering long, thus answered brief.
   I heard thee in the garden, and of thy voice
Afraid, being naked, hid myself. To whom
The gracious judge without revile replied.
   My voice thou oft hast heard, and hast not feared,
But still rejoiced, how is it now become   120
So dreadful to thee? that thou art naked, who
Hath told thee? hast thou eaten of the tree
Whereof I gave thee charge thou shouldst not eat?
   To whom thus Adam sore beset replied.
O heaven! in evil strait this day I stand
Before my judge, either to undergo
My self the total crime, or to accuse
My other self, the partner of my life;
Whose failing, while her faith to me remains,
I should conceal, and not expose to blame   130
By my complaint; but strict necessity
Subdues me, and calamitous constraint
Lest on my head both sin and punishment,
However insupportable, be all
Devolved; though should I hold my peace, yet thou
Wouldst easily detect what I conceal.
This woman whom thou mad'st to be my help,
And gav'st me as thy perfect gift, so good,
So fit, so acceptable, so divine,
That from her hand I could suspect no ill,   140
And what she did, whatever in itself,
Her doing seemed to justify the deed;
She gave me of the tree, and I did eat.
   To whom the sovereign presence thus replied.
Was she thy God, that her thou didst obey
Before his voice, or was she made thy guide,
Superior, or but equal, that to her
Thou didst resign thy manhood, and the place
Wherein God set thee above her made of thee,
And for thee, whose perfection far excelled   150

Hers in all real dignity: adorned
She was indeed, and lovely to attract
Thy love, not thy subjection, and her gifts
Were such as under government well seemed,
Unseemly to bear rule, which was thy part
And person, hadst thou known thyself aright.
   So having said, he thus to Eve in few:
Say woman, what is this which thou hast done?
   To whom sad Eve with shame nigh overwhelmed,
Confessing soon, yet not before her judge   160
Bold or loquacious, thus abashed replied.
   The serpent me beguiled and I did eat.
   Which when the Lord God heard, without delay
To judgment he proceeded on the accused
Serpent though brute, unable to transfer
The guilt on him who made him instrument
Of mischief, and polluted from the end
Of his creation; justly then accursed,
As vitiated in nature: more to know
Concerned not man (since he no further knew)   170
Nor altered his offence; yet God at last
To Satan first in sin his doom applied,
Though in mysterious terms, judged as then best:
And on the serpent thus his curse let fall.
   Because thou hast done this, thou art accursed
Above all cattle, each beast of the field;
Upon thy belly grovelling thou shalt go,
And dust shalt eat all the days of thy life.
Between thee and the woman I will put
Enmity, and between thine and her seed;   180
Her seed shall bruise thy head, thou bruise his heel.
   So spake this oracle, then verified
When Jesus son of Mary second Eve,
Saw Satan fall like lightning down from heaven,
Prince of the air; then rising from his grave
Spoiled principalities and powers, triumphed
In open show, and with ascension bright
Captivity led captive through the air,
The realm itself of Satan long usurped,
Whom he shall tread at last under our feet;   190
Even he who now foretold his fatal bruise,

And to the woman thus his sentence turned.
　　Thy sorrow I will greatly multiply
By thy conception; children thou shalt bring
In sorrow forth, and to thy husband's will
Thine shall submit, he over thee shall rule.
　　On Adam last thus judgment he pronounced.
Because thou hast hearkened to the voice of thy wife,
And eaten of the tree concerning which
I charged thee, saying: Thou shalt not eat thereof,　　200
Cursed is the ground for thy sake, thou in sorrow
Shalt eat thereof all the days of thy life;
Thorns also and thistles it shall bring thee forth
Unbid, and thou shalt eat the herb of the field,
In the sweat of thy face shalt thou eat bread,
Till thou return unto the ground, for thou
Out of the ground wast taken, know thy birth,
For dust thou art, and shalt to dust return.
　　So judged he man, both judge and saviour sent,
And the instant stroke of death denounced that day　　210
Removed far off; then pitying how they stood
Before him naked to the air, that now
Must suffer change, disdained not to begin
Thenceforth the form of servant to assume,
As when he washed his servants' feet so now
As father of his family he clad
Their nakedness with skins of beasts, or slain,
Or as the snake with youthful coat repaid;
And thought not much to clothe his enemies:
Nor he their outward only with the skins　　220
Of beasts, but inward nakedness, much more
Opprobrious, with his robe of righteousness,
Arraying covered from his father's sight.
　　　·　　·　　·　　·　　·　　·　　·

From Book XII

[ADAM TO MICHAEL]

How soon hath thy prediction, seer blessed,
Measured this transient world, the race of time,
Till time stand fixed: beyond is all abyss,
Eternity, whose end no eye can reach.
Greatly instructed I shall hence depart,
Greatly in peace of thought, and have my fill
Of knowledge, what this vessel can contain;
Beyond which was my folly to aspire.   560
Henceforth I learn, that to obey is best,
And love with fear the only God, to walk
As in his presence, ever to observe
His providence, and on him sole depend,
Merciful over all his works, with good
Still overcoming evil, and by small
Accomplishing great things, by things deemed weak
Subverting worldly strong, and worldly wise
By simply meek; that suffering for truth's sake
Is fortitude to highest victory,   570
And to the faithful death the gate of life;
Taught this by his example whom I now
Acknowledge my redeemer ever blessed.
   To whom thus also the angel last replied:
This having learned, thou hast attained the sum
Of wisdom; hope no higher, though all the stars
Thou knew'st by name, and all the ethereal powers,
All secrets of the deep, all nature's works,
Or works of God in heaven, air, earth, or sea,
And all the riches of this world enjoyed'st,   580
And all the rule, one empire; only add
Deeds to thy knowledge answerable, add faith,
Add virtue, patience, temperance, add love,
By name to come called Charity, the soul
Of all the rest: then wilt thou not be loath
To leave this Paradise, but shalt possess
A paradise within thee, happier far.
Let us descend now therefore from this top

Of speculation; for the hour precise
Exacts our parting hence; and see the guards,   590
By me encamped on yonder hill, expect
Their motion, at whose front a flaming sword,
In signal of remove, waves fiercely round;
We may no longer stay: go, waken Eve;
Her also I with gentle dreams have calmed
Portending good, and all her spirits composed
To meek submission: thou at season fit
Let her with thee partake what thou hast heard,
Chiefly what may concern her faith to know,
The great deliverance by her seed to come   600
(For by the woman's seed) on all mankind.
That ye may live, which will be many days,
Both in one faith unanimous though sad,
With cause for evils past, yet much more cheered
With meditation on the happy end.

   He ended, and they both descend the hill;
Descended, Adam to the bower where Eve
Lay sleeping ran before, but found her waked;
And thus with words not sad she him received.

   Whence thou return'st, and whither went'st, I know;   610
For God is also in sleep, and dreams advise,
Which he hath sent propitious, some great good
Presaging, since with sorrow and heart's distress
Wearied I fell asleep: but now lead on;
In me is no delay; with thee to go,
Is to stay here; without thee here to stay,
Is to go hence unwilling; thou to me
Art all things under heaven, all places thou,
Who for my wilful crime art banished hence.
This further consolation yet secure   620
I carry hence; though all by me is lost,
Such favour I unworthy am vouchsafed,
By me the promised seed shall all restore.

   So spake our mother Eve, and Adam heard
Well pleased, but answered not; for now too nigh
The archangel stood, and from the other hill
To their fixed station, all in bright array
The cherubim descended; on the ground
Gliding meteorous, as evening mist

Risen from a river o'er the marish glides,   630
And gathers ground fast at the labourer's heel
Homeward returning. High in front advanced,
The brandished sword of God before them blazed
Fierce as a comet; which with torrid heat,
And vapour as the Lybian air adust,
Began to parch that temperate clime; whereat
In either hand the hastening angel caught
Our lingering parents, and to the eastern gate
Led them direct, and down the cliff as fast
To the subjected plain; then disappeared.   640
They looking back, all the eastern side beheld
Of Paradise, so late their happy seat,
Waved over by that flaming brand, the gate
With dreadful faces thronged and fiery arms:
Some natural tears they dropped, but wiped them soon;
The world was all before them, where to choose
Their place of rest, and providence their guide:
They hand in hand with wandering steps and slow,
Through Eden took their solitary way.

SAMSON AGONISTES

OF THAT SORT OF DRAMATIC POEM
WHICH IS CALLED TRAGEDY

Tragedy, as it was anciently composed, hath been ever held the gravest, moralest, and most profitable of all other poems: therefore said by Aristotle to be of power by raising pity and fear, or terror, to purge the mind of those and such-like passions, that is to temper and reduce them to just measure with a kind of delight, stirred up by reading or seeing those passions well imitated. Nor is nature wanting in her own effects to make good his assertion: for so in physic things of melancholic hue and quality are used against melancholy, sour against sour, salt to remove salt humours. Hence philosophers and other gravest writers, as Cicero, Plutarch and others, frequently cite out of tragic poets, both to adorn and illustrate their discourse. The Apostle Paul himself thought it not unworthy to insert a verse of Euripides into the text of Holy Scripture, I Cor. 15: 33, and Paraeus commenting on the *Revelation*, divides the whole book as a tragedy, into acts distinguished each by a chorus of heavenly harpings and song between. Heretofore men in highest dignity have laboured not a little to be thought able to compose a tragedy. Of that honour Dionysius the elder was no less ambitious, than before of his attaining to the tyranny. Augustus Caesar also had begun his *Ajax*, but unable to please his own judgement with what he had begun, left it unfinished. Seneca the philosopher is by some thought the author of those tragedies (at least the best of them) that go under that name. Gregory Nazianzen a Father of the church, thought it not unbeseeming the sanctity of his person to write a tragedy, which he entitled, *Christ Suffering*. This is mentioned to vindicate tragedy from the small esteem, or rather infamy, which in the account of many it undergoes at this day with other common interludes; happening through the poet's error of intermixing comic stuff with tragic sadness and gravity; or introducing trivial and vulgar persons, which by all judicious hath been counted absurd; and brought in without discretion, corruptly to gratify the people. And though ancient tragedy use no prologue, yet using sometimes, in case of self-defence, or explanation, that which Martial calls an epistle; in behalf of this tragedy coming forth after the ancient manner, much different from what among us passes for best, thus much beforehand may be epistled; that chorus is here introduced after the Greek manner, not ancient only but modern, and still in use among the Italians. In the modelling therefore of this poem, with good reason, the ancients and Italians are rather followed, as of much more authority and fame. The measure of verse used in the chorus is of all sorts, called by the Greeks monostrophic, or rather *apolelymenon*, without regard had to strophe, antistrophe or epode, which were a kind of stanzas framed only for the music, then used with the chorus that sung; not essential to the poem, and therefore not material; or being divided into stanzas or pauses, they may be called *alleostropha*. Division into act and scene referring chiefly to the stage (to which this work never was intended) is here omitted. It suffices if the whole drama be found not produced beyond the fifth act.

Of the style and uniformity, and that commonly called the plot, whether intricate or explicit, which is nothing indeed but such economy, or disposition of the fable as may stand best with verisimilitude and decorum; they only will best judge who are not unacquainted with Aeschylus, Sophocles, and Euripides, the three tragic poets unequalled yet by any, and the best rule to all who endeavour to write tragedy. The circumscription of time wherein the whole drama begins and ends, is according to ancient rule, and best example, within the space of twenty-four hours.

THE ARGUMENT

Samson made captive, blind, and now in the prison at Gaza, there to labour as in a common workhouse, on a festival day, in the general cessation from labour, comes forth into the open air, to a place nigh, somewhat retired there to sit a while and bemoan his condition. Where he happens at length to be visited by certain friends and equals of his tribe, which make the Chorus, who seek to comfort him what they can; then by his old father Manoa, who endeavours the like, and withal tells him his purpose to procure his liberty by ransom; lastly, that this feast was proclaimed by the Philistines as a day of thanksgiving for their deliverance from the hands of Samson, which yet more troubles him. Manoa then departs to prosecute his endeavour with the Philistian lords for

Samson's redemption; who in the meanwhile is visited by other
persons; and lastly by a public officer to require his coming to the
feast before the lords and people, to play or show his strength in
their presence; he at first refuses, dismissing the public officer with
absolute denial to come; at length persuaded inwardly that this was
from God, he yields to go along with him, who came now the
second time with great threatenings to fetch him; the Chorus yet
remaining on the place, Manoa returns full of joyful hope, to
procure ere long his son's deliverance: in the midst of which
discourse an Hebrew comes in haste confusedly at first; and
afterward more distinctly relating the catastrophe, what Samson
had done to the Philistines, and by accident to himself; wherewith
the tragedy ends.

THE PERSONS

Samson
Manoa, the father of Samson
Dalila his wife
Harapha of Gath
Public Officer
Messenger
Chorus of Danites

The Scene before the Prison in Gaza

Sam. A little onward lend thy guiding hand
To these dark steps, a little further on;
For yonder bank hath choice of sun or shade,
There I am wont to sit, when any chance
Relieves me from my task of servile toil,
Daily in the common prison else enjoined me,
Where I a prisoner chained, scarce freely draw
The air imprisoned also, close and damp,
Unwholesome draught: but here I feel amends,
The breath of heaven fresh blowing, pure and sweet,   10
With day-spring born; here leave me to respire.
This day a solemn feast the people hold
To Dagon their sea-idol, and forbid
Laborious works, unwillingly this rest
Their superstition yields me; hence with leave
Retiring from the popular noise, I seek
This unfrequented place to find some ease,

Ease to the body some, none to the mind
From restless thoughts, that like a deadly swarm
Of hornets armed, no sooner found alone,   20
But rush upon me thronging, and present
Times past, what once I was, and what am now.
O wherefore was my birth from heaven foretold
Twice by an angel, who at last in sight
Of both my parents all in flames ascended
From off the altar, where an offering burned,
As in a fiery column charioting
His godlike presence, and from some great act
Or benefit revealed to Abraham's race?
Why was my breeding ordered and prescribed   30
As of a person separate to God,
Designed for great exploits; if I must die
Betrayed, captived, and both my eyes put out,
Made of my enemies the scorn and gaze;
To grind in brazen fetters under task
With this heaven-gifted strength? O glorious strength
Put to the labour of a beast, debased
Lower than bond-slave! Promise was that I
Should Israel from Philistian yoke deliver;
Ask for this great deliverer now, and find him   40
Eyeless in Gaza at the mill with slaves,
Himself in bonds under Philistian yoke;
Yet stay, let me not rashly call in doubt
Divine prediction; what if all foretold
Had been fulfilled but through mine own default,
Whom have I to complain of but myself?
Who this high gift of strength committed to me,
In what part lodged, how easily bereft me,
Under the seal of silence could not keep,
But weakly to a woman must reveal it,   50
O'ercome with importunity and tears.
O impotence of mind, in body strong!
But what is strength without a double share
Of wisdom, vast, unwieldy, burdensome,
Proudly secure, yet liable to fall
By weakest subtleties, not made to rule,
But to subserve where wisdom bears command.
God, when he gave me strength, to show withal

How slight the gift was, hung it in my hair.
But peace, I must not quarrel with the will   60
Of highest dispensation, which herein
Haply had ends above my reach to know:
Suffices that to me strength is my bane,
And proves the source of all my miseries;
So many, and so huge, that each apart
Would ask a life to wail, but chief of all,
O loss of sight, of thee I most complain!
Blind among enemies, O worse than chains,
Dungeon, or beggary, or decrepit age!
Light the prime work of God to me is extinct,   70
And all her various objects of delight
Annulled, which might in part my grief have eased,
Inferior to the vilest now become
Of man or worm; the vilest here excel me,
They creep, yet see, I dark in light exposed
To daily fraud, contempt, abuse and wrong,
Within doors, or without, still as a fool,
In power of others, never in my own;
Scarce half I seem to live, dead more than half.
O dark, dark, dark, amid the blaze of noon,   80
Irrecoverably dark, total eclipse
Without all hope of day!
O first-created beam, and thou great word,
Let there be light, and light was over all;
Why am I thus bereaved thy prime decree?
The sun to me is dark
And silent as the moon,
When she deserts the night
Hid in her vacant interlunar cave.
Since light so necessary is to life,   90
And almost life itself, if it be true
That light is in the soul,
She all in every part; why was the sight
To such a tender ball as the eye confined?
So obvious and so easy to be quenched,
And not as feeling through all parts diffused,
That she might look at will through every pore?
Then had I not been thus exiled from light;
As in the land of darkness yet in light,

To live a life half dead, a living death,   100
And buried; but O yet more miserable!
Myself, my sepulchre, a moving grave,
Buried, yet not exempt
By privilege of death and burial
From worst of other evils, pains and wrongs,
But made hereby obnoxious more
To all the miseries of life,
Life in captivity
Among inhuman foes.
But who are these? for with joint pace I hear   110
The tread of many feet steering this way;
Perhaps my enemies who come to stare
At my affliction, and perhaps to insult,
Their daily practice to afflict me more.
Chor. This, this is he; softly awhile,
Let us not break in upon him;
O change beyond report, thought, or belief!
See how he lies at random, carelessly diffused,
With languished head unpropped,
As one past hope, abandoned,   120
And by himself given over;
In slavish habit, ill-fitted weeds
O'er-worn and soiled;
Or do my eyes misrepresent? Can this be he,
That heroic, that renowned,
Irresistible Samson? whom unarmed
No strength of man, or fiercest wild beast could withstand;
Who tore the lion, as the lion tears the kid,
Ran on embattled armies clad in iron,
And weaponless himself,   130
Made arms ridiculous, useless the forgery
Of brazen shield and spear, the hammered cuirass,
Chalybean-tempered steel, and frock of mail
Adamantean proof;
But safest he who stood aloof,
When insupportably his foot advanced,
In scorn of their proud arms and warlike tools,
Spurned them to death by troops. The bold Ascalonite
Fled from his lion ramp, old warriors turned
Their plated backs under his heel;   140

Or grovelling soiled their crested helmets in the dust.
Then with what trivial weapon came to hand,
The jaw of a dead ass, his sword of bone,
A thousand foreskins fell, the flower of Palestine
In Ramath-lehi famous to this day:
Then by main force pulled up, and on his shoulders bore
The gates of Azza; post, and massy bar
Up to the hill by Hebron, seat of giants old,
No journey of a sabbath-day, and loaded so;
Like whom the Gentiles feign to bear up heaven.   150
Which shall I first bewail,
Thy bondage or lost sight,
Prison within prison
Inseparably dark?
Thou art become (O worst imprisonment!)
The dungeon of thyself; thy soul
(Which men enjoying sight oft without cause complain)
Imprisoned now indeed,
In real darkness of the body dwells,
Shut up from outward light   160
To incorporate with gloomy night;
For inward light alas
Puts forth no visual beam.
O mirror of our fickle state,
Since man on earth unparalleled!
The rarer thy example stands,
By how much from the top of wondrous glory,
Strongest of mortal men,
To lowest pitch of abject fortune thou art fallen.
For him I reckon not in high estate   170
Whom long descent of birth
Or the sphere of fortune raises;
But thee whose strength, while virtue was her mate,
Might have subdued the earth,
Universally crowned with highest praises.
Sam. I hear the sound of words, their sense the air
Dissolves unjointed ere it reach my ear.
Chor. He speaks, let us draw nigh. Matchless in might,
The glory late of Israel, now the grief;
We come thy friends and neighbours not unknown   180
From Eshtaol and Zora's fruitful vale

To visit or bewail thee, or if better,
Counsel or consolation we may bring,
Salve to thy sores, apt words have power to suage
The tumours of a troubled mind,
And are as balm to festered wounds.
Sam. Your coming, friends, revives me, for I learn
Now of my own experience, not by talk,
How counterfeit a coin they are who friends
Bear in their superscription (of the most   190
I would be understood), in prosperous days
They swarm, but in adverse withdraw their head
Not to be found, though sought. Ye see, O friends,
How many evils have enclosed me round;
Yet that which was the worst now least afflicts me,
Blindness, for had I sight, confused with shame,
How could I once look up, or heave the head,
Who like a foolish pilot have shipwrecked,
My vessel trusted to me from above,
Gloriously rigged; and for a word, a tear,   200
Fool, have divulged the secret gift of God
To a deceitful woman: tell me friends,
Am I not sung and proverbed for a fool
In every street, do they not say, how well
Are come upon him his deserts? yet why?
Immeasurable strength they might behold
In me, of wisdom nothing more than mean;
This with the other should, at least, have paired,
These two proportioned ill drove me transverse.
Chor. Tax not divine disposal, wisest men   210
Have erred, and by bad women been deceived;
And shall again, pretend they ne'er so wise.
Deject not then so overmuch thyself,
Who hast of sorrow thy full load besides;
Yet truth to say, I oft have heard men wonder
Why thou shouldst wed Philistian women rather
Than of thine own tribe fairer, or as fair,
At least of thy own nation, and as noble.
Sam. The first I saw at Timna, and she pleased
Me, not my parents, that I sought to wed,   220
The daughter of an infidel: they knew not
That what I motioned was of God; I knew

From intimate impulse, and therefore urged
The marriage on; that by occasion hence
I might begin Israel's deliverance,
The work to which I was divinely called;
She proving false, the next I took to wife
(O that I never had! fond wish too late)
Was in the vale of Sorec, Dalila,
That specious monster, my accomplished snare.   230
I thought it lawful from my former act,
And the same end; still watching to oppress
Israel's oppressors: of what now I suffer
She was not the prime cause, but I myself,
Who vanquished with a peal of words (O weakness!)
Gave up my fort of silence to a woman.
Chor. In seeking just occasion to provoke
The Philistine, thy country's enemy,
Thou never wast remiss, I bear thee witness:
Yet Israel still serves with all his sons.   240
Sam. That fault I take not on me, but transfer
On Israel's governors, and heads of tribes,
Who seeing those great acts which God had done
Singly by me against their conquerors
Acknowledged not, or not at all considered
Deliverance offered: I on the other side
Used no ambition to commend my deeds,
The deeds themselves, though mute, spoke loud the doer;
But they persisted deaf, and would not seem
To count them things worth notice, till at length   250
Their lords the Philistines with gathered powers
Entered Judea seeking me, who then
Safe to the rock of Etham was retired,
Not flying, but forecasting in what place
To set upon them, what advantaged best;
Meanwhile the men of Judah to prevent
The harass of their land, beset me round;
I willingly on some conditions came
Into their hands, and they as gladly yield me
To the uncircumcised a welcome prey,   260
Bound with two cords; but cords to me were threads
Touched with the flame: on their whole host I flew
Unarmed, and with a trivial weapon felled

Their choicest youth; they only lived who fled.
Had Judah that day joined, or one whole tribe,
They had by this possessed the towers of Gath,
And lorded over them whom now they serve;
But what more oft in nations grown corrupt,
And by their vices brought to servitude,
Than to love bondage more than liberty,   270
Bondage with ease than strenuous liberty;
And to despise, or envy, or suspect
Whom God hath of his special favour raised
As their deliverer; if he aught begin,
How frequent to desert him, and at last
To heap ingratitude on worthiest deeds?
Chor. Thy words to my remembrance bring
How Succoth and the fort of Penuel
Their great deliverer contemned,
The matchless Gideon in pursuit   280
Of Madian and her vanquished kings;
And how ingrateful Ephraim
Had dealt with Jephtha, who by argument,
Not worse than by his shield and spear
Defended Israel from the Ammonite,
Had not his prowess quelled their pride
In that sore battle when so many died
Without reprieve adjudged to death,
For want of well pronouncing *shibboleth*.
Sam. Of such examples add me to the roll,   290
Me easily indeed mine may neglect,
But God's proposed deliverance not so.
Chor. Just are the ways of God,
And justifiable to men;
Unless there be who think not God at all,
If any be, they walk obscure;
For of such doctrine never was there school,
But the heart of the fool,
And no man therein doctor but himself.
     Yet more there be who doubt his ways not just,   300
As to his own edicts, found contradicting,
Then give the reins to wandering thought,
Regardless of his glory's diminution;
Till by their own perplexities involved

They ravel more, still less resolved,
But never find self-satisfying solution.
   As if they would confine the interminable,
And tie him to his own prescript,
Who made our laws to bind us, not himself,
And hath full right to exempt   310
Whom so it pleases him by choice
From national obstriction, without taint
Of sin, or legal debt;
For with his own laws he can best dispense.
   He would not else who never wanted means,
Nor in respect of the enemy just cause
To set his people free,
Have prompted this heroic Nazarite,
Against his vow of strictest purity,
To seek in marriage that fallacious bride,   320
Unclean, unchaste.
   Down reason then, at least vain reasonings down,
Though reason here aver
That moral verdict quits her of unclean:
Unchaste was subsequent, her stain not his.
   But see here comes thy reverend sire
With careful step, locks white as down,
Old Manoa: advise
Forthwith how thou ought'st to receive him.
   Sam. Ay me, another inward grief awaked,   330
With mention of that name renews the assault.
Man. Brethren and men of Dan, for such ye seem,
Though in this uncouth place; if old respect,
As I suppose, towards your once gloried friend,
My son now captive, hither hath informed
Your younger feet, while mine cast back with age
Came lagging after; say if he be here.
Chor. As signal now in low dejected state,
As erst in highest, behold him where he lies.
Man. O miserable change! is this the man,   340
That invincible Samson, far renowned,
The dread of Israel's foes, who with a strength
Equivalent to angel's walked their streets,
None offering fight; who single combatant
Duelled their armies ranked in proud array,

Himself an army, now unequal match
To save himself against a coward armed
At one spear's length. O ever-failing trust
In mortal strength! and O what not in man
Deceivable and vain! Nay what thing good   350
Prayed for, but often proves our woe, our bane?
I prayed for children, and thought barrenness
In wedlock a reproach; I gained a son,
And such a son as all men hailed me happy;
Who would be now a father in my stead?
O wherefore did God grant me my request,
And as a blessing with such pomp adorned?
Why are his gifts desirable, to tempt
Our earnest prayers, then given with solemn hand
As graces, draw a scorpion's tail behind?   360
For this did the angel twice descend? for this
Ordained thy nurture holy, as of a plant;
Select, and sacred, glorious for awhile,
The miracle of men: then in an hour
Ensnared, assaulted, overcome, led bound,
Thy foes' derision, captive, poor, and blind
Into a dungeon thrust, to work with slaves?
Alas methinks whom God hath chosen once
To worthiest deeds, if he through frailty err,
He should not so o'erwhelm, and as a thrall   370
Subject him to so foul indignities,
Be it but for honour's sake of former deeds.
Sam. Appoint not heavenly disposition, father,
Nothing of all these evils hath befall'n me
But justly; I myself have brought them on,
Sole author I, sole cause: if aught seem vile,
As vile hath been my folly, who have profaned
The mystery of God given me under pledge
Of vow, and have betrayed it to a woman,
A Canaanite, my faithless enemy.   380
This well I knew, nor was at all surprised,
But warned by oft experience: did not she
Of Timna first betray me, and reveal
The secret wrested from me in her height
Of nuptial love professed, carrying it straight
To them who had corrupted her, my spies,

And rivals? In this other was there found
More faith? who also in her prime of love,
Spousal embraces, vitiated with gold,
Though offered only, by the scent conceived   390
Her spurious first-born; treason against me?
Thrice she assayed with flattering prayers and sighs,
And amorous reproaches to win from me
My capital secret, in what part my strength
Lay stored, in what part summed, that she might know:
Thrice I deluded her, and turned to sport
Her importunity, each time perceiving
How openly, and with what impudence
She purposed to betray me, and (which was worse
Than undissembled hate) with what contempt   400
She sought to make me traitor to myself;
Yet the fourth time, when mustering all her wiles,
With blandished parleys, feminine assaults,
Tongue-batteries, she surceased not day nor night
To storm me over-watched, and wearied out.
At times when men seek most repose and rest,
I yielded, and unlocked her all my heart,
Who with a grain of manhood well resolved
Might easily have shook off all her snares:
But foul effeminacy held me yoked   410
Her bond-slave; O indignity, O blot
To honour and religion! servile mind
Rewarded well with servile punishment!
The base degree to which I now am fall'n,
These rags, this grinding, is not yet so base
As was my former servitude, ignoble,
Unmanly, ignominious, infamous,
True slavery, and that blindness worse than this,
That saw not how degenerately I served.
Man. I cannot praise thy marriage-choices, son,   420
Rather approved them not; but thou didst plead
Divine impulsion prompting how thou might'st
Find some occasion to infest our foes.
I state not that; this I am sure; our foes
Found soon occasion thereby to make thee
Their captive, and their triumph; thou the sooner
Temptation found'st, or over-potent charms

To violate the sacred trust of silence
Deposited within thee; which to have kept
Tacit, was in thy power; true; and thou bear'st 430
Enough, and more the burden of that fault;
Bitterly hast thou paid, and still art paying
That rigid score. A worse thing yet remains,
This day the Philistines a popular feast
Here celebrate in Gaza, and proclaim
Great pomp, and sacrifice, and praises loud
To Dagon, as their god who hath delivered
Thee Samson bound and blind into their hands,
Them out of thine, who slew'st them many a slain.
So Dagon shall be magnified, and God, 440
Besides whom is no god, compared with idols,
Disglorified, blasphemed, and had in scorn
By the idolatrous rout amidst their wine;
Which to have come to pass by means of thee,
Samson, of all thy sufferings think the heaviest,
Of all reproach the most with shame that ever
Could have befall'n thee and thy father's house.
Sam. Father, I do acknowledge and confess
That I this honour, I this pomp have brought
To Dagon, and advanced his praises high 450
Among the heathen round; to God have brought
Dishonour, obloquy, and oped the mouths
Of idolists, and atheists; have brought scandal
To Israel, diffidence of God, and doubt
In feeble hearts, propense enough before
To waver, or fall off and join with idols;
Which is my chief affliction, shame and sorrow,
The anguish of my soul, that suffers not
Mine eye to harbour sleep, or thoughts to rest.
This only hope relieves me, that the strife 460
With me hath end; all the contest is now
'Twixt God and Dagon; Dagon hath presumed,
Me overthrown, to enter lists with God,
His deity comparing and preferring
Before the God of Abraham. He, be sure,
Will not connive, or linger, thus provoked,
But will arise and his great name assert:
Dagon must stoop, and shall ere long receive

Such a discomfit, as shall quite despoil him
Of all these boasted trophies won on me,   470
And with confusion blank his worshippers.
Man. With cause this hope relieves thee, and these words
I as a prophecy receive: for God,
Nothing more certain, will not long defer
To vindicate the glory of his name
Against all competition, nor will long
Endure it, doubtful whether God be Lord,
Or Dagon. But for thee what shall be done?
Thou must not in the meanwhile here forgot
Lie in this miserable loathsome plight   480
Neglected. I already have made way
To some Philistian lords, with whom to treat
About thy ransom: well they may by this
Have satisfied their utmost of revenge
By pains and slaveries, worse than death inflicted
On thee, who now no more canst do them harm.
Sam. Spare that proposal, father, spare the trouble
Of that solicitation; let me here,
As I deserve, pay on my punishment;
And expiate, if possible, my crime,   490
Shameful garrulity. To have revealed
Secrets of men, the secrets of a friend,
How heinous had the fact been, how deserving
Contempt, and scorn of all, to be excluded
All friendship, and avoided as a blab,
The mark of fool set on his front!
But I God's counsel have not kept, his holy secret
Presumptuously have published, impiously,
Weakly at least, and shamefully: a sin
That Gentiles in their parables condemn   500
To their abyss and horrid pains confined.
Man. Be penitent and for thy fault contrite,
But act not in thy own affliction, son,
Repent the sin, but if the punishment
Thou canst avoid, self-preservation bids;
Or the execution leave to high disposal,
And let another hand, not thine, exact
Thy penal forfeit from thyself; perhaps
God will relent, and quit thee all his debt;

Who evermore approves and more accepts   510
(Best pleased with humble and filial submission)
Him who imploring mercy sues for life,
Than who self-rigorous chooses death as due;
Which argues over-just, and self-displeased
For self-offence, more than for God offended.
Reject not then what offered means, who knows
But God hath set before us, to return thee
Home to thy country and his sacred house,
Where thou may'st bring thy off'rings, to avert
His further ire, with prayers and vows renewed.   520
Sam. His pardon I implore; but as for life,
To what end should I seek it? when in strength
All mortals I excelled, and great in hopes
With youthful courage and magnanimous thoughts
Of birth from heaven foretold and high exploits,
Full of divine instinct, after some proof
Of acts indeed heroic, far beyond
The sons of Anak, famous now and blazed,
Fearless of danger, like a petty god
I walked about admired of all and dreaded   530
On hostile ground, none daring my affront.
Then swoll'n with pride into the snare I fell
Of fair fallacious looks, venereal trains,
Softened with pleasure and voluptuous life;
At length to lay my head and hallowed pledge
Of all my strength in the lascivious lap
Of a deceitful concubine who shore me
Like a tame wether, all my precious fleece,
Then turned me out ridiculous, despoiled,
Shaven, and disarmed among my enemies.   540
Chor. Desire of wine and all delicious drinks,
Which many a famous warrior overturns,
Thou couldst repress, nor did the dancing ruby
Sparkling, out-poured, the flavour, or the smell,
Or taste that cheers the heart of gods and men,
Allure thee from the cool crystalline stream.
Sam. Wherever fountain or fresh current flowed
Against the eastern ray, translucent, pure
With touch ethereal of heaven's fiery rod
I drank, from the clear milky juice allaying   550

Thirst, and refreshed; nor envied them the grape
Whose heads that turbulent liquor fills with fumes.
Chor. O madness, to think use of strongest wines
And strongest drinks our chief support of health,
When God with these forbidden made choice to rear
His mighty champion, strong above compare,
Whose drink was only from the liquid brook.
Sam. But what availed this temperance, not complete
Against another object more enticing?
What boots it at one gate to make defence,   560
And at another to let in the foe
Effeminately vanquished? by which means,
Now blind, disheartened, shamed, dishonoured, quelled,
To what can I be useful, wherein serve
My nation, and the work from heaven imposed,
But to sit idle on the household hearth,
A burdenous drone; to visitants a gaze,
Or pitied object, these redundant locks
Robustious to no purpose clustering down,
Vain monument of strength; till length of years   570
And sedentary numbness craze my limbs
To a contemptible old age obscure.
Here rather let me drudge and earn my bread,
Till vermin or the draff of servile food
Consume me, and oft-invocated death
Hasten the welcome end of all my pains.
Man. Wilt thou then serve the Philistines with that gift
Which was expressly given thee to annoy them?
Better at home lie bed-rid, not only idle,
Inglorious, unemployed, with age outworn.   580
But God who caused a fountain at thy prayer
From the dry ground to spring, thy thirst to allay
After the brunt of battle, can as easy
Cause light again within thy eyes to spring,
Wherewith to serve him better than thou hast;
And I persuade me so; why else this strength
Miraculous yet remaining in those locks?
His might continues in thee not for naught,
Nor shall his wondrous gifts be frustrate thus.
Sam. All otherwise to me my thoughts portend,   590
That these dark orbs no more shall treat with light,

Nor the other light of life continue long,
But yield to double darkness nigh at hand:
So much I feel my genial spirits droop,
My hopes all flat, nature within me seems
In all her functions weary of herself;
My race of glory run, and race of shame,
And I shall shortly be with them that rest.
Man. Believe not these suggestions, which proceed
From anguish of the mind and humours black,   600
That mingle with thy fancy. I however
Must not omit a father's timely care
To prosecute the means of thy deliverance
By ransom or how else: meanwhile be calm,
And healing words from these thy friends admit.
Sam. O that torment should not be confined
To the body's wounds and sores
With maladies innumerable
In heart, head, breast, and reins;
But must secret passage find   610
To the inmost mind,
There exercise all his fierce accidents,
And on her purest spirits prey,
As on entrails, joints, and limbs,
With answerable pains, but more intense,
Though void of corporal sense.
    My griefs not only pain me
As a lingering disease,
But finding no redress, ferment and rage,
Nor less than wounds immedicable   620
Rankle, and fester, and gangrene,
To black mortification.
Thoughts my tormentors armed with deadly stings
Mangle my apprehensive tenderest parts,
Exasperate, exulcerate, and raise
Dire inflammation which no cooling herb
Or med'cinal liquor can assuage,
Nor breath of vernal air from snowy alp.
Sleep hath forsook and given me o'er
To death's benumbing opium as my only cure.   630
Thence faintings, swoonings of despair,
And sense of heaven's desertion.

I was his nursling once and choice delight,
His destined from the womb,
Promised by heavenly message twice descending.
Under his special eye
Abstemious I grew up and thrived amain;
He led me on to mightiest deeds
Above the nerve of mortal arm
Against the uncircumcised, our enemies.   640
But now hath cast me off as never known,
And to those cruel enemies,
Whom I by his appointment had provoked,
Left me all helpless with the irreparable loss
Of sight, reserved alive to be repeated
The subject of their cruelty, or scorn.
Nor am I in the list of them that hope;
Hopeless are all my evils, all remediless;
This one prayer yet remains, might I be heard,
No long petition, speedy death,   650
The close of all my miseries, and the balm.
Chor. Many are the sayings of the wise
In ancient and in modern books enrolled;
Extolling patience as the truest fortitude;
And to the bearing well of all calamities,
All chances incident to man's frail life
Consolatories writ
With studied argument, and much persuasion sought
Lenient of grief and anxious thought,
But with the afflicted in his pangs their sound   660
Little prevails, or rather seems a tune,
Harsh, and of dissonant mood from his complaint,
Unless he feel within
Some source of consolation from above;
Secret refreshings, that repair his strength,
And fainting spirits uphold.
    God of our fathers, what is man!
That thou towards him with hand so various,
Or might I say contrarious,
Temper'st thy providence through his short course,   670
Not evenly, as thou rul'st
The angelic orders and inferior creatures mute,
Irrational and brute.

Nor do I name of men the common rout,
That wand'ring loose about
Grow up and perish, as the summer fly,
Heads without name no more remembered,
But such as thou hast solemnly elected,
With gifts and graces eminently adorned
To some great work, thy glory,   680
And people's safety, which in part they effect:
Yet toward these thus dignified, thou oft
Amidst their height of noon,
Changest thy countenance, and thy hand with no regard
Of highest favours past
From thee on them, or them to thee of service.
   Nor only dost degrade them, or remit
To life obscured, which were a fair dismission,
But throw'st them lower than thou didst exalt them high,
Unseemly falls in human eye,   690
Too grievous for the trespass or omission,
Oft leav'st them to the hostile sword
Of heathen and profane, their carcases
To dogs and fowls a prey, or else captived:
Or to the unjust tribunals, under change of times,
And condemnation of the ingrateful multitude.
If these they scape, perhaps in poverty
With sickness and disease thou bow'st them down,
Painful diseases and deformed,
In crude old age;   700
Though not disordinate, yet causeless suffering
The punishment of dissolute days, in fine,
Just or unjust, alike seem miserable,
For oft alike, both come to evil end.
   So deal not with this once thy glorious champion,
The image of thy strength, and mighty minister.
What do I beg? how hast thou dealt already?
Behold him in this state calamitous, and turn
His labours, for thou canst, to peaceful end.
   But who is this, what thing of sea or land?   710
Female of sex it seems,
That so bedecked, ornate, and gay,
Comes this way sailing
Like a stately ship

Of Tarsus, bound for th' isles
Of Javan or Gadire
With all her bravery on, and tackle trim,
Sails filled, and streamers waving,
Courted by all the winds that hold them play,
An amber scent of odorous perfume   720
Her harbinger, a damsel train behind;
Some rich Philistian matron she may seem,
And now at nearer view, no other certain
Than Dalila thy wife.
Sam. My wife, my traitress, let her not come near me.
Chor. Yet on she moves, now stands and eyes thee fixed,
About t' have spoke, but now, with head declined
Like a fair flower surcharged with dew, she weeps
And words addressed seem into tears dissolved,
Wetting the borders of her silken veil: 730
But now again she makes address to speak.
Dal. With doubtful feet and wavering resolution
I came, still dreading thy displeasure, Samson,
Which to have merited, without excuse,
I cannot but acknowledge; yet if tears
May expiate (though the fact more evil drew
In the perverse event than I foresaw)
My penance hath not slackened, though my pardon
No way assured. But conjugal affection
Prevailing over fear, and timorous doubt   740
Hath led me on desirous to behold
Once more thy face, and know of thy estate.
If aught in my ability may serve
To lighten what thou suffer'st, and appease
Thy mind with what amends is in my power,
Though late, yet in some part to recompense
My rash but more unfortunate misdeed.
Sam. Out, out hyena; these are thy wonted arts,
And arts of every woman false like thee,
To break all faith, all vows, deceive, betray,   750
Then as repentant to submit, beseech,
And reconcilement move with feigned remorse,
Confess, and promise wonders in her change,
Not truly penitent, but chief to try
Her husband, how far urged his patience bears,

His virtue or weakness which way to assail:
Then with more cautious and instructed skill
Again transgresses, and again submits;
That wisest and best men full oft beguiled
With goodness principled not to reject   760
The penitent, but ever to forgive,
Are drawn to wear out miserable days,
Entangled with a poisonous bosom snake,
If not by quick destruction soon cut off
As I by thee, to ages an example.
Dal. Yet hear me Samson; not that I endeavour
To lessen or extenuate my offence,
But that on the other side, if it be weighed
By itself, with aggravations not surcharged,
Or else with just allowance counterpoised,   770
I may, if possible, thy pardon find
The easier towards me, or thy hatred less.
First granting, as I do, it was a weakness
In me, but incident to all our sex,
Curiosity, inquisitive, importune
Of secrets, then with like infirmity
To publish them, both common female faults:
Was it not weakness also to make known
For importunity, that is for naught,
Wherein consisted all thy strength and safety?   780
To what I did thou show'dst me first the way.
But I to enemies revealed, and should not.
Nor shouldst thou have trusted that to woman's frailty:
Ere I to thee, thou to thyself wast cruel.
Let weakness then with weakness come to parle
So near related, or the same of kind,
Thine forgive mine; that men may censure thine
The gentler, if severely thou exact not
More strength from me, than in thyself was found.
And what if love, which thou interpret'st hate,   790
The jealousy of love, powerful of sway
In human hearts, nor less in mine towards thee,
Caused what I did? I saw thee mutable
Of fancy, feared lest one day thou wouldst leave me
As her at Timna, sought by all means therefore
How to endear, and hold thee to me firmest:

No better way I saw than by importuning
To learn thy secrets, get into my power
Thy key of strength and safety: thou wilt say,
Why then revealed? I was assured by those   800
Who tempted me, that nothing was designed
Against thee but safe custody, and hold:
That made for me; I knew that liberty
Would draw thee forth to perilous enterprises,
While I at home sat full of cares and fears
Wailing thy absence in my widowed bed;
Here I should still enjoy thee day and night
Mine and love's prisoner, not the Philistines',
Whole to myself, unhazarded abroad,
Fearless at home of partners in my love.   810
These reasons in love's law have passed for good,
Though fond and reasonless to some perhaps;
And love hath oft, well meaning, wrought much woe,
Yet always pity or pardon hath obtained.
Be not unlike all others, not austere
As thou art strong, inflexible as steel.
If thou in strength all mortals dost exceed,
In uncompassionate anger do not so.
Sam. How cunningly the sorceress displays
Her own transgressions, to upbraid me mine!   820
That malice not repentance brought thee hither,
By this appears: I gave, thou say'st, the example,
I led the way; bitter reproach, but true,
I to myself was false ere thou to me,
Such pardon therefore as I give my folly,
Take to thy wicked deed: which when thou seest
Impartial, self-severe, inexorable,
Thou wilt renounce thy seeking, and much rather
Confess it feigned, weakness is thy excuse,
And I believe it, weakness to resist   830
Philistian gold: if weakness may excuse,
What murderer, what traitor, parricide,
Incestuous, sacrilegious, but may plead it?
All wickedness is weakness: that plea therefore
With God or man will gain thee no remission.
But love constrained thee; call it furious rage
To satisfy thy lust: love seeks to have love;

My love how couldst thou hope, who took'st the way
To raise in me inexpiable hate,
Knowing, as needs I must, by thee betrayed?   840
In vain thou striv'st to cover shame with shame,
Or by evasions thy crime uncover'st more.
Dal. Since thou determin'st weakness for no plea
In man or woman, though to thy own condemning,
Hear what assaults I had, what snares besides,
What sieges girt me round, ere I consented;
Which might have awed the best-resolved of men,
The constantest to have yielded without blame.
It was not gold, as to my charge thou lay'st,
That wrought with me; thou know'st the magistrates   850
And princes of my country came in person,
Solicited, commanded, threatened, urged,
Adjured by all the bonds of civil duty
And of religion, pressed how just it was,
How honourable, how glorious to entrap
A common enemy, who had destroyed
Such numbers of our nation: and the priest
Was not behind, but ever at my ear,
Preaching how meritorious with the gods
It would be to ensnare an irreligious   860
Dishonourer of Dagon: what had I
To oppose against such powerful arguments?
Only my love of thee held long debate;
And combated in silence all these reasons
With hard contest: at length that grounded maxim
So rife and celebrated in the mouths
Of wisest men; that to the public good
Private respects must yield; with grave authority
Took full possession of me and prevailed;
Virtue, as I thought, truth, duty so enjoining.   870
Sam. I thought where all thy circling wiles would end;
In feigned religion, smooth hypocrisy.
But had thy love, still odiously pretended,
Been, as it ought, sincere, it would have taught thee
Far other reasonings, brought forth other deeds.
I before all the daughters of my tribe
And of my nation chose thee from among
My enemies, loved thee, as too well thou knew'st,

Too well, unbosomed all my secrets to thee,
Not out of levity, but overpowered   880
By thy request, who could deny thee nothing;
Yet now am judged an enemy. Why then
Didst thou at first receive me for thy husband?
Then, as since then, thy country's foe professed:
Being once a wife, for me thou wast to leave
Parents and country; nor was I their subject,
Nor under their protection but my own,
Thou mine, not theirs: if aught against my life
Thy country sought of thee, it sought unjustly,
Against the law of nature, law of nations,   890
No more thy country, but an impious crew
Of men conspiring to uphold their state
By worse than hostile deeds, violating the ends
For which our country is a name so dear;
Not therefore to be obeyed. But zeal moved thee;
To please thy gods thou didst it; gods unable
To acquit themselves and prosecute their foes
But by ungodly deeds, the contradiction
Of their own deity, gods cannot be:
Less therefore to be pleased, obeyed, or feared,   900
These false pretexts and varnished colours failing,
Bare in thy guilt how foul must thou appear!
Dal. In argument with men a woman ever
Goes by the worse, whatever be her cause.
Sam. For want of words no doubt, or lack of breath,
Witness when I was worried with thy peals.
Dal. I was a fool, too rash, and quite mistaken
In what I thought would have succeeded best.
Let me obtain forgiveness of thee, Samson,
Afford me place to show what recompense   910
Towards thee I intend for what I have misdone,
Misguided; only what remains past cure
Bear not too sensibly, nor still insist
To afflict thyself in vain: though sight be lost,
Life yet hath many solaces, enjoyed
Where other senses want not their delights
At home in leisure and domestic ease,
Exempt from many a care and chance to which
Eyesight exposes daily men abroad.

I to the lords will intercede, not doubting   920
Their favourable ear, that I may fetch thee
From forth this loathsome prison-house, to abide
With me, where my redoubled love and care
With nursing diligence, to me glad office,
May ever tend about thee to old age
With all things grateful cheered, and so supplied,
That what by me thou hast lost thou least shalt miss.
Sam. No, no, of my condition take no care;
It fits not; thou and I long since are twain;
Nor think me so unwary or accursed   930
To bring my feet again into the snare
Where once I have been caught; I know thy trains
Though dearly to my cost, thy gins, and toils;
Thy fair enchanted cup, and warbling charms
No more on me have power, their force is nulled,
So much of adder's wisdom I have learnt
To fence my ear against thy sorceries.
If in my flower of youth and strength, when all men
Loved, honoured, feared me, thou alone could hate me
Thy husband, slight me, sell me, and forgo me;   940
How wouldst thou use me now, blind, and thereby
Deceivable, in most things as a child
Helpless, thence easily contemned, and scorned,
And last neglected? How wouldst thou insult
When I must live uxorious to thy will
In perfect thraldom, how again betray me,
Bearing my words and doings to the lords
To gloss upon, and censuring, frown or smile?
This jail I count the house of liberty
To thine whose doors my feet shall never enter.   950
Dal. Let me approach at least, and touch thy hand.
Sam. Not for thy life, lest fierce remembrance wake
My sudden rage to tear thee joint by joint.
At distance I forgive thee, go with that;
Bewail thy falsehood, and the pious works
It hath brought forth to make thee memorable
Among illustrious women, faithful wives:
Cherish thy hastened widowhood with the gold
Of matrimonial treason: so farewell.
Dal. I see thou art implacable, more deaf   960

To prayers than winds and seas, yet winds to seas
Are reconciled at length, and sea to shore:
Thy anger, unappeasable, still rages,
Eternal tempest never to be calmed.
Why do I humble thus myself, and suing
For peace, reap nothing but repulse and hate?
Bid go with evil omen and the brand
Of infamy upon my name denounced?
To mix with thy concernments I desist
Henceforth, nor too much disapprove my own.   970
Fame if not double-faced is double-mouthed,
And with contrary blast proclaims most deeds,
On both his wings, one black, the other white,
Bears greatest names in his wild airy flight.
My name perhaps among the circumcised
In Dan, in Judah, and the bordering tribes,
To all posterity may stand defamed,
With malediction mentioned, and the blot
Of falsehood most unconjugal traduced.
But in my country where I most desire,   980
In Ecron, Gaza, Asdod, and in Gath
I shall be named among the famousest
Of women, sung at solemn festivals,
Living and dead recorded, who to save
Her country from a fierce destroyer, chose
Above the faith of wedlock-bands, my tomb
With odours visited and annual flowers.
Not less renowned than in Mount Ephraim,
Jael, who with inhospitable guile
Smote Sisera sleeping through the temples nailed.   990
Nor shall I count it heinous to enjoy
The public marks of honour and reward
Conferred upon me, for the piety
Which to my country I was judged to have shown.
At this whoever envies or repines
I leave him to his lot, and like my own.
Chor. She's gone, a manifest serpent by her sting
Discovered in the end, till now concealed.
Sam. So let her go, God sent her to debase me,
And aggravate my folly who committed   1000
To such a viper his most sacred trust

Of secrecy, my safety, and my life.
Chor. Yet beauty, though injurious, hath strange power,
After offence returning, to regain
Love once possessed, nor can be easily
Repulsed, without much inward passion felt
And secret sting of amorous remorse.
Sam. Love-quarrels oft in pleasing concord end,
Not wedlock-treachery endangering life.
Chor. It is not virtue, wisdom, valour, wit,   1010
Strength, comeliness of shape, or amplest merit
That woman's love can win or long inherit;
But what it is, hard is to say,
Harder to hit
(Which way soever men refer it),
Much like thy riddle, Samson, in one day
Or seven, though one should musing sit;
    If any of these or all, the Timnian bride
Had not so soon preferred
Thy paranymph, worthless to thee compared,   1020
Successor in thy bed,
Nor both so loosely disallied
Their nuptials, nor this last so treacherously
Had shorn the fatal harvest of thy head.
Is it for that such outward ornament
Was lavished on their sex, that inward gifts
Were left for haste unfinished, judgment scant,
Capacity not raised to apprehend
Or value what is best
In choice, but oftest to affect the wrong?   1030
Or was too much of self-love mixed,
Of constancy no root infixed,
That either they love nothing, or not long?
    Whate'er it be, to wisest men and best
Seeming at first all heavenly under virgin veil,
Soft, modest, meek, demure,
Once joined, the contrary she proves, a thorn
Intestine, far within defensive arms
A cleaving mischief, in his way to virtue
Adverse and turbulent, or by her charms   1040
Draws him awry enslaved
With dotage, and his sense depraved

To folly and shameful deeds which ruin ends.
What pilot so expert but needs must wreck
Embarked with such a steers-mate at the helm?
   Favoured of heaven who finds
One virtuous rarely found,
That in domestic good combines:
Happy that house! his way to peace is smooth:
But virtue which breaks through all opposition,   1050
And all temptation can remove,
Most shines and most is acceptable above.
   Therefore God's universal law
Gave to the man despotic power
Over his female in due awe,
Nor from that right to part an hour,
Smile she or lour:
So shall he least confusion draw
On his whole life, not swayed
By female usurpation, nor dismayed.   1060
   But had we best retire, I see a storm?
Sam. Fair days have oft contracted wind and rain.
Chor. But this another kind of tempest brings.
Sam. Be less abstruse, my riddling days are past.
Chor. Look now for no enchanting voice, nor fear
The bait of honeyed words; a rougher tongue
Draws hitherward, I know him by his stride,
The giant Harapha of Gath, his look
Haughty as is his pile high-built and proud.
Comes he in peace? what wind hath blown him hither   1070
I less conjecture than when first I saw
The sumptuous Dalila floating this way:
His habit carries peace, his brow defiance.
Sam. Or peace or not, alike to me he comes.
Chor. His fraught we soon shall know, he now arrives.
Har. I come not Samson, to condole thy chance,
As these perhaps, yet wish it had not been,
Though for no friendly intent. I am of Gath,
Men call me Harapha, of stock renowned
As Og or Anak and the Emims old   1080
That Kiriathaim held, thou know'st me now
If thou at all art known. Much I have heard
Of thy prodigious might and feats performed

Incredible to me, in this displeased,
That I was never present on the place
Of those encounters, where we might have tried
Each other's force in camp or listed field:
And now am come to see of whom such noise
Hath walked about, and each limb to survey,
If thy appearance answer loud report.   1090
Sam. The way to know were not to see but taste.
Har. Dost thou already single me? I thought
Gyves and the mill had tamed thee. O that fortune
Had brought me to the field where thou art famed
To have wrought such wonders with an ass's jaw;
I should have forced thee soon wish other arms,
Or left thy carcase where the ass lay thrown:
So had the glory of prowess been recovered
To Palestine, won by a Philistine
From the unforeskinned race, of whom thou bear'st   1100
The highest name for valiant acts, that honour
Certain to have won by mortal duel from thee,
I lose, prevented by thy eyes put out.
Sam. Boast not of what thou wouldst have done, but do
What then thou wouldst, thou seest it in thy hand.
Har. To combat with a blind man I disdain,
And thou hast need much washing to be touched.
Sam. Such usage as your honourable lords
Afford me assassinated and betrayed,
Who durst not with their whole united powers   1110
In fight withstand me single and unarmed,
Nor in the house with chamber ambushes
Close-banded durst attack me, no not sleeping,
Till they had hired a woman with their gold
Breaking her marriage faith to circumvent me.
Therefore without feigned shifts let be assigned
Some narrow place enclosed, where sight may give thee,
Or rather flight, no great advantage on me;
Then put on all thy gorgeous arms, thy helmet
And brigandine of brass, thy broad habergeon,   1120
Vantbrace and greaves, and gauntlet, add thy spear
A weaver's beam, and seven-times-folded shield,
I only with an oaken staff will meet thee,
And raise such outcries on thy clattered iron,

Which long shall not withhold me from thy head,
That in a little time while breath remains thee,
Thou oft shalt wish thyself at Gath to boast
Again in safety what thou wouldst have done
To Samson, but shalt never see Gath more.
Har. Thou durst not thus disparage glorious arms   1130
Which greatest heroes have in battle worn,
Their ornament and safety, had not spells
And black enchantments, some magician's art
Armed thee or charmed thee strong, which thou from heaven
Feign'dst at thy birth was given thee in thy hair,
Where strength can least abide, though all thy hairs
Were bristles ranged like those that ridge the back
Of chafed wild boars or ruffled porcupines.
Sam. I know no spells, use no forbidden arts;
My trust is in the living God who gave me   1140
At my nativity this strength, diffused
No less through all my sinews, joints and bones,
Than thine, while I preserved these locks unshorn,
The pledge of my unviolated vow.
For proof hereof, if Dagon be thy god,
Go to his temple, invocate his aid
With solemnest devotion, spread before him
How highly it concerns his glory now
To frustrate and dissolve these magic spells,
Which I to be the power of Israel's God   1150
Avow, and challenge Dagon to the test,
Offering to combat thee his champion bold,
With the utmost of his godhead seconded:
Then thou shalt see, or rather to thy sorrow
Soon feel, whose God is strongest, thine or mine.
Har. Presume not on thy God, whate'er he be,
Thee he regards not, owns not, hath cut off
Quite from his people, and delivered up
Into thy enemies' hand, permitted them
To put out both thine eyes, and fettered send thee   1160
Into the common prison, there to grind
Among the slaves and asses thy comrades,
As good for nothing else, no better service
With those thy boisterous locks, no worthy match
For valour to assail, nor by the sword

Of noble warrior, so to stain his honour,
But by the barber's razor best subdued.
Sam. All these indignities, for such they are
From thine, these evils I deserve and more,
Acknowledge them from God inflicted on me   1170
Justly, yet despair not of his final pardon
Whose ear is ever open; and his eye
Gracious to readmit the suppliant;
In confidence whereof I once again
Defy thee to the trial of mortal fight,
By combat to decide whose god is God,
Thine or whom I with Israel's sons adore.
Har. Fair honour that thou dost thy God, in trusting
He will accept thee to defend his cause,
A murderer, a revolter, and a robber.   1180
Sam. Tongue-doughty giant, how dost thou prove me these?
Har. Is not thy nation subject to our lords?
Their magistrates confessed it, when they took thee
As a league-breaker and delivered bound
Into our hands: for hadst thou not committed
Notorious murder on those thirty men
At Ascalon, who never did thee harm,
Then like a robber stripp'dst them of their robes?
The Philistines, when thou hadst broke the league,
Went up with armèd powers thee only seeking,   1190
To others did no violence nor spoil.
Sam. Among the daughters of the Philistines
I chose a wife, which argued me no foe;
And in your city held my nuptial feast:
But your ill-meaning politician lords,
Under pretence of bridal friends and guests,
Appointed to await me thirty spies,
Who threatening cruel death constrained the bride
To wring from me and tell to them my secret,
That solved the riddle which I had proposed.   1200
When I perceived all set on enmity,
As on my enemies, wherever chanced,
I used hostility, and took their spoil
To pay my underminers in their coin.
My nation was subjected to your lords.
It was the force of conquest; force with force

Is well ejected when the conquered can.
But I a private person, whom my country
As a league-breaker gave up bound, presumed
Single rebellion and did hostile acts.   1210
I was no private but a person raised
With strength sufficient and command from heaven
To free my country; if their servile minds
Me their deliverer sent would not receive,
But to their masters gave me up for nought,
The unworthier they; whence to this day they serve.
I was to do my part from heaven assigned,
And had performed it if my known offence
Had not disabled me, not all your force:
These shifts refuted, answer thy appellant   1220
Though by his blindness maimed for high attempts,
Who now defies thee thrice to single fight,
As a petty enterprise of small enforce.
Har. With thee a man condemned, a slave enrolled,
Due by the law to capital punishment?
To fight with thee no man of arms will deign.
Sam. Cam'st thou for this, vain boaster, to survey me,
To descant on my strength, and give thy verdict?
Come nearer, part not hence so slight informed;
But take good heed my hand survey not thee.   1230
Har. O Baal-zebub! can my ears unused
Hear these dishonours, and not render death?
Sam. No man withholds thee, nothing from thy hand
Fear I incurable; bring up thy van,
My heels are fettered, but my fist is free.
Har. This insolence other kind of answer fits.
Sam. Go baffled coward, lest I run upon thee,
Though in these chains, bulk without spirit vast,
And with one buffet lay thy structure low,
Or swing thee in the air, then dash thee down   1240
To the hazard of thy brains and shattered sides.
Har. By Astaroth ere long thou shalt lament
These braveries in irons loaden on thee.
Chor. His giantship is gone somewhat crestfall'n,
Stalking with less unconscionable strides,
And lower looks, but in a sultry chafe.
Sam. I dread him not, nor all his giant-brood,

Though fame divulge him father of five sons
All of gigantic size, Goliah chief.
Chor. He will directly to the lords, I fear, 1250
And with malicious counsel stir them up
Some way or other yet further to afflict thee.
Sam. He must allege some cause, and offered fight
Will not dare mention, lest a question rise
Whether he durst accept the offer or not,
And that he durst not plain enough appeared.
Much more affliction than already felt
They cannot well impose, nor I sustain;
If they intend advantage of my labours,
The work of many hands, which earns my keeping 1260
With no small profit daily to my owners.
But come what will, my deadliest foe will prove
My speediest friend, by death to rid me hence,
The worst that he can give, to me the best.
Yet so it may fall out, because their end
Is hate, not help to me, it may with mine
Draw their own ruin who attempt the deed.
Chor. O how comely it is and how reviving
To the spirits of just men long oppressed!
When God into the hands of their deliverer 1270
Puts invincible might
To quell the mighty of the earth, the oppressor,
The brute and boisterous force of violent men
Hardy and industrious to support
Tyrannic power, but raging to pursue
The righteous and all such as honour truth;
He all their ammunition
And feats of war defeats
With plain heroic magnitude of mind
And celestial vigour armed, 1280
Their armouries and magazines contemns,
Renders them useless, while
With wingèd expedition
Swift as the lightning glance he executes
His errand on the wicked, who surprised
Lose their defence distracted and amazed.
    But patience is more oft the exercise
Of saints, the trial of their fortitude,

Making them each his own deliverer,
And victor over all   1290
That tyranny or fortune can inflict,
Either of these is in thy lot,
Samson, with might endued
Above the sons of men; but sight bereaved
May chance to number thee with those
Whom patience finally must crown.
This idol's day hath been to thee no day of rest,
    Labouring thy mind
More than the working day thy hands,
And yet perhaps more trouble is behind.   1300
For I descry this way
Some other tending, in his hand
A sceptre or quaint staff he bears,
Comes on amain, speed in his look.
By his habit I discern him now
A public officer, and now at hand.
His message will be short and voluble.
Off. Hebrews, the prisoner Samson here I seek.
Chor. His manacles remark him, there he sits.
Off. Samson, to thee our lords thus bid me say;   1310
This day to Dagon is a solemn feast,
With sacrifices, triumph, pomp, and games;
Thy strength they know surpassing human rate,
And now some public proof thereof require
To honour this great feast, and great assembly;
Rise therefore with all speed and come along,
Where I will see thee heartened and fresh clad
To appear as fits before the illustrious lords.
Sam. Thou know'st I am an Hebrew, therefore tell them,
Our law forbids at their religious rites   1320
My presence; for that cause I cannot come.
Off. This answer, be assured, will not content them.
Sam. Have they not sword-players, and every sort
Of gymnic artists, wrestlers, riders, runners,
Jugglers and dancers, antics, mummers, mimics,
But they must pick me out with shackles tired,
And over-laboured at their public mill,
To make them sport with blind activity?
Do they not seek occasion of new quarrels

On my refusal to distress me more,   1330
Or make a game of my calamities?
Return the way thou cam'st, I will not come.
Off. Regard thyself, this will offend them highly.
Sam. Myself? my conscience and internal peace.
Can they think me so broken, so debased
With corporal servitude, that my mind ever
Will condescend to such absurd commands?
Although their drudge, to be their fool or jester,
And in my midst of sorrow and heart-grief
To show them feats, and play before their god,   1340
The worst of all indignities, yet on me
Joined with extreme contempt? I will not come.
Off. My message was imposed on me with speed,
Brooks no delay: is this thy resolution?
Sam. So take it with what speed thy message needs.
Off. I am sorry what this stoutness will produce.
Sam. Perhaps thou shalt have cause to sorrow indeed.
Chor. Consider, Samson; matters now are strained
Up to the height, whether to hold or break;
He's gone, and who knows how he may report   1350
Thy words by adding fuel to the flame?
Expect another message more imperious,
More lordly thundering than thou well wilt bear.
Sam. Shall I abuse this consecrated gift
Of strength, again returning with my hair
After my great transgression, so requite
Favour renewed, and add a greater sin
By prostituting holy things to idols;
A Nazarite in place abominable
Vaunting my strength in honour to their Dagon?   1360
Besides, how vile, contemptible, ridiculous,
What act more execrably unclean, profane?
Chor. Yet with this strength thou serv'st the Philistines,
Idolatrous, uncircumcised, unclean.
Sam. Not in their idol-worship, but by labour
Honest and lawful to deserve my food
Of those who have me in their civil power.
Chor. Where the heart joins not, outward acts defile not.
Sam. Where outward force constrains, the sentence holds
But who constrains me to the temple of Dagon,   1370

Not dragging? the Philistian lords command,
Commands are no constraints. If I obey them,
I do it freely; venturing to displease
God for the fear of man, and man prefer,
Set God behind: which in his jealousy
Shall never, unrepented, find forgiveness.
Yet that he may dispense with me or thee
Present in temples at idolatrous rites
For some important cause, thou need'st not doubt.
Chor. How thou wilt here come off surmounts my reach.   1380
Sam. Be of good courage, I begin to feel
Some rousing motions in me which dispose
To something extraordinary my thoughts.
I with this messenger will go along,
Nothing to do, be sure, that may dishonour
Our law, or stain my vow of Nazarite.
If there be aught of presage in the mind,
This day will be remarkable in my life
By some great act, or of my days the last.
Chor. In time thou hast resolved, the man returns.   1390
Off. Samson, this second message from our lords
To thee I am bid say. Art thou our slave,
Our captive, at the public mill our drudge,
And dar'st thou at our sending and command
Dispute thy coming? come without delay;
Or we shall find such engines to assail
And hamper thee, as thou shalt come of force,
Though thou wert firmlier fastened than a rock.
Sam. I could be well content to try their art,
Which to no few of them would prove pernicious.   1400
Yet knowing their advantages to many,
Because they shall not trail me through their streets
Like a wild beast, I am content to go.
Masters' commands come with a power resistless
To such as owe them absolute subjection;
And for a life who will not change his purpose?
(So mutable are all the ways of men)
Yet this be sure, in nothing to comply
Scandalous or forbidden in our law.
Off. I praise thy resolution, doff these links: 1410
By this compliance thou wilt win the lords

To favour, and perhaps to set thee free.
Sam. Brethren farewell, your company along
I will not wish, lest it perhaps offend them
To see me girt with friends; and how the sight
Of me as of a common enemy,
So dreaded once, may now exasperate them
I know not. Lords are lordliest in their wine;
And the well-feasted priest then soonest fired
With zeal, if aught religion seem concerned: 1420
No less the people on their holydays
Impetuous, insolent, unquenchable;
Happen what may, of me expect to hear
Nothing dishonourable, impure, unworthy
Our God, our law, my nation, or myself,
The last of me or no I cannot warrant.
Chor. Go, and the holy one
Of Israel be thy guide
To what may serve his glory best, and spread his name
Great among the heathen round: 1430
Send thee the angel of thy birth, to stand
Fast by thy side, who from thy father's field
Rode up in flames after his message told
Of thy conception, and be now a shield
Of fire; that spirit that first rushed on thee
In the camp of Dan
Be efficacious in thee now at need.
For never was from heaven imparted
Measure of strength so great to mortal seed,
As in thy wondrous actions hath been seen.   1440
But wherefore comes old Manoa in such haste
With youthful steps? much livelier than erewhile
He seems: supposing here to find his son,
Or of him bringing to us some glad news?
Man. Peace with you brethren; my inducement hither
Was not at present here to find my son,
By order of the lords new parted hence
To come and play before them at their feast.
I heard all as I came, the city rings
And numbers thither flock, I had no will,   1450
Lest I should see him forced to things unseemly.
But that which moved my coming now, was chiefly

To give ye part with me what hope I have
With good success to work his liberty.
Chor. That hope would much rejoice us to partake
With thee; say reverend sire, we thirst to hear.
Man. I have attempted one by one the lords
Either at home, or through the high street passing,
With supplication prone and father's tears
To accept of ransom for my son their prisoner,   1460
Some much averse I found and wondrous harsh,
Contemptuous, proud, set on revenge and spite;
That part most reverenced Dagon and his priests,
Others more moderate seeming, but their aim
Private reward, for which both god and state
They easily would set to sale, a third
More generous far and civil, who confessed
They had enough revenged, having reduced
Their foe to misery beneath their fears,
The rest was magnanimity to remit,   1470
If some convenient ransom were proposed.
What noise or shout was that? it tore the sky.
Chor. Doubtless the people shouting to behold
Their once great dread, captive, and blind before them,
Or at some proof of strength before them shown.
Man. His ransom, if my whole inheritance
May compass it, shall willingly be paid
And numbered down: much rather I shall choose
To live the poorest in my tribe, than richest,
And he in that calamitous prison left.   1480
No, I am fixed not to part hence without him.
For his redemption all my patrimony,
If need be, I am ready to forgo
And quit: not wanting him, I shall want nothing.
Chor. Fathers are wont to lay up for their sons,
Thou for thy son art bent to lay out all;
Sons wont to nurse their parents in old age,
Thou in old age car'st how to nurse thy son,
Made older than thy age through eyesight lost.
Man. It shall be my delight to tend his eyes,   1490
And view him sitting in the house, ennobled
With all those high exploits by him achieved,
And on his shoulders waving down those locks,

That of a nation armed the strength contained:
And I persuade me God had not permitted
His strength again to grown up with his hair
Garrisoned round about him like a camp
Of faithful soldiery, were not his purpose
To use him further yet in some great service,
Not to sit idle with so great a gift   1500
Useless, and thence ridiculous about him.
And since his strength with eyesight was not lost,
God will restore him eyesight to his strength.
Chor. Thy hopes are not ill founded nor seem vain
Of his delivery, and thy joy thereon
Conceived, agreeable to a father's love,
In both which we, as next participate.
Man. I know your friendly minds and—O what noise!
Mercy of heaven what hideous noise was that!
Horribly loud unlike the former shout.   1510
Chor. Noise call you it or universal groan
As if the whole inhabitation perished,
Blood, death, and deathful deeds are in that noise,
Ruin, destruction at the utmost point.
Man. Of ruin indeed methought I heard the noise,
O it continues, they have slain my son.
Chor. Thy son is rather slaying them, that outcry
From slaughter of one foe could not ascend.
Man. Some dismal accident it needs must be;
What shall we do, stay here or run and see?   1520
Chor. Best keep together here, lest running thither
We unawares run into danger's mouth.
This evil on the Philistines is fall'n,
From whom could else a general cry be heard?
The sufferers then will scarce molest us here,
From other hands we need not much to fear.
What if his eyesight (for to Israel's God
Nothing is hard) by miracle restored,
He now be dealing dole among his foes,
And over heaps of slaughtered walk his way?   1530
Man. That were a joy presumptuous to be thought.
Chor. Yet God hath wrought things as incredible
For his people of old; what hinders now?
Man. He can I know, but doubt to think he will;

Yet hope would fain subscribe, and tempts belief.
A little stay will bring some notice hither.
Chor. Of good or bad so great, of bad the sooner;
For evil news rides post, while good news baits.
And to our wish I see one hither speeding,
An Hebrew, as I guess, and of our tribe.   1540
Messenger. O whither shall I run, or which way fly
The sight of this so horrid spectacle
Which erst my eyes beheld and yet behold;
For dire imagination still pursues me.
But providence or instinct of nature seems,
Or reason though disturbed, and scarce consulted
To have guided me aright, I know not how,
To thee first reverend Manoa, and to these
My countrymen, whom here I knew remaining,
As at some distance from the place of horror,   1550
So in the sad event too much concerned.
Man. The accident was loud, and here before thee
With rueful cry, yet what it was we hear not,
No preface needs, thou seest we long to know.
Mess. It would burst forth, but I recover breath
And sense distract, to know well what I utter.
Man. Tell us the sum, the circumstance defer.
Mess. Gaza yet stands, but all her sons are fall'n,
All in a moment overwhelmed and fall'n.
Man. Sad, but thou know'st to Israelites not saddest   1560
The desolation of a hostile city.
Mess. Feed on that first, there may in grief be surfeit.
Man. Relate by whom.
Mess.   By Samson.
Man.   That still lessens
The sorrow, and converts it nigh to joy.
Mess. Ah Manoa I refrain, too suddenly
To utter what will come at last too soon;
Lest evil tidings with too rude irruption
Hitting thy agèd ear should pierce too deep.
Man. Suspense in news is torture, speak them out.
Mess. Then take the worst in brief, Samson is dead.   1570
Man. The worst indeed, O all my hope's defeated
To free him hence! but death who sets all free
Hath paid his ransom now and full discharge.

What windy joy this day had I conceived
Hopeful of his delivery, which now proves
Abortive as the first-born bloom of spring
Nipped with the lagging rear of winter's frost.
Yet ere I give the reins to grief, say first,
How died he? death to life is crown or shame.
All by him fell thou say'st, by whom fell he,   1580
What glorious hand gave Samson his death's wound?
Mess. Unwounded of his enemies he fell.
Man. Wearied with slaughter then or how? explain.
Mess. By his own hands.
Man.   Self-violence? what cause
Brought him so soon at variance with himself
Among his foes?
Mess.   Inevitable cause
At once both to destroy and be destroyed;
The edifice where all were met to see him
Upon their heads and on his own he pulled.
Man. O lastly over-strong against thyself!   1590
A dreadful way thou took'st to thy revenge.
More than enough we know; but while things yet
Are in confusion, give us if thou canst,
Eye-witness of what first or last was done,
Relation more particular and distinct.
Mess. Occasions drew me early to this city,
And as the gates I entered with sunrise,
The morning trumpets festival proclaimed
Through each high street: little I had dispatched
When all abroad was rumoured that this day   1600
Samson should be brought forth to show the people
Proof of his mighty strength in feats and games;
I sorrowed at his captive state, but minded
Not to be absent at that spectacle.
The building was a spacious theatre,
Half round on two main pillars vaulted high,
With seats where all the lords and each degree
Of sort, might sit in order to behold,
The other side was open, where the throng
On banks and scaffolds under sky might stand;   1610
I among these aloof obscurely stood.
The feast and noon grew high, and sacrifice

Had filled their hearts with mirth, high cheer, and wine,
When to their sports they turned. Immediately
Was Samson as a public servant brought,
In their state livery clad; before him pipes
And timbrels, on each side went ar|armèd guards,
Both horse and foot before him and behind
Archers, and slingers, cataphracts and spears.
At sight of him the people with a shout   1620
Rifted the air clamouring their god with praise,
Who had made their dreadful enemy their thrall.
He patient but undaunted where they led him,
Came to the place, and what was set before him
Which without help of eye might be assayed,
To heave, pull, draw, or break, he still performed
All with incredible, stupendious force,
None daring to appear antagonist.
At length for intermission sake they led him
Between the pillars; he his guide requested   1630
(For so from such as nearer stood we heard)
As over-tired to let him lean awhile
With both his arms on those two massy pillars
That to the archèd roof gave main support.
He unsuspicious led him; which when Samson
Felt in his arms, with head a while inclined,
And eyes fast fixed he stood, as one who prayed,
Or some great matter in his mind revolved.
At last with head erect thus cried aloud,
Hitherto, lords, what your commands imposed   1640
I have performed, as reason was, obeying,
Not without wonder or delight beheld.
Now of my own accord such other trial
I mean to show you of my strength, yet greater;
As with amaze shall strike all who behold.
This uttered, straining all his nerves he bowed,
As with the force of winds and waters pent,
When mountains tremble, those two massy pillars
With horrible convulsion to and fro,
He tugged, he shook, till down they came and drew   1650
The whole roof after them, with burst of thunder
Upon the heads of all who sat beneath,
Lords, ladies, captains, counsellors, or priests,

Their choice nobility and flower, not only
Of this but each Philistian city round
Met from all parts to solemnize this feast.
Samson with these inmixed, inevitably
Pulled down the same destruction on himself;
The vulgar only scaped who stood without.
Chor. O dearly-bought revenge, yet glorious! 1660
Living or dying thou hast fulfilled
The work for which thou wast foretold
To Israel, and now li'st victorious
Among thy slain self-killed
Not willingly, but tangled in the fold,
Of dire necessity, whose law in death conjoined
Thee with thy slaughtered foes in number more
Than all thy life had slain before.
Semichor. While their hearts were jocund and sublime,
Drunk with idolatry, drunk with wine, 1670
And fat regorged of bulls and goats,
Chanting their idol, and preferring
Before our living dread who dwells
In Silo his bright sanctuary:
Among them he a spirit of frenzy sent,
Who hurt their minds,
And urged them on with mad desire
To call in haste for their destroyer;
They only set on sport and play
Unweetingly importuned 1680
Their own destruction to come speedy upon them.
So fond are mortal men
Fall'n into wrath divine,
As their own ruin on themselves to invite,
Insensate left, or to sense reprobate,
And with blindness internal struck.
Semichor. But he though blind of sight,
Despised and thought extinguished quite,
With inward eyes illuminated
His fiery virtue roused 1690
From under ashes into sudden flame,
And as an evening dragon came,
Assailant on the perchèd roosts,
And nests in order ranged

Of tame villatic fowl; but as an eagle
His cloudless thunder bolted on their heads.
So virtue given for lost,
Depressed, and overthrown, as seemed,
Like that self-begotten bird
In the Arabian woods embossed,   1700
That no second knows nor third,
And lay erewhile a holocaust,
From out her ashy womb now teemed,
Revives, reflourishes, then vigorous most
When most unactive deemed,
And though her body die, her fame survives,
A secular bird ages of lives.
Man. Come, come, no time for lamentation now,
Nor much more cause, Samson hath quit himself
Like Samson, and heroically hath finished   1710
A life heroic, on his enemies
Fully revenged, hath left them years of mourning,
And lamentation to the sons of Caphtor
Through all Philistian bounds. To Israel
Honour hath left, and freedom, let but them
Find courage to lay hold on this occasion,
To himself and father's house eternal fame;
And which is best and happiest yet, all this
With God not parted from him, as was feared,
But favouring and assisting to the end.   1720
Nothing is here for tears, nothing to wail
Or knock the breast, no weakness, no contempt,
Dispraise, or blame, nothing but well and fair,
And what may quiet us in a death so noble.
Let us go find the body where it lies
Soaked in his enemies' blood, and from the stream
With lavers pure, and cleansing herbs wash off
The clotted gore. I with what speed the while
(Gaza is not in plight to say us nay)
Will send for all my kindred, all my friends   1730
To fetch him hence and solemnly attend
With silent obsequy and funeral train
Home to his father's house: there will I build him
A monument, and plant it round with shade
Of laurel ever green, and branching palm,

With all his trophies hung, and acts enrolled
In copious legend, or sweet lyric song.
Thither shall all the valiant youth resort,
And from his memory inflame their breasts
To matchless valour, and adventures high: 1740
The virgins also shall on feastful days
Visit his tomb with flowers, only bewailing
His lot unfortunate in nuptial choice,
From whence captivity and loss of eyes.
Chor. All is best, though we oft doubt,
What the unsearchable dispose
Of highest wisdom brings about,
And ever best found in the close.
Oft he seems to hide his face,
But unexpectedly returns   1750
And to his faithful champion hath in place
Bore witness gloriously; whence Gaza mourns
And all that band them to resist
His uncontrollable intent,
His servants he with new acquist
Of true experience from this great event
With peace and consolation hath dismissed,
And calm of mind all passion spent.

Notes

ABBREVIATIONS

Aen.   [Virgil] *Aeneid*
ELH   *Journal of English Literary History*
FQ   [Spenser] *Faerie Queene*
Il.   [Homer] *Iliad*
Met.   [Ovid] *Metamorphoses*
OED   *Oxford English Dictionary*
Od.   [Homer] *Odyssey*
PL   *Paradise Lost*
PMLA   *Publications of the Modern Language Association of America*
SA   *Samson Agonistes*

POEMS (1645)

1 *On the Morning of Christ's Nativity.* The poem stands first both in 1645 and 1673; it is dated 1629 in a headnote in 1645. This is the only poem in the 1645 volume that Milton can be shown to have revised for the 1673 edition; we therefore print the revised text.

l. 5. *holy sages*: Old Testament prophets of redemption, but perhaps also Virgil, who predicts the birth of a peace-bearing child in *Eclogues*, iv.

l. 6. *forfeit*: crime, transgression.   *release*: cancel, grant remission of.

l. 8. *unsufferable*: unendurable (because 'going beyond all natural limits' (*OED*)).

l. 10. *wont*: was accustomed.

l. 11. *the midst . . . unity*: as the middle figure of the Trinity.

l. 14. *mortal clay*: flesh; in Gen. 2: 7, Adam is created from dust; cf. l. 138.

l. 15. *muse*: usually identified as Urania, muse of astronomy and hence of heavenly matters. See *PL*, i. 6.   *vein*: poetic genius.

l. 16. *Afford*: furnish.

l. 19. *sun's team*: horses of Apollo's chariot.

l. 21. *spangled host*: the stars, although the imagery is also applied to the angelic orders; cf. ll. 112–14, 243.

l. 23. *wizards*: wise men, the Magi.

l. 24. *prevent*: come before (Lat. *praevenire*), anticipate (and, by implication, delay; cf. l. 239).

2 l. 28. *From out his secret altar* . . . The syntax is inverted; he asks to be touched with hallowed fire drawn from the secret altar (as Isaiah had been, Isa. 6: 6–7).   *secret*: set apart.

l. 36. *wanton*: play amorously, heedlessly, idly.

l. 39. *guilty*. Nature is guilty because corrupted by the Fall.   *front*: face, demeanour.

ll. 39–42. *To hide* . . . *throw*: cf. Rev. 3: 18.

l. 41. *Pollute*: polluted.

l. 45. *cease*: commonly used transitively in the seventeenth century.

l. 47. *olive green*. Olive branches were emblematic of peace.

l. 48. *turning sphere*. In the Ptolemaic scheme of the universe, the outermost of the hollow spheres that revolved around the earth bearing the heavenly bodies (cf. ll. 75, 102); a stage machine of the sort used in court masques may also be implied (cf. ll. 141–8).

l. 50. *turtle wing*: wing of the turtledove.

l. 51. *myrtle*: an attribute of Venus.

l. 56. *hookèd*: armed with hooks, as in Spenser's description of the Souldan's chariot, *FQ*, v. xxviii. 5.

3 l. 59. *awful*: filled with awe.

l. 64. *whist*: hushed.

l. 68. *birds of calm*: halcyons, or kingfishers; the sea was said to remain calm during their winter nesting period.   *brooding*: nesting. *charmèd*: under a spell.

l. 71. *influence*: forces emanating from the stars and planets and affecting mankind.

l. 73. *For all*: despite, notwithstanding.

l. 74. *Lucifer*: the morning star (Hesperus, Venus) as well as the devil; cf. Isa. 14: 12 and l. 119.

l. 78. *room*: space.

l. 81. *As*: as if.

l. 84. *axle-tree*: axle of the sun's chariot.

l. 86. *Or ere*. Both words mean before; the doubling is for emphasis.

l. 89. *Pan*: god of nature, patron of shepherds; Pan is glossed as Christ in Spenser's *Shepheardes Calender*, 'May'.

l. 90. *kindly*: both according to his nature and lovingly.

4 l. 92. *silly*: simple, rustic.

4 l. 95. *strook*: struck; the form was still in use in the seventeenth century.

l. 100. *close*: conclusion of a musical phrase, cadence.

ll. 102–3. *round ... seat*: the sphere of the moon.   *Cynthia*. Diana, the moon goddess (from her birthplace on Mount Cynthus).

l. 104. *won*: rescued, delivered.

ll. 112–13. *cherubim ... seraphim*: lower and higher orders of angels respectively.

l. 116. *unexpressive*: inexpressible, indescribable.

l. 122. *on hinges*: on its axis.

5 l. 124. *welt'ring*: surging.

ll. 125–7. *Ring out ... so*. The lines allude to the Pythagorean idea that the turning spheres make a music inaudible to human ears.

l. 130. *base of heaven*: earth, invoked (with a play on 'bass') to join in the heavenly harmony.   *organ*: the instrument used to play the ground bass in a musical composition; also, since it was thought of as the universal instrument, an image for the universe as a musical structure.

l. 131. *ninefold*: the number of both the spheres and the angelic orders.

l. 132. *Make up full consort to*: complete the harmony of.   *consort*: 'The accord or harmony of several instruments or voices playing or singing in tune' (*OED*).

l. 135. *Time will run back*: cf. the return to the golden age prophesied in Virgil, *Eclogues*, iv.

l. 136. *speckled*: blemished, opposite of immaculate.

l. 140. *mansions*: dwelling places (not necessarily buildings).

l. 141. *Justice*. The return of the goddess of justice, Astraea, is announced in Virgil, *Eclogues*, IV.

l. 146. *tissued*: as if made of a cloth interwoven with gold or silver.

l. 147. *as*: as if.

6 l. 155. *ychained*: Spenserian archaism.

ll. 157–64. *With such ... throne*. Exod. 19: 16–20 describes the effects of the delivery of the law to Moses on Mount Sinai; Matt. 24: 29–31 predicts similar events at Christ's second coming.

l. 163. *session*: three syllables.

l. 168. *the old dragon*. 'The dragon, that old serpent, which is the Devil' (Rev. 20: 2).

l. 172. *Swinges*: lashes.

l. 173. *The oracles are dumb*. The pagan oracles were said to have ceased functioning after the advent of Christ.

l. 178. *Delphos*. Delphi, site of Apollo's oracle, was generally called Delphos in the period, though the two places were not confused.

l. 186. *genius*: the *genius loci*, guardian spirit of a place; cf. *Lycidas*, l. 183.

7 l. 191. *lars*: Roman tutelary deities of home and family.   *lemures*: Roman spirits of the dead.

l. 194. *flamens*: Roman priests.   *quaint*: strange, curious.

l. 196. *peculiar*: particular.

l. 197. *Peor, and Baalim*. The Canaanite sun god Baal was worshipped at Peor as Baal-Peor (see *PL*, i. 412, 421–3); Baalim is a plural designating various other manifestations of the god.

l. 199. *twice battered god*: Dagon, the Philistine god, whose idol was twice thrown down in 1 Sam. 5: 3–4 and whose followers were defeated by Samson, who destroys his temple in Judg. 16: 23–30.

l. 200. *Ashtaroth*: a plural form of the Syrian goddess of the moon and fertility (also called Astarte), paired with Baalim in *PL*, i. 421–3 and described in *PL*, i. 437–46.

l. 203. *Libyc Hammon*: Ammon, Lybian (and Egyptian) god represented as a horned ram.

l. 204. *Tyrian*: Phoenician (from Tyre, the capital).   *Thammuz*: lover of Astarte, the Phoenician version of Adonis. His death was celebrated annually.

l. 205. *Moloch*: an Ammonite god (the name literally means king) whose rites included child sacrifice to a calf-headed brass idol filled with fire; cf. *PL*, i. 392–9.

l. 211. *brutish*: in animal form.

l. 212. *Isis*: Egyptian moon goddess.   *Orus*: Horus, offspring of Isis and her brother Osiris.   *Anubis*: dog-headed offspring of Osiris and Nepthys, also his sister.

ll. 213–20. *Nor is . . . ark*. See Plutarch's account in *Isis and Osiris* (in his *Moralia*); at Memphis, Osiris was worshipped as the bull Apis.

l. 218. *Shroud*: both a place of shelter and a winding cloth.

8 l. 223. *eyn*: eyes; not an archaic usage.

l. 226. *Typhon*: both an Egyptian god and a monster from Greek mythology.

ll. 227–8. *Our babe . . . crew*: as Hercules in his infancy strangled two snakes.

8 l. 231. *orient*: eastern, hence the source of light.

l. 236. *night-steeds*: horses of the chariot of Night.

l. 239. *Time is*: it is time.   *tedious*: wearisome; also dilatory, slow.

l. 240. *teemèd*: born.

l. 244. *harnessed*: armoured.

On Time. A subtitle, 'To be set on a clock case', appears, crossed out, in the Trinity MS of the poem. Usually dated 1633.

ll. 2–3. *leaden-stepping . . . plummet's pace.* The plummet is the weight, often made of lead, whose slow descent moves a clock.

l. 4. *womb.* The word was used of the stomach and bowels, as well as of the uterus.

9 l. 9. *whenas*: when.

l. 12. *individual*: indivisible, i.e. everlasting, and also, as proper to each soul.

l. 18. *happy-making sight*: beatific vision.

l. 20. *quit*: having been left behind.

At a Solemn Music. Like *On Time* usually dated 1633.

l. 1. *sirens.* Plato imagined (*Republic*, x. 616–17) that the celestial spheres were moved by sirens who produced the music of the spheres. *pledges.* Earthly music; the 'voice and verse' of l. 2 are conceived as both offspring and anticipatory assurances of heavenly harmony.

l. 2. *Sphere-born.* MSS have 'sphere-borne', suggesting sirens conveyed by or on the spheres.

l. 5. *fantasy*: imagination, the image-making capacity.

l. 6. *concent*: harmony.

l. 7. *Ay*: ever.   *sapphire-coloured throne*: cf. Ezek. 1: 26.

l. 17. *That*: so that.

10 l. 23. *diapason*: the harmonic interval of an octave; perfect concord.

l. 27. *consort*: a group of musicians (here angels), but also musical harmony, or a marriage partner.

On Shakespeare. Milton's first published poem; it appeared anonymously in the second folio (1632) of Shakespeare's plays.

l. 4. *ypointing.* Imitating Spenser, but inaccurately: the Middle English prefix 'y-' was used before a past participle, not before a present participle.

l. 10. *easy numbers.* In the prefatory epistle to the first Shakespeare folio (1623), Heminge and Condell remark: 'His mind and hand went together; and what he thought, he uttered with that easiness, that we have scarce received from him a blot in his papers.' Numbers are metrical periods, hence lines, verses.

ll. 10–14. *Thy . . . conceiving.* 'Because each reader's heart bears the impress of your wisdom, your powers replace our own; so that, being merely the material on which your thought is carved, we become your monument'. For the metaphor, compare *Il Penseroso*, ll. 40–2.

l. 11. *unvalued*: invaluable.

l. 12. *Delphic.* Delphi was the site of the oracle of Apollo, god of poetry.

L'Allegro. 'The Happy Man'. As with its companion poem, *Il Penseroso*, 'The Melancholy Man', the title designates a personification or abstraction for the state of mind invoked in the poem. Usually dated *c.*1631.

l. 1. *Melancholy.* As a physiological condition caused by an excess of black bile, melancholy was associated with depression as well as genius.

ll. 2–3. *Of Cerberus . . . forlorn.* The genealogy is invented. *Cerberus* was the three-headed hound, guardian of hell; the name means heart-devouring in Greek (cf. l. 135, below). Virgil depicts Cerberus in a cave overlooking the river Styx in *Aen.*, vi. 417–18.

l. 5. *uncouth*: unknown, desolate, wild.   *cell*: technically, a single-room dwelling; by the seventeenth century, poetic usage for a humble cottage (not applied to prisons until the eighteenth century).

11 l. 10. *Cimmerian desert.* The Homeric land of the Cimmerians was a place of perpetual night in *Od.*, xi. 13–19.

l. 12. *yclept*: named; a Spenserian archaism.   *Euphrosyne*: (Mirth) with Aglaia (Brightness) and Thalia (Bloom), one of the three graces, usually associated with Venus (although not always as her offspring), and implying love, beauty, and generosity.

l. 17. *some sager.* No source has been identified for this alternative genealogy.

l. 19. *Zephyr . . . Aurora*: the west wind and the dawn.

l. 24. *buxom, blithe, and debonair.* Three characteristics of Mirth with much semantic overlap; buxom suggests pliability; blithe, kindliness as well as good-humour; debonair, affability.

l. 27. *Quips*: witty remarks.   *cranks*: verbal tricks.   *wanton wiles*: unrestrained, playful tricks.

l. 28. *becks*: beckonings, 'come-ons'.

l. 29. *Hebe*: goddess of youth.

11 l. 34. *fantastic*: fanciful, elaborately conceived, perhaps alluding to dances in masques that executed complicated designs bearing philosophical meanings, as in Jonson's *Pleasure Reconciled to Virtue*.

ll. 37–40. *And if . . . pleasures free*: echoing Marlowe, 'The Passionate Shepherd to his Love', ll. 19–20; cf. ll. 151–2 below, and *Il Penseroso*, ll. 175–6.

l. 39. *her*: Liberty.

l. 40. *unreprovèd*: unreprovable, blameless.

l. 41. *the lark*: traditionally the first bird to sing in the morning.

ll. 45–6. *to come . . . good morrow*. Editorial opinion has been divided over whether it is L'Allegro who comes to his window and bids good morrow to the day, or the lark who bids good morrow to L'Allegro; most critics favour the former interpretation, which accords most easily with the syntax.

12 l. 49. *the cock*. The crowing of the rooster signals dawn. Cf. l. 114.

l. 50. *Scatters the rear*. The image is of a retreating army.

l. 51. *stack*: haystack.

l. 55. *hoar*: grey, either with frost or mist.

l. 60. *state*: stately march, as of a monarch.

l. 62. *dight*: clothed.

l. 67. *tells his tale*: counts the number of his flock and/or recounts his story.

l. 71. *fallows*: unploughed, fallow land.

l. 75. *trim*: neat.   *pied*: variegated.

l. 80. *cynosure*: centre of attraction (the name of the constellation otherwise called Ursa Minor, containing the North Star).

ll. 83–8. *Where Corydon . . . sheaves*. The pastoral names here appear in Virgil's *Eclogues*, and in countless Renaissance poems.

l. 85. *herbs*: vegetables.   *messes*: food.

13 l. 91. *secure*: free from care (from Lat. *sine cura*).

l. 92. *upland*: on the hills, above the meadows.

l. 94. *rebecks*: three-stringed instruments, like fiddles.

l. 98. *sunshine*: sunny.

l. 102. *Mab*: Queen of the fairies, as in *Romeo and Juliet*, 1. iv. 54 ff.   *junkets*: cream-cheeses, or other forms of cream.

l. 104. *friar's lantern*: the will-o'-the-wisp.

l. 105. *drudging goblin*. Robin Goodfellow, a folklore figure noted for both household help and mischievous pranks, and propitiated with offerings of cream; he is Shakespeare's Puck (called a 'hobgoblin' in *A Midsummer Night's Dream*, II. i. 40).

l. 110. *lubber*: loutish.

l. 111. *chimney*: fireplace.

l. 113. *crop-full*: totally satiated.   *flings*: rushes.

l. 120. *weeds*: clothing, here the costumes appropriate to these courtly celebrations.

l. 121. *store of*: many.

l. 122. *influence*. The eyes are imagined as stars with their supposed power to affect destiny; cf. 'Nativity Ode', l. 71.

l. 125. *Hymen*: Roman god of marriage, with his usual attributes of saffron-coloured robe and torch.

l. 126. *taper clear*. If the torch burned without smoke, the omens for the marriage were propitious.

14 l. 132. *sock*: the slipper worn by the Greek comic actor, as opposed to the tragic actor's buskin; here, a synedoche for comedy.

l. 133. *fancy*: imagination, fantasy; cf. *Il Penseroso*, l. 6.

l. 136. *Lydian*: Greek musical mode associated in Plato primarily with laxness, conviviality, 'softness and sloth' (but also with 'dirges and lamentations').

l. 137. *Married*: cf. the similar overlap with musical terms in 'At a Solemn Music', ll. 2, 27.

l. 138. *meeting*: responsive, outgoing.

l. 139. *bout*: 'a roundabout way' (*OED*).

ll. 145–50. *That Orpheus' . . . Eurydice*. The story of Orpheus and Eurydice is in Ovid, *Met.*, 10 and 11, and in Virgil, *Georgics*, iv. 453–527. Orpheus, the archetypal poet, attempts to regain his wife Eurydice, who has been killed by a serpent; Pluto, the god of hell, grants his wish, but on condition that Orpheus not look back at Eurydice; he does, and loses her again. Ultimately, he is decapitated by the frenzied maenads. Virgil ends the story with the wailing of the severed head; Ovid reunites the couple in Elysium.

l. 145. *Orpheus' self*: Orpheus himself.

l. 149. *quite*: entirely.

Il Penseroso

l. 3. *bestead*: avail.

l. 4. *toys*: idle thoughts.

l. 6. *fond*: foolish.   *shapes*: the images of fancy, or imagination.

14 l. 10. *pensioners*: military attendants.   *Morpheus*: god of dreams. *train*: entourage.

15 l. 14. *hit*: suit.

l. 18. *Memnon's sister.* Memnon was an Ethiopian (hence black) king who fought on the Trojan side and was killed by Achilles; in *Od.*, xi. 522 he is a paradigm of manly beauty. His sister Himera (or Hemera) is mentioned in later redactions of the Troy story.

l. 19. *starred Ethiop queen.* Cassiopeia, wife of the Ethiopian king Cepheus, and mother of Andromeda; boasting of her beauty (or in some accounts, of her daughter's) offended the gods and provoked her metamorphosis into the constellation that bears her name.

l. 23. *Vesta*: goddess of the hearth and the chaste daughter of Saturn. The story of the genesis of Melancholy is Milton's invention.

l. 24. *solitary Saturn.* As patron of melancholics (those with a saturnine temperament), the god was represented as unsociable.

ll. 29–30. *Ida's . . . Jove.* In the Golden Age, Saturn ruled the world from atop Mount Ida, in Crete. Jove was born there, and subsequently overthrew and expelled his father.

l. 31. *nun*: 'a priestess or votaress of some pagan deity' (*OED*).

l. 33. *grain*: dye.

l. 35. *cypress lawn*: fine black linen.

l. 39. *commercing*: conversing, communicating.

ll. 40–2. *Thy rapt . . . till*: cf. 'On Shakespeare', ll. 13–14.

l. 43. *sad*: both melancholy and serious, grave; cf. l. 103.   *leaden*: Saturn was associated with lead.

l. 44. *fast*: fixedly.

l. 48. *Ay*: always.

l. 53. *fiery-wheelèd throne*: perhaps alluding to Ezekiel's vision (Ezek. I).

16 l. 55. *hist*: summon silently.

l. 56. *Philomel.* The nightingale; her rape and transformation are recounted in *Met.*, vi.

l. 59. *Cynthia*: goddess of the moon, similarly represented with a dragon-drawn chariot in Marlowe's *Hero and Leander*, l. 107 ff., though the dragons more usually conveyed the underworld goddess Hecate through the skies.

l. 68. *noon*: apogee.

l. 73. *plat*: plot, patch.

l. 76. *sullen.* The word also meant solemn.

l. 77. *air*: weather, climate.

l. 78. *still removèd place*: either an equally remote place, or a remote quiet place.

l. 83. *bellman*: watchman.   *charm*: both song (Lat. *carmen*) and spell (OE *cierm*).

l. 87. *Bear*: Ursa Major, visible until daybreak.

l. 88. *With . . . Hermes.* With the works of Hermes Trismegistus, supposed author of the *Corpus Hermeticum*, a series of mystical writings, for the most part composed in Alexandria in the second and third centuries; they were the first Neoplatonic texts translated into Latin by Ficino in 1463, and were regarded as the founding texts for Renaissance Neoplatonism.

ll. 88–9. *unsphere . . . Plato.* Plato's spirit is presumed to occupy its own heavenly sphere, from which the mystical practitioner attempts to summon it.

l. 92. *mansion*: dwelling (not necessarily a building).   *fleshly nook*: mortal place; *nook* means here a remote part of the world.

l. 93. *daemons*: daemons, sublunary spirits, here assigned control of the four elements.

17 ll. 95–6. *Whose . . . element.* i.e. the daemons control the mystical correspondence and harmony between the elements and the heavens. *consent*: sympathy, harmony.

l. 98. *pall*: mantle of the Greek tragic actor.

l. 99. *Thebes*: where Oedipus ruled.   *Pelops' line*: the house of Agamemnon, Pelops' grandson.

l. 102. *buskined*: tragic (lit. wearing the buskin or high boot of the Greek tragic actor).

l. 104. *Musaeus.* Mythical poet, sometimes described as the son of Orpheus and a priest of Demeter, and hence as the founder of religious poetry; the late classical poem on Hero and Leander from which Marlowe's poem derives was until the early seventeenth century generally ascribed to him.

ll. 105–8. *Orpheus . . . seek.* See *L'Allegro*, ll. 145–50.

l. 109 ff. *him . . . half-told*: Chaucer, in the uncompleted *Squire's Tale*, continued by Spenser in *FQ*, iv.

l. 113. *virtuous*: magical.

l. 121. *career*: course; 'pale' because moonlit.

l. 122. *civil-suited*: soberly attired.   *Morn.* Aurora, who seduced Cephalus ('the Attic boy', l. 124).

l. 123. *tricked and frounced*: adorned and curled.

17 l. 125. *kerchiefed*: covered as with a shawl.

l. 127. *still*: gentle.

l. 134. *Sylvan*: Sylvanus, the Roman woodland deity.

18 l. 145. *consort*: harmony.

l. 154. *genius*: the spirit of the place (*genius loci*).

l. 155. *due*: proper, dutiful.

l. 156. *pale*: enclosure.

l. 157. *embowèd*: vaulted, as a cathedral.

l. 158. *antic*: fantastic, quaint; many editors modernize to 'antique'. *massy proof*: massive strength.

l. 159. *storied*: pictorial, stained-glass.   *dight*: decorated.

l. 170. *spell*: decipher, with an overtone of its magical sense.

ll. 175–6. *These pleasures . . . live*. See *L'Allegro*, ll. 37–40, 151–2.

19 *Sonnet 1* ('*O nightingale*'). *c.* 1628–30.

l. 4. *hours*: Horae, the deities whose dance led the months and seasons, and determined the course of the year.

ll. 6–7. *First . . . love*. It was considered lucky to hear the nightingale before the cuckoo, which was associated with cuckoldry.

l. 6. *shallow*: shrill, thin.

l. 9. *timely*: early, promptly.   *bird of hate*: cuckoo.

Sonnet 7 ('*How soon hath time*'). Date: either 9 Dec. 1631, Milton's twenty-third birthday, or 9 Dec. 1632, when he ceased being 23 (see l. 2).

l. 3. *full career*: swift course.

l. 5. *deceive*: misrepresent.

l. 8. *timely-happy*: seasonable, perhaps precocious.

l. 9. *it*. If there is a definite antecedent, this refers to 'inward ripeness'; there are similar difficulties with 'it' at l. 13.

l. 10. *still*: always.   *even*: equal, appropriate.

20 *Sonnet 8* ('*Captain or colonel, or knight in arms*'). In the Trinity MS, a subtitle, 'on his door when the City expected an assault', has been crossed out and replaced with a substitute in Milton's hand, 'When the assault was intended to the City'. In Oct. 1642, the king's forces approached London.

l. 1. *colonel*: three syllables, usually pronounced coronel.

l. 5. *charms*: both spells (OE *cierm*) and songs (Lat. *carmen*).

l. 10. *Emathian conqueror*. Emathia is a district in Macedon; the conqueror is Alexander the Great. Pliny tells the story of how he spared Pindar's house in Thebes.

l. 13. *Electra's poet*: Euripides. Plutarch reports in his *Life of Lysander* (15) that Athens was spared when one of Lysander's generals pleaded for the city by reciting a chorus from *Electra*.

Sonnet 9 ('*Lady, that in the prime*'). The subject's identity is unknown; *c*. 1642–5.

l. 1. *prime . . . youth*: 'the "springtime" of human life; the time of early manhood or womanhood, from about 21 to 28 years of age' (*OED*).

l. 2. *the broad way*: cf. Matt. 7: 13.

l. 5. *Mary*. Jesus praises Mary, the sister of Martha, for choosing 'that good part, which shall not be taken away from her' (Luke 10: 42) by attending to him rather than to household chores.   *Ruth*. Ruth abandoned her home in Moab to live with Naomi, her Hebrew mother-in-law.

l. 6. *overween*: are presumptuous.

l. 7. *fret their spleen*. 'Fret' = irritate, aggravate; the spleen was considered the seat of ill temper or melancholy.

ll. 9–14. *Thy care . . . pure*: alluding to one of the parables of the kingdom in Matt. 25: 1–13, of the wise and foolish virgins, half of whom kept their lamps burning in readiness for the midnight return of the bridegroom summoning them to the marriage feast.

21 *Sonnet 10* ('*Daughter to that good earl*'). Titled in the Trinity MS, 'To the Lady Margaret Ley'; she was the daughter of James Ley (1550–1629), the Lord Chief Justice who presided over the trial of Francis Bacon; he was briefly Lord High Treasurer and Lord President of the Council under Charles I, who created him Earl of Marlborough in 1626. Lady Margaret married John Hobson in Dec. 1641 and was for a time Milton's neighbour; Edward Phillips reports the intimacy between the two families in the 1640s.

l. 5. *sad breaking of that parliament*. On 10 Mar. 1629, Charles I dissolved a hostile parliament, but members held the speaker in his chair while they passed three resolutions condemning the king's policies. The earl died four days later.

l. 6. *dishonest*: from Lat. *inhonestus*, inglorious.

l. 7. *Chaeronea*: where Philip of Macedon destroyed the armies of Athens and Thebes, and thereby Greek liberty, in 338 BC.

l. 8. *old man eloquent*: Isocrates, who starved himself to death on hearing the news.

21 l. 9. *later . . . than*: born too late.

Lycidas. The name Milton assigns his 'learned friend' Edward King is a commonplace one in classical and Renaissance pastorals. King (1612–37) entered Christ's College, Cambridge, in 1626 at the age of 14; he and Milton had the same tutor, William Chappell. In 1630, upon receiving his BA, King was made a Fellow of Christ's at the instigation of King Charles I; the appointment was due largely to politics and family connections rather than scholastic excellence, though some Latin poems of King's ('wholly undistinguished' according to Douglas Bush in the *Variorum*) are extant. In Aug. 1637, as he was on his way home to Dublin for the long vacation, King was drowned in a shipwreck near the coast of Wales; his body was not recovered. The Trinity MS of *Lycidas* is dated Nov. 1637, three months after King's death; the poem was first published in a commemorative volume, *Justa Edouardo King naufrago* (1638), as the last poem in a final section of English elegies entitled *Obsequies to the memorie of Mr Edward King, Anno Dom, 1638*, and is signed J.M.

l. 1. *laurels*: sacred to Apollo and traditional crown of poets.

l. 2. *myrtles*: sacred to Venus and hence emblematic of love poetry. *ivy*: sacred to Bacchus, patron of ecstatic poetry.   *never sere*: all three plants are evergreen.

l. 3. *crude*: unripe (Lat. *crudus*).

l. 4. *rude*: unskilled.

l. 5. *Shatter*: originally a variant form of scatter, hence both destroy and fling about.

l. 6. *dear*: both severe and precious.

l. 10. *Who . . . Lycidas?* Cf. Virgil, *Eclogues*, x. 3: '*neget quis carmina Gallo?*', 'Who would not sing for Gallus?'.

l. 11. *to sing*: how to sing.

l. 13. *welter*: roll or toss about.

l. 14. *meed*: honour, something merited.   *melodious tear*: elegy; the metaphor was a common one (cf. e.g. Spenser's title *The Teares of the Muses*).

ll. 15–17. *Begin then . . . string*. Cf. Virgil, *Eclogues*, iv. 1: '*Sicilides Musae, paulo maiora canamus*', 'Sicilian Muses, let us sing a somewhat loftier strain.' The muses are invoked from one of their sacred fountains, either Aganippe on Mount Helicon, where there was a shrine to Jove, or the Pierian spring on Mount Olympus, their birthplace.

22 l. 17. *somewhat loudly*: as in Virgil's 'somewhat loftier', an allusion to pastoral constraints upon a higher poetic mode.

l. 18. *coy*: modest, reserved.

l. 19. *muse*: poet (one inspired by the muse), and hence male in l. 21.

l. 20. *lucky*: well-omened; 'felicitous' has also been suggested.

l. 21. *he*: refers to muse, l. 19 above.

l. 25. *lawns*: untilled, grass-covered land; cf. *L'Allegro*, l. 71.

l. 28. *What time*: a Latinism (*quo tempore*): at what time, when. *winds*: blows.

l. 29. *Battening*: feeding, fattening.　　　*dews*: grass with the dew still on it; Virgil (*Eclogues*, viii. 14–15) mentions the flocks' preference for grass on which the dew remains.

l. 30. *the star*: Venus as Hesperus, the evening star.

l. 31. *westering*: moving westward.

l. 33. *Tempered*: attuned.　　　*oaten flute*: the traditional pastoral wind instrument, made of oat reeds.

l. 36. *Damaetas*. A conventional pastoral name; commentators have attempted to identify him with a particular Cambridge figure, e.g. William Chappell, Milton's and King's Cambridge tutor.

l. 40. *gadding*: straggling.

l. 46. *taint-worm*. The modern term is 'husk', an intestinal parasite fatal to newly weaned calves.

l. 48. *whitethorn*: hawthorn.

l. 51. *Closed . . . head*: introducing the comparison of Lycidas with Orpheus (see ll. 58–63), decapitated by the maenads when his songs offended them. For Orpheus, cf. *L'Allegro*, ll. 145–50, *Il Penseroso*, ll. 103–8.

l. 55. *Deva . . . stream*: the river Dee, on which Chester stands, said to have magical properties.

l. 56. *fondly*: foolishly.

23　l. 58. *the muse*: Calliope.

l. 61. *rout*: disorderly crowd, here the maenads.

ll. 62–3. *His gory . . . shore*. Orpheus was torn to bits by the enraged women, and his head was thrown into the river Hebrus and eventually washed up on the island of Lesbos.

l. 64. *boots*: avails.

l. 65. *tend*: attend to.

l. 68. *Amaryllis*: a conventional pastoral figure, notably in Virgil, where the woods resound the name (*Eclogues*, i. 4–5), and where Corydon considers whether it would not have been better to suffer her rage rather than the scorn of his beloved Alexis (*Eclogues*, ii. 14–15).

23 l. 69. *Neaera*. The name appears in Virgil, *Eclogues*, iii. 3, and as the name of the poet's mistress in numerous classical and Renaissance pastorals.

l. 70. *clear*: noble (Lat. *clarus*); blameless.

l. 73. *guerdon*: reward.

l. 75. *Fury*: Atropos, the Fate who cuts the thread of life.

l. 77. *Phoebus*: Apollo, god of poetry, who similarly touches the poet's ear in Virgil, *Eclogues*, vi. 3–5, restraining him from epic and enjoining him to feed his sheep and sing.

l. 79. *glistering foil*: the glittering leaf of metal used to set off a jewel and enhance its lustre.

l. 85. *Arethuse*: Sicilian river, whose nymph was wooed and pursued by Alpheus (see l. 132, below); associated with Theocritean pastoral.

l. 86. *Mincius*: the river of Mantua, Virgil's birthplace.

l. 87. *mood*: musical mode.

l. 88. *oat*: the oaten flute of l. 33.

l. 89. *herald*: Triton.

l. 90. *plea*: Triton is conceived either as gathering evidence for Neptune's court, or as exonerating Neptune, who is on trial.

l. 91. *felon*: savage, wild, criminal.

l. 96. *Hippotades*: Aeolus (son of Hippotas), god of winds, who keeps them in a cave (the dungeon of l. 97).

24 l. 99. *Panope*: one of the fifty sea nymphs (nereids) born to the sea deities Nereus and Doris.

l. 101. *eclipse*: portent of disaster.

l. 103. *Camus*: the river Cam imagined as a classical river god.

l. 104. *hairy*: Here, alluding to the river reeds; Milton associates the hairy mantle with studiousness: cf. *Il Penseroso*, l. 169.

l. 105. *Inwrought*: inscribed or embroidered.

l. 106. *sanguine flower*: the hyacinth, inscribed AI AI by Apollo to record his grief for his dead and metamorphosed beloved, Hyacinthus.

l. 107. *pledge*: a person acting as a surety for another, thus, figuratively, Lycidas as token of Cambridge's care (as a child is token of its parents' love), and as promise of futurity.

l. 109. *the pilot*. St Peter, the founder of the Church; the keys in l. 110 are his usual attribute, deriving from Matt. 16: 18–28. Peter was a fisherman on Lake Galilee when Christ called him (see Luke 5: 3–11); when Christ walks on Lake Galilee (in Matt. 14: 25–31; cf. l. 173), he rebukes Peter for lacking faith. In his final appearance to

Peter, Christ commands him to 'feed my lambs' (John 21: 15); cf. ll. 114–25.

l. 111. *amain*: forcefully.

l. 112. *mitred*: wearing the mitre, the bishop's ceremonial head-dress.

l. 114. *Enow*: enough.

l. 119. *Blind mouths*: i.e. pure gluttony. Ruskin comments in *Sesame and Lilies*: 'A "Bishop" means "a person who sees." A "Pastor" means one who feeds. The most unbishoply character . . . is therefore to be blind. The most unpastoral is, instead of feeding, to want to be fed, —to be a mouth.'

l. 122. *What recks it them?* What do they care?   *They are sped*: they succeed and thrive; they are promoted or furthered; also, they are dispatched, destroyed.

l. 123. *list*: choose, please.

l. 124. *scrannel*: thin, meagre, harsh; probably a dialect word.

l. 126. *draw*: inhale, breathe.

l. 128. *wolf*: regularly identified with Catholicism in Renaissance Protestant rhetoric.   *privy*: secret, hidden.

ll. 130–1. *But that . . . no more.* A 'two-handed engine' is a sword so large that wielding it requires two hands; Michael similarly wields a sword 'with two-handed sway' (*PL*, vi. 251), and Peter's power here seems to extend to the threat of ultimate judgment.   *engine*: machine or instrument (of war).

l. 132. *Alpheus*: see l. 85 n., above.

l. 135. *bells*: bell-shaped flowers.

l. 136. *use*: frequent, habitually resort.

l. 137. *wanton*: unrestrained.

l. 138. *swart star*: Sirius, the dog star, associated with summer heat, and hence black (swart), alluding to the effect of heat.

25 l. 142. *rathe*: early blooming.

l. 143. *crow-toe*: variously identified as the hyacinth, wild hyacinth, and buttercup.   *jessamine*: Jasmine.

l. 144. *pink*: dianthus.   *freaked*: striped, variegated.

l. 157. *whelming*: overthrowing violently, submerging, sinking.

l. 159. *moist vows*: tearful prayers (Lat. *votum*).

l. 160. *Bellerus*. Bellerium was the Latin name of Land's End, the south-west tip of England; Milton apparently invented Bellerus from the place-name.

25 l. 161. *vision . . . mount.* Camden reports that on St Michael's Mount,
off the Cornish coast near Land's End, the archangel himself
appeared in a vision to the monks. He is conceived as keeping guard
against the Spanish Catholic threat implied in l. 162.

l. 162. *Namancos and Bayona's hold*: a district (properly Nemancos) and
fortress town ('hold') in north-western Spain, facing Cornwall.

l. 163. *Look homeward.* The injunction is, presumably, to St Michael,
either to return his gaze from distant Spain to England and its tragic
loss immediately northward, or, perhaps to heaven; some commen-
tators, however, have felt that the grammar of ll. 154 ff. requires
'angel' to refer back to 'thou' (at ll. 157, 159), i.e. Lycidas, who is
being asked to look to his heavenly (or perhaps to his earthly) home.

l. 164. *waft*: 'convey safely by water' (*OED*), as the poet Arion was
rescued by dolphins charmed with his songs.

l. 168. *day-star*: the sun, or conceivably Lucifer, the morning star.

l. 170. *tricks*: adorns, or trims.

l. 176. *unexpressive*: inexpressible, indescribable; perhaps, too, inappre-
hensible.   *nuptial song*: combining the song of the 144,000
virgins in Rev. 14: 1–5 and the song for the mystic marriage with the
lamb in Rev. 19: 6–9.

26 l. 183. *genius*: the spirit of the place (*genius loci*), the guardian.

l. 184. *In . . . recompense*: as your reward.

l. 186. *uncouth*: unknown, untutored, rustic.

l. 188. *tender stops*: frail, responsive holes in the reed pipe.   *quills*:
reeds.

l. 189. *Doric*: the dialect of Theocritus, Bion, and Moschus; hence
'pastoral'.

l. 192. *twitched*: pulled around his shoulders.

A Masque . . . Presented at Ludlow Castle ['*Comus*']. Milton's masque
was commissioned as an entertainment for the Earl of Bridgewater
and his family at Ludlow Castle in Herefordshire. It was performed
on 29 Sept. 1634. The earl had recently been appointed Lord
Lieutenant of Wales and President of the Council; the masque is often
said to celebrate his investiture, which, however, took place several
months earlier. His three children were among the principal per-
formers: Lady Alice Egerton, aged 15, played the Lady, and her
brothers John, Viscount Brackley, aged 11, and Lord Thomas Egerton,
aged 9, played the two brothers. The children's music master, Henry
Lawes, composed the music for the masque, and took the role of the
Attendant Spirit. Lawes was acquainted with Milton and may have

been instrumental in arranging the commission for him to write the text; Milton had already contributed verses to *Arcades*, an entertainment for Bridgewater's mother-in-law the Dowager Countess of Derby, the music for which is presumed to have been by Lawes as well. The Bridgewater children had twice performed in masques at the court at Whitehall. In 1632 they appeared in Aurelian Townshend's and Inigo Jones's *Tempe Restored*, which is about Circe and the transformation of men into animals and has strong affinities with Milton's masque; and in 1634 the two boys served as torchbearers in the most splendid of the Caroline court productions, Thomas Carew's and Jones's *Coelum Britannicum*. Milton's masque is deeply imbued with a sense of the genre, but it differs significantly from masques intended for the court. Courtiers never took speaking roles in royal masques; to do so would have constituted a violation of aristocratic decorum—the fact that the Bridgewater children spoke, and at length, reveals just how intimate a family affair this entertainment was. The text survives in several stages of composition. Milton, moving towards publication, turned his masque increasingly away from family intimacy and towards philosophical reasoning and Neoplatonic symbolism, adding about one hundred lines in the process. Our text is the final, much revised text included in Milton's 1645 *Poems*. The title *Comus* was given to the work in the eighteenth century, when an operatic version was prepared by John Dalton, with music by Thomas Arne.

[stage direction] *discovers*: reveals.   *Attendant Spirit*: in the manuscripts, 'a guardian spirit or daemon'. 'Daemon' transliterates the Greek term for a tutelary deity or genius, in Christian terms a guardian angel.

l. 2. *mansion*: dwelling (not necessarily a building); also an astrological term for one of the 28 divisions of the ecliptic.

l. 3. *ensphered*: in the sphere of heaven.

27 l. 7. *pestered*: crowded, encumbered.   *pinfold*: lit. a cattle pen; hence 'a place of confinement, a pen, a trap' (*OED*).

l. 11. *enthroned . . . seats*. As in *PL*, Milton conceives the classical gods as versions of the angels.

l. 16. *ambrosial*: divine (lit. pertaining to the immortals).   *weeds*: garments.

l. 17. *sin-worn mould*: earth worn out with sin.

l. 19. *salt flood*: ocean.

l. 20. *Took . . . Jove*. After the victory of the Olympian gods over the Titans, Jove and his brothers Neptune and Pluto (in Greek Zeus, Poseidon, and Hades) drew lots to divide the universe among themselves. Jove drew the heavens, Neptune the waters and islands, Pluto (the 'nether Jove') the underworld.

27 l. 24. *to grace . . . gods*: to show favour to the lesser gods (those of rivers and islands) who pay him tribute.

l. 25. *several*: various.

l. 28. *main*: ocean.

l. 29. *quarters*: gives as their dwelling.   *blue-haired deities.* The tritons, Neptune's children, represented as blue-haired in Jonson's *Masque of Blackness* (1605; pub. 1608). Ovid, whom Jonson cites as his source, describes them as entirely blue (*caeruleum*) in *Met.*, i. 333.

ll. 30–1. *tract . . . peer.* As Lord Lieutenant, the Earl of Bridgewater had administrative responsibility for Herefordshire and the Welsh counties, in the west of England.   *mickle*: great; archaic, and Spenserian, usage.

l. 32. *tempered awe*: temperately used authority. 'Awe' = 'power to inspire fear or reverence' (*OED*).

l. 33. *nation*: Wales.

l. 35. *state*: combining the senses of throne and high rank.

l. 37. *perplexed*: intricate, entangled.

l. 38. *horror*: with an overtone of its Latin meaning, 'bristling'.

28 l. 46. *Bacchus*: the Greek Dionysus, god of wine, theatre, and ecstatic poetry.

l. 48. *After . . . transformed.* The seventh Homeric Hymn *To Dionysus*, elaborated by Ovid, *Met.*, iii. 650–91, tells how the god was captured by Italian ('Tuscan') pirates, but he turned them into dolphins and their ship into a grape arbour. (The syntax is Latin.)   *transformed*: had been transformed.

l. 49. *Tyrrhene shore*: the Italian coast north of Sicily, opposite Sardinia and Corsica.   *listed*: wished.

l. 50. *Circe's island*: Aeaea (*Od.*, x. 135); Homer is vague about its location.

l. 51. *The daughter of the Sun.* Circe's father was Helios, the sun god.

ll. 51–3. *Whose . . . swine.* The account of Circe's transformation of Odysseus' men into swine is in *Od.*, x. 238. It is also the subject of William Browne's *Inner Temple Masque* (1615), which Milton certainly knew, and of Aurelian Townshend's and Inigo Jones's masque *Tempe Restored*, performed at court in 1632, and in which the three Bridgewater children danced.

l. 58. *Comus.* The name is a Latinization of the Greek *komos*, meaning 'revelry', and cognate with 'comedy'. In Philostratus' *Icones* (or

Imagines, l. 2), he is described as a charming and graceful youth crowned with roses and sleepy from wine, presiding over a wedding celebration. In Jonson's masque *Pleasure Reconciled to Virtue* (1618), he is presented as a gross belly-god and his revelry as a danger to the pursuit of virtue. The story of his birth is original with Milton.

l. 59. *frolic of*: merry in.

l. 60. *Celtic, and Iberian*: French and Spanish.

l. 65. *orient*: shining.

l. 66. *drought of Phoebus*: thirst caused by the hot sun.

l. 67. *fond*: foolish.

ll. 69-70. *changed . . . form*. In Renaissance moralizations of the Circe story, her victims were transformed not into swine but into whatever animal most truly expressed their inner bestial natures.

l. 71. *ounce*: lynx.

l. 73. *perfect is their misery*: complete is their depravity.

l. 79. *advent'rous*: hazardous.

l. 83. *Iris' woof*: the rainbow.

l. 84. *weeds*: garments.   *swain*. The word had a wide variety of meanings, of which the relevant ones here are young man, rustic, attendant, shepherd.

29 ll. 86-8. *soft pipe . . . waving woods*. The role was played by the musician and composer Henry Lawes; the swain's control over nature analogizes him to the arch-musician Orpheus.

l. 87. *knows to*: knows how to.

l. 88. *nor of less faith*: no less trustworthy (than musically talented).

l. 90. *present*: immediate.

l. 92. *viewless*: invisible.

l. 93. *The star . . . fold*. The appearance of Venus (or Hesperus) as the evening star is the signal for the shepherd to lead his flock to the sheepfold.

l. 95. *gilded car of day*: sun's chariot.

l. 96. *allay*: cool down.

l. 97. *steep*: flowing precipitously.

l. 98. *slope*: sloping, setting.

l. 99. *pole*: sky.

l. 110. *saws*: sententious wisdom.

l. 112. *choir*: 'a band of dancers, or of dancers and singers' (*OED*).

l. 115. *sounds*: straits, inlets.

29 l. 116. *morris*: morris-dance, a lively group dance.

l. 117. *shelves*: banks.

l. 121. *wakes*: nocturnal revels.

30 l. 123. *prove*: experience.

l. 129. *Cotytto*: a Thracian earth goddess whose cult spread throughout Greece and Rome.

l. 131. *dragon womb*. Dragons were associated with Hecate, queen of the underworld (see l. 135).

l. 132. *Stygian*: hellish (from the River Styx, which flows through the underworld).

l. 134. *ebon*: black.

l. 137. *dues*: rites.

l. 139. *nice*: relevant senses are ignorant, tender, delicate, coy, shy, over-modest, and over-fastidious.   *steep*: mountain.

l. 140. *cabined loophole*: small window; *cabined* = confined, *loophole* = a hole to peer through.

l. 141. *descry*: reveal.

l. 142. *solemnity*: ceremonies.

l. 144. *round*: circular dance.

[stage direction] *Measure*. The term denoted any rhythmical performance; here, both the dance and the music.

l. 147. *shrouds*: hiding places.

l. 151. *trains*: lit. the bait for luring wild animals into a trap.

l. 154. *dazzling spells*. The Trinity MS reads 'powdered spells', suggesting that Comus here threw some sparkling powder, the 'magic dust' of l. 165, into the air.   *spongy*: absorbent, receptive.

l. 155. *blear*: dimming or confusing the sight.

l. 156. *presentments*: images, displays.

l. 157. *quaint habits*: strange garments.

31 l. 161. *glozing*: flattering.

l. 163. *Wind me*: insinuate myself; but, taken with *hug* (l. 164), including overtones of a constrictor snake.

l. 165. *virtue*: power.

l. 168. *fairly*: quietly.

l. 174. *loose*: unrestrained, wanton.   *unlettered hinds*: uneducated farm labourers.

l. 175. *teeming*: fertile, breeding.

l. 176. *Pan*: god of nature, patron of shepherds, and especially associated with licentious sexuality.

l. 178. *swilled*: drunken; *OED*'s only citation for the adjective, but 'swilled with drink' [= drunk to excess] was in common usage.

l. 179. *wassailers*: revellers.

l. 180. *inform*: direct.   *unacquainted*: unfamiliar (with the way).

l. 188. *Even*: evening.

l. 189. *sad votarist*: solemn pilgrim.   *in palmer's weed*: dressed like a palmer, a pilgrim who carried a palm branch in token of his visit to the Holy Land.

l. 190. *Phoebus' wain*: the chariot of the sun.

l. 193. *engaged*: committed.

l. 197. *dark lantern*: 'a lantern with a slide or arrangement by which the light can be concealed' (*OED*).

32 l. 203. *rife*: abundant, strong, loud-sounding.   *perfect*: absolutely distinct.

l. 204. *single*: total.

l. 210. *astound*: stun, stupefy.

l. 212. *siding*: supporting (taking one's side).

l. 215. *Chastity*. The Lady invokes as the third of the triad the classical Chastity, the virtue of adherence to the highest Reason, rather than the expected Christian Charity, divine or holy love.

l. 230. *Echo*: a nymph who was so talkative that Juno commanded her to speak only when spoken to, and then to repeat only what she heard. She fell in love with Narcissus, who spurned her, and whom Venus punished by making him fall in love with his own image in a pool. Echo pined away with grief until only her voice remained. Echo songs, in which the refrain repeats the end of the line preceding it, were common; and the invocation of the nymph leads one to expect a refrain which never comes.

l. 231. *airy shell*: the sphere of the sky.

l. 232. *Meander*: a river in Phrygia to which Echo wandered in her despair.

l. 234. *love-lorn nightingale*. Philomela, raped and mutilated by her brother-in-law Tereus, was transformed into the nightingale, who sings nightly of the grief of love.

33 l. 241. *parley*: speech, alluding to her notorious loquacity.   *sphere*: the sky, the 'airy shell' of l. 231.

l. 244. *mould*: clay.

33 l. 247. *air*: both song and atmosphere.

l. 248. *his*: its, the 'something holy' of l. 246.

l. 251. *fall*: cadence.

l. 253. *Sirens*: in *Od.*, xii. 39-72, beautiful sea nymphs who drew sailors to their destruction by the power of their songs.

l. 254. *Naiades*: nymphs of streams and springs.

l. 257. *Scylla*: a nymph who was changed by Circe (or in some versions of the story by Amphitrite), her rival in love, into a monster with ferocious dogs sprouting from her lower body. She ultimately became a dangerous rock off the Sicilian coast.

l. 259. *fell*: cruel, savage.   *Charybdis*: a violent whirlpool opposite Scylla.

l. 262. *home-felt*: heartfelt, apparently a Miltonic coinage.

l. 265. *Hail foreign wonder*: echoing Ferdinand on his first sight of Miranda, 'O you wonder!' (*Tempest*, i. ii. 427).

l. 267. *Unless the goddess.* i.e. unless you are she; the suggestion recalls Aeneas' reaction to seeing Venus after the Trojan shipwreck, '*O dea certe*' (*Aen.*, i. 328), and Ferdinand's response to his first sight of Miranda, 'Most sure the goddess | On whom these airs attend' (*Tempest*, i. ii. 422-3).

l. 268. *Sylvan*: Sylvanus, god of woods.

l. 273. *shift*: expedient.

34 l. 286. *hit*: guess.

l. 287. *Imports their loss*: does their loss matter?

l. 290. *Hebe*: lit. 'youth', the daughter of Zeus and Hera, and cupbearer to the gods.

ll. 291-2. *what time . . . came*: i.e. at evening, when the oxen were unyoked.   *traces*: harness.

l. 293. *swinked*: wearied with toil (from *swink*, labour).   *hedger*: workman in charge of maintaining hedges and fences.

l. 294. *mantling*: enveloping, covering.

l. 297. *port*: bearing.

l. 299. *element.* The word was used both for the sky and the air.

l. 301. *plighted*: pleated.

l. 312. *Dingle*: woodland hollow.

l. 313. *bosky bourn*: stream bordered by shrubs.

l. 315. *attendance*: companions (those who attend you).

l. 316. *shroud*: sheltered (past participle of *shroud*, to take shelter).

l. 318. *thatched pallet*: nest of straw.

35 l. 325. *it*: courtesy, which derives from 'court'.

l. 326. *yet*: both 'still' and 'nevertheless'.

l. 329. *square*: adjust, adapt.

l. 332. *wont'st*: are used to.   *benison*: blessing.

l. 334. *disinherit*: dispossess.

l. 335. *shades*: shadows.

l. 338. *rush-candle*: a candle made by dipping a rush in tallow or oil, which gave a very weak light.   *wicker hole*: window filled with wicker-work (instead of glass, hence implying a very poor dwelling).

l. 340. *rule*: ray, beam.

ll. 341–2. *star . . . Cynosure.* North Star: the Cynosure is the constellation Ursa Minor, the little bear, which has the North Star in its tail; it is *Tyrian* because the Tyrians, or Phoenicians (from their capital Tyre), used it to steer by, unlike the Greeks, who steered by Ursa Major; it is the *star of Arcady* because the Arcadian prince Arcas was transformed by Zeus into Ursa Minor when he was about to kill his mother Callisto, who had been metamorphosed into a bear, and who thereupon became the constellation Ursa Major.

l. 344. *folded*: i.e. in their sheepfolds.   *wattled cotes*: sheds constructed of woven twigs.

l. 345. *pastoral . . . stops*: the shepherd's pipe, traditionally made of oat stalks; the *stops* are the finger holes.

l. 349. *innumerous*: innumerable.

36 l. 359. *over-exquisite*: over-elaborate or unreasonably precise.

l. 360. *cast*: forecast.

l. 361. *so*: as they have been predicted.

l. 362. *forestall*: anticipate; 'think of, deal with, or introduce before the appropriate time; "to meet [misfortune, etc.] halfway"' (*OED*).

l. 366. *to seek*: lacking, at a loss.

l. 367. *unprincipled in*: ignorant of the principles of.

l. 368. *bosoms*: embraces, holds in its bosom.

l. 369. *single*: mere.

l. 372. *misbecoming*: unbecoming.

l. 375. *flat*: including the sense of lifeless, dull.

l. 376. *seeks*: resorts.

l. 378. *plumes*: dresses or preens.

36 l. 379. *resort*: 'Concourse or assemblage of people' (*OED*).

l. 380. *all to-*: utterly; both words are intensives.

l. 382. *centre*: of the earth (hence as far as possible from daylight).

l. 386. *affects*: prefers.

l. 387. *cell*: technically, a single-chamber dwelling, often with monastic implications; by the late sixteenth century used poetically for 'a small and humble dwelling, a cottage' (*OED*). Not applied to prisons until the eighteenth century.

l. 388. *haunt*: companionship, society.

l. 390. *weeds*: clothing.

l. 391. *beads*: rosary.   *maple dish*: wooden bowl.

l. 393. *Hesperian tree.* The tree, which bore golden apples, was a wedding gift from the earth goddess Ge to Hera when she married Zeus. Hera planted it in the garden of the Hesperides, daughters of the evening star Hesperus, and set the dragon Ladon to guard it. Stealing the golden apples was one of the labours of Hercules. In some versions, he succeeded by persuading Atlas, the brother of Hesperus, to bring him the apples; in others, he killed the dragon and took the fruit himself.

l. 395. *unenchanted eye.* Hercules used charms to put the dragon to sleep.

37 l. 397. *Incontinence*: specifically, in the seventeenth century, uncontrolled sexual passion.

l. 398. *unsunned*: hidden.

l. 401. *wink on*: wink at, overlook.

l. 404. *Of . . . not.* 'It is not night or loneliness that worry me.'

l. 407. *unowned*: lost.

l. 408. *Infer, as if*: imply that.

l. 410. *equal . . . fear.* The metaphor is of a balance weighing hope against fear.

l. 411. *arbitrate the event*: decide the outcome.

l. 413. *squint*: not looking straight.

l. 420. *chastity*: see l. 215.

l. 422. *quivered nymph*: on the model of the chaste Diana, goddess of the hunt (see l. 441).

l. 423. *trace*: travel through.   *unharboured*: without shelter.

l. 426. *mountaineer*: mountain dweller.

l. 428. *very desolation*: utter desolation, desolation itself.

l. 429. *shagged*: shaggy.

l. 430. *unblenched*: unflinching.

l. 431. *Be it*: so long as it is.

l. 433. *fire*: the will-o'-the-wisp.   *moorish*: marshy.

l. 434. *Blue*: 'the colour of plagues and things hurtful' (*OED*). *stubborn unlaid ghost*: ghost that refuses to remain buried.

38 l. 435. *curfew*: the evening bell, rung at nine o'clock in Milton's time, originally as a signal to extinguish all household fires (the word derives from *couvre feu*), but by the sixteenth century merely marking the hour. Spirits were free to walk either then or at midnight, and to continue till the first cock-crow.

l. 436. *swart . . . mine*: black underground fairy; cf. the underground demons in *Il Penseroso*, ll. 93–4.

l. 439. *old schools*: philosophical academies.

l. 443. *brinded*: tawny and streaked or spotted.

l. 444. *pard*: the word was used for both the panther and leopard.

l. 445. *bolt*: arrow.

ll. 447–8. *What . . . wore*. Minerva carried on her shield the snake-haired head of the Gorgon Medusa, which turned those who looked at it to stone.

ll. 459–63. *Till oft . . . immortal*: in *PL*, v. 497–503, Raphael similarly offers Adam the hope that his body may ultimately be refined into pure spirit.

l. 459. *oft converse*: frequent conversation.

ll. 465–75. *But most . . . state*. The argument follows that of Socrates in the *Phaedo*, 81: virtuous souls rejoice in their liberation from the body at death, but the souls of carnal and worldly people fear the realms of the spirit and are dragged back to this world, where they haunt their graves and are visible as ghosts.

l. 468. *Embodies, and imbrutes*: becomes physical and bestial.

39 l. 479. *nectared*: both deliciously sweet and heavenly; nectar was the food of the gods.

l. 480. *crude*: indigestible.

l. 483. *night-foundered*: submerged in night.

l. 491. *iron stakes*: i.e. their weapons, swords or daggers.

l. 494. *Thyrsis*: a singer-shepherd in Theocritus' *Idyll* i and Virgil's *Eclogue* vii, hence alluding again to Lawes (see ll. 86–8).

l. 495. *huddling*: pressing together.   *Madrigal*: technically a part song for three or more voices, but here simply music.

39 l. 501. *next*: closest, dearest.

l. 502. *toy*: trifle.

l. 506. *To*: compared with.

l. 509. *sadly*: in earnest.

l. 511. *me unhappy*: imitating the Latin *me miserum*; cf. Satan's 'Me miserable!', *PL*, iv. 73.

40 l. 513. *fabulous*: mere fables.

l. 517. *chimeras*. The chimera was a composite monster with three heads of lion, goat, and dragon.

l. 520. *navel*: centre.

l. 530. *Charactered*: lit. engraved or imprinted, continuing the coining metaphor.

l. 531. *hard*: close.   *crofts*: enclosed fields.

l. 532. *brow*: form the brow of, overlook.

l. 534. *stabled*. The word apparently meant simply 'in their lairs' for Milton; cf. *PL*, ix. 748, where sea-monsters are described as 'stabled'.

l. 535. *Hecate*: queen of the underworld, patroness of sorcerers (see l. 135).

l. 539. *unweeting*: not knowing, or unwittingly.

l. 542. *knot-grass*: a common weed with intricately branched creeping stems and pink flowers (*polygonum aviculare*).

l. 545. *flaunting*: 'waving gaily or proudly like a plume or banner' (*OED*).

l. 546. *melancholy*: the serious mood associated with artistic composition: see *Il Penseroso*, ll. 11 ff.

l. 547. *meditate*: exercise, with an echo of Virgil's '*musam meditari*' (*Eclogues*, i. 2), to occupy oneself with song or poetry.

l. 548. *close*: cadence.

l. 551. *listened them*. 'Listen' was regularly used transitively until the nineteenth century.

41 l. 558. *took . . . ware*: captured before she knew it.

ll. 559–60. *never . . . displaced*. (1) [Silence was willing to be] annihilated if such music could always replace her; (2) [Silence was willing to] cease being silent if she could be superseded in this way.

l. 585. *period*: sentence, or full stop (hence, 'not even a punctuation mark . . .').

42 l. 599. *stubble*: the short stalks of grain left after reaping, i.e. not a solid foundation.

l. 604. *sooty*: black.   *Acheron*: hell; Acheron was one of the four rivers of the underworld.

l. 605. *Harpies and hydras.* The harpies, who attacked Aeneas and his men and destroyed their food, had the faces of women and the bodies and talons of birds; the hydra was a many-headed poisonous serpent killed by Hercules.

l. 606. *Ind*: India.

l. 607. *purchase*: prey or plunder; the word literally means the pursuit of game in hunting.

l. 608. *curls*: curled hair, an attribute of Bacchus, was considered a sign of licentiousness or effeminacy.

l. 610. *emprise*: chivalric enterprise.

l. 611. *stead*: service.

l. 617. *shifts*: expedients.

l. 618. *surprisal*: being surprised.

l. 620. *Of small regard to see to*: unimpressive in appearance.

l. 621. *virtuous*: potent, capable of producing great effects.

l. 626. *scrip*: 'a small bag, especially one carried by . . . a shepherd' (*OED*).

l. 627. *simples*: medicinal herbs.

43 l. 635. *clouted shoon*: either patched shoes, or shoes with clouted soles, studded with broad-headed nails.

ll. 636–7. *moly . . . gave.* In *Od.*, x. 287–303, Hermes gives Odysseus the magic herb moly, with a white flower and a black root, to protect him against the charms of Circe. Moly was often allegorized in the Renaissance as temperance or prudence.

l. 638. *haemony*. Various derivations for the name have been proposed, from Haemonia, or Thessaly, traditionally the home of witchcraft, or from the Greek *haimon*, skilful, or from *haimonios*, blood-red (suggesting Christ's redemptive blood).

l. 646. *lime-twigs*: traps; lit. twigs smeared with the sticky substance birdlime, used for catching birds.

l. 647. *came off*: got away.

l. 651. *brandished blade*: following Hermes' instructions to Odysseus that he must approach Circe with his sword drawn.

l. 655. *sons of Vulcan*: the underground spirits that cause volcanoes to erupt. Vulcan was god of fire, and kept the forges of the gods.

l. 657. *apace*: quickly.

[stage direction] *puts . . . about*: pushes away and begins.

43   l. 660. *nerves*: muscles.

ll. 661–2. *Daphne . . . Apollo*. Daphne was a chaste nymph pursued by Apollo. As he was about to catch her, the gods answered her prayers and transformed her into a laurel.

l. 664. *corporal rind*: bodily shell; *rind* = the skin of a person or animal (still in use in 'bacon rind').

44   l. 669. *fancy*: imagination in the sense of fantasy (of which it is originally a variant spelling); often applied to love.

l. 672. *cordial julep*: restorative drink; both words had medicinal overtones.

l. 673. *his*: its.

l. 674. *balm*: specifically, balsam, an aromatic resin 'much prized for its fragrance and medicinal properties' (*OED*), and more generally any fragrant and healing substance or agency.

ll. 675–6. *nepenthes . . . Helena*. Returning from Troy, Menelaus and Helen stopped in Egypt, where they were hospitably received by Thone and his wife Polydamna. Polydamna gave Helen the drug *nepenthes*, which could banish grief from the mind, and she administered it to Menelaus.   *Jove-born Helena*: Helen was the child of Jove by Leda.

l. 685. *unexempt condition*: condition to which there can be no exceptions.

l. 688. *That have*: you who have.

l. 694. *aspects*: both faces and looks.

l. 698. *vizored*: masked.   *forgery*: deception.

l. 700. *lickerish*: tempting, delicious, lecherous.

45   l. 707. *budge doctors*: stodgy or pompous teachers (probably alluding to the lambswool fur, called *budge*, that trimmed academic gowns). *Stoic*: the philosophical school that advocated renunciation of worldly things.   *fur*: academic discipline (alluding again to the trimming of university gowns).

l. 708. *Cynic tub*. The Cynics counselled a life of poverty and renunciation of pleasure; in pursuit of these ideals Diogenes made a tub his home.

l. 714. *curious*: fastidious, difficult to satisfy.

l. 716. *shops*: workshops.

l. 719. *hutched*: stored.

l. 720. *store*: furnish.

l. 721. *pet*: ill-humoured fit.   *pulse*: legume seeds; beans, peas, lentils, etc., typifying the simplest foods.

l. 722. *frieze*: rough wool.

l. 730. *cumbered*: overwhelmed, blocked up.

l. 733. *the forehead of the deep*: that part of the earth's core nearest the surface. 'Deep' usually signified the ocean, but could mean the depths of the earth as well, and diamonds come from the earth not the sea.

l. 737. *coy*: shy.

ll. 737–8. *cozened* | *With*: deceived by.

l. 740. *current*: in circulation, as currency.

l. 745. *brag*: display, with an overtone of boastfulness.

46 l. 750. *sorry grain*: poor colour.   *ply*: work at.

l. 751. *tease*: comb out, for spinning.

l. 752. *vermeil*: scarlet.

l. 759. *pranked*: dressed up.

l. 760. *bolt*: sift, as in running flour through a sieve (thereby separating the attractive from the unattractive arguments, letting only the 'refined' ones appear).

l. 769. *beseeming*: befitting.

l. 770. *lewdly*: wickedly, with an overtone of lasciviously.

l. 774. *no whit*: not a bit.

l. 775. *the giver*: God, not Nature (see 'His', l. 776).

l. 782. *sun-clad*: radiant.

l. 785. *high mystery*: holy doctrine.

47 l. 791. *fence*: fencing skill.

l. 793. *uncontrollèd*: uncontrollable.

l. 794. *rapt*: enraptured.

l. 797. *brute . . . shake*. Alluding to Horace's '*bruta tellus . . . concutitur*', the brute earth was shaken so violently by a thunderbolt that the existence of the gods seemed to be confirmed (*Odes*, 1. xxxiv. 9–12). *nerves*: strength, energy.

l. 803. *Dips me*: suffuses me with moisture.

l. 804. *Speaks . . . chains*: i.e. has a voice of thunder and pronounces a sentence of chains.   *Erebus*: primeval darkness, the son of Chaos, according to Hesiod; here used for the underworld.

l. 805. *Saturn's crew*. The giants and Titans: with Saturn (the Greek Cronos) they made war on Saturn's son Jove (or Zeus), who defeated them and imprisoned them in the underworld.

l. 806. *try her*: test her strength.

47 l. 808. *canon laws*: Fundamental principles; but the use is ironic, since the term literally means the laws of the church as established by an ecclesiastical council.

l. 809. *suffer*: permit.

ll. 809–10. *lees . . . blood.* The melancholic humour, the part of blood associated with the element earth, was conceived to precipitate as sediment, causing depression or madness.

l. 811. *straight*: immediately.

l. 816. *reversed*: turned backwards or upside down; Circe's charms were similarly undone by reversing her wand.

l. 817. *backward . . . power*: i.e. his spells can only be undone by reciting them backwards.

l. 822. *Meliboeus*: in Virgil's *Eclogues* i and vii, an old shepherd/poet; the name was often used as the type of the wise shepherd in Renaissance pastorals. Since the Sabrina story (ll. 824 ff.) derives most directly from *FQ*, commentators have usually identified Meliboeus with Spenser.

l. 823. *soothest*: wisest.

48 l. 825. *with . . . sways*: with watery power controls: a *curb* is the leash or reins used to control an animal.

ll. 826–31. *Sabrina . . . flood.* Sabrina is the Latin name of the River Severn. Milton's immediate source for the story of the death of the girl who became the tutelary nymph of the river is in *FQ*, II. x. 17–19; the account ultimately derives from Geoffrey of Monmouth's *Historia Regum Britanniae*. Sabrina was the illegitimate child of King Locrine by his beloved mistress Estrildis; both she and Sabrina were drowned on the orders of Locrine's queen Gwendolen after she had defeated and killed her husband in battle. In Geoffrey, the story is about thwarted love and destructive jealousy; sixteenth-century versions, of which there are several, generally stress Sabrina's innocence and the pathos of her situation.

l. 827. *Whilom*: formerly (i.e. before she became a nymph).

l. 828. *Brute*: Brutus, great-grandson of Aeneas and legendary founder of Britain.

l. 831. *Commended*: entrusted.   *flood*: river.

l. 832. *stayed*: hindered.

l. 835. *Nereus*: a sea-god, the 'old man of the sea' in Homer and, unlike the other sea deities Neptune and Proteus, wise and generous.

l. 836. *lank*: drooping, languid (*OED* 3).

l. 837. *his daughters*: the Nereids, recalling Spenser's account of the wounded Marinell cured by the Nereids with 'sovereign balm and nectar good', *FQ*, III. iv. 40.

l. 838. *nectared lavers*: perfumed basins.   *asphodel*: immortal flower found in the Elysian Fields.

l. 839. *porch and inlet*: both mean entrance; a distinction between outer and inner openings seems to be intended.

l. 840. *ambrosial*: heavenly, hence restorative.

l. 841. *quick*: both swift and living.   *immortal change*: change to an immortal.

l. 845. *urchin blasts*: wounds or illnesses caused by goblins: an urchin is a hedgehog, and goblins were called urchins because they were said to assume that shape.

l. 846. *shrewd*: malignant, mischievous.

l. 849. *lays*: songs.

l. 852. *the old swain*: Meliboeus (see l. 822).

l. 858. *adjuring*: entreating.

49 l. 863. *amber-dropping hair*: (1) flowing hair the colour of amber; (2) hair perfumed with ambergris.

l. 864. *honour's*: Chastity's.

l. 865. *lake*. The word could mean a running stream, but Milton may be thinking of Virgil, who refers to the Tiber as a lake (*lacus*) in *Aen.*, viii. 74.

l. 868. *Oceanus*: One of the Titans, father of the rivers and in Homer the progenitor of the Olympian gods.

l. 869. *earth-shaking*: Homer's standard epithet for Neptune.

l. 870. *Tethys*: wife of Oceanus.

l. 871. *Nereus*: see l. 835.

l. 872. *Carpathian wizard's hook*. Proteus could change his shape, lived, according to Virgil, in the Carpathian sea, was a *vates*, or seer, and, with his shepherd's crook, herded Neptune's flocks of sea-lions.

l. 873. *Triton*: Neptune's herald (see *Lycidas*, l. 89), who plays a conch shell.   *winding*: both played like a trumpet and twisted.

l. 874. *Glaucus*: Boeotian fisherman transformed into a sea god by eating a magic herb, which also endowed him with the power of prophecy.

l. 875. *Leucothea*: lit. 'white goddess', the sea deity into whom Neptune transformed Ino, aunt of Dionysus/Bacchus (and his foster mother after the death of his mother Semele), to save her from the wrath of Juno. She is generous to mortals, and gave Odysseus her magic scarf to keep him from drowning.

49 l. 876. *her son*: Melicertes, transformed with Ino into the sea god Palaemon, the Roman Portunus, guardian of ports and harbours.

l. 877. *Thetis*: a Nereid, the mother of Achilles.   *tinsel-slippered feet.* Homer calls Thetis 'silver-footed'; *tinsel* (lit. 'sparkling') was originally cloth made with silver or gold threads; subsequently any glittering cloth or decoration, usually with disparaging connotations.

l. 878. *Sirens*: sea creatures whose singing was irresistible; but unlike the other sea creatures invoked, these are not beneficent, and Milton has already alluded to their dangerous attractions and their association with Circe and Comus (l. 253). Odysseus did, however, through wisdom and cunning, hear their songs and escape unharmed.

l. 879. *Parthenope*: one of the Sirens. According to post-Homeric legend, after the escape of Odysseus the Sirens drowned themselves, and Parthenope was washed up on the shore near Naples. A tomb was erected for her and the city originally bore her name.

l. 880. *Ligea*: another Siren, according to Eustathius' commentary on Homer, and a river nymph with lustrous hair in Virgil.

l. 884. *wily*: cunning, artful—apparently not used pejoratively here.

l. 892. *sliding*: gliding.   *stays*: stops.

l. 893. *azurn*: azure, Milton's coinage; cf. '*cedarn*', l. 990.

l. 896. *fleet*: swift.

50 l. 904. *charmèd band*: magic bonds.

l. 907. *unblessed*: unholy, wicked.

l. 913. *of precious cure*: valuable for healing.

l. 917. *glutinous heat*: heat sufficient to make the gums like glue.

l. 921. *Amphitrite*: a nereid, the wife of Neptune.

l. 923. *Anchises*: father of Aeneas, hence ancestor of Locrine and Sabrina.

l. 924. *brimmèd*: brimming.

l. 926. *petty*: little.

l. 928. *singèd*: scorching.

l. 930. *torrent*: torrential.

l. 933. *beryl*: general name for a group of greenish and blue-green precious and semi-precious stones, including the emerald and aquamarine.

51 l. 941. *device*: trick.

l. 942. *waste*: superfluous.

l. 949. *gratulate*: welcome.

l. 959. *sunshine*: sunny.

l. 960. *duck or nod*: curtsy or bow, the graces of courtly dances.

l. 961. *trippings*: dances.

l. 962. *Of*: by.   *court guise*: courtly style or behaviour.

l. 963. *Mercury . . . devise.* Hermes/Mercury was the inventor of the lyre, but there is no classical source crediting him with the invention of dancing. However, Milton may be thinking of the masque tradition: Mercury introduces the final dances of Jonson's *Pleasure Reconciled to Virtue*, and in Jonson's *Pan's Anniversary* (1621), Hermes is cited as the archetype choreographer, exceeded only by Pan.

l. 964. *mincing*: dainty, elegant (apparently not pejorative).
Dryades: wood nymphs.

l. 965. *lawns . . . leas*: glades . . . meadows.

l. 970. *timely*: early.

l. 971. *patience*: lit. 'endurance of suffering'.   *truth*: constancy, fidelity.

l. 972. *assays*: trials.

52   l. 980. *liquid*: clear, bright.

ll. 981–3. *gardens . . . tree*: see l. 393.

l. 984. *crispèd*: a poetic word 'applied to trees: sense uncertain' (*OED* 4). The word generally means curled, crinkled, or puckered.

l. 985. *spruce*: lively.

l. 986. *Graces . . . Hours*: or Charites and Horae, goddesses respectively of natural beauty and of the seasons (see *PL*, iv. 267).

l. 988. *That*: so that.

l. 989. *west winds*: zephyrs, gentle breezes.   *musky*: fragrant.

l. 990. *cedarn alleys*: walks between rows of cedars; *cedarn* is apparently Milton's coinage (cf. *azurn*, l. 893).

l. 991. *Nard, . . . cassia*: aromatic plants: nard, or spikenard, is a root, cassia a bark.

l. 992. *Iris*: goddess of the rainbow.

l. 993. *that blow*: where bloom.

l. 995. *purfled*: multi-coloured.

l. 996. *Elysian*: heavenly; from Elysium, in classical myth the fields where the spirits of the blessed live after death.

l. 997. *List*: hearken.   *true*: 'of the right kind' (*OED*), i.e. capable of apprehending spiritual things.

52 l. 999. *Adonis*: lover of Venus, killed by a boar and restored to immortal life in the Garden of Adonis. See *PL*, ix. 439–40.

l. 1000. *Waxing*: growing.

l. 1002. *Assyrian queen*: Venus, or Aphrodite, first worshipped, according to Pausanias, in Assyria.

l. 1004. *advanced*: raised high.

ll. 1004–8. *Cupid ... bride*. The story is in Apuleius' *Golden Ass*; Psyche was a mortal woman so beautiful that Venus, envious of her, sent Cupid to make her fall in love with someone loathsome, but Cupid fell in love with her instead. He visited her only in the dark at night, and forbade her to see him. Her sisters convinced her that her lover was a monster, and one night as he slept beside her she lit a candle to look at him, and, overcome with his beauty, let some wax drop on him, waking him. For her disobedience she was punished with many trials and wanderings, but Jove finally relented and allowed her to marry Cupid and live with him in heaven.

ll. 1010–11. *Two ... Joy*. In Apuleius, their child is Voluptas.

53 l. 1015. *bowed welkin*: arch of the sky.

l. 1017. *corners*: farthest extremities (on the analogy of 'the four corners of the earth'); but Milton may also be taking the word in its etymological sense of horns, from Latin *cornu*.

l. 1021. *Higher ... chime*: above the music of the spheres, hence to the highest heaven.

ENGLISH POEMS ADDED IN 1673

54 *Sonnet 11* ('A book was writ of late'). In the Trinity MS, Sonnet 11 follows Sonnet 12. The MS subtitle, 'On the Detraction Which Followed Upon My Writing Certain Treatises', refers to the four divorce tracts, *Doctrine and Discipline of Divorce* (1643, 1644), *Judgment of Martin Bucer* (1644), *Tetrachordon*, and *Colasterion* (both 1645). The sonnet would thus date from late 1645 or early 1646.

l. 1. *Tetrachordon*. Lit. a four-note scale, or a musical instrument with four strings; here, the four places in scripture relevant to the question of divorce 'harmonized' to present the argument for divorce on the basis of incompatibility.

l. 4. *Numbering*: either determining the number of, or comprising (as its readers).

l. 5. *stall-reader*: who reads the book at the bookstall, and has not purchased it.

ll. 6–7. *in file ... false*: stand in a row misreading.

ll. 7-8. *Mile-End Green*: located a mile beyond Aldgate, the eastern end of London.

ll. 8-9. *Gordon ... Galasp*: rough Scottish names (Colkitto is a nickname, 'lefty Colin', and Galasp seems to be a version of Gillespie). They have been identified, at least plausibly, as three Royalist followers of the Marquis of Montrose and a leader of the Westminster Assembly; but more broadly, Milton's allusion would be both to the general assimilation of the Scots in England after the Stuarts ascended the throne, and to the more immediate ubiquitousness of Scottish Presbyterians.

l. 10. *rugged*: harsh; the manuscript originally read 'barbarous'.

l. 11. *Quintilian*: Late first-century author of an important treatise on rhetoric, *The Institutes*, which has a section (1. v. 8) condemning the importation of foreign words into Latin.

l. 12. *Sir John Cheke*: mid-sixteenth-century English humanist, first Professor of Greek at Cambridge, and tutor of Edward VI.

Sonnet 12. On the Same ('I did but prompt the age'). Date: see Sonnet 11.

l. 1. *clogs*: prisoners' restraints.

l. 2. *ancient liberty*. This implies not only the laws in scripture, but also those inscribed internally and naturally, reason and the promptings of nature, the Christian liberty central to Milton's thought.

l. 4. *owls*: considered stupid birds in Renaissance birdlore.
cuckoos: noisy birds associated with cuckoldry.

ll. 5-7. *hinds ... fee.* Latona, or Leto, transformed two peasants ('hinds') into frogs when they refused to give her a drink for her infants, Apollo and Diana, who were destined to control ('hold in fee') the sun and moon.

l. 8. *casting pearl to hogs*: alluding to Matt. 7: 6.

l. 10. *truth ... free*: cf. John 8: 32.

l. 13. *mark*: target.

l. 14. *For*: despite.

55 *Sonnet 13. To Mr H. Lawes* ('Harry whose tuneful'). The poem first appeared in *Choice Psalms* (1648) by Henry and William Lawes; the volume was dedicated to King Charles and commemorated William Lawes, who had died in his cause. Henry Lawes wrote the music for *Comus* and played the part of the Attendant Spirit.

ll. 2-3. *span ... accent*: give words their proper measure of length and stress.   *scan*: count.

55 l. 4. *Midas' ears*. Midas was punished with the ears of an ass for preferring Pan's music to Apollo's.   *committing*: joining together (*OED* 7), joining in conflict (*OED* 9); the Trinity MS originally read 'misjoyning'.   *short and long*: syllables or notes; the metrical values of words and music.

l. 8. *humour*: fit, suit.

l. 10. *Phoebus*: Apollo, as god of music.

l. 11. *story*. According to a marginal note in *Choice Psalms*, this alludes to 'The story of Ariadne set by him in music': Lawes's setting of William Cartwright's *Complaint of Ariadne*.

ll. 12–13. *Dante ... Casella*. Dante's meeting with the musician Casella is described in *Purgatorio*, ii. 76–117; Casella sings his setting of one of Dante's *canzoni*.

Sonnet 14 ('When faith and love which parted from thee never'). There are three MSS of this poem; one in Milton's hand is titled 'On the religious memory of Mrs Catharine Thomason my Christian friend deceased 16 December 1646'. She was the wife of George Thomason, a London bookseller; both she and her husband were collectors of contemporary pamphlets (the present Thomason Collection in the British Library contains over 22,000 items from 1640 to 1660, including several works by Milton inscribed as gifts of the author).

l. 4. *from life*: i.e. from eternal life.

l. 8. *Followed thee*: cf. Rev. 14: 13.

56 *Sonnet 15. On the Late Massacre in Piedmont*. On 24 Apr. 1655, the Duke of Savoy's troops slaughtered the Vaudois, or Waldensians, a Protestant sect regarded by contemporaries as the repository of primitive Christianity (modern historians find their origins in the twelfth-century followers of Valdes of Lyons, founder of a mendicant order). They had been granted limited rights in Savoy and, on the pretext that they had settled in territory forbidden them, were massacred. Cromwell issued a protest composed by Milton in May 1655. Later that summer the remaining Waldensian forces were able to defeat their persecutors and to secure their rights.

l. 4. *stocks and stones*: idols made of wood and stone.

l. 5. *thy book*: the book of God's judgments, recording those who are to have eternal life.

l. 10. *martyred blood ... sow*: recalling Tertullian's famous dictum 'The blood of the martyrs is the seed of the Church', as well as the parable of the sower, and the myth of Cadmus, who sowed the teeth of a serpent from which armed men arose.

l. 12. *triple Tyrant*: the pope; his mitre is composed of a triple crown.

l. 14. *Babylonian woe*. Babylon was the place of Jewish exile, the city of reprobation throughout Revelation, and was often identified by Protestants with papal Rome.

Sonnet 16 ('When I consider how my light is spent'). The date of this poem has occasioned much debate. Assuming that the order of the sonnets in the 1673 edition is chronological, its placement appears to date it after 1655; yet many readers have felt that the attitudes expressed would seem more appropriate to the onslaught of blindness in 1652. Neither date fits well with the second line of the sonnet, 'Ere half my days . . .': Milton was 44 in 1652. The usual subtitle, 'On his blindness', is an eighteenth-century addition.

l. 2. *Ere half my days*. If the biblical allotment of 70 years is meant, the poem would date from before 1643, at which time, however, Milton was not yet blind.

ll. 3–6. *talent . . . chide*: punning on the double sense of 'talent', ability, and the valuable coin of the ancient world. Milton alludes here to the parable of the talents, Matt. 25.

l. 7. *day-labour*: cf. John 9: 4 and the parable of the bridegroom that immediately precedes the parable of the talents.

l. 8. *fondly*: foolishly.   *prevent*: forestall, preclude.

l. 12. *Thousands*: the angels.

57   *Sonnet 17* ('Lawrence of virtuous father virtuous son'). Edward Lawrence (1633–57) was the elder son of Henry Lawrence, who became President of Cromwell's Council of State in 1654; his studious and literary son became a Member of Parliament in the last year of his life. Generally dated *c.*1655.

l. 4. *waste*: spend, pass; not necessarily pejorative.

l. 6. *Favonius*: the west wind.

l. 9. *neat*: elegant, tasteful, not excessive.

l. 10. *Of Attic taste*: as would have pleased the Athenians, with their refined food and conversation.

l. 12. *Tuscan air*: Italian music.

ll. 13–14. *spare | To interpose*: ambiguous—either refrain from or find time for.

Sonnet 18 ('Cyriack whose grandsire on the royal bench'). Cyriack Skinner (1627–1700), was the grandson of Sir Edward Coke (1552–1634), Chief Justice of Common Pleas and, from 1613 to 1616, of the

King's Bench, the most important legal mind of his time, especially as an advocate of the privileges of Parliament. Skinner may have been a student of Milton's, and is perhaps the author of an anonymous early life; he became an intimate friend. Written *c.*1655.

57 l. 2. *Themis*: goddess of justice.

l. 3. *volumes*: among Coke's books are *The Institutes of the Law of England*.

l. 4. *others*: other judges.

l. 5. *resolve* ... The verb is an imperative addressed to Skinner; the syntax is, 'resolve with me to drench deep thoughts in mirth.'

l. 8. *Swede* ... *French*. Skinner's interest in international politics is exemplified by reference to Charles X of Sweden's recent attack on Poland, and Cromwell's negotiations with Cardinal Mazarin, resulting in the Treaty of Westminster. Cf. Horace, *Odes*, II. xi. 1–6, in which the poet urges his friend to remember that youth is fleeting, and to forget the foreign adventures of 'the warlike Cantabrian ... and the Scythian'.

l. 9. *betimes*: early.

58 *Sonnet 19* ('Methought I saw my late espousèd saint'). Commentators have debated the identity of the 'late espousèd saint'. Readers who insist on the literalness of the allusions to childbirth in ll. 5–6 opt for Milton's first wife Mary Powell, who died in childbirth in 1652; however, Katherine Woodcock, Milton's second wife, who died of a fever in Feb. 1658, several months after delivering a child, would nevertheless have lived long enough to fulfil the prescribed period of purification alluded to in the poem. The reference to ritual purification in fact can be used to support either identification—it was *Mary* who brought Jesus to the temple 'when the days of her purification according to the law of Moses were accomplished' (Luke 2: 22); on the other hand, 'pure' (l. 9) is linked etymologically to the name Katherine by way of Gk. *katharos*, pure, and the purification in the poem is in any case being used as a simile: the woman is dressed in white *like* one who had been purified. Similar difficulties attend the question of whether the wife that he hopes to see again is a wife he ever, literally, saw—Milton was blind by the time he married Katherine Woodcock; on the other hand, the fact that the figure's face is veiled may imply that he has not in fact seen her. In the light of such ambiguous evidence, it might be worth entertaining the possibility that Milton is thinking of both his marriages in the poem.

l. 1. *late*: both recently (modifying 'espousèd'), and deceased.

l. 2. *Alcestis*: the wife of Admetus; she sacrificed her life to save her husband from death, and was rescued from the grave by Hercules ('Jove's great son', l. 3).

l. 5. *as whom*: as one whom.

l. 6. *Purification . . . law*. Rules for purification after childbirth are detailed in Lev. 12. Cleansing (the 'washing' of l. 5) occurred one week after the birth of a son, two weeks after the birth of a daughter; purification after another 33 or 66 days respectively. During that period, the woman could not enter the temple.

l. 10. *veiled*: Alcestis also returns veiled from the grave.

On the New Forcers of Conscience under the Long Parliament. Episcopacy was abolished in 1643, and after long and acrimonious debate the ordinances establishing Presbyterianism were finally formulated in 1646. Usually dated 1646.

l. 1. *prelate lord*: bishops were 'lords spiritual'.

l. 3. *plurality*: holding more than one benefice, an episcopal abuse that was continued by the Presbyterians.

l. 5. *adjure*: charge, bind (as to an oath): the Presbyterians demanded the enforcement of conformity to the reformed Church.

l. 7. *classic hierarchy*: the division of parishes into classes (presbyteries), which were below the synod and national assembly in the Church hierarchy.

l. 8. *A. S.* Adam Stewart, a Scottish divine who replied to the Independent position.   *Rutherford*: Samuel Rutherford, a Scottish member of the Westminster Assembly, whose *Divine Right of Church-Government* (1646) argued against toleration.

l. 10. *Paul*: St Paul, from whom Milton derived the concept of liberty of conscience against which Rutherford argued in his 1649 *Free Disputation Against pretended Liberty of Conscience*.

l. 12. *Edwards*: Thomas Edwards, who attacked Milton's views on divorce in *Gangrena . . . a Catalogue of . . . Heresies* (1646).   *Scotch What-d'ye-call*: cf. the generic Scots names in Sonnet 11; here, although editors have proposed various particular members of the Assembly, a general allusion to Scottish presbyters seems more likely to be intended—'any old Scot'.

l. 14. *packing*: manipulation by packing the meetings of the assembly in order to outnumber the dissenters.   *Trent*: the Council of Trent.

59 l. 17. *phylacteries*: small leather case containing texts from Exod. and Deut. worn by Jews in prayer; here, as an outward and hypocritical display.   *balk your ears*: stop short of clipping your ears.

59 l. 19. *they*: parliament.   *charge*: indictment.

l. 20. *old Priest*. Etymologically, 'priest' is a contracted form of 'presbyter'.

UNCOLLECTED ENGLISH POEMS

60 *On the Lord General Fairfax* ('Fairfax, whose name in arms through Europe rings'). First printed in *Letters of State* (1694), ed. Edward Phillips. The Trinity MS in Milton's hand (our text here) titles it 'On the Lord General Fairfax at the siege of Colchester'; the siege occurred in the summer of 1648. Sir Thomas Fairfax was commander-in-chief of the New Model Army.

l. 1. *rings*: resounds.

l. 5. *virtue*: retaining the sense of Lat. *virtus*, physical strength, courage, manliness; Phillips's 1694 version reads 'valour'.

l. 6. *Victory*. Besides Colchester, Fairfax's victories included the battles of Marston Moor and Naseby, decisive events in the war.

l. 7. *hydra*: a mythical beast with many heads; when one head was cut off, two sprouted as replacements. Hercules slew it.   *false north*: the Scots, who broke the Solemn League and Covenant, and sent troops in support of Charles I in 1648.

l. 8. *imp*: graft new feathers on. Although the hydra was not usually depicted as winged, its sister the sphinx was, as were other offspring of its mother, the monstrous Echidna, half woman, half snake.

l. 9. *a nobler task*. Fairfax, in fact, did not serve in the government. After Charles I was executed he resigned his position and retired to his estate at Nun Appleton; Marvell's *Upon Appleton House* celebrates that part of his career.

To the Lord General Cromwell ('Cromwell, our chief of men'). Like the preceding sonnet to Fairfax, this poem first appeared in *Letters of State* (1694). In the Trinity MS (our text here) it is titled, in the hand of a scribe, 'To the Lord General Cromwell May 1652 | On the proposals of certain ministers at the Committee for Propagation of the Gospel'. The Committee's business included regulating worship and promulgating basic tenets of belief; Cromwell was a member of the committee along with the other Independent ministers who championed a nationally supported church with limited toleration for dissent.

l. 4. *peace and truth*. The phrase appeared on a coin struck in celebration of Cromwell's victories; the words were also used to summarize the aims of the Solemn League and Covenant (1643).

ll. 5–6. *on the neck . . . pursued*. Cromwell overcame 'crowned fortune' by defeating not only Charles I, but also Charles II, crowned in Scotland in 1651 and defeated at Worcester in that year (see l. 9). Of that victory, Cromwell said, 'the dimensions of this mercy are above my thoughts. It is, for aught I know, a crowning mercy.'   *reared . . . trophies*: erected memorials to God's triumph.

l. 7. *Darwen*: the river in Lancashire near which the battle of Preston (Aug. 1648) was fought against the Scots.   *imbrued*: stained with blood.

l. 8. *Dunbar*: where Cromwell won a decisive victory over the Scots (Sept. 1650).

l. 9. *laureate wreath*: the laurel crown of victory.

l. 10. *peace . . . victories*. The sentiment goes back at least as far as Cicero, *De officiis*, in which the achievements of peace are extolled over victories in war.

ll. 11-12. *foes . . . chains*: alluding to those ministers who petitioned Parliament in 1652 to enforce conformity to a state-controlled Church.

l. 14. *hireling*. Under the proposals of 1652, the clergy were to be paid by the government. Cf. *Lycidas*, ll. 113-22.   *maw*: belly, mouth, appetite.

61 *To Sir Henry Vane the Younger* ('Vane, young in years, but in sage counsel old'). The title is from the Trinity MS (our text here), where the poem is in a scribe's hand. Vane had been Governor of Massachusetts (1635-7), Treasurer of the Navy (1639), and was a member of the Council of State concerned with foreign affairs in 1652 when the poem was written. He was executed in 1662 after the restoration of Charles II. The poem was first published in George Sikes, *The Life and Death of Sir Henry Vane* (1662), introduced as follows: 'The character of this deceased statesman . . . I shall exhibit to you in a paper of verses, composed by a learned gentleman, and sent him, July 3, 1652.'

l. 1. *young in years*. Vane was born in 1613, and was therefore almost 40. He was called 'the Younger' because his father, with the same name, was still alive.

l. 3. *gowns*: Roman senatorial togas.

l. 4. *Epirot . . . African*: Pyrrhus, King of Epirus, and Hannibal; both invaded Italy and were defeated.

ll. 5-6. *unfold . . . spelled*: uncover designs not easily deciphered. *hollow*: untrustworthy; punning, most commentators contend, on Holland, with whom Vane had urged an alliance, and against whom, when negotiations failed, he prepared the navy, suspecting their peace envoys.

61 l. 8. *nerves*: sinews.   *iron and gold*. Milton had noted in his commonplace book Machiavelli's dictum that arms, not money, are the sinews ('*il nervo*') of war.

l. 9. *equipage*: war machinery.

l. 12. *either sword*: of 'spiritual power and civil', l. 9, above.

To Mr Cyriack Skinner Upon his Blindness ('Cyriack, this three years' day these eyes'). For Skinner, see headnote to Sonnet 18, above. The poem was first published in Phillips's *Letters of State* (1694), titled 'To Mr Cyriack Skinner Upon his Blindness'. Our text is that of the Trinity MS, where the poem is probably in Skinner's hand. Date: 1655 (see ll. 1–3).

l. 1. *three years' day*. Milton became totally blind in 1651–2.   *clear*. In the *Second Defence*, Milton remarks that his eyes gave no outward sign of blindness.

l. 3. *light*. The 1694 text reads 'sight'.

ll. 4–6. *Nor . . . woman*: cf. descriptions of his blindness in *PL*, iii. 22–55.

l. 8. *bear up*: including the nautical meaning of sailing with the wind.

l. 10. *conscience*: including the sense of 'consciousness'.   *over-plied*: overworked; the nautical sense is steering against the wind.

l. 13. *mask*: perhaps in the theatrical sense (masque), especially for its royalist associations and its extravagant and ephemeral quality; also masquerade, false show, disguise.

MAJOR POEMS

62 *Paradise Lost*. The earliest subjects Milton seems to have considered for an epic were drawn from British history and legend, and his admiration for 'our sage and serious poet Spenser', the obvious English epic model, is expressed in *Areopagitica*—Dryden reports that Milton told him that 'Spenser was his original'. In the early 1640s he was thinking of biblical material as a subject not for epic but for tragedy: the Trinity MS includes four outlines of a drama on the fall, two of which are entitled *Paradise Lost* and *Adam Unparadized*. Milton's nephew Edward Phillips reports being shown some lines of Satan's soliloquy in Book IV (ll. 32–41) some years before Milton began the composition of his epic; the speech at that time was the beginning of a tragedy. But by the time Milton was writing the epic *Paradise Lost* he was representing the move away from chivalric legend (and, ultimately, from rhymed stanzas) as an affirmation of truth and

liberty. As an immediate model of the Protestant biblical epic, he had Guillaume Salluste, Sieur du Bartas' enormously influential *Les Semaines et les Jours* (1578), which appeared in English in Joshua Sylvester's translation as *Divine Weeks and Days* in 1605; Milton admired the poem, and declares his indebtedness to it by many allusions.

Milton clearly worked on some version of *Paradise Lost*, however intermittently, from the early 1640s on. John Aubrey reports that the composition of the poem in its final form took Milton four or five years, roughly from 1658 to 1663. This was a period of both total blindness and considerable danger for Milton; his sense of his situation is keenly conveyed in the opening section of Book VII. He worked by dictating to whatever willing scribe was at hand; Phillips corrected the spelling and punctuation of at least some of the manuscript. By 1667 it was ready for the printer—Milton's early biographer John Toland reports that the censor objected to it because of a passage in Book I (ll. 597-9) about the ominous implications of solar eclipses for the fate of monarchs, but it nevertheless was duly licensed and appeared in a first edition of six variant issues in 1667, 1668, and 1669, and in a second edition in 1674, the year of Milton's death. It sold relatively quickly, and by the time Dryden approached Milton, in the last year of his life, to declare his intention of turning the poem into an opera, it had established itself as a classic.

In its first published version, *Paradise Lost* was a poem in ten books; it did not include either Milton's introductory note on the verse or the arguments of the individual books, and had no prefatory commendatory poems. The note on the verse and the arguments, all grouped together at the beginning, were added in 1668, apparently at the request of the publisher. We have omitted them from our selection. For the second edition of 1674, Milton had revised the poem into twelve books. To accomplish this, Books VII and X were simply split in two; the rewriting involved was small, but not insignificant, and a few other minor revisions were made. The volume included a Latin prefatory poem by Milton's friend the physician Samuel Barrow, and Andrew Marvell's 'On Paradise Lost'. Some commentators have seen in the ten-book version a vestige of Milton's original dramatic scheme, a double five-act structure; the change to twelve books clearly reflects Milton's Virgilian model.

BOOK I

l. 4. *one greater man*: Jesus, as the Messiah.

l. 6. *heavenly muse*. Urania, the muse of astronomy, and therefore of heavenly matters generally, invoked by name in Book VII: as the inspiration of Moses, she is identified here with the divine word.

62 *secret top*: summit hidden from public view, where God spoke alone with Moses.

l. 7. *of Oreb, or of Sinai.* God delivered the Ten Commandments to Moses either on Mount Horeb (Deut. 4: 10) or on nearby Mount Sinai (Exod. 19: 20). Here, as throughout, Milton uses the Vulgate form of biblical names.

l. 8. *shepherd.* Moses is identified as the shepherd of Jethro's flock in Exod. 3, but the term is also used figuratively for him as leader of his people.   *seed*: literally translating *semen*, God's offspring, the children of Israel.

l. 9. *In the beginning*: the opening words of Genesis and John.

l. 10. *out of chaos.* Technically a heretical position: orthodox doctrine held that God created the world not out of unformed matter (the *chaos* of Neoplatonic philosophy) but *ex nihilo*, out of nothing, the 'void' of Gen. 1: 2.   *Sion hill*: the sacred Mount Zion, on which Solomon's Temple stood.

l. 11. *Siloa's brook*: the Pool of Siloam, which flows alongside the Temple mountain, and with whose waters Jesus cured a blind man.

l. 12. *Fast by*: close.

l. 15. *Aonian mount*: Helicon, in Aonia in Boeotia, sacred to the classical muses.

ll. 17–22. *And chiefly thou . . . pregnant*: the Holy Spirit, who in Gen. 1: 2 'moved upon the waters' and was the agent of creation. Milton's 'brooding' (l. 21) gives a more precise translation of the Hebrew.

l. 21. *Dove-like.* The Holy Spirit is a dove descending on Jesus in John 1: 32.

l. 24. *height.* Milton's normal spelling, and standard usage in the seventeenth century, is 'highth'.   *argument*: subject.

l. 28. *Nor*: not even.

63 l. 36. *what time*: when; the diction is Latinate, but the expression was in common English usage.

l. 48. *adamantine*: unbreakable; adamant was a mythical substance of impenetrable hardness.

l. 50. *Nine times . . . night.* The nine days of the rebel angels' fall is based not on biblical authority but on Hesiod's account of the fall of the Titans who rebelled against Zeus, which was considered another version of the same event.

l. 56. *baleful*: both malign and full of pain.

l. 57. *witnessed*: both regarded and testified to.

l. 60. *dismal*: ominous, disastrous.

l. 66. *hope never comes*: recalling Dante's inscription on the gate of hell, '*Lasciate ogni speranza, voi ch'entrate*' ('Abandon all hope, you who enter', *Inferno*, iii. 9).

l. 68. *Still urges*: continuously presses.

l. 72. *utter*: both total and outer.

l. 75. *As from the centre . . . pole.* Milton imagines a Ptolemaic universe with the earth at the centre of nine concentric spheres. The distance from hell to heaven is three times as far as the centre of the earth is from a point on the outermost sphere.

64 l. 78. *weltering*: writhing.

l. 81. *Beelzebub.* The name in Hebrew means 'god of flies'.

l. 82. *And thence . . . called Satan.* The name means 'enemy'; his original name was Lucifer, 'bringer of light'.

l. 84. *If . . . changed.* The words contain a double echo, of Aeneas seeing a vision of the dead Hector on the night Troy fell, '*quantum mutatus ab illo | Hectore*' ('how changed from that other Hector', *Aen.*, ii. 274–5), and of Isa. 14: 12, 'How art thou fallen from heaven, Lucifer, son of the morning.'

l. 87. *if he.* 'Thou beest' is understood.

l. 104. *dubious*: 'of uncertain issue or result' (*OED*).

l. 107. *study of*: zeal for (Lat. *studium*).

l. 114. *Doubted*: feared for.

65 l. 117. *empyreal*: heavenly (lit. made of fire, the purest element).

l. 132. *proof*: test.

l. 144. *Of force*: perforce.

l. 148. *suffice*: satisfy.

66 l. 158. *Doing or suffering*: whether active or passive.

l. 167. *fail*: mistake.

l. 172. *laid*: put down.

l. 178. *slip*: neglect.

l. 186. *afflicted*: lit. 'cast down'.

l. 187. *offend*: injure.

l. 196. *rood*: or rod, a variable measure, from six to eight yards.

67 ll. 198–9. *Titanian . . . Typhon.* The hundred-armed Briareos was a Titan, the monster Typhon (or Typhoeus) a giant with a hundred serpent-heads. Both Titans and giants made war on the Olympian gods and were thrown back to earth and crushed or cast into the classical hell, Tartarus. The Typhon story was moralized by

Renaissance mythographers as an allegory of the destructive potential of ambition.

67   l. 200. *Tarsus*. According to Pindar, Typhon dwelt in a cave in Cilicia, of which Tarsus was the principal city (*Pythian Odes*, i. 17).

l. 201. *Leviathan*: a mysterious sea-monster in Job 41, a 'piercing' and 'crooked serpent' in Isa. 27: 1, hence associated with Satan; also frequently identified as a whale. The story of the whale appearing a safe haven to unwary sailors was often cited as a parallel to the dangerous deceptiveness of Satan.

l. 206. *rind*: the skin of an animal.

l. 207. *under the lee*: in its shelter.

l. 208. *Invests*: envelops.

l. 210. *Chained on*: confined to.

l. 226. *incumbent*: lying (lit. 'pressing upon'; see l. 227).

l. 228. *lights*: alights.   *ever*: always.

l. 231. *subterranean wind*. Ovid describes underground winds creating a hill in *Met.*, xv. 296–377; seventeenth-century meteorology held that the earth is 'full of wind . . . which, sometimes breaking out, causeth horrible earthquakes' (Burton, *Anatomy of Melancholy*, II. ii. 3).

ll. 232–3. *Pelorus . . . Aetna*: Cape Faro, in north-east Sicily, and the volcano nearby.

l. 235. *Sublimed with mineral fury*: Vaporized by the volcano's violence.

68   l. 239. *Stygian flood*: the Styx, one of the four rivers of hell. *Stygian* implies impenetrable darkness.

l. 256. *What matter where*: 'I am' understood.

l. 266. *astonished*: stunned.   *oblivious*: producing forgetfulness.

l. 268. *mansion*: dwelling-place (not necessarily a building).

l. 276. *edge*: front line (Lat. *acies*).

69   l. 282. *pernicious*: ruinous, fatal.

l. 285. *Ethereal temper*: tempered in heavenly fire.

l. 288. *optic glass*: telescope.   *Tuscan artist*: Galileo, who first devised a telescope sufficiently powerful to reveal the surface of the moon. Milton alludes to a visit to him in *Areopagitica*.

l. 289. *Fesole*: Fiesole, a hill-town near Florence.

l. 290. *Valdarno*: the Arno valley, in which Florence is located.

l. 294. *admiral*: flagship.

l. 296. *marl*: soil.

l. 299. *Natheless*: nevertheless.

l. 303. *Vallombrosa*: lit. 'valley of shadows', near Florence.
Etrurian shades: Tuscan foliage.

l. 304. *sedge*: seaweed.

l. 305. *Orion*: one of the giants, a great hunter slain by Diana and transformed into a constellation. It was associated with storms because its evening rising during autumn signals the approach of winter.

ll. 306–7. *whose waves . . . chivalry.* After Moses parted the Red Sea and the Israelites passed safely to the opposite shore, the waters closed over the pursuing Egyptians, destroying Pharaoh's army.   *Busiris.* Pharaoh, here given the name of a legendary Egyptian tyrant.

l. 307. *Memphian chivalry*: Egyptian cavalry.

l. 309. *Goshen*: the area in Egypt where Jacob and his descendants settled, and from which the Israelites were fleeing.

l. 313. *amazement*: stupefaction.

l. 317. *astonishment*: 'loss of sense . . . mental prostration, stupor' (*OED*; cf. l. 266).

l. 320. *virtue*: strength.

70 l. 324. *Cherub and seraph*: the two highest orders of angels, first established by Dionysius the Pseudo-Areopagite (fourth-century AD).

l. 333. *whom*: the one whom.

l. 339. *Amram's son*: Moses, whose 'potent rod' invoked the plague of locusts on the Egyptians.

l. 341. *warping*: whirling.

l. 345. *cope*: canopy.

l. 353. *Rhene . . . Danaw*: Rhine, Danube.

l. 360. *erst*: formerly.

71 l. 363. *books of life.* The term is used in the Old and New Testaments for the record of God's faithful, those destined for eternal life in heaven.

l. 365. *Got them new names.* The transformation of the fallen angels into pagan deities is attested by many Church Fathers.

l. 372. *religions*: religious rites.

l. 373. *devils . . . deities.* 'They sacrificed unto devils, not to God' (Deut. 32: 17).

l. 376. *then*: i.e. subsequently, in the 'heathen world' of l. 375.

l. 380. *promiscuous*: 'massed together without order' (*OED*).

l. 392. *Moloch*: the name means *king*; cf. 'Nativity Ode', l. 205 ff.

ll. 394–5. *Though for the noise . . . unheard.* The cries of sacrificial children were drowned out by the sound of drums and timbrels.

71 l. 396. *Ammonite.* The Ammonites were enemies of Israel, ultimately conquered by Jephtha.

l. 397. *Rabba*: Rabbah, the Ammonite capital; modern Amman, in Jordan.

ll. 398-9. *Argob . . . Basan . . . Arnon*: the lands east of the Dead Sea, roughly the northern section of modern Jordan.

71-2 ll. 401-3. *Of Solomon . . . that hill.* 'Solomon loved many strange [i.e. foreign] women'; among his seven hundred wives were Ammonites and Moabites, who 'turned away his heart after other gods', and he built a temple 'for Moloch, the abomination of the children of Ammon' on the Mount of Olives, hence 'that opprobrious hill' (1 Kgs. 11: 1-7).

72 ll. 404-5. *Hinnom, Tophet . . . Gehenna.* The valley of Hinnom runs along the western and southern edges of Jerusalem. Tophet, in the valley's south, was the site of Moloch's shrine where the child sacrifices of ll. 394-5 were performed. The Hebrew name of the valley, Ge-hinnom, was transliterated into Greek as Geenna, in its English form *Gehenna*, and, because of the abominations practised there, this became the New Testament word for hell.

l. 406. *Chemos.* 'Chemosh, the abomination of Moab', also worshipped at Solomon's shrine.

l. 407. *Aroar.* Aroer (modern Arair, in Jordan), an important northern Moabite city.   *Nebo.* The name of both a southern Moabite town and the mountain in Moab from which Moses saw the promised land of Canaan.

ll. 408-9. *Abarim*: a range of hills, including Mount Nebo, at the western edge of Moab, overlooking the Jordan valley and the Dead Sea.   *Hesebon . . . Horonaim . . . Seon's realm.* Heshbon and Horonaim were Amorite cities; Sihon (*Seon*) was king of the amorites.

ll. 410-11. *Sibma . . . Eleale.* Sibma, east of the Jordan in the Moabite hills, was famous for its wine; Elealeh was a nearby city.   *the Asphaltic Pool*: the Dead Sea, which casts up bitumen, or asphalt.

l. 412. *Peor*: more fully Baal-Peor, the Moabite deity identified with Chemosh.

ll. 413-14. *Sittim . . . wanton rites*: Shittim, on the east bank of the Jordan opposite Jericho, the last encampment of the Israelites before crossing into Canaan, where 'the people began to commit whoredom with the daughters of Moab . . . and Israel joined himself unto Baal-peor' (Num. 25: 1-3).

ll. 415-16. *Yet thence . . . hill of scandal*: the Mount of Olives, the 'opprobrious hill' of l. 403 (see note to ll. 404-5).

l. 417. *hard by*: adjacent to.

l. 418. *good Josiah*: extirpated idolatry from Israel and destroyed the shrine of Topheth.

ll. 420–1. *Euphrates . . . Syrian ground*: from the northernmost to the southernmost border of Syria (the River Besor), including modern Jordan.

l. 422. *Baalim and Ashtaroth*. Baal (plural Baalim) was the general name given to the chief god of the Canaanite pantheon, particularized in various cults by the addition of a surname (e.g. Baal-peor; cf. l. 412); Ashtoreth (plural Ashtaroth) is the biblical form of Ishtar or Astarte, analogous to Venus in the Roman pantheon, goddess of sex and, in the middle-eastern cults, of war. Cf. 'Nativity Ode', ll. 197 ff.

l. 428. *cumbrous*: cumbersome.

l. 433. *their living strength*: i.e. the God of Israel.

l. 435. *bestial*: because they were worshipped in the form of animals.

ll. 438–9. *Astoreth . . . Astarte*: worshipped as the moon goddess, hence 'with crescent horns', l. 439.

l. 441. *Sidonian*: Phoenician (from Sidon, the chief city of Phoenicia).

73 l. 444. *uxorious king*: Solomon, who had seven hundred wives.

ll. 446–9. *Thammuz . . . summer's day*. Astarte's lover Tammuz, a god of fertility and vegetation, was identified with Adonis. His death was annually celebrated at the summer solstice.

ll. 450–1. *Adonis . . . purple*. The River Adonis, in Lebanon, becomes discoloured with reddish mud each summer.

ll. 457–9. *came one . . . brute image*. The Philistines placed the captured ark of the Lord in the temple of their god Dagon; the next morning the idol of Dagon was found destroyed. Cf. *SA*, 13.

l. 460. *groundsel*: threshold.

ll. 464–6. *Azotus . . . Ascalon . . . Accaron*: Vulgate names of the Authorized Version's Ashdod, Askelon, Ekron; these, with Gath and Gaza, were the five principal Philistine cities.   *coast*: Philistia lay along the Mediterranean coast.   *frontier bounds*: Ekron was the northernmost of the five cities, Gaza the southernmost.

l. 467. *Rimmon*: the chief Syrian deity.

l. 471. *A leper once he lost*. When Elisha told the Syrian general Naaman that washing in the Jordan would cure his leprosy, Naaman scoffed, but when he subsequently followed the prophet's advice and was cured, he acknowledged the God of Israel.

ll. 471–6. *a king . . . vanquished*. King Ahaz in alliance with the king of Assyria conquered Damascus, but he then converted to the cult of Rimmon and placed a Syrian altar in the temple of Jerusalem.

73 l. 472. *sottish*: foolish.

l. 478. *Osiris, Isis, Orus.* Isis, Egyptian moon goddess, represented with the horns of a cow, was the mother of Orus (or Horus), a hawk-headed god, and wife and mother of the sun god Osiris. See the 'Nativity Ode', ll. 211-20 and notes.

ll. 483-4. *borrowed gold . . . Oreb.* While Moses was on Mount Sinai receiving the ten commandments, his brother Aaron, the high priest, erected a golden idol of a calf, claiming it as the god who had delivered Israel from Egypt. The worship of the golden calf so enraged Moses when he returned that he broke the tablets of the law and destroyed the idol.

73-4 ll. 484-5. *rebel king . . . Dan.* When Jereboam led the rebellion of the Ten Tribes of Israel against King Rehoboam, he set up two golden calves, in Bethel and Dan, as alternative centres of worship to the temple at Jerusalem.

74 ll. 487-9. *Jehovah . . . bleating gods.* For God's destruction of the Egyptian firstborn, see Exod. 12: 12.

l. 488. *equalled*: i.e. made equal by destroying.

l. 490. *Belial.* Not a god in the Old Testament, but a personification: the Hebrew word means 'worthless', and the biblical 'sons of Belial' were not worshippers at a particular shrine but good-for-nothings. Milton is partly aware of this: see ll. 492-3.

ll. 495-6. *Eli's sons . . . God.* Eli was a priest at Shiloh, who took the young Samuel into his care. His two profligate sons 'lay with the women that assembled at the door of the tabernacle'; for this iniquity God pronounced the irremediable doom of Eli's house (1 Sam. 2-4).

l. 502. *flown*: swollen.

ll. 503-5. *Sodom . . . rape.* The story is in Judg. 19: a Levite travelling with his concubine was given shelter by an old man in the city of Gibeah, and 'certain sons of Belial beset the house round about, and beat at the door' demanding to be allowed to rape the Levite. They were given the concubine instead (the 'matron' of l. 505) and raped her to death. Milton's notion that there are preferable kinds of rape is entirely consistent with the biblical account.

l. 508. *Ionian*: Greek.   *Javan*: son of Japhet and grandson of Noah, here identified with Ion, progenitor of the Ionian Greeks.

ll. 509-10. *Heaven and Earth . . . parents.* Uranus and Ge (in Latin, Coelus and Terra) were the parents of the Titans, and grandparents of Zeus (Jove) and the Olympian gods.

ll. 510–13. *Titan . . . found.* Titan, the oldest of Uranus' children, was overthrown by his younger brother Saturn, who in turn was overthrown by his son Jove.   *Rhea*: Saturn's wife, Jove's mother.

ll. 514–15. *Crete . . . Ida.* Jove was born on Mount Ida in Crete.

ll. 517–18. *Delphian cliff . . . Dodona.* The oracle of Apollo was at Delphi, that of Zeus at Dodona.

l. 519. *Doric land*: Greece.   *Saturn . . . fled*: Saturn was banished from heaven by Jove, and roamed the earth.

l. 520. *Adria*: the Adriatic Sea.

l. 520. *Hesperian fields*: Italy.

l. 521. *Celtic*: French.   *utmost isles*: Britain and Ireland.

l. 523. *damp*: depressed, 'with dampened spirits'.

75 l. 528. *recollecting*: summoning up, rallying.

l. 532. *clarions*: shrill-sounding trumpets with a narrow tube, 'formerly much used as a signal in war' (*OED*).

l. 534. *Azazel*: not an angel in the Bible, but in Cabbalistic writers one of four standard-bearers of Satan's army; the name means 'scapegoat'.

l. 537. *meteor*: in the seventeenth century both a shooting star and a comet.

l. 538. *emblazed*: 'adorned with heraldic devices' (*OED*).

l. 542. *concave*: vault.

l. 543. *reign . . . Night.* In ii. 894 ff. Chaos and Night rule over a Kingdom of 'eternal anarchy', the formless void between hell and heaven.

l. 546. *orient*: bright.

l. 547. *helms*: helmets.

l. 550. *phalanx*: 'a body of heavy-armed infantry drawn up in close order, with shields joined and long spears overlapping' (*OED*).
Dorian mode: the gravest of the Greek musical modes, considered especially suitable to men preparing for battle.

l. 557. *swage*: assuage.

l. 563. *horrid.* The word retains its etymological sense of 'bristling' (with the 'forest huge of spears' of l. 546).

76 l. 568. *traverse*: all across.

l. 573. *created man*: man was created.

ll. 575–6. *small infantry . . . cranes.* Homer describes the pygmies slaughtered by cranes in *Il.*, iii. 1–5.   *infantry.* The word also meant a group of infants and puns on their size.

76 ll. 576–7. *Giant . . . Phlegra.* The giants battled the gods on the plains of Phlegra in Macedonia.

ll. 577–8. *heroic race . . . Ilium*: the Seven Against Thebes, heroes of the Trojan War and epic subject of Statius' *Thebaid* and of Aeschylus' play.

l. 579. *auxiliar*: assisting.

l. 580. *Uther's son*: King Arthur, son of Uther Pendragon.

l. 581. *Armoric*: from Brittany.

l. 583. *Aspramont or Montalban*: castles in the chivalric romances.

l. 584. *Damasco* [Damascus] *. . . Morocco, or Trebizond*: scenes of jousts between Christian and pagan knights in chivalric romances. Trebizond was a Byzantine city on the Black Sea taken by the Turks in 1461.

l. 585. *whom Bizerta sent.* The Saracens who invaded Spain and defeated Charlemagne's army embarked from Bizerta, in Tunisia.

ll. 586–7. *Charlemagne . . . Fontarabia.* Charlemagne did not fall, but his troops led by Roland were destroyed at Roncesvalles near Fontarabia (the modern Fuenterrabia) in Spain.

ll. 598–9. *with fear . . . monarchs.* Solar eclipses were from earliest times taken to be premonitions of the death of kings, as the king was identified with the sun.

l. 603. *considerate*: deliberate.

77 ll. 609–10. *amerced | Of heaven*: both 'deprived of heaven' and 'punished by heaven'.

l. 613. *scathed*: injured.

l. 617. *From wing to wing*: from one end of the phalanx to the other.

l. 624. *event*: outcome.

l. 636. *different*: disagreeing; *counsels* and *danger* are both objects of *shunned*: Satan denies that he either ignored alternative proposals or avoided danger.

l. 641. *still*: always.

l. 646. *close*: secret.

78 l. 651. *fame*: rumour.

l. 656. *eruption*: lit. 'breaking out'.

l. 672. *scurf*: crust.

l. 673. *his*: its.

l. 674. *The work of sulphur.* Sulphur was a basic ingredient in the refining of metals.

l. 676. *pioneers*: lit. 'diggers', originally the foot-soldiers who preceded the main body of the army to dig protective trenches.

l. 678. *Mammon.* Not a biblical devil but Aramaic for 'wealth', and this is how the word appears in the New Testament. But as a personification, the figure was associated with the Greek god of wealth, Plutus, and in turn identified with Pluto, god of the underworld.

l. 686. *Ransacked the centre*: mined the earth for precious metals.

79 l. 690. *ribs*: veins.   *admire*: marvel.

l. 694. *Of Babel . . . kings*: the tower in Nimrod's capital, and the Egyptian pyramids, monuments to earthly vanity.

l. 697. *reprobate*: 'rejected by God' (*OED*).

l. 700. *cells*: individual containers.

l. 703. *founded*: melted down (as in a foundry).

l. 706. *various*: complex.

l. 707. *strange*: wonderful.

l. 710. *fabric*: edifice.

l. 711. *exhalation*: mist.

l. 712. *symphonies.* Harmonious music; the city is built as the walls of Thebes were raised by the songs of the legendary musician Amphion.

l. 713. *pilasters*: columns attached to the walls.

l. 714. *Doric pillars*: the least ornate and most dignified of the Greek columns; cf. Satan's martial music in the Dorian mode, l. 550; but note also the elaborate ornamentation of the building as a whole.

l. 715. *architrave*: the beam resting on the columns that supports the roof; the lowest section of the entablature.

l. 716. *Cornice or frieze*: the decorative upper sections of the entablature.   *bossy . . . graven*: sculptures carved in relief.

l. 717. *fretted*: ornamented with decorative patterns in relief.

l. 718. *Alcairo*: modern Cairo, famous for its luxurious buildings.

l. 720. *Belus*: Babylonian version of Baal.   *Serapis*: Osiris as god of the underworld.

l. 724. *folds*: 'the leaves of a folding door' (*OED*).   *discover*: reveal.

l. 728. *cressets*: iron baskets used as lanterns.

l. 729. *naphtha and asphaltus*: lamp oil and pitch, fuel for the lamps and lanterns.

80 l. 739. *Ausonian land*: Italy.

80 l. 740. *Mulciber*: or Vulcan (the Greek Hephaestos), smith and artisan of the gods.

ll. 740–1. *how . . . fabled*. For Hephaestos' fall see *Il.*, i. 588–95.

l. 750. *engines*: devices.

l. 756. *Pandaemonium*: Milton's coinage from the Greek, meaning 'all the devils'.

l. 758. *squarèd regiment*: squadron.

l. 764. *Wont*: were wont to.   *soldan's*: Sultan's.

l. 765. *paynim*: pagan.

l. 766. *To . . . lance*: either a fight to the death or a joust for a prize.   *career*: gallop.

l. 769. *sun . . . rides*. The sun enters Taurus in April.

81 l. 774. *expatiate*: both walk about and talk at length.   *confer*: discuss.

l. 785. *arbitress*: as judge.

l. 795. *close*: private.

l. 797. *Frequent*: crowded.

l. 798. *consult*: consultation.

BOOK II

l. 508. *paramount*: chief.

l. 512. *globe*: 'a compact body (of persons)' (*OED*), hence the phalanx.

l. 513. *emblazonry*: heraldry.   *horrent*: bristling.

82 l. 517. *alchemy*: 'a metallic composition imitating gold', hence 'a trumpet of such metal, or of brass' (*OED*).

l. 521. *raised*: cheered, made bold.

l. 528. *sublime*: high above.

l. 530. *Pythian fields*: near Delphi, where the Pythian games, celebrating Apollo's victory over the Python, were held.

l. 531. *shun the goal*: avoid touching the track posts as they take the turn in their chariots.

l. 532. *fronted*: facing each other.

l. 535. *van*: vanguard.

l. 536. *Prick*: spur their horses.   *couch*: lower into the attack position.

l. 537. *close*: engage in battle.

l. 538. *welkin*: sky.

l. 539. *Typhoean*: monstrous, from Typhon or Typhoeus (see i. 198–9 and note, and see below, l. 541).   *fell*: fierce, cruel.

l. 541. *whirlwind.* The word for a whirlwind was *typhon* (not cognate with *typhoon*, but later associated with it).

l. 542. *Alcides*: Hercules (from his grandfather Alcaeus).

ll. 542–6. *from Oechalia . . . Euboic sea.* Returning victorious from Oechalia, in Laconia, Hercules was brought a gift of the cloak of the centaur Nessus, whom he had years earlier fought and killed. The cloak, however, was poisoned, and destroyed him, and in his death agony he hurled Lichas, the innocent deliverer of the gift, into the sea.   *Oeta*: a mountain in Thessaly, now called Banina.
Euboic: Euboean; Milton combines two versions of the story, in which the action takes place on the island of Euboea, and in which it is in Thessaly.

l. 552. *partial*: in parts, i.e. harmonized, with a pun on 'prejudiced'.

l. 554. *Suspended*: enraptured.

83 l. 564. *apathy*: the Stoic ideal, to be free from passion and unmoved by suffering.

l. 568. *obdurèd*: obdurate, 'hardened in wickedness or sin; persistently impenitent' (*OED*).

l. 570. *gross*: large.

ll. 577–83. *Abhorrèd Styx . . . oblivion*: etymologizing the names of the rivers of the classical underworld.

l. 590. *heap*: into heaps.

l. 591. *pile*: building.

l. 592. *Serbonian bog*: the quicksands surrounding Lake Serbonis, in Egypt.

l. 593. *Damietta*: a city at the mouth of the Nile.

l. 595. *frore*: frozen, an archaic past participle.

84 l. 596. *harpy-footed Furies.* The harpies, who attacked Aeneas and his men, had the faces and breasts of young women, the wings and bodies of birds, and talons for hands. The Furies were the classical agents of divine retribution.

l. 597. *certain revolutions*: see l. 603.

l. 600. *starve*: cause to die.

l. 604. *sound*: strait.

l. 611. *Medusa with gorgonian terror.* Medusa, one of the three gorgons, had snakes for hair and a look so terrible that it turned mortals to stone.

84 l. 613. *wight*: person.

l. 614. *Tantalus*: condemned in hell to suffer intense thirst in a pool whose water was just out of reach.

l. 625. *prodigious*: unnatural, abnormal.

l. 628. *Gorgons . . . hydras . . . chimeras*. The hydra was a nine-headed dragon, the chimera breathed fire; for gorgons, see l. 611.

l. 632. *Explores*: tries, puts to proof.

85 l. 638. *Bengala*. Bengal: the ships are following the spice route, from India south and west around the Cape of Good Hope.

l. 639. *Ternate and Tidore*: two of the Moluccas, or Spice Islands, near New Guinea.

l. 641. *Ethiopian*: the Indian Ocean.

l. 642. *stemming*: making headway.

l. 645. *folds*: layers.

l. 647. *impaled*: surrounded.

l. 653. *mortal*: deadly.

ll. 653–4. *about . . . hounds*. Milton's figure of Sin is based on the classical Scylla (see l. 660), a nymph who was changed by the witch Circe into a monster with ferocious dogs sprouting from her lower body.

l. 654. *cry*: pack.

l. 655. *Cerberian*: from Cerberus, three-headed watchdog of hell.

l. 656. *list*: wished.

ll. 660–1. *Scylla . . . shore*. Scylla ultimately became a dangerous rock off the Sicilian coast.   l. 661. *Trinacrian*: Sicilian.

l. 662. *Night-hag*: the chief witch, or Hecate, goddess of the underworld.   *called*: invoked.

l. 665. *Lapland*: especially associated with witches.   *labouring*: suffering (because in eclipse, l. 666).

l. 677. *admired*: wondered.

86 l. 686. *proof*: experience.

l. 688. *goblin*: demon.

l. 693. *Conjured*: sworn together (Lat. *coniuro*).

l. 706. *deform*: deformed.

l. 709. *Ophiuchus*: the constellation of the Serpent-Bearer, in the northern sky.

l. 710. *horrid hair*. *Horrid* retains its etymological meaning of 'bristling'; *hair* alludes to the etymology of *comet*, from the Greek for long-haired.

l. 711. *Shakes . . . war.* Comets were considered omens of disaster.

87   l. 735. *pest*: plague.

l. 739. *spares*: forbears.

ll. 757–8. *a goddess . . . sprung.* The birth of Sin from the head of Satan parallels the birth of Athena from the head of Zeus.

88   l. 761. *Portentous*: ominous.

l. 772. *pitch*: height.

l. 783. *that*: so that.

l. 798. *list*: wish.

89   l. 801. *conscious terrors*: terrors born of knowledge.

l. 813. *mortal dint*: death-dealing blow.

l. 815. *lore*: lesson.

l. 825. *pretences*: claims.

l. 827. *uncouth*: unfamiliar, uncertain.

l. 829. *unfounded*: bottomless.

l. 833. *purlieus*: outskirts.

l. 835. *removed*: distant.

l. 836. *surcharged*: overcrowded.

l. 837. *hap . . . broils*: chance to precipitate new quarrels.

90   l. 842. *buxom*: unresisting, a Spenserian usage.   *embalmed*: balmy, perhaps with an overtone of the usual sense associating the word with death.

l. 847. *famine*: hunger.   *maw*: voracious appetite.

l. 859. *office*: service.

l. 874. *portcullis*: outer grate.

l. 877. *wards*: the notches in a key, which correspond to those of the lock and permit it to be opened.

91   l. 883. *Erebus*: hell.

l. 885. *That*: so that.   *wings*: flanks of the squadron.

l. 889. *redounding*: overflowing.

l. 898. *Hot . . . Dry*: the characteristics of the four humours, corresponding to the four elements of fire, earth, water, and air.

l. 900. *embryon*: as yet unformed.

l. 904. *Barca . . . Cyrene*: cities in the Libyan desert.

ll. 905–6. *Levied . . . wings.* The atoms are used as ballast for the winds.   *poise*: add weight to.

91 l. 919. *frith*: firth, inlet.

l. 920. *pealed*: deafened.

l. 922. *Bellona*: goddess of war.

92 l. 927. *vans*: fans, i.e. wings.

l. 930. *cloudy chair*: the cloud machinery of masque scenery, in which deities ascended to the stage's heaven.

l. 933. *pennons*: feathers, wings.   *plumb*: directly, like a plumb line.

l. 937. *Instinct*: infused.

l. 939. *Syrtis*: dangerous shifting sands on the North African coast.

l. 943. *griffin*: a fabulous monster with the body of a winged lion and the head of an eagle.

l. 944. *moory*: marshy.

ll. 945–7. *Pursues . . . gold*. Griffins were the guardians of hoards of gold, which the Arimaspi, a Scythian tribe, continually attempted to steal.

l. 961. *wasteful*: desolate.

l. 964. *Orcus and Ades* [Hades]: gods of the underworld.

93 l. 965. *Demogorgon*. The mysterious primal god of pagan mythology, dreadful and unknowable.

l. 977. *Confine with*: border on (lit. 'share a boundary with').

l. 982. *behoof*: benefit.

l. 988. *anarch old*: chaos.

l. 989. *incomposed*: discomposed.

l. 1001. *intestine*: internal.

93–4 ll. 1005–6. *linked . . . heaven*. The notion of the world hanging by a golden chain from the floor of heaven derives originally from Homer and was greatly elaborated in Platonic and Neoplatonic philosophy. See ll. 1051–2.

94 l. 1008. *speed*: the word also means 'succeed'.

ll. 1017–18. *Argo . . . rocks*. When the Argo, the ship of Jason and the Argonauts, passed through the Bosphorus, it was nearly crushed by the huge floating islands of the Symplegades.

l. 1019. *larboard*: port, or left side (as he sailed through the Straits of Messina, between Italy and Sicily).

l. 1020. *Charybdis*: the whirlpool on the Italian side of the Straits, opposite Scylla, the 'other whirlpool'.

l. 1024. *amain*: at full speed.

l. 1043. *holds*: approaches.

l. 1044. *shrouds*: sails.

95 l. 1048. *undetermined . . . round*: i.e. Satan cannot make out its shape.

l. 1050. *Of*: with.   *living*: 'native, in its natural condition' (*OED*).

l. 1051. *fast by*: beside it.

l. 1052. *This pendent world*: not the earth, but the whole created universe.

BOOK III

ll. 2–3. *Or . . . unblamed?* Or may I, without incurring blame, call you equally eternal with God?   *express*: describe.   *since God is light*: quoting the First Epistle of John 1: 5.

l. 6. *effluence*: radiance.   *increate*: never created.

l. 7. *hear'st thou rather*: would you rather be called.

l. 8. *fountain*: source.

l. 10. *invest*: envelop.

ll. 17–18. *Orphean . . . Night.* The poet Orpheus went to the underworld and succeeded in recovering his dead wife Eurydice. He was the legendary founder of the Orphic mystical tradition and a *Hymn to Night* was ascribed to him.

l. 19. *the heavenly Muse*: Urania, Muse of astronomy (see i. 6, and vii. 1).

l. 23. *Revisit'st not these eyes.* Milton had been totally blind since 1652.

ll. 25–6. *drop serene . . . suffusion*: medical terms for Milton's blindness: the *gutta serena*, in which the eye appears normal, and the cataract, which covers it with an opaque film.

96 l. 30. *Sion*: the sacred mountain, source of Hebrew poetry (as opposed to the Greek spring Helicon and Mount Parnassus).

l. 34. *So were I*: if I were.

l. 35. *Thamyris*: legendary bard mentioned by Homer.   *Maeonides*: Homer, said to have been born in Maeonia (or Lydia) in Asia Minor.

l. 36. *Tiresias*: the blind prophet in the Oedipus story.   *Phineus*: blind Thracian prophet-king.

l. 37. *voluntary*: freely; of their own volition.

l. 38. *numbers*: poetic units, hence verses.   *wakeful bird*: the nightingale.

l. 39. *darkling*: in the dark.

l. 60. *sanctities*: sacred creatures, the angels.

96 l. 61. *his sight*: both from his eyes, and from seeing him.

97 l. 72. *sublime*: aloft.

l. 73. *stoop*: descend.

l. 74. *outside of this world*: outer shell of the universe.

l. 75. *embosomed*: enclosed.   *firmament*: sky.

l. 76. *Uncertain . . . air*: i.e. it is unclear to Satan whether the land is surrounded by water or air.

l. 84. *interrupt*: 'forming an interval or breach' (*OED*).

l. 93. *glozing*: flattering, cajoling.

l. 106. *would*: wished to do.

98 l. 120. *least impulse*: in any way being forced.

l. 129. *first sort*: i.e. the fallen angels.   *suggestion*: temptation.

l. 136. *spirits elect*: the unfallen angels, who are therefore God's chosen.

l. 140. *Substantially*: in his substance; i.e. he partakes of the divine nature.

99 l. 170. *effectual might*: my agent, through whom my power takes effect.

l. 174. *of*: through.

l. 176. *lapsèd*: lit. 'fallen'.

l. 177. *exorbitant*: 'erring, faulty, transgressing' (*OED*).

l. 179. *mortal*: deadly.

100 l. 204. *fealty*: obligation, fidelity: a feudal term.

l. 206. *Affecting godhead*: assuming divinity.

l. 208. *sacred and devote*: dedicated and condemned.

l. 219. *Patron*: protector, advocate.

l. 222. *redemption*: lit. 'buying back'.

l. 224. *doom*: sentence.

l. 231. *unprevented*: unanticipated.

101 l. 234. *meet*: suitable.

l. 248. *unspotted*: untainted.

l. 251. *spoiled*: despoiled.

l. 255. *maugre*: in spite of.

l. 270. *attends*: both awaits and serves.

102 l. 276. *complacence*: source of pleasure.

ll. 281–2. *Thou . . . join.* The syntax is, 'therefore join to thy nature the nature of those whom only thou canst redeem'.

l. 285. *room*: place.

l. 291. *Imputed*: assigned, transferred; technical theological language, alluding to the doctrine of imputed righteousness, whereby Christ's virtue is transferred to Christians through their faith.

l. 299. *Giving*: both yielding and giving (Christ) to.

l. 303. *assume*: take on.

l. 307. *fruition*. 'Enjoyment . . . the pleasure arising from possession' (*OED*), possibly with a pun on *fruit* (cf. i. 1), though the words are etymologically unrelated.

103 ll. 318–19. *assume | Thy merits*. Take on the honours you merit.

l. 320. *Thrones . . . dominions*: angelic orders, with *princedoms* replacing its synonym *principalities*.

ll. 324 ff. The account of judgement and paradise liberally paraphrases Revelation.

l. 326. *from all winds*: i.e. from the four points of the compass.

l. 327. *cited*: summoned.

l. 328. *doom*: judgement.

l. 340. *need*: be needed.

l. 341. *gods*: angels.

l. 418. *opacous*: opaque.

l. 419. *first convex*: the outer shell of the created universe, 'the bare outside of this world' where Satan was about to land at l. 72.

l. 420. *luminous inferior orbs*: the inner spheres of the stars, planets, sun, and moon.

104 l. 431. *Imaus*: the Himalayas.

l. 434. *yeanling*: newborn.

l. 436. *Hydaspes*: now the Jhelum river, a tributary of the Indus.

l. 438. *Sericana*: China; the 'barren plains' (l. 437) are the Gobi Desert.

l. 444. *store*: many.

l. 449. *fond*: foolish.

l. 452. *painful*: including the sense of laborious.

l. 456. *unkindly*: unnaturally.

l. 457. *fleet*: fly.

l. 459. *in . . . dreamed*. Giordano Bruno, Jerome Cardan, and Henry More had seriously postulated lunar inhabitants, and the idea was satirized by Ariosto, who located a fool's paradise in the moon in

Orlando Furioso (1532), and by Ben Jonson's masque *News from the New World Discovered in the Moon* (1620).

104 l. 460. *argent*: silver.

l. 461. *Translated saints*: such Old Testament heroes and prophets as Enoch and Elijah, who were transported to heaven.

ll. 462–4. *Betwixt . . . came*. Gen. 6: 4 describes how 'the sons of God came in unto the daughters of men', who bore their children, a race of giants.

l. 467. *Sennaar*: Shinar; the story is in Gen. 10: 10.

105 l. 470. *fondly*: foolishly.

l. 471. *Empedocles*: Sicilian pre-Socratic philosopher (fifth century BC).

l. 473. *Cleombrotus*: a youth said to have drowned himself after reading the *Phaedo*.

l. 474. *eremites*: hermit friars.

l. 475. *White, black and grey*: Carmelite, Dominican, and Franciscan, from the colour of their habits.

l. 477. *Golgotha*: site of Christ's crucifixion and burial.

l. 479. *weeds*: garments.

l. 481. *the fixed*: the sphere of the fixed stars.

ll. 482–3. *that crystalline . . . talked*. The crystalline sphere contains the constellation Libra, 'the balance'; this is said to measure the amount of 'trepidation', i.e. irregular motion in the Ptolemaic system. *talked*: so-called.   *that first moved*: the *primum mobile*, the tenth and outermost sphere.

l. 484. *wicket*: gate; the diminutive term is ironic.

l. 489. *devious*: both distant and erratic.

l. 491. *beads*: rosaries.

l. 492. *dispenses*: dispensations.   *bulls*: papal decrees.

l. 495. *limbo*: lit. border region.

l. 506. *frontispiece*: façade.

l. 507. *orient*: lustrous, brilliant.

105–6 ll. 510–15. *The stairs . . . heaven*. After Jacob had deceived his father Isaac into giving him the blessing intended for his older brother Esau, and supplanted him as the heir, he had a dream of angels upon a ladder reaching to heaven, and a vision of God promising to make him prosper.

106 l. 513. *Padan-Aram*: in Syria, where Jacob was fleeing to the protection of his uncle Laban in order to escape Esau's rage.   *Luz*: in the Judaean hills; after the vision Jacob renamed the place Bethel.

l. 516. *stair*: step.   *mysteriously*: symbolically; allegorical interpretations of Jacob's ladder commonly related it to the golden chain of Jupiter (see ii. 1005 and 1051), linking heaven to earth and establishing and justifying the natural and social hierarchies.

l. 522. *Rapt*: transported.

l. 534. *choice*: careful.

l. 535. *Paneas*: Greek name for the city of Dan, at the source of the Jordan, and the northern boundary of Canaan.

l. 536. *Beersaba*: Beersheba, the southern boundary.

l. 546. *Obtains*: reaches.

l. 547. *discovers*: reveals.

107 l. 552. *though after heaven seen*: though he had seen heaven.

l. 558. *Libra . . . star*: the constellations of the scales and Aries.

l. 559. *Andromeda*: the constellation next to Aries.

l. 562. *world's first region*: uppermost region of the atmosphere.

l. 563. *precipitant*: precipitous.

l. 564. *marble*: the relevant connotations are cold, smooth, shining.

l. 566. *nigh hand*: nearby.

l. 568. *Hesperian gardens*: the earthly paradise, where the daughters of Hesperus kept the golden apples of immortality.

l. 575. *By centre, or eccentric*: i.e. depending on whether the earth is at the centre of the universe or not: Milton declines to choose between the Ptolemaic and Copernican systems.

l. 576. *longitude*: how far he flew horizontally (as opposed to 'up or down', l. 574).

l. 577. *Aloof*: standing apart from.

l. 580. *numbers*: (musical) measures.

l. 586. *virtue*: force.

ll. 588–90. *a spot . . . saw*. Galileo had reported his observation of sunspots in 1613.

108 l. 595. *clear*: bright.

l. 596. *carbuncle*: used for a variety of red stones, including the garnet and ruby, and also 'applied to a mythical gem said to emit light in the dark' (*OED*).   *chrysolite*: used for various green stones, including tourmaline, zircon, and topaz; the two terms may be in apposition with *Ruby or topaz*, l. 597.

l. 597. *to*: i.e. and so on, to.

l. 598. *Aaron's breastplate*: the ceremonial raiment of Moses' brother, the high priest. Each stone was inscribed with the name of one of the twelve tribes.

108 ll. 600–1. *that which . . . sought*: the Philosopher's Stone, which was said by alchemists ('philosophers') to be able to change base metal into gold.

l. 603. *Hermes*: or mercury, the crucial element in alchemical processes.

l. 604. *Proteus*: sea-god capable of infinite changes of shape.

l. 605. *limbeck*: chemical retort.

l. 607. *elixir pure*: the final product of the alchemical process, which would effect the transformation into gold.

l. 608. *Potable*: liquid.   *virtuous*: powerful.

l. 609. *arch-chemic*: archetypical alchemist.

ll. 610–12. *Produces . . . glorious.* The theory was that precious stones are created by the action of the sun's rays penetrating underground.

l. 610. *terrestrial humour*: earthly moisture.

l. 617. *Culminate from the equator*: shine directly overhead, from the celestial equator (and hence produce no shadows to interfere with Satan's view).

l. 622. *ken*: range of vision.

l. 623. *The same whom John saw*: see Rev. 19: 17.

l. 625. *tiar*: crown.

l. 627. *Illustrious*: lustrous.   *fledge*: featured.

109 l. 634. *casts*: both casts about and casts off his present shape.

l. 637. *Not of the prime*: (1) not yet mature; (2) not one of the important angels.

l. 643. *succinct*: girded up, not voluminous.

l. 644. *decent*: both graceful and decorous, modest.

l. 648. *Uriel*: lit. 'light of God', a cabbalistic name, not in the Bible.

l. 656. *authentic*: authoritative.

110 l. 690. *held*: considered.

l. 694. *tends*: intends.

l. 699. *mansion*: dwelling.

l. 712. *his second bidding*: God's second command was 'Let there be light.'

111 l. 717. *spirited*: inanimate.

l. 718. *orbicular*: in a circle.

l. 729. *still . . . still*: always . . . always.

l. 730. *countenance triform.* The moon has three faces, or phases, the new crescent, the full moon, and the waning crescent. Its three forms were personified by three goddesses, Diana, Lucina (or Luna), and Hecate.

l. 731. *Hence*: from here (i.e. the sun).

l. 732. *checks*: restrains.

l. 740. *ecliptic*: the path of the sun.

l. 742. *Niphates*: a mountain in Armenia, near the Assyrian border.

BOOK IV

ll. 1–3. *which ... rout.* St John's vision of a new battle in heaven culminating in another defeat of the dragon Satan is in Rev. 12: 3–12.

l. 6. *while time was*: while there was still time.

112 l. 11. *wreak*: avenge.

l. 17. *engine*: cannon.

ll. 27–8. *Eden ... Lay pleasant. Eden* means 'pleasure' in Hebrew.

l. 30. *meridian*: noon.

l. 31. *revolving*: contemplating.

l. 50. *'sdained*: disdained.

113 l. 51. *quit*: cancel.

ll. 53–4. *still*: always.

l. 56. *still*: nevertheless.

l. 87. *dearly*: painfully.   *abide*: abide by, or await the issue of; suffer, bear.

114 l. 94. *By act of grace*: by a concession of God's.

ll. 114–15. *each passion ... despair*: i.e. each of the three passions brought pallor ('*pale*') to his face.

l. 118. *distempers*: disorders.

l. 123. *couched*: (lying) hidden.

l. 126. *the Assyrian mount*: Niphates (see iii. 742).

115 l. 134. *champaign head*: open country.

l. 136. *grotesque*: like a grotto.

l. 149. *enamelled*: bright.

l. 151. *humid bow*: rainbow.

l. 153. *of*: from.

l. 157. *odoriferous*: scent-bearing.

115 l. 160. *Cape of Hope*: Cape of Good Hope; the ships are travelling the spice route to Asia.

l. 162. *Sabean*: from Sheba (modern Yemen), in southern Arabia.

l. 163. *Araby the blest*. Or *Arabia Felix*, applied to the main part of the Arabian peninsula and particularly to Yemen.

l. 165. *grateful*: gratifying.   *Ocean*: Oceanus, one of the Titans, father of the rivers and in Homer the progenitor of the Olympian gods.

l. 167. *bane*: poison.

ll. 168–71. *Asmodeus . . . bound*. The story is from the apocryphal Book of Tobit: Tobit's son Tobias, travelling in Media, in Persia, on the advice of the archangel Raphael married Sara, whose seven previous husbands had been murdered on their wedding night by her incubus Asmodeus. Raphael enabled Tobias to escape their fate by instructing him to burn the heart and liver of a fish, and the smell drove the demon 'into the utmost parts of Egypt, and the angel bound him' (Tobit 8: 3).   *post*: quickly (cf. post-haste).

116 l. 175. *brake*: thicket.

l. 176. *had perplexed*: would have perplexed, rendered impassable.

l. 182. *sheer*: entirely.

l. 186. *hurdled cotes*: fenced shelters.   *secure*: with an ironic overtone: the sheep are secured, the shepherds too sure of themselves.

l. 192. *clomb*: climbed; a Spenserian archaism.

l. 193. *lewd*: the original meaning was 'lay or non-clerical', generalized to 'ignorant' and thence to 'wicked, unprincipled'.   *hirelings*: mercenaries (i.e. salaried ministers).

l. 198. *virtue*: power.

l. 211. *Auran*: Haran, on the eastern boundary of ancient Israel.

l. 212. *Seleucia*: in modern Iraq, on the Tigris.

l. 214. *Telassar*: a city in Eden.

117 l. 228. *kindly*: natural.

l. 237. *crispèd*: rippling.

l. 239. *error*: wandering.

l. 241. *nice*: meticulous, delicate.

l. 242. *curious knots*: complex designs.   *boon*: bountiful.

l. 250. *Hesperian fables*: the golden apples of Hesperus, which conferred immortality.

l. 255. *irriguous*: well-watered.

118 l. 257. *umbrageous*: shady.

l. 264. *apply*: both join and practise (as in 'applied art').   *airs*: both breezes and melodies.

l. 266. *Pan*: god of nature; the word in Greek means 'all'.

l. 267. *Graces ... Hours*: or Charites and Horae, goddesses respectively of natural beauty and of the seasons.

ll. 269–72. *Enna ... world*. Dis, or Pluto, god of the underworld, abducted Proserpina, daughter of the grain goddess Ceres, from the meadow of Enna, in Sicily. Ceres, in mourning, searched for her, and during this time no crops would grow. Dis agreed to return Proserpina to her mother for half of each year, and in this period the earth is fertile. The story was considered a pagan analogue to Eve's fall.

ll. 273–4. *Daphne ... spring*. The grove of Daphne on the River Orontes in Syria had a spring named for the Castalian Spring of the Muses on Mount Parnassus, and an oracle of Apollo (hence '*inspired*').

ll. 275–9. *Nyseian ... eye*. Diodorus records how Ammon, the son of Saturn and king of Lybia, loved the nymph Amalthea and had a son, Bacchus, by her. To protect them from the jealousy of his wife Rhea, he hid them on the island of Nysa, in the River Triton, in modern Tunisia. Ammon was identified by the Romans with Jove, and by Christian commentators with Noah's son Ham, or Cham in the Vulgate.

l. 278. *florid*: ruddy: Bacchus is god of wine.

l. 280. *Abassin*: Abyssinian.   *issue*: children.

ll. 281–2. *Mount ... line*. Amara, a sandstone hill in modern Ethiopia, was thought in Milton's time to be on or near the Equator, the 'Ethiop line', and sometimes identified with Eden.

l. 283. *Nilus' head*: the source of the Nile.

l. 294. *filial freedom*: freedom deriving from their status as God's children.

l. 295. *Whence*: i.e. from God.

119 l. 300. *front*: forehead.   *sublime*: 'of lofty ... aspect' (*OED*).

l. 301. *hyacinthine locks*: hair as beautiful as that of Hyacinthus, the youth loved by Apollo.

l. 306. *wanton*: here, luxuriant, unrestrained, but the word is most often used pejoratively in the period.

l. 310. *coy*: 'shyly reserved' (*OED*), perhaps again with an ironic overtone.

l. 312. *mysterious*: both secret and sacred, as in a religious mystery.

l. 313. *dishonest*: including the sense 'unchaste'.

119   ll. 323–4. *since ... sons*: since his descendants were born (before which time there was no one to compare him with).   *her daughters*: i.e. all women.

l. 329. *zephyr*: the west wind.

l. 332. *Nectarine*: sweet as nectar.

l. 333. *recline*: reclining.

l. 337. *gentle*: both kindly and noble.   *purpose*: conversation.

120   l. 341. *chase*: hunting ground.

l. 343. *ramped*: reared up.

l. 344. *ounces, pards*: lynxes (or any similar small wildcats), leopards.

l. 347. *sly*: the word could mean merely clever or skilful, but the pejorative sense was the primary one by Milton's time.

l. 348. *Insinuating*: moving sinuously; like '*sly*', with both neutral and pejorative implications.   *with Gordian twine*: as convoluted as the Gordian knot (which could not be untied, and was only undone when it was cut by Alexander).

l. 349. *braided*: tangled, intricate.

l. 352. *ruminating*: chewing the cud.

l. 353. *prone career*: sinking course.

l. 354. *Ocean Isles*: in the western Atlantic, identified as the Azores in l. 592.

l. 359. *room*: place.

121   l. 404. *purlieu*: 'a place where one has the right to range at large ... or which one habitually frequents' (*OED*).

l. 410. *Turned ... ear*. The syntax is ambiguous: either Adam's speech compelled Satan's full attention, or Eve turned fully attentive to Adam ('him' in the latter case would be dative). The first gives the easier sense, but both constructions are elliptical, and in any case the confusion of Eve's attention with Satan's may be part of the point.

l. 411. *sole part*: unrivalled part, with the additional implication that Eve is all his joy.

122   l. 447. *odds*: 'the amount ... by which one thing exceeds, or excels ... another' (*OED*); like *news*, a plural substantive treated as a singular noun.

122–3 ll. 460–9. *As ... goes*: recalling Narcissus, vainly yearning for his own image reflected in a pool.

123   l. 470. *shadow stays*: image awaits.

l. 478. *platan*: plane tree.

l. 486. *individual*: inseparable.

l. 500. *impregns*: impregnates.

124   l. 511. *pines*: torments (me).

l. 530. *A . . . chance*: a bit of mere luck.

l. 539. *in utmost longitude*: at the greatest distance, 'the ends of the earth'.

ll. 541–2. *with . . . Against*: i.e. directly facing.

125   l. 548. *Still*: always.

l. 549. *Gabriel*: with Michael, Uriel, and Raphael, one of the four archangels; the name means 'strength of God'.

l. 557. *thwarts*: both crosses (the literal meaning) and defeats.
vapours fired: fiery exhalations from the earth, thought to be the cause of shooting stars.

l. 567. *described*: descried.

l. 568. *gait*: course, bearing.

126   l. 590. *now raised*. The beam points upward because the sun has now moved below the horizon.

ll. 592–5. *whether . . . there*: whether through the movement of the sun or the earth; Milton once again declines to choose between the Ptolemaic and Copernican systems.   *Diurnal*: in a single day.
voluble: 'capable of ready rotation on a centre or axis' (*OED*).

l. 600. *Silence accompanied*: both an absolute construction, for 'silence accompanied evening', and an oxymoron, 'silence was accompanied', by the song of the nightingale of l. 602.

l. 603. *descant*: 'a melodious accompaniment to a simple musical theme' (*OED*).

l. 605. *Hesperus*: the evening star.

l. 608. *Apparent*: manifest, and playing on 'heir apparent'.

l. 612. *Mind us*: put us in mind.

127   l. 628. *manuring*: cultivation (lit. 'working with the hands').

l. 632. *Ask riddance*: need to be cleared.

l. 635. *author*: one 'who originates or gives existence'; 'one who authorizes or instigates'; 'an authority, an informant' (*OED*).

l. 640. *seasons*: not seasonal changes, which began only after the fall, but times of day, as the next eight lines indicate.

l. 642. *charm*: including senses derived from its double etymology, from Anglo Saxon *cierm*, magic spell, and Lat. *carmen*, song.

128   l. 669. *foment*: 'cherish with heat' (*OED*).

128 l. 676. *want . . . want*: lack . . . lack.

l. 698. *jessamine*: jasmine.

l. 699. *flourished*: flowered.

l. 703. *emblem*: both inlaid work and symbolic image.

l. 706. *feigned*: invented (by poets).

129 l. 707. *Pan . . . Sylvanus*: gods respectively of all nature and of woods and gardens.

l. 708. *Faunus*: Roman farm and forest deity.

l. 711. *hymenean*: marriage song (from Hymen, god of marriage).

l. 712. *genial*: presiding over marriage, generative.

l. 714. *Pandora*: lit. 'all gifts'; the first woman, created at Jove's command and sent with Hermes as a gift for Epimetheus ('hindsight') to avenge the audacity of his brother Prometheus ('foresight'), who had stolen fire from the gods to give to man. Pandora came with a box filled with evils; when Epimetheus opened the box, these were let loose throughout the world.

l. 716. *event*: outcome.

l. 717. *Japhet*: the Titan Iapetus, father of Prometheus and Epimetheus; he was identified with Noah's son Japhet.

l. 719. *authentic*: original.

l. 724. *pole*: sky, heavens.

l. 730. *wants*: lacks.

l. 736. *unanimous*: lit. 'with one mind'.

l. 739. *Handed*: holding hands.   *eased the putting off*: not needing to take off.

l. 743. *Mysterious*: sacred.

l. 747. *commands to some*. In 1 Cor. 7, marriage is enjoined upon those who otherwise would be unable to avoid fornication (see l. 753).

130 l. 748. *Our . . . increase*: in Gen. 1: 28.

l. 751. *sole propriety*: i.e. marriage was the only property exclusively ordained for Adam and Eve in paradise—the relation of husband to wife is conceived as a property relationship.

l. 756. *charities*: natural affections.

l. 763. *Love*: personified as Cupid.   *shafts*: arrows.

l. 764. *purple*: imperial, royal; also bright-hued, brilliant, splendid.

l. 769. *starved*: deprived (of love).

l. 773. *repaired*: renewed on the branches.

l. 777. *sublunar*: beneath the moon.

l. 778. *port*: gate.

l. 782. *Uzziel*: lit. 'strength of god'; a human name in the Bible, an angel in the cabbalistic tradition.

l. 785. *shield . . . spear*: the sides on which these were held, left and right.

l. 786. *these*: the latter.

l. 788. *Ithuriel and Zephon*: lit. 'discovery of God' and 'searcher'. Ithuriel is not a biblical name, and the biblical Zephon is not an angel.

131 l. 791. *secure*: 'feeling no care or apprehension' (*OED*).

l. 793. *Who*: one who.

l. 805. *animal spirits*. Burton explains the relationship of the bodily spirits: 'The natural are begotten in the liver, and thence dispersed through the veins . . . The vital spirits are made in the heart . . . The animal spirits formed of the vital, brought up to the brain, and diffused by the nerves, to the subordinate members, give sense and motion to them all.' (*Anatomy of Melancholy*, 1. i. 2. 2.) *Animal* = of the spirit or soul.

l. 809. *high conceits*: fanciful, excessive conceptions.

l. 812. *celestial temper*: both the weapon, tempered in heaven, and Ithuriel's angelic nature.

l. 813. *Of force*: perforce, necessarily.

l. 815. *nitrous powder*: gunpowder.

l. 816. *Fit for the tun*: ready for storage; *tun* = barrel.   *magazine*: storehouse for explosives.

l. 817. *Against*: in anticipation of.   *smutty*: black; smut is a fungus disease affecting grain that turns it to black powder.

133 l. 879. *transgressions*: the word includes its etymological sense of crossing boundaries.   *charge*: both the duty and those whom the angels are charged to care for, Adam and Eve.

l. 886. *hadst . . . wise*: were considered wise.

l. 899. *durance*: imprisonment.   *thus . . . asked*: so much for your question.

l. 904. *O . . . wise*: 'what a judge of wisdom you are, what a loss to heaven'.

l. 911. *However*: in whatever way he can.

134 l. 930. *at random*: i.e. missing the point.

l. 939. *afflicted powers*: weakened forces—both his own diminished strength and his crippled army.

134 l. 942. *gay*: showy, gaudy.

l. 945. *practised distances*: keeping a deferential distance.

ll. 947–9. *To say . . . traced*. Gabriel is mistaken (as he is again at ll. 1011–12): Satan's two claims do not contradict each other.

135 l. 962. *aread*: warn.   *avaunt*: begone.

l. 967. *facile*: easily opened.

l. 971. *limitary*: stationed on the boundary; also, setting limits, and limited.

l. 976. *progress*: ceremonial procession.

l. 978. *moonèd horns*: formation like the crescent moon.

l. 980. *ported spears*. Spears carried 'diagonally across and close to the body, so that the blade is opposite the middle of the left shoulder'; the military command is 'port arms' (*OED*). The point is that the spears therefore are not in the attack position.

l. 981. *Ceres*: the grain goddess.

l. 983. *careful*: worried.

l. 987. *Tenerife or Atlas*: mountains in the Canary Islands and Morocco respectively.   *unremoved*: 'fixed in place, firmly stationed' (*OED*).

l. 989. *wanted*: lacked.

136 ll. 997–8. *scales . . . Scorpion*: the constellation Libra, between Virgo and Scorpio.   *Astraea*: goddess of justice, who fled from earth after the Golden Age, identified here with the constellation Virgo.

l. 1001. *ponders*: lit. weighs.

l. 1004. *kicked the beam*: struck the crossbar.

ll. 1011–13. *read . . . resist*. Gabriel misinterprets the sign, which does not weigh Satan against the angels but fighting against parting, and shows parting to be preferable—for Gabriel as well as for Satan.

ll. 1013–14. *knew . . . scale*. Satan accepts Gabriel's interpretation.

BOOK V

ll. 5–7. *which . . . dispersed*: i.e. the mere sound of wind in the leaves and water was enough to wake Adam.   *Aurora*: goddess of dawn.

l. 12. *cordial*: lit. from the heart.

137 l. 15. *peculiar*: special, all its own.

l. 16. *Zephyrus . . . Flora*: the west wind and the goddess of flowers.

l. 21. *prime*: the first morning hour, beginning at six o'clock.

l. 22. *blows*: blooms.

l. 23. *balmy reed*: balsam.

l. 41. *love-laboured*: produced with love.

l. 47. *still*: always.

138 l. 61. *reserve*: restriction.

l. 66. *vouched with*: confirmed by.

139 l. 467. *what compare?* How can they be comparable?

l. 468. *hierarch*: archangel (lit. 'holy leader').

l. 472. *one first matter*: i.e. the world was created not *ex nihilo*, out of nothing, but of an original essential matter (see i. 10).

ll. 478–9. *bounds . . . kind*: stages appropriate to each form of life.

l. 481. *consummate*: perfected.

l. 483. *sublimed*: refined; an alchemical term.

ll. 484–5. *vital . . . intellectual*: the three kinds of fluids that enable and control the bodily and intellectual functions.

l. 488. *Discursive*: through the reasoning process.

l. 493. *proper*: my own.

140 l. 498. *tract*: length.

BOOK VII

l. 1. *Urania*: classical muse of astronomy, but here used in a more literal sense: the name means 'heavenly', from Greek *ouranos*, the sky, and Milton invokes 'The meaning, not the name' (l. 5).

l. 3. *Olympian hill*: Olympus, a favourite haunt of the muses and the home of the classical gods.

l. 4. *Pegasean wing*: the winged horse Pegasus, who created the muses' sacred fountain Hippocrene by stamping his hoof on Mount Helicon, and was therefore associated with poetic inspiration. His rider was Bellerophon (l. 18).

l. 9. *converse*: the word retains its literal meaning, 'dwell'.

l. 15. *Thy tempering*: tempered by you.

ll. 17–18. *as once Bellerophon*. Bellerophon attempted to fly to heaven on Pegasus, and Zeus punished him by sending a gadfly to sting the horse and cause it to throw its rider; though he survived his fall he lived out his last years, according to the mythographers, in blindness and alone (hence perhaps Milton's choice of him as an appropriate heroic model).

l. 19. *Aleian field*: in Lycia, in modern Turkey, where Bellerophon fell.

l. 20. *Erroneous*: lit. 'wandering'.

l. 22. *visible diurnal sphere*: the visible universe, which revolves diurnally, or daily, around the earth.

140 l. 23. *rapt*: transported.

141 ll. 25–6. *though fallen ... tongues*. Milton, as an important spokesman for the revolution, was under attack in the last year of the Commonwealth, and in danger of arrest and indictment after the restoration of the monarchy in 1660.

l. 27. *In darkness*: Milton had been totally blind since 1652.

l. 33. *Bacchus*: the Greek Dionysus, god of wine, theatre, and ecstatic poetry, patron of the legendary poet Orpheus, but also leader of the 'barbarous ... rout' of Bacchantes, his murderers.

ll. 34–8. *Thracian bard ... son*. Orpheus had offended the Bacchantes by spurning women after the death of his wife Eurydice and his failure to bring her back from Hades. Instead he turned to boys, and was credited with the introduction of pederasty into Greece. In revenge, the Thracian maenads attacked him and tore him to pieces. See *Lycidas*, ll. 58–63.

l. 35. *Rhodope*: a Thracian mountain.

ll. 35–6. *woods ... rapture*. According to Ovid, nature was so entranced with Orpheus' songs that not only the animals but the rocks and trees stopped to listen, and wept at his fate.

l. 37. *muse*: Calliope, muse of epic poetry and mother of Orpheus.

BOOK VIII

l. 256. *reeking*: vaporous (without its modern pejorative sense).

l. 263. *lapse*: lapping, flow.

l. 268. *went*: walked.

142 l. 296. *mansion*: dwelling (not necessarily a building).   *wants*: lacks.

l. 299. *seat*: residence.

143 l. 316. *Submiss*: submissive.

ll. 320–30. *To till ... die*: paraphrasing Gen. 2: 15–17.

l. 337. *purpose*: matter, discourse.

BOOK IX

144 l. 2. *familiar*: including the sense of familial.

l. 5. *Venial*: pardonable: the implication is that Adam is at fault (e.g. for his inquisitiveness about astronomy), but not seriously.

l. 13. *argument*: subject.

l. 15. *his foe*: Hector.

l. 16. *fugitive*: fleeing; for Achilles' pursuit of and victory over Hector see *Il.*, xxii.

ll. 16–17. *rage . . . disespoused.* Lavinia, the daughter of the king of Latium, was betrothed to Turnus, King of the Rutuli. Her father Latinus, however, in deference to a divine warning that he should marry her to a stranger, gave her to Aeneas instead, thus precipitating hostility and conflict between the Rutuli and the Trojans (*Aen.*, vii).

l. 19. *the Greek . . . son*: Odysseus and Aeneas, son of Venus or Cytherea, so-called from her association with the island of Cythera.

l. 20. *answerable*: appropriate.

l. 21. *celestial patroness*: Urania, muse of astronomy (see vii. 1 ff.).

ll. 25–6. *this . . . late.* Milton's earliest sketches for *Paradise Lost* were in the early 1640s, as the subject of a drama.

l. 27. *sedulous*: eager, diligent.

145 l. 28. *argument*: subject-matter.

l. 29. *dissect*: analyse.

l. 31. *feigned*: invented, as in the *Faerie Queene*.

l. 34. *tilting furniture*: jousting weapons.

l. 35. *Impresas quaint*: complex heraldic symbols.   *caparisons*: ornamental coverings for horses.

l. 36. *Bases*: cloth coverings for horses.

l. 38. *sewers, and seneschals*: the sewer (lit. 'seater') 'superintended the arrangement of the table, the seating of the guests, and the tasting and serving of the meal' (*OED*); the seneschal was the major-domo, or chief steward of the household.

l. 44. *That name*: of epic.

l. 49. *Hesperus*: Venus as the evening star.

l. 54. *improved*: increased, aggravated (*OED*).

l. 56. *maugre*: despite.

ll. 64–5. *thrice . . . circled.* Satan circles the earth at the equator, keeping ahead of the sun and thereby remaining in darkness.

l. 66. *colure.* The colures are two longitudinal circles intersecting at right angles at the poles and dividing the ecliptic into four equal parts.

146 l. 77. *Pontus*: the Black Sea.

l. 78. *Maeotis*: the Sea of Azov.   *river Ob*: in the Siberian arctic.

l. 80. *Orontes*: a river in Lebanon, Syria, and Turkey.

l. 81. *Darien*: Panama.

l. 90. *suggestions*: temptations to evil.

l. 95. *Doubt*: suspicion.

146 l. 104. *officious*: dutiful, though here perhaps with its modern pejorative overtone.

147 l. 112. *gradual*: gradated, in stages.

l. 121. *siege*: both seat and attack.

l. 145. *virtue*: power.

ll. 146–7. *if . . . created*: i.e. if the angels are not self-created, or did not always exist.

l. 148. *room*: place.

l. 150. *original*: origin.

148 ll. 170–1. *obnoxious . . . To*: exposed to harm from; the modern sense was apparently not yet in use.

l. 173. *reck*: care.

l. 174. *higher*: i.e. when I aim at God.

l. 186. *Nor nocent*: both not harmful and innocent.

l. 188. *brutal*: animal.

l. 191. *close*: secretly.

149 l. 197. *grateful*: including the meaning 'pleasing'.

l. 199. *wanting*: lacking.

l. 209. *Luxurious*: luxuriant, though the word was most commonly pejorative, and must have such an overtone here.

l. 211. *wanton*: unrestrained; like *luxurious* above, with pejorative overtones.

l. 218. *spring*: grove.

l. 219. *redress*: 'set upright again' (*OED*).

l. 229. *motioned*: suggested.

150 l. 265. *Or . . . worse*: whether his intention be this or something worse.

l. 270. *virgin*: innocent.

151 l. 292. *entire*: 'free from reproach, unblemished, blameless' (*OED*).

l. 296. *asperses*: slanders.

l. 310. *Access*: increase.

152 l. 326. *still*: always.

l. 330. *front*: lit. 'face', but punning on 'affronts', l. 328.

l. 334. *event*: outcome.

l. 353. *still erect*: always alert.

153 l. 358. *mind*: both remind, admonish, and pay attention to.

l. 361. *specious*: deceptively attractive.

l. 367. *approve*: prove, test.

l. 371. *securer*: less careful.

l. 387. *Oread or dryad*: mountain or wood nymph.   *Delia*: Diana, so called from her birthplace on Delos.

l. 390. *bow and quiver*: Diana was goddess of the hunt.

l. 392. *Guiltless*: innocent, without experience.

l. 393. *Pales*: goddess of pastures.   *Pomona*: goddess of orchards.

l. 395. *Vertumnus*: more properly Vortumnus, god of gardens, who presided over the changes of the year. Variously disguised, he pursued and wooed Pomona, ultimately successfully.   *Ceres*: goddess of agriculture (cf. iv. 268 ff.).

l. 396. *Proserpina*: child of Ceres by Jove.

154 l. 405. *event perverse*: evil outcome.

l. 413. *Mere*: wholly a.

l. 419. *Their tendance*: the object of their care.

l. 431. *mindless*: both unaware and inattentive (cf. l. 358).

l. 436. *voluble*: undulating.

l. 437. *arborets*: shrubs.

155 l. 438. *hand*: handiwork.

ll. 439-40. *gardens . . . Adonis*. Adonis was the lover of Venus. When hunting he was killed by a boar, and Venus made the anemone (or in some versions, the rose) spring from his blood. After his death, in response to the pleas of both Venus and Proserpina, Jove restored him to life and allowed him to live half the year with each—the myth, like that of Proserpina herself, was from the earliest times said to allude to the cycles of the crops. The Garden of Adonis became a proverbial expression for the swift passing of earthly beauty; however, in Spenser's version of the tale, it is the secret garden where Adonis and Venus make love, a place of 'perpetual spring and harvest' (*FQ*, III. vi. 29).

l. 441. *Alcinous . . . son*. Homer describes the visit of Odysseus, son of Laertes, to Alcinous, king of the Phaeacians, and his marvellous gardens, in *Od.*, vii. 112 ff.

l. 442. *not mystic*: real, not fabled or allegorical.   *sapient king*: Solomon.

l. 443. *Egyptian spouse*: Solomon married the daughter of Pharaoh (1 Kgs. 3: 1); for Solomon's garden see S. of S. 6: 2.

l. 450. *tedded*: cut and dried, for use as hay.   *kine*: cattle.

l. 453. *for*: because of.

155 l. 456. *plat*: plot of ground.

l. 472. *gratulating*: rejoicing.

l. 476. *for*: in exchange for.

156 l. 481. *opportune*: open, conveniently located.

l. 483. *intellectual*: intellect.

l. 484. *haughty*: lofty, high-minded.

l. 488. *to*: in comparison with.

l. 500. *carbuncle*: 'a mythical gem said to emit light in the dark' (*OED*).

l. 502. *spires*: coils.

l. 503. *redundant*. The word had the senses of both 'wavelike' and 'copious'.

ll. 505-6. *those . . . Cadmus*. For the metamorphosis of Harmonia (or Hermione) and Cadmus into serpents see *Met.*, iv. 563 ff.

ll. 506-7. *god . . . Epidaurus*: Aesculapius, god of healing, who appeared in his shrine at Epidaurus in the form of a serpent (*Met.*, xv. 760-4).

ll. 508-10. *Ammonian . . . Scipio*. Jupiter Ammon made love to Olympias, the mother of Alexander the Great, in the form of a serpent, as Jupiter Capitolinus (so named from his shrine on the Capitoline in Rome) did to the mother of the Roman hero Scipio Africanus.   *height of Rome*: greatest Roman.   *tract*: path, course.

157 l. 522. *at . . . disguised*. The sorceress Circe transformed her victims into fawning animals.

l. 530. *Organic*: being used as an organ or instrument (of speech, because snakes have no vocal chords).   *impulse . . . air*: impelling the air to make the sounds of speech.

l. 549. *glozed*: flattered.

l. 558. *demur*: am doubtful about.

158 l. 580. *Grateful*: pleasing.

l. 581. *fennel . . . teats*. Snakes were said to be especially fond of fennel, and of milk sucked directly from the teat.

l. 586. *defer*: delay.

l. 601. *Wanted*: lacked.

159 l. 605. *middle*: the air between.

l. 616. *virtue*: combining the meanings of power, innate excellence, and nature.   *proved*: tested.

l. 623. *their provision*: what they provide.

l. 624. *birth*. Milton uses 'bearth', an etymologizing spelling not in normal usage, but appropriate to trees which 'bear' fruit.

l. 629. *blowing*: blooming.

l. 635. *Compact . . . vapour*: composed of oily gasses; referring to the *ignis fatuus*, or will o' the wisp.

160 l. 668. *Fluctuates*: changes his aspect.

ll. 675–6. *Sometimes . . . brooking*: i.e. began at the height of the argument, without any preface.

l. 680. *science*: knowledge.

161 ll. 685–7. *ye . . . knowledge*: paraphrasing Gen. 3: 4–5.   *To knowledge*: eventuating in knowledge.

l. 695. *denounced*: threatened.

l. 717. *participating*: partaking of.

l. 722. *they*: 'produce' understood.

162 l. 732. *humane*: both benevolent and human: the spellings were not yet fully distinguished in the seventeenth century.

l. 737. *impregned*: impregnated.

l. 742. *Inclinable*: inclined, disposed.

l. 754. *infers*: implies.

l. 758. *In plain*: in plain words.

163 l. 771. *author unsuspect*: trustworthy authority.

l. 793. *boon*: jovial.

l. 797. *To sapience*: in producing knowledge, with a pun on the etymological meaning of sapience, 'taste' (*sapere*, taste, know). *infamed*: slandered.

164 l. 821. *wants*: is wanting.

l. 837. *sciential*: endowed with or bestowing knowledge.

l. 845. *divine of*: divining.

l. 846. *faltering measure*: of his heart, which 'misgave him'.

165 l. 876. *erst*: formerly.

l. 887. *distemper*: disorder, intoxication.

166 l. 890. *Astonied*: stunned (lit. 'turned to stone').   *blank*: speechless, nonplussed, helpless.

l. 901. *devote*: condemned.

l. 928. *fact*: crime, the most usual seventeenth-century sense.

167 l. 951. *Matter . . . foe.* 'He would not give the enemy grounds for contempt.'

167 l. 953. *Certain*: resolved (Lat. *certus*).

168 l. 980. *oblige thee*: make you subject to a penalty, involve you in guilt.   *fact*: deed.

l. 984. *event*: outcome.

l. 987. *to*: in comparison with.

l. 999. *fondly*: foolishly.

169 l. 1016. *dalliance*: sport, trifling, with implications of wanton or lascivious flirtation.

l. 1018. *elegant*: refined.

l. 1019. *each meaning*: of 'taste', judgment, and savour; cf. l. 797, above.

l. 1028. *meet*: appropriate.

l. 1034. *toy*: 'light caress' (*OED*).

l. 1047. *bland*: 'pleasing to the senses' (*OED*).

l. 1050. *unkindly*: both unnatural and immoral.   *conscious*: guilty.

170 ll. 1059–62. *so rose . . . strength*. For Delilah's treachery in cutting off Samson's hair see Judg. 16.   *Danite*. Samson was from the tribe of Dan.   *Dalilah*. Milton uses a variant of the Vulgate form Dalila.

l. 1078. *evil store*: a multitude of evils.

l. 1081. *erst*: formerly.

171 l. 1094. *obnoxious*: exposed (to evil or harm).

l. 1101. *fig-tree*: the banyan, or *ficus indica*.

l. 1111. *Amazonian targe*: the shields of Amazons.

172 l. 1140. *approve*: test, demonstrate.

l. 1141. *owe*: either possess, or are obliged to render.

ll. 1164–5. *expressed* | *Immutable*: (my love) which I declared was unalterable.

l. 1175. *secure*: overconfident.

BOOK X

173 l. 92. *cadence*: setting, sinking, with an overtone of the musical sense—cf. 'airs', l. 93.

l. 97. *voice of God*: as viceregent, Christ speaks with God's voice, and is called God throughout the scene.

174 l. 118. *revile*: abuse.

175 ll. 155–6. *part* | *And person*: theatrical terms, role and character.

l. 157. *in few*: in few words.

ll. 165–7. *unable . . . mischief*. Since the serpent cannot speak, he cannot accuse Satan; and hence the first instance of God's justice after the fall is the condemnation of the only wholly innocent party to the crime. Milton undertakes no mitigation of the biblical account in Gen. 3: 14–15, though he acknowledges its 'mysterious terms' (l. 173).

l. 184. *Saw . . . heaven*. Jesus reports Satan's fall in Luke 10: 18.

ll. 186–7. *Spoiled . . . show*: cf. St Paul's account of Christ's victory, Col. 2: 15.

ll. 187–8. *with ascension . . . captive*: alluding to Ps. 68: 18.

176 ll. 198–208. The passage quotes Gen. 3: 17–19 almost verbatim.

l. 210. *denounced*: pronounced (as a judge passing a sentence).

l. 215. *washed . . . feet*. Jesus washes his disciples' feet in John 13: 5.

ll. 217–18. *or slain . . . repaid*. Milton offers alternative possibilities for the source of the first clothing, a subject on which the scripture gives no guidance: either Christ killed animals for their pelts, or the animals sloughed off their skins as snakes do.   *repaid*: recompensed (for losing its skin).

BOOK XII

177–8 ll. 588–9. *top | Of speculation*: both mountain-top vantage point and high philosophical inquiry.

178 ll. 591–2. *expect . . . motion*: await their orders to move.

l. 629. *meteorous*: meteoric.

179 l. 630. *marish*: marsh.

l. 635. *adust*: scorched.

l. 640. *subjected*: lying below.

SAMSON AGONISTES

180 Preface: 'Of that Sort of Dramatic Poem . . .'

Aristotle: in *Poetics*, vi, describing the cathartic effect of tragedy.

a verse of Euripides: 'Evil communications corrupt good manners' (1 Cor. 15: 33), a Euripidean fragment that became proverbial in late classical times.

Paraeus: David Paraeus (1548–1622), German Calvinist.

Dionysius the elder: tyrant of Syracuse (431–367 BC), author of a tragedy awarded first prize in the Athenian competition.

180 *Augustus Caesar.* Suetonius reports that Augustus destroyed his incomplete tragedy.

Seneca. There was debate over whether the ten tragedies ascribed to Seneca were the work of the philosopher or of a dramatist with the same name.

Gregory Nazianzen. Fourth-century bishop of Constantinople and supposed author of *Christ Suffering.*

sadness: seriousness.

prologue: prefatory address, apology.

181 Martial . . . epistle: *Ad Lectorem*, prefaced to his first book of Epigrams.

monostrophic . . . apolelymenon: A single stanza employing a free strophic pattern, rather than the usual strict pattern of strophe, antistrophe, epode.

alleostropha: irregular strophes.

produced . . . act: extended beyond the action that would be appropriate to the final act of a traditional tragedy.

plot, . . . explicit. Aristotle classes plots as simple and complex in *Poetics*, vi.

rule: a neo-classic dictum (deriving in part from Aristotle, but more significantly from Horace's *Ars Poetica*) that the action of a drama should take place in a single day.

The Argument. While the 'fable' behind *SA* is the story in Judges, the 'argument' summarizes the play, emphasizing its classic form—it most resembles Sophocles' *Oedipus at Colonus*, the story of the final days of Oedipus, blind and in banishment.

Manoa. Here as throughout, Milton uses the Vulgate form of proper names.

182 catastrophe: the event that produces the denouement of the drama.

by accident. As a secondary effect; in Judg. 16: 30, Samson prays, 'Let me die with the Philistines'; Milton is perhaps concerned to remove the implication that the hero's intentions include suicide.

l. 6. *else*: otherwise.

l. 11. *day-spring*: dawn.

l. 13. *Dagon their sea-idol*: the chief Philistine deity, described in *PL*, i. 462–3, as a 'sea monster, upward man | And downward fish.'

l. 16. *popular noise*: noise of the populace.

183 ll. 23–4. *foretold | Twice*: in Judg. 13: 3–5 and 10–23; cf. ll. 361, 635, below.

l. 27. *charioting*: carrying off as if in a chariot.

l. 31. *separate*: literally translating Nazarite, one who is set apart and dedicated to God's service, as his uncut hair witnesses (from Hebrew *nazar*, to separate; cf. Num. 6: 2).

l. 34. *gaze*: spectacle; cf. l. 112, below.

l. 38. *Promise was*: see Judg. 13: 5.

ll. 50–1. *to . . . tears*. Milton conflates Dalila's treachery with Samson's earlier betrayal by the woman of Timnath (Judg. 14: 17).

l. 55. *secure*: overconfident.

184 l. 63. *bane*: evil, destruction.

ll. 65–6. *each . . . wail*: each by itself would require a lifetime to deplore.

l. 70. *prime work*: first creation; see Gen. 1: 3, and cf. ll. 83 ff., below.   *extinct*: extinguished.

l. 77. *still*: always.

l. 87. *silent*: 'Of the moon: Not shining' (*OED*); see l. 89.

l. 89. *vacant interlunar cave*. The moon is conceived as resting in a dark cave in the period between the old and new moon; *vacant* = not at work (cf. 'vacation').

l. 93. *She . . . part*: i.e. the soul is diffused throughout the body.

l. 95. *obvious*: exposed.

185 l. 106. *obnoxious*: exposed to harm.

l. 118. *at random*: in disorder.   *diffused*: spread out.

l. 122. *In slavish habit*: dressed like a slave.   *weeds*: clothing.

l. 128. *tore the lion*: see Judg. 14: 5–6.

l. 129. *embattled*: ready for battle.

l. 131. *forgery*: forging.

l. 132. *cuirass*: breastplate.

l. 133. *Chalybean*. The Chalybes were famous metal workers.

l. 134. *Adamantean proof*: capable of withstanding adamant, a substance of impregnable hardness.

l. 136. *insupportably*: irresistibly.

l. 138. *Ascalonite*: Ascalon (Ashkelon) was one of the five principal Philistine cities, where Samson slew thirty men (Judg. 14: 19).

l. 139. *lion ramp*: leonine attack.   *old*: experienced.

l. 140. *plated*: armoured.

186 ll. 142–3. *trivial . . . ass*: see Judg. 15: 15–16.

l. 144. *foreskins*. The Philistines were uncircumcised.

186 l. 145. *Ramath-lehi*: where Samson discarded the jawbone.

l. 147. *Azza*: variant form of Gaza.

l. 148. *Hebron . . . giants*: see Num. 13: 33.

l. 149. *journey of a sabbath-day.* The sabbath's day journey—the distance permissible to travel on the sabbath—was variously computed at 2,000, 3,000, and 4,000 cubits (a cubit was at various times from 18 to 22 inches); the point is that Samson carried the massive gates a considerable distance.

l. 150. *whom . . . heaven*: Atlas, the Titan who bore the sky on his shoulders.

l. 161. *incorporate*: become one with.

l. 163. *visual beam.* Ancient and Renaissance science held that sight derives from rays emitted by the eye.

ll. 164–5. *O mirror . . . unparalleled*: i.e. there has been no symbol of the uncertainty of the human condition to equal Samson since the time that man first appeared on earth.

l. 170. *in high estate*: a necessary quality of the tragic hero according to Aristotle, *Poetics*, xiii.

l. 181. *Eshtaol . . . Zora*: Danite cities. Samson's father Manoah was of the tribe of Dan; Samson was born in Zora.

187 l. 185. *tumours*: lit. 'swellings', often applied to the effects of passion on the mind.

l. 190. *superscription*: lit. 'the inscription on a coin'.

ll. 190–1. *of . . . understood*: i.e. this applies to most people.

l. 207. *mean*: average.

l. 208. *paired*: been equal.

l. 209. *transverse*: off course.

l. 210. *Tax*: blame.

l. 212. *pretend . . . wise*: however wise they may claim to be.

l. 219. *first . . . Timna*: see Judg. 14: 1–20 and ll. 382 ff.

188 l. 223. *intimate*: inmost, deep-seated.

l. 228. *fond*: foolish.

l. 230. *specious*: deceptively attractive.   *accomplished*: both effective and cultured.

l. 235. *peal*: discharge (as of artillery).

l. 247. *ambition.* The word retains its Latin sense, from *ambitio*, going about to seek votes or support.

l. 254. *forecasting*: planning.

l. 258. *on some conditions*. The Israelites agreed that they would not attack him themselves; see Judg. 15: 12.

l. 263. *trivial weapon*: the jaw bone of an ass; cf. l. 142 above.

189 l. 266. *by this*: by this time.   *Gath*: one of the five principal Philistine cities.

l. 275. *frequent*: usual.

l. 278. *Succoth and . . . Penuel*. Their inhabitants refused to aid Gideon in pursuit of the kings of Midian (see Judg. 8: 5–9).

l. 282. *ingrateful Ephraim*. The Ephraimites refused to aid Jephtha and his Gileadite supporters against the Ammonites (Judg. 11: 12–33, 12: 1–6); Jephtha slaughtered the Ephraimites, who revealed themselves by their inability to pronounce the word 'shibboleth' (Judg. 12: 5–6).

l. 291. *mine*: my countrymen.

l. 295. *think not God*: think that there is no God.

l. 299. *doctor*: teacher.

l. 300. *doubt*: suspect.

190 l. 305. *ravel*: become entangled.

l. 307. *interminable*: infinite.

l. 312. *obstriction*: obligation (to marry only Jewish women); the word is Milton's coinage.

l. 313. *legal debt*: what is owed to the (Mosaic) law.

l. 320. *fallacious*: deceitful.

l. 324. *quits . . . unclean*: acquits her of the charge that she was unclean: a gentile marriage partner was, according to Mosaic law, unclean (see Deut. 7: 3), however impeccable her moral or sexual behaviour.

l. 327. *careful*: full of care.

l. 333. *uncouth*: strange, unknown.

l. 335. *informed*: directed.

l. 338. *signal*: conspicuous, remarkable.

191 l. 360. *graces*: favours.

l. 373. *Appoint not*: either 'do not attempt to prescribe', or 'do not dispute'.

l. 377. *profaned*: retains its original sense, 'sacrilegiously made public' (from Lat. *profanus*, outside the temple).

l. 384. *secret*: the riddle of the lion and the honeycomb; see Judg. 14: 8–9, 12–18. For the subsequent narrative, see Judg. 16: 6–20.

192 l. 389. *vitiated*: corrupted.

192 ll. 390–1. *by . . . treason*: i.e. the mere smell of gold caused her to 'give birth to' treason.

l. 394. *capital*: of the head; principal; fatal.

l. 395. *summed*: concentrated.

l. 405. *over-watched*: exhausted by staying awake too long.

l. 423. *infest*: plague.

l. 424. *state not*: do not comment upon.

193 l. 430. *Tacit*: silent.

l. 433. *rigid score*: stiff (Lat. *rigidus*) debt; 'score' also connotes cutting or marking.

l. 434. *popular*: public.

l. 439. *Them out of thine*: the Philistines out of Samson's hands.

l. 454. *diffidence*: distrust.

l. 455. *propense*: inclined.

l. 466. *connive*: shut his eyes, pretend ignorance (Lat. *conniveo*).

194 l. 469. *discomfit*: defeat.

l. 471. *blank*: confound.

ll. 481–3. *I already . . . ransom.* Manoa's negotiation with the Philistines and the plan to ransom Samson have no basis in the biblical account.

l. 493. *fact*: deed.

l. 496. *front*: forehead.

ll. 500–1. *Gentiles . . . confined.* Tantalus was condemned to eternal punishment in Hades for revealing divine secrets.

l. 509. *quit thee*: cancel.

195 l. 514. *argues over-just*: shows one to be excessively just.

l. 515. *self-offence*: offence against oneself.

l. 516. *what . . . knows*: whatever means are offered which, for all one knows . . .

l. 526. *instinct*: impulse.

l. 528. *sons of Anak*: the giants of l. 148, above.   *blazed*: celebrated.

l. 533. *fallacious*: deceptive.   *venereal trains*: sexual traps.

l. 535. *pledge*: sign, i.e. his unshorn hair, the token of his status as a Nazarite.

l. 538. *wether*: castrated ram.

l. 541. *wine.* Nazarites were required to abstain from wine.

l. 549. *fiery rod*: sunbeam.

l. 550. *milky juice*: water (as nourishment).

196 l. 557. *liquid*: clear.

l. 560. *What boots it . . .* Of what use is it.

l. 567. *gaze*: spectacle.

l. 568. *redundant*: both superfluous and flowing or abundant.

l. 569. *Robustious*: strong.

l. 571. *craze*: render infirm.

l. 574. *draff*: garbage, swill.

l. 578. *annoy*: injure.

l. 581. *a fountain*: see Judg. 15: 18–19.

l. 591. *treat*: have to do (lit. 'negotiate').

197 l. 594. *genial*: vital.

l. 600. *humours black.* In the old physiology, an excess of the black bile humour caused a disposition to melancholy.

l. 601. *fancy*: imagination.

l. 603. *prosecute*: pursue.

l. 604. *how else*: whatever other means.

l. 609. *reins*: kidneys.

l. 612. *accidents*: symptoms of a disease.

l. 615. *answerable*: corresponding.

l. 622. *mortification*: gangrene.

l. 624. *apprehensive*: sensate.

l. 625. *exasperate*: irritate.   *exulcerate*: cause ulcers.

l. 628. *alp*: high mountain.

198 l. 635. *message*: messenger, angel (see Judg. 13 and ll. 23–9, above).

l. 639. *nerve*: strength.

l. 645. *repeated*: repeatedly.

l. 657. *Consolatories*: consoling treatises.

l. 659. *Lenient*: soothing.

199 l. 677. *Heads without name*: unknown people.

l. 687. *remit*: send them back.

l. 688. *dismission*: dismissal.

l. 700. *crude*: premature.

l. 701. *Though not disordinate*: though they have not been intemperate.

l. 702. *in fine*: in conclusion.

199 l. 706. *minister*: servant, agent.

199–200 ll. 714–15. *ship | Of Tarsus*: a common biblical phrase exemplifying pride; Tarsus was a Spanish port.

200 l. 716. *Javan*: Greece (after Noah's grandson Javan, who supposedly sired the Ionians; cf. *PL*, i. 505).   *Gadire*: Cadiz.

l. 717. *bravery*: finery.

l. 719. *hold them play*: keep them in play.

l. 720. *amber*: ambergris, the basis of perfume.

l. 731. *makes address*: prepares.

l. 736. *fact*: deed.

l. 737. *perverse event*: untoward or unexpected outcome.

l. 748. *hyena*: proverbial example of deceitfulness.

l. 752. *move*: propose.

201 l. 769. *with . . . surcharged*: not overburdened with exaggerations.

l. 775. *importune*: persistent in solicitation.

l. 785. *parle*: parley (discussion of truce).

l. 786. *the . . . kind*: of the same nature.

l. 794. *fancy*: affection.

202 ll. 800–2. *I . . . custody*. In Judg. 15: 5, the Philistines tell Delilah their aim is to 'bind him to afflict him'.

l. 803. *made for me*: suited me.

l. 812. *fond*: foolish.

l. 826. *which*: refers to pardon, l. 825.

203 l. 847. *awed*: struck with fear.

l. 865. *grounded*: established.

204 l. 897. *acquit themselves*: perform their offices.

l. 901. *varnished colours*: false rhetoric.

l. 906. *worried*: assailed.   *peals*: outbursts (cf. l. 235, above).

l. 910. *place*: opportunity.

l. 913. *sensibly*: intensely.

l. 916. *want*: lack.

205 l. 926. *grateful*: pleasing.

ll. 932–3. *trains . . . gins . . . toils*: all words for traps.

l. 934. *enchanted . . . charms*. Dalila is compared with Circe and various Renaissance descendants of the sorceress; see *Comus*, ll. 50 ff. *charms*: including the Latinate sense, songs.

l. 936. *adder*: proverbially deaf.

l. 944. *insult*: 'exult proudly or contemptuously' (*OED*).

l. 948. *gloss upon*: comment on.

l. 950. *To*: compared to.

206 l. 967. *evil omen*: the sarcastic prediction that she will be 'memorable | Among illustrious women', ll. 956–7.

l. 968. *denounced*: pronounced.

l. 969. *concernments*: concerns.

ll. 971–3. *Fame . . . white*. Fame is the Latin *fama*, rumour, unreliable and hence 'double-mouthed'. In all classical and Renaissance sources, however, the figure is female; the black and white wings are also Milton's invention.   *blast*: as of a trumpet.

l. 975. *circumcised*: Israelites.

l. 981. *Ecron . . . Gath*: major Philistine cities.

l. 987. *odours*: incense.

ll. 988–90. *Mount Ephraim . . . nailed*. The reference is to the song of the prophetess Deborah, who lived on Mount Ephraim (Judg. 4: 5), a hymn of praise for Jael, who slew the Canaanite general Sisera when she had given him refuge after his defeat by the Israelites (see Judg. 4: 17–21, 5: 24).

l. 1000. *aggravate*: lit. 'add to the weight of'.

207 l. 1012. *inherit*: possess.

l. 1016. *thy riddle*: the riddle proposed at his first wedding to the woman of Timnath, 'Out of the eater came forth meat, and out of the strong came forth sweetness' (Judg. 14: 14); Samson gave the Philistines seven days to find the solution.

l. 1018. *any of these*: any of the virtues in ll. 1010–11.

l. 1020. *paranymph*: best man, friend of the groom; in Judg. 14: 20, the woman of Timnath is, in Samson's absence, 'given to his companion, whom he had used as his friend'.

l. 1022. *both*: both wives.   *disallied*: dissolved; Milton's coinage.

l. 1025. *for that*: because.

l. 1037. *joined*: married.

l. 1038. *Intestine*: internal; here, domestic.

l. 1039. *cleaving*: clinging, but also self-dividing.

208 l. 1048. *in . . . combines*: joins (with him) in domestic happiness.

l. 1058. *confusion*: ruin, destruction.

l. 1062. *contracted*: suffered (as in 'contract a disease').

208 l. 1068. *Harapha*. Not in the scriptural narrative; the name appears to derive from the Hebrew *ha raphah*, the giant, sometimes treated by biblical commentators as a proper name.

l. 1069. *pile*: mass, stature (as of a building); cf. l. 1239 below.

l. 1073. *habit*: clothing (he is unarmed).

l. 1075. *fraught*: freight, i.e. what he brings.

l. 1076. *condole thy chance*: lament your fate.

l. 1080. *Og . . . Anak . . . Emims*: biblical giants; cf. ll. 148, 528, above.

l. 1081. *Kiriathaim*: in Gen. 14: 5, where the Emims dwelt.

l. 1082. *If . . . known*: if you know anything at all; but cf. also Satan to Ithuriel, 'Not to know me argues yourself unknown' (*PL*, iv. 830).

209 l. 1087. *camp . . . field*: either on the battlefield or in the lists, at a tournament.

ll. 1088-9. *noise . . . about*: reports have circulated.

l. 1092. *single*: challenge to single combat.

l. 1105. *in thy hand*: within reach.

l. 1109. *assassinated*: treacherously stricken.

l. 1113. *Close-banded*: secretly leagued together.

l. 1120. *brigandine*: body armour.   *habergeon*: sleeveless coat of chain mail.

l. 1121. *Vantbrace and greaves*: arm and leg armour.   *gauntlet*: mailed glove.

ll. 1121-2. *spear | A weaver's beam*: spear as big as the roller on a loom; cf. the description of Goliath in 1 Sam. 17: 7.   *seven-times-folded*: made of seven layers of hide.

210 l. 1138. *chafed*: enraged.   *~ruffled*: both angered, and with their quills standing on end.

l. 1147. *spread*: lay.

l. 1164. *boisterous*: coarse-growing, rank (*OED* 6).

211 l. 1169. *thine*: thy people.

ll. 1183-5. *took . . . hands*: see Judg. 15: 11-13, and ll. 253 ff., above.

ll. 1186-8. *murder . . . robes*. At his wedding feast, Samson had promised thirty Philistines new garments if they could solve the riddle he proposed. They succeeded by persuading his wife to extract the answer from him, and to fulfil his vow he slew thirty men of Askalon and gave their garments to the Philistines. See Judg. 14: 12, 19, and ll. 382 ff., above.

ll. 1196-7. *Under . . . spies*. Josephus adds this detail to the story, that the thirty men were offered to Samson 'in pretence to be his companions, but in reality to be a guard upon him' (*Antiquities*, v. 8).   *await*: wait upon.

ll. 1201–3. *When ... hostility.* 'When I saw that everyone was determined to be my enemy, I was hostile at every opportunity, as I would be with my enemies.'

l. 1204. *underminers*: betrayers.

212 l. 1220. *appellant*: challenger to combat.

l. 1221. *maimed for*: rendered incapable of.

l. 1223. *of small enforce*: easy to perform.

l. 1231. *Baal-zebub*: lit. 'god of flies', one of the many forms of the Philistine sun god Baal, whose shrine was in Ekron, the northern-most Philistine city; he appears as Satan's companion Beelzebub in *PL.*   *unused*: i.e. to hearing 'dishonours' (l. 1232).

l. 1234. *van*: vanguard, first line of battle; i.e. start fighting.

l. 1237. *baffled*: publicly disgraced (*OED* 1. 1).

l. 1238. *vast.* The adjective modifies 'bulk'.

l. 1242. *Astaroth*: collective name for the many forms of Astarte, the fertility goddess and female counterpart of Baal; cf. 'Nativity Ode', ll. 200–2.

l. 1243. *braveries*: boasts.

l. 1245. *unconscionable*: excessive.

213 l. 1248. *divulge*: proclaim.

l. 1249. *Goliah*: the Authorized Version's Goliath.

l. 1277. *ammunition*: war supplies.

l. 1283. *expedition*: speed.

l. 1287. *patience.* The word literally means suffering; cf. *PL*, ix. 31–3.

l. 1288. *saints*: in the Protestant sense, holy persons, especially 'the elect', those chosen for salvation; the term was regularly used by seventeenth-century puritans self-referentially; cf. Sonnet 15.

214 l. 1300. *behind*: yet to come.

l. 1303. *quaint*: curious.

l. 1305. *habit*: dress.

l. 1307. *voluble*: fluent.

l. 1309. *remark*: mark out, distinguish.

l. 1317. *heartened*: refreshed.

l. 1320. *law forbids.* The second commandment forbids worship of idols or service to other gods (Exod. 20: 4–5).

214 l. 1325. *antics*: clowns.   *mummers*: mimes.

215 l. 1333. *Regard thyself*: look to your own interests.

l. 1342. *Joined*: enjoined, imposed.

l. 1344. *Brooks*: permits.

l. 1346. *sorry what*: sorry to think what.   *stoutness*: obstinacy, defiance.

l. 1369. *sentence holds*: maxim holds true.

216 l. 1375. *jealousy*: cf. Exod. 20: 5, 'I the Lord thy God am a jealous God'.

ll. 1377–8. *dispense . . . Present*: give a dispensation for me or thee to be present.

l. 1380. *come off*: escape.

l. 1399. *art*: skill.

l. 1402. *Because*: so that.

217 l. 1420. *aught*: at all (modifying 'concerned').

l. 1450. *I had no will*: I had no will to go there.

218 l. 1453. *give ye part*: let you share.

l. 1454. *With good success*: successfully.

l. 1457. *attempted*: entreated.

l. 1459. *With supplication prone*: prostrating myself as I pleaded.

l. 1470. *The . . . remit*: to give up the rest (of their revenge) would be magnanimous.

l. 1478. *numbered down*: counted out.

l. 1484. *wanting*: lacking.

219 l. 1503. *to*: in addition to.

l. 1507. *next*: next of kin, tribesmen (like Samson, they are Danites).

l. 1515. *ruin*: in its literal sense, collapse.

l. 1529. *dole*: grief, pain, with a pun on dole as what is dealt.

220 l. 1535. *subscribe*: agree.

l. 1536. *stay*: pause.

l. 1538. *post*: quickly (as on post horses).   *baits*: travels slowly ('to bait' originally meant to pause on a journey to feed the horses).

l. 1539. *to*: in accordance with.

l. 1543. *erst*: just now.

l. 1552. *accident*: occurrence (lit. 'happening').

l. 1567. *irruption*: bursting in.

221 l. 1574. *windy*: empty.

l. 1585. *at variance*: in conflict.

l. 1596. *Occasions*: business.

l. 1599. *little I had dispatched*: I had accomplished little.

l. 1603. *minded*: intended.

l. 1605. *theatre*. The temple of Dagon is called a 'house' in Judg. 16: 26–7; but the pillars (16: 25–9) and the presence of 3000 spectators (16: 27) may have suggested a theatrical structure to Milton.

ll. 1607–8. *each . . . sort*: everyone of high rank.

l. 1610. *banks*: benches.   *scaffolds*: platforms.

222 l. 1619. *cataphracts*: soldiers in full armour.   *spears*: spearsmen.

l. 1627. *stupendious*: stupendous.

l. 1646. *nerves*: sinews.

ll. 1647–8. *with . . . tremble*. Earthquakes and volcanoes were explained as the effects of the volatile elements trapped underground; cf. *PL*, i. 230–7.

223 l. 1659. *vulgar*: common people.

l. 1669. *sublime*: elated.

l. 1671. *regorged*: regurgitated.

l. 1674. *Silo*: Shiloh, where the ark of the covenant was kept.

l. 1682. *fond*: foolish.

l. 1685. *Insensate . . . reprobate*: left senseless, or left to a godless ('reprobate') sense.

l. 1692. *evening dragon*: firedrake, a meteorological phenomenon similar to the will-o'-the-wisp.

224 l. 1695. *villatic*: farmyard; Milton's coinage.

l. 1699. *self-begotten bird*: the phoenix, a mythical bird continually reborn out of its own ashes.

l. 1700. *embossed*: imbosked, hidden in the woods.

l. 1701. *no . . . third*: only one phoenix existed at a time.

l. 1702. *lay . . . holocaust*: was a short while ago wholly consumed by fire.

l. 1703. *teemed*: born.

l. 1707. *secular*: lasting for ages.

l. 1709. *quit*: acquitted.

l. 1713. *sons of Caphtor*: the Philistines, who emigrated to Canaan from Caphtor, generally thought to be Crete.

l. 1715. *hath*: he hath.

224 l. 1727. *lavers*: washbasins.

l. 1728. *what speed*: with as much speed as possible.

l. 1729. *plight*: condition.

225 ll. 1736–7. *enrolled . . . legend*: fully written out (*legend* = something to be read).

l. 1746. *dispose*: disposition.

l. 1751. *in place*: here.

l. 1753. *band them*: band together.

l. 1755. *acquist*: acquisition.

Further Reading

THERE is no authoritative modern edition of Milton's poetry; frequently cited are: Merritt Y. Hughes (ed.), *John Milton: Complete Poems and Major Prose* (New York, 1957), and John Carey and Alastair Fowler (eds.), *The Poems of John Milton* (New York and London, 1968). Both editions offer annotations fully in tune with traditional Milton scholarship. A summary of such criticism on the shorter poems and on *Paradise Regained* can be found in Douglas Bush and A. S. P. Woodhouse, *A Variorum Commentary on the Poems of John Milton* (New York, 1970). The standard edition of the prose is the Yale edition, *The Complete Prose Works of John Milton*, 8 vols. (New Haven, Conn., 1953–82), which offers much information on the historical contexts. A full-scale modern biography is William Riley Parker, *Milton: A Biography* (Oxford, 1968), worth supplementing with the seven volumes of David Masson, *The Life of John Milton* (Cambridge and London, 1859–94) and Helen Darbishire (ed.), *The Early Lives of Milton* (London, 1932).

A strong collection of recent criticism is Mary Nyquist and Margaret W. Ferguson (eds.), *Re-Membering Milton* (New York and London, 1987). Catherine Belsey offers a good introduction to current critical concerns in *John Milton: Language, Gender, Power* (Oxford and New York, 1988). Other recommended studies:

Francis Barker, *The Tremulous Private Body* (New York and London, 1984).
Harold Bloom, *The Anxiety of Influence* (London and New York, 1973).
—— *A Map of Misreading* (London and New York, 1975).
Anthony Easthope, 'Towards the Autonomous Subject in Poetry: Milton's "On His Blindness"', in R. Machin and C. Norris (eds.), *Post-Structuralist Readings of English Poetry* (Cambridge, 1987).
William Empson, *Milton's God* (London, 1961, 1965; Cambridge, 1981).
—— *Some Versions of Pastoral* (London, 1935).
Stanley Fish, *Surprised by Sin: The Reader in Paradise Lost* (London and Berkeley, Calif., 1967).
—— 'The Temptation to Action in Milton's Poetry', *ELH* 48 (1981), 516–31.
—— 'Things and Actions Indifferent: The Temptation to Plot in *Paradise Regained*', *Milton Studies*, 17 (1983), 163–85.
Angus Fletcher, *The Transcendental Masque: An Essay on Milton's Comus* (Ithaca, NY, 1971).
Jonathan Goldberg, 'Dating Milton', in K. E. Maus and E. D. Harvey (eds.), *Soliciting Interpretation* (Chicago, 1990).

Jonathan Goldberg, *Voice Terminal Echo: Postmodernism and English Renaissance Texts* (New York and London, 1986).

Kenneth Gross, '"Each heav'nly close": Mythologies and Metrics in Spenser and the Early Poetry of Milton', *PMLA* 98 (1983), 21–36.

John Guillory, 'Dalila's House: *Samson Agonistes* and the Sexual Division of Labor', in M. W. Ferguson, M. Quilligan, and N. J. Vickers (eds.), *Rewriting the Renaissance* (Chicago, 1986).

—— *Poetic Authority: Spenser, Milton, and Literary History* (New York, 1983).

Geoffrey Hartman, 'Adam on the Grass with Balsamum', and 'Milton's Counter-plot', in *Beyond Formalism* (New Haven, Conn., 1970).

Christopher Hill, *Milton and the English Revolution* (London and New York, 1978).

Christopher Kendrick, *Milton: A Study in Ideology and Form* (New York and London, 1986).

William Kerrigan, 'The Heretical Milton: From Assumption to Mortalism', *English Literary Renaissance*, 5 (1975), 125–66.

—— *The Prophetic Milton* (Charlottesville, Va., 1974).

—— *The Sacred Complex: On the Psychogenesis of Paradise Lost* (Cambridge, Mass., 1983).

Edward Semple LeComte, *Milton's Unchanging Mind* (Port Washington, NY, 1973).

Mary Nyquist, 'Fallen Differences, Phallogocentric Discourses: Losing *Paradise Lost* to History', in D. Attridge, G. Bennington, and R. Young (eds.), *Post-Structuralism and the Question of History* (Cambridge, 1987).

—— 'The Father's Word/Satan's Wrath', *PMLA* 100 (1985), 187–202.

—— 'Textual Overlapping and Dalilah's Harlot-Lap', in P. Parker and D. Quint (eds.), *Literary Theory/Renaissance Texts* (Baltimore, 1986).

Patricia Parker, *Inescapable Romance* (Princeton, NJ, 1979).

C. A. Patrides (ed.), *Milton's Lycidas: The Tradition and the Poem* (Columbia, Miss., 1983).

John Shawcross, 'Milton and Diodati: An Essay in Psychodynamic Meaning', *Milton Studies*, 7 (1975), 127–63.

Index of Titles and First Lines